Gender in the Middle Ages

Volume 5

MONSTERS, GENDER, AND SEXUALITY IN MEDIEVAL ENGLISH LITERATURE

Monsters abound in Old and Middle English literature, from Grendel and his mother in *Beowulf* to those found in medieval romances such as *Sir Gowther*. Through a close examination of the way in which their bodies are sexed and gendered, and drawing from postmodern theories of gender, identity, and subjectivity, this book interrogates medieval notions of the body and the boundaries of human identity. Case studies of *Wonders of the East*, *Beowulf*, *Mandeville's Travels*, the *Alliterative Morte Arthure*, and *Sir Gowther* reveal a shift in attitudes toward the gendered and sexed body, and thus toward identity, between the two periods: while Old English authors and artists respond to the threat of the gendered, monstrous form by erasing it, Middle English writers allow transgressive and monstrous bodies to transform and therefore integrate into society. This metamorphosis enables redemption for some monsters, while other monstrous bodies become dangerously flexible and invisible, threatening the communities they infiltrate. These changing cultural reactions to monstrous bodies demonstrate the precarious relationship between body and identity in medieval literature.

DANA M. OSWALD is Assistant Professor of English, University of Wisconsin-Parkside.

Gender in the Middle Ages

ISSN 1742–870X

Series Editors
Jacqueline Murray
Diane Watt

Editorial Board
John Aenold   Clare Lees
Katherine Lewis   Karma Lochrie

This series investigates the representation and construction of masculinity and feminity in the Middle Ages from a variety of disciplinary and interdisciplinary perspectives. It aims in particular to explore the diversity of medieval genders, and such interrelated contexts and issues of sexuality, social class, race and ethnicity, and orthodoxy and hereodoxy.

Proposals or queries should be sent in the first instance to the editors or to the publisher, at the addresses given below; all submissions receive prompt and informed consideration.

Professor Jacqueline Murray, Department of History, University of Guelph, Guelph, Ontario, N1G 2W1, Canada

Professor Diane Watt, Department of English, Aberystwyth University, Penglais, Aberystwyth, SY23 3DY, UK

Boydell & Brewer Limited, PO Box 9, Woodbridge, Suffolk IP12 3DF, UK

Also in this series

MONSTERS, GENDER, AND SEXUALITY
IN MEDIEVAL ENGLISH LITERATURE

Dana Oswald

D. S. BREWER

First published 2010
D. S. Brewer

ISBN 978–1–84384–232–3

D. S. Brewer is an imprint of Boydell & Brewer Ltd
PO Box 9, Woodbridge, Suffolk IP12 3DF, UK
and of Boydell & Brewer Inc.
668 Mt Hope Avenue, Rochester, NY 14620, USA
website: www.boydellandbrewer.com

A catalogue record for this title is available
from the British Library

This publication is printed on acid-free paper

Typeset by Pru Harrison, Hacheston, Suffolk
Printed in Great Britain by
CPI Antony Rowe, Chippenham and Eastbourne

CONTENTS

For Drew – who opened the eyes of my eyes

ACKNOWLEDGEMENTS

I am grateful for the many intellectual communities that sustained me throughout this project. Nick Howe's readings of medieval texts and of the world inform many aspects of my thinking in this work. I could not have completed this book without his notes on the page and his voice in my head. I am deeply sad that he is no longer here to read it. I am honored by the commitment of wisdom, time, and support from the Department of English at The Ohio State University, particularly from my generous advisors Drew Jones, Lisa Kiser, and Ethan Knapp. The community I encountered at the University of Wisconsin-Parkside was crucial to my development of this project: I extend thanks to Walt Graffin, Fran Kavenik, Jay McRoy, Mary Lenard, and Patrick McGuire, who supported my research with advice, course releases, and research funding, and to Sandy Moats and Teresa Coronado, who talked and wrote with me.

I thank the manuscript curators at The British and Bodleian Libraries, who allowed me access to their amazing manuscript collections. I am inspired by my colleagues in monster studies, especially Asa Mittman, Susan Kim, and Debra Strickland, and am thankful for their insight and advice. It is Tom Bredehoft who first set me on the path of medieval studies, for which I am forever grateful.

I would like to thank my readers, first and foremost Jennifer Camden, who read every word on every page of this book. I also received the advice of Robyn Malo-Johnston, Eileen Joy, Robin Norris, Tom Bredehoft, Mary Ramsey, Theresa Kulbaga, Melissa Ianetta, Suzanna Schroeder, Amy Lenegar, and my anonymous reviewers: thanks for your many hours of work. I would also like to thank my writing group at OSU, especially Susan Williams, whose commitment to collegiality and intellectual rigor is unparalleled.

The ideas in this book have often begun in the classroom, so I must thank my students, particularly those in Literary Analysis, who worked so diligently with the text of *Beowulf* and the theories of Freud, Lacan, Kristeva, Sedgwick, Halberstam, Rubin, and Derrida. Their fresh ideas and enthusiasm remain an inspiration for my work.

Finally, thanks to my dear friends and family, who listened endlessly to discussions regarding monsters' genitals. Special thanks to my mother, who taught me the spirit of adventure in the pages of a book, and to my husband and best friend, Drew Carmichael, who has been with me for every step of this odyssey.

My thanks go to the Series Editor of Gender in the Middle Ages, Diane Watt, and my editors at Boydell & Brewer, Caroline Palmer and Rohais Haughton, who have given me endless patience and support.

LIST OF FIGURES

INTRODUCTION

Sex and the Single Monster

The mind needs monsters. Monsters embody all that is dangerous and horrible in the human imagination. – David Gilmore (1)

For all of the famed restrictions of Christian doctrine and medieval modes of social conduct, the Middle Ages was, perhaps paradoxically, a period that appears to have accommodated, in ways our liberal society does not or seems not to, what we might broadly call the rude, bawdy or obscene. But that does not mean that, at different times and in different ways, it was not contentious nor that it was devoid of the power to shock or offend, as well as to titillate and excite. – Nicola McDonald (2)

JOHANNES HARTLIEB's 1461 portrait of Alexander the Great shows us a surprising version of the Greek leader (as reprinted in Petzoldt and Neubauer 41). This Alexander wears an elaborate three-peaked crown and a well-cut tunic, neither unusual nor inappropriate attire. His nose is decidedly Roman and his eyebrows pinch together in consternation over light-colored eyes that look intelligent. Despite all the signs of royalty and refinement, this Alexander bears two signs of barbarity: slender tusks protruding from his cheeks and an unkempt beard and hair. His clothes tell us of his wealth and political significance, but his crude animal attributes interrupt and contradict this story. Hartlieb portrays Alexander as a man overtaken by the mysterious East he hoped to conquer. Just as the lands that he conquered were known as barbarous to medieval readers and viewers, so too does Alexander's physical form in this image reflect the perceived qualities of these lands. Contact with the savage lands of the East has changed a leader of civilization into the monster as represented by Hartlieb. Though dressed in the proper attire and still obviously human in his facial features, this Alexander cannot hide his corruption. It peeks through in tousled hair, an untidy beard, and, most strikingly, those intractable tusks.

This fifteenth century German painting offers one perspective of the monstrous human body in medieval culture. The image suggests that congress with the dangerous lands of the East visibly contaminates the human body of Alexander – and indeed, in much early medieval literature, the monstrous exists only in distant places like the marvel-filled East. As the image also implies, humans like Alexander desire contact with the monstrous and find its very liminality fascinating and

1

inviting. These two problems are fundamentally related: humans are both fascinated and repelled by monstrous forms. Alexander's infamous desire to see,
describe, and thereby possess the wondrous creatures of the East, as represented by
his letters to his teacher Aristotle,[1] has redounded upon him and he, at least in the
Hartlieb image, becomes one of them. Like Alexander, humans want to witness
strange bodies, but they also wish to control, to circumscribe these bodies, in order
to keep them somehow at a safe distance. This control is enacted textually and
visually through the representation and the erasure of the monstrous body.
Through practices of erasure, the text allows both distance and proximity to the
monstrous, standing in as a kind of protection for the viewer or reader that enables
safe indulgence in the pleasure provided by the monstrous form.

*erasure → or rather
reduction?*

MONSTROSITY DEFINED

*places
monsters
below*

Over halfway through the Middle English travel narrative, *Mandeville's Travels*,
the narrator, Sir John Mandeville, defines the term 'monster' for his readers: Sir
John tells us that 'a monster is a þing difformed aȝen kynde bothe of man or of best
or of ony þing elles & þat is cleped a Monstre' [a monster is a thing deformed
against kind, both of man or of beast or of anything else, and that is called a
monster] (Hamelius 30). A monster is therefore an outlier within its race or 'kind,'
*external
to
kin*
whether that kin-group is human or animal. The monster is always read against
the bodies of those who are not monstrous – the so-called 'normal' humans or
'normal' animals.[2] I do not seek to reify the concept of normalcy here, but rather to
point to the ways monstrous bodies represent the problems inherent in human
bodies, particularly the problems of sex, gender, and reproduction. The term 'normal' holds a great deal of current political capital, particularly in disability studies.
As Lennard Davis argues, 'even in texts that do not appear to be about disability,
the issue of normalcy is fully deployed. One can find in almost any novel ... a kind
of surveying of the terrain of the body, an attention to difference – physical,

---

[1] The Alexander tradition in medieval England, and indeed medieval Europe, is well established. See especially the chapter, 'The Alexander-Legend in Anglo-Saxon England' in
Orchard, *Pride and Prodigies.*

[2] As Lennard Davis points out, the term 'normal' is one that does not come into popular use
until the nineteenth century, after statistics, as a branch of knowledge, came to influence
public policy in Europe (4). He sets the term against notions of the ideal and the grotesque,
ultimately linking the notion of ideal or average to nationalism and politics. Davis ultimately
wants to demonstrate that 'the very term that permeates our contemporary life – the normal –
is a configuration that arises in a particular historical moment' (15). While the term 'normal'
does not exist in the medieval lexicon, the notion of uniformity and difference is certainly
known and articulated, much as Mandeville defines creatures as being 'against kind.'
Disability was often perceived in this period, and many following it, as a kind of monstrosity. I
do not wish to perpetuate this perception, and note that there is much to be gained from an
examination of medieval bodies through the lens of disability studies.

mental, and national' (15). While medieval responses to disabled bodies are hardly sensitive, medieval texts most certainly do explore 'the terrain of the body' and examine what it means for a body to appear *different*.

Monsters, because they do appear different, help humans define themselves.[3] In 'Man-Eating Monsters and Ants as Big as Dogs,' Susan Kim builds from the work of Bruno Roy to clearly articulate this philosophy:

> … monster catalogues can reassure their readers. Roy follows Augustine in his argument that the depiction of monsters is an articulation of the fear of the loss of corporal integrity. As they provide a normalizing context for aberrant human births, monsters demonstrate what can happen to the human body – what can come off, what can be unnaturally added on. But with the same gesture the catalogue reassures: the articulation of the fear of disintegration allows that fear to be put to rest, because as the monstrosities define the norm, they confirm it, and thus quiet the fear of its dissolution. (40)

Monsters do more than provide a delicious terror for their viewers. They assure viewers that their humanity is more complete than that possessed by the monster, but they also notify viewers that variations are possible, and that humanity is available on a kind of sliding scale. Thus, they demand that viewers appraise the status of their own humanity, and the integrity of their bodies and identities. Monsters remind humans of what it means to be human – they may threaten the human body, but they also confirm notions of its relative cohesion.

Because human monsters are in part human, authors and scholars demonstrate significant concerns over their position in the spiritual hierarchy. When considering the nature of monstrous humans, most scholars of medieval monsters turn initially and immediately to Augustine's admonition in book sixteen of *De Civitate Dei*:

> Verum quisquis uspiam nascitur homo, id est animal rationale mortale, quamlibet nostris inusitatem sensibus gerat corporis formam seu colorem sive motum sive sonum sive qualibet vi, qualibet parte, qualibet qualitate naturam, ex illo uno protoplasto originem ducere nullus fidelium dubitaverit. (42–5)

---

[3] For example, Lesley Kordecki argues that 'Animals in discourse for the most part show the shaping of human subjectivity, and the lost monsters of the mediaeval text demonstrate what we do not want to be, but perhaps, as in Marie's fable, we realize we are not so far removed from them after all' (36–7). For studies of medieval monstrosity, see Cohen, 'Monster Culture'; Daston and Park, *Wonders*; Orchard, *Pride and Prodigies*; Tolkien, 'Monsters and the Critics'; Roy, 'En Marge'; Thompson, *Freakery*; Wittkower, 'Marvels of the East'; Bildhauer and Mills, *Monstrous Middle Ages*; Bynum, *Metamorphosis*; Williams, *Deformed Discourse*; Olsen and Houwen, *Monsters and the Monstrous*; Bovey, *Monsters and Grotesques*; Verner, *Epistemology*; Kline, *Maps*; Jones and Sprunger, *Marvels*; and Knoppers and Landes, *Monstrous Bodies*. Other studies of monstrosity, particularly those related to film, are Creed, *Monstrous Feminine*; Schildrick, *Embodying the Monster*; Saunders, *Imps*; Lant and Thompson, *Imagining*; Benshoff, *Monsters in the Closet*; and Kirkup et al., *Cyborg*.

3

[Yet whoever is born anywhere as a human being, that is, as a rational mortal creature, however strange he may appear to our senses in bodily form or colour or motion or utterance, or in any faculty, part or quality of his nature whatsoever, let no true believer have any doubt that such an individual is descended from the one man who was first created.]

Augustine writes to assure his readers that the races of monsters, at least those that are 'rational,' have the potential to be saved, and thus are human. According to Augustine, a body that is 'formed against kind' is not counted out of the human race, just so long as the being inside of it is capable of higher thinking. However, if the idea of rationality separates human from animal, monsters continue to occupy a difficult middle ground – how and when do we decide if monstrous humans are rational? Does it have to do with their ability to speak? To live in communities? Must all monstrous humans act rationally – and do, indeed, all humans act rationally? If monsters do not act in a way that is perceived to be rational, are they to be considered beasts, even if their bodies seem to be human? The animal is distinguished from the human, according to Joyce Salisbury, following Thomas Aquinas, by the ability to reason: animals act according to instinct where humans act according to reason (5). In her book, *The Beast Within*, she elucidates the complicated medieval understandings of animal behavior – and the lengths to which philosophers would go to deny animals' rationality.[4] Jan Ziolkowski also demonstrates the difficulty of distinguishing human from beast, saying 'the line between human and animal in the Middle Ages was at once sharply drawn and porous' ('Literary' 22).[5]

If the line between animal and human was problematic for medieval thinkers, despite the oft-cited Augustinian injunction concerning rationality, then the divisions among animals, monsters, and humans were considerably more troubling. As Salisbury notes, monsters were largely understood as hybrid creatures, a comment that serves as an 'example of the growth of the idea (and fear) of the blurring of the lines between animal and human' (145). Monsters are particularly difficult to categorize, Augustine acknowledges, because their appearances can be

---

4   Salisbury argues that sharp delineation began to decline after the twelfth century. Because animals were a way to think about the nature of human identity, this shift required an altered understanding of humanity: 'When early Christian thinkers established what they believed to be clear categories that separated animals from humans, they were not only making a theological statement of humanity's dominance over the natural world, but they were actually defining what it meant to be human. ... The increasing popularity of the metaphoric linking of humans and animals seems to have opened the possibility for redefining humanity in a way that eliminated the categoric separation of the species' (Salisbury 149).

5   See both 'Literary Genre and Animal Symbolism' and *Talking Animals*. Other studies also examine the relationship between humans and animals, including Cohen's *Medieval Identity Machines*, which theorizes the intimate relationships, for example, between horse and rider. Susan Crane, too, has spoken of the nature of animals through a study of the hunt, and particularly dogs' behavior in the hunt as intermediate between human and prey ("Medieval Hunting").

misleading; this difficulty is exacerbated when monsters are animal–human hybrids. The inclusion of animal parts on a recognizably human form, however, seems not to have led to a monster being classified as an animal. Indeed, the Anglo-Saxon listing of monsters, *Liber Monstrorum*, carefully divides its monsters into three categories: monstrous men, monstrous beasts, and monstrous serpents. Included among the humans are the person of both sexes (Orchard, "*Liber*" I.1), fauns (I.5), sirens (I.6), hippocentaurs (I.7), Ethiopians (I.9), Cyclops (I.11), Hercules (I.12), and the Cynocephali (I.16). Among the beasts, we find the lion (II.1), leopards (II.6), chimaera (said to be a 'bestiam triplicis monstruosa corporis foeditate terribilum' [terrible beast of triple body with monstrous hideousness] (Orchard 294–5)) (II.11), the two-headed dog Cerberus (II.14), horse-fishes (II.28), and fox-sized mice (II.29). These lists reveal that both monstrous humans and monstrous beasts can be hybrid, but that those creatures that possess both animal and human features, like fauns, sirens, hippocentaurs, and the Cynocephali, are still considered human. Moreover, the lists imply that Hercules, a man of excessive strength, is just as monstrous as a creature that is half goat and half man, or that a crocodile is as monstrous as a chimaera. It seems that monstrous humans are not to be identified as animals; they are, rather, incomplete or over-determined humans.

According to Augustine's definition as well as to the divisions of *Liber Monstrorum*, humans who possess animal parts are not to be classified as animals, but as monsters; however, by virtue of their animal parts, they are also not entirely human. John Block Friedman, in *The Monstrous Races in Medieval Art and Thought*, claims that monstrous humans were not conceived of as truly human: 'it was not possible to grant full and equal humanity to an alien race ... As long as the definition of "man" was based upon a Western model, the monstrous races could only be assigned a subordinate place in the Chain of Being' (196). Thus, for most medieval thinkers and writers, humanoid and rational monsters had the possibility of salvation as Augustine claimed,[6] but they existed somewhere between human and animal in the spiritual and social hierarchy.

Common among all of these writers and thinkers is the notion that monstrous bodies are those that exceed human norms. Physical norms, however, are not built on subtle differences, but rather on visible ones – ones that help a community decide who fits the norm, and who exceeds it. Consequently, I argue that monstrosity is a primarily physical and visible category: in order to be monstrous, one must manifest a clear and usually visible physical difference from that which is 'normal.' Some critics delimit the category by declaring that monsters only exist in fantasy or imagination (Gilmore 6), while others focus on more amorphous qualities, such as 'inherent *evil* [sic], that is, unmotivated wickedness toward humanity'

---

6 For a discussion of a hierarchy of salvation, see Austin, 'Marvelous Peoples or Marvelous Races? Race and the Anglo-Saxon *Wonders of the East*', discussed at greater length in chapter one.

(Waterhouse, quoted in Gilmore 6), or that 'they are dangerous objects of fear, but that this fear includes "the primal fear of being eaten"' (Andriano, quoted in Gilmore 6). These vague definitional concepts are problematic; how shall we decide what is evil, or, indeed, unmotivated? How does our fear of being consumed define what is monstrous? Is this the only human fear that monsters invoke? Even Joseph Campbell turns to hard-to-quantify qualities: 'By a monster I mean some horrendous presence or apparition that explodes all of your standards for harmony, order, and ethical condition' (quoted in Gilmore 7). Standards for harmony, order, or ethical condition are not only socially constructed; they differ at individual levels. I propose a physical and therefore more concrete boundary for monstrosity, in concert with Mandevillian, and, I would argue, medieval tenets.

A monstrous body can differ from a human body in three ways, and we see across medieval literature examples of each of these kinds of difference: they can be more than human, less than human, and human plus some other element not intrinsic to an individual human body. Thus, three types of monstrous humans exist: monsters of excess, monsters of lack, and hybrid monsters. Monsters of excess include the giants of Middle English romance, whose bodies are excessively large, excessively hairy, and usually excessively violent. The *sciapods* (one-footed men) and *blemmye* (men with no heads and faces in their chests) featured in both *Wonders of the East* and *Mandeville's Travels*, are monsters of lack – they do not have all the body parts expected of normal humans. Finally, monsters of hybridity combine attributes of different creatures, different species, or even different sexes into one body. They most often combine animal and human body parts, as the Hartlieb portrait of Alexander depicts him as a human man with tusks like those of a boar. These elements can be more complex, as with the tusked, hooved, and tailed women of *Wonders*, or the horse-footed and fanged men of *Mandeville*. This type of monster also includes sex hybrids, such as the hermaphrodites in *Mandeville* or the bearded huntresses in *Wonders*. Each of these types of monster may present a different kind of commentary, culturally and contextually contingent, regarding the human body. However, at a more abstract level, we can perhaps see the monsters of lack indicating the vulnerability of the human body (for what happens to us if we lose a leg, or worse still, our head?), while those of excess demonstrate its inadequacies. The monsters of hybridity, however, represent a more complex problem; they show the permeability of the human body: the very lack of integrity that permits it to be taken over by parts of other creatures, creating a whole that is neither one thing nor the other. The hybrid monster shows the instability of the categories and organizational principles that drive human societies.

While physical aberration is the primary attribute of monstrosity, deviant behavior can serve to emphasize or exaggerate monstrosity. Monstrous behaviors help to mark the monster as a cultural as well as a physical Other. Some such behaviors include habits of eating, grooming, and dressing, reactions to human approach, use of human language, and transgressing gender roles. For example, a particular group of enormous men in *Wonders* catch fish with their hands and

6

consume them raw, while another group of large lion-headed men consume passing travelers, luring them with human speech. A community of bearded women, hybrid because they possess male and female physical attributes, also engage in transgressive gender roles because they hunt, whereas another group of monstrous women – the Amazons – lack a breast and thereby function as both creatures of lack and also potentially as hybrid because they attempt to take on a male physical characteristic (breastlessness), perform their monstrosity in that they govern themselves, and act as warriors. Grendel's mother, too, a monster of excess like her son, performs a hybrid kind of monstrosity when she takes on the male privilege of getting revenge for her son's death. While these behaviors certainly oppose social norms, they do not make women into monsters *unless* they are accompanied by a physically different body.

Monstrous action or behavior alone does not make the actor a monster. In order to be a monster, one must possess a monstrous body, largely because actions are temporary and can be changed. Aberrant behavior holds the possibility for reform, whereas a monstrous body allows far less possibility of such modification. Women with transgressive behaviors but human bodies may be reformed, as is true of Thryth in *Beowulf,* or even of the Amazons in Chaucer's *Knight's Tale* (who seem to possess both breasts). Reform is considerably more problematic, however, when a woman possesses a tail or tusks. Like their female counterparts, many male monsters, particularly giants, transgress gender roles through excess sexuality in addition to their already excessively large bodies. Thus, transgressive behaviors, when linked with aberrant physicality, reinforce human allegorical or metaphorical interpretations of the monstrous body. However, these actions alone cannot identify a person as a monster.

If this definition of the monster seems to rely on essential categories, that is because it does. A monster, in the Middle Ages, is a creature with a body that differs from the norm in significant ways. The category of the monster implies that there is a set of characteristics that defines the bodies of humans. If a creature possesses *more of, less of,* or *different from* this essence, then the creature is a monster – but the category of monstrous humans depends upon its relation to the category of humanity. Lisa Verner explicates Mandeville's definition of 'deformed against kind,' suggesting that it means 'deformed against the nature of the general category of creature under consideration' (5). Thus, this definition requires a certain level of agreement regarding what it means to be human.

The category of human is one often perceived as complete and independent, in no need of being propped up by external supports. The monster, however, takes the category of humanity, and exploits its boundaries and explores and challenges its integrity. Jeffrey Jerome Cohen argues that the monster always manages to escape (being caught, being killed) because its body cannot be easily categorized or understood – 'the monster is dangerous, a form suspended between forms that threatens to smash distinctions' ('Monster Culture' 6). Because monsters contest cultural categories of 'normality,' they help to rewrite cultural beliefs. However, Cohen states that the monster simultaneously 'prevents mobility, delimiting the

[handwritten margin notes: "weaker argument"; "Oswald seems to follow Verner + Mandeville"; bottom: "Oswald's thesis: VISIBLE difference is necessary for monstrosity"]

7

Cohen: monsters make space
monsters limit space

social spaces through which private bodies can move,' under threat of those creatures that serve as 'border patrol' (12). Monstrous humans, then, reify what it
means to be fully human, but they also delimit the possibilities for the human
body. Because they are simultaneously human and not human, their very indeter-
minacy makes the monstrous a location for displacing fears about bodies that are
all too human.

SEX, GENDER, SEXUALITY, AND REPRODUCTION

While monsters are depositories for all kinds of human fears and anxieties, the
nexus of many of these fears is sexuality. Judith Halberstam argues that 'Where
sexuality becomes identity, other "others" become invisible and the multiple
features of monstrosity seem to degenerate back into a primeval sexual sludge.
Class, race, and nation are subsumed, in other words, within the monstrous sexual
body' (*Skin Shows* 7). This is not to suggest that issues like race, class, or nation do
not contribute to the meaning or function of the monster; rather, sexuality can be
a focal point at which these various concerns meet. Racial and social concerns can
be carried out through the medium of the sexualized monstrous body.[7]

However, sexuality remains an elusive term, one which theorists struggle to
define. As Eve Sedgwick claims, 'Sex, gender, sexuality: three terms whose usage
relations and analytical relations are almost irremediably slippery' (27). The difficulty in pinning down sexuality stems from the troubled relationship between
categories of sex and gender. The biologist and feminist scholar Anne
Fausto-Sterling notes that

> In 1972 the sexologists John Money and Anke Ehrhardt popularized the idea that
> sex and gender are separate categories. Sex, they argued, refers to physical attrib-
> utes and is anatomically and physiologically determined. Gender they saw as a
> psychological transformation of the self – the internal conviction that one is
> either male or female (gender identity) and the behavioral expressions of that
> conviction. (3)

Sex, then, is biological, supposedly indisputable, while gender is more amorphous,
and perhaps more culturally constructed – or at least can be defined in relation to
cultural constraints. Sedgwick states that sex differences:

> include (or are ordinarily thought to include) more or less marked dimorphisms
> of genital formation, hair growth …, fat distribution, hormonal function, and
> reproductive capacity. 'Sex' in this sense … is seen as the relatively minimal raw
> material on which is then based the social construction of *gender*. Gender, then,

---

7   Although Halberstam's concerns are with monsters in Gothic novels and their specific social
    and historical context, her description of the literary experience of monstrous bodies is simi-
    larly apt for medieval audiences.

is the far more elaborated, more fully and rigidly dichotomized social produc-
tion and reproduction of male and female identities and behaviors. (27)

Sedgwick, and most cultural scholars, treat sex as an easy-to-identify category,
placing gender as more difficult to identify or categorize. However, Fausto-
Sterling argues that even the basic physical facts of human bodies are complex and
contradictory: 'Our bodies are too complex to provide clear-cut answers about
sexual difference. The more we look for a simple physical basis for "sex," the more
it becomes clear that "sex" is not a pure physical category. What bodily signals and
functions we define as male or female come already entangled in our ideas about
gender' (4). In other words, what we expect to see because of our socialized
notions of gender affects what we will identify as sex characteristics. Thus, while
our expectations about gender are based on sex, so too are our expectations of sex
based on gender. Moreover, as Judith Butler rightly reminds us, gender extends

[margin handwriting: → there is no "normal" human body]

> beyond that naturalized binary. The conflation of gender with masculine/femi-
> nine, man/woman, male/female, thus performs the very naturalization that the
> notion of gender is meant to forestall. Thus, a restrictive discourse on gender that
> insists on the binary of man and woman as the exclusive way to understand the
> gender field performs a *regulatory* operation of power that naturalizes the hege-
> monic instance and forecloses the thinkability of its disruption.
>
> (*Undoing Gender* 43)

In other words, to rely only on categories of masculinity and femininity as options
for gender is as reductive as conflating sex and gender.

When the lines between sex and gender are difficult to draw, definitions and
understandings of sexuality become necessarily culturally contingent. Sedgwick
struggles to define sexuality in a way that removes from it elements of gender. She
claims that sexuality is 'the array of acts, expectations, narratives, pleasures, identity formations, and knowledges, in both women and men, that tends to cluster
most densely around certain genital sensations but is not adequately defined by
them' (29). Sexuality is not just about what is done, but what is desired, expected,
preferred, and known. Because of our binary systems of both sex (male/female)
and gender (homo-/heterosexual),[8] it becomes almost impossible to discuss sexuality without invoking these categories and turning sexuality into merely a question of 'object-choice' (30), that is, who or what one desires to engage with
sexually. Sedgwick does her best to eschew this means of thinking about sexuality,
stating 'sexuality extends along so many dimensions that aren't well described in
terms of the gender of object-choice at all' (35). Thus, untangling the web of sex,

[margin handwriting: Sexuality is more than the "object choice" of desire]

---

8 As Sedgwick argues, although bi-sexuality and hermaphroditism are alternate categories, they
rely upon these binary systems because they must define themselves in relation to them.
Without the binary system, these concepts possess no meaning (though, of course, the bodies
and behaviors they describe continue to exist).

gender, and sexuality is a risky and potentially impossible undertaking. However, thinking about the matrix of these elements of identity – elements that 'can be expressed only in the terms of the other' (30) – yields to us a better sense of biological, social, and cultural expectations about bodies and the identities that are attached to them.

These complex interrelations among sex, gender, and sexuality complicate my earlier definition of the monstrous – a definition that relies on the primacy of physicality, with behavior and performance acting as auxiliary components. However, Ruth Mazo Karras argues:

> It is important for our purposes here to recognize that in the Middle Ages the distinction among the three was not just blurred, it did not exist. If someone deviated from the expected models of sexual behavior, people did not assume that the variation was a matter of biology *or* gender identity *or* sexual desire; the three worked together ... For them, sexuality was not separate from sex and gender. (6)

She claims that medieval people saw inextricable relations among these three categories, and that just as a body indicated certain expectations of behavior, so too did any behavior or performance articulate certain truths about the body. In the following chapters, I demonstrate that while monsters may perform transgressive genders and sexualities, what makes them truly monstrous is the bodies they possess. While Butler and many postmodern feminist writers rightly resist such essentialism, insisting that we cannot be reduced to our bodies, medieval notions of the body as represented in the literature regarding monsters are indeed rather essentialist. Although I reiterate this essentialist vision of identity as constructed by the body, I do so for a larger feminist purpose. I believe the very flexibility of the monstrous sexed body – its ability to defy and subvert norms – serves as a kind of predecessor for Butler's notions of performativity and iteration. The bodies of medieval monsters exceed the boundaries of humanity, and in stretching these boundaries they expand what it means to be human, but also what it means to be male and/or female, masculine and/or feminine, or, indeed, something else entirely.

I explore the limits of the binaries of masculinity and femininity not because these are the only options represented in medieval literature, but rather because they are the predominant social categories. As Karras argues, 'The line between active and passive partner in the Middle Ages was very sharp, and closely related to gender roles. To be active was to be masculine, regardless of the gender of one's partner, and to be passive was to be feminine' (23). This is not to say that all people sexed as women would be gendered feminine, but rather it confirms that these categories and the qualities that define them are culturally entrenched. Medieval bodies, behaviors, and desires do exceed these categories, yet the binary is established as natural, or as a kind of norm, in order to prescribe and proscribe behavior. The wide array of scholarship on medieval queerness, however, illustrates the variety of actions and choices depicted across medieval literature.

10

monsters as QUEER

Queerness, Carolyn Dinshaw states, is 'a relation to a norm, and both the norm and the particular queer lack of fit [within the norm] will vary according to specific instances' ('Got Medieval' 21). In other words, queerness and its variation from the norm shift, relative to the circumstances in which they exist. For Dinshaw, among others, medieval sexuality and queerness are not determined just by who one chooses or desires, but also if one chooses a partner at all.[9] Karma Lochrie, too, challenges the idea of a heteronormativity, suggesting that

> Because of the implicit association of the feminine with desire and the pathologizing of all sexuality in medieval theology, though, the Middle Ages was in the peculiar position of vacuating the category of normal sex. Heterosexuality as a normative principle simply did not exist; fornication as a perversion that coexisted with sodomy and gender infractions did. In this area at least, nature seems to have created nothing but perversions. (*Covert* 225)

Because sexual desire and sexuality in any form is figured as transgressive and perhaps even feminine, no actual sexuality is normative.[10] All sexuality, then, can be conceived of as perverse and unacceptable. Thus, medieval sexuality contests the binary norm in a variety of ways that both resist and reiterate social mores, much like monstrosity.

Indeed, the links between the sexual body and the monstrous one are very strong. As Amy Hollywood notes, 'recent studies suggest that the determining term for sexuality is *natura*, with sexual activity judged according to whether it is natural or against nature' (176).[11] Therefore, like the monstrous body defined by Mandeville, the sexed body is judged as being either like its kind, or against it.

---

9   Virginity is a significant sexual category in this period, and choosing Jesus rather than a human sexual partner is a viable and indeed valuable choice – whether it is made by the individual or the family. Virginity might rightly be identified as another valid gender (as well as a part of sexual identity), and can also be considered queer. The virginal body, like the monstrous body, is a body that defies norms. See Weston, 'Queering Virginity.' Judith Bennett further argues that contemporary assumptions about sexuality cannot be applied to the Middle Ages, saying 'Insofar as there *were* sexual identities in the Middle Ages, the best articulated might have been those of the celibate and the virginal' (116).

10 For discussion of heteronormativity and how it functions (or perhaps does not) in medieval Europe, see Lochrie, *Covert Operations*; Watts, *Amoral Gower*; Schultz, 'Heterosexuality as a Threat to Medieval Studies,' and Burger and Kruger, *Queering the Middle Ages*. While these scholars argue convincingly that heterosexuality and heteronormativity are not entirely functional ideologies in medieval Europe, they also affirm complex understandings of and expectations regarding gender. I argue in this book that monsters act as challenges to heteronormative gender expectations; while they may be representations meant to shore up ideas of gender based solely on assumptions about reproduction and hierarchy, they also expand the catalog of sexual and gender possibility in the Middle Ages.

11 Dinshaw has said her primary concern in *Getting Medieval* 'was on people who were and are disadvantaged by being left out of reigning classification (in particular, dominant sexual categories)' ('Got Medieval' 204). She thus confirms the power of the system of 'reigning classifications,' articulating who falls inside these categories (those who stay within the binary system of sex, gender, and sexuality) and who exceeds them (the queer).

What is most troubling in bodies that are both monstrous and sexual is the capacity for reproduction. While emphasis on reproduction can imply a kind of heterosexual norm, such a system accounts for medieval sexuality in a limited way, as James A. Schultz suggests:

> That children were born in the Middle Ages does suggest that medieval women and men had sex with each other. And there is, it would seem, a trivial sense in which one could label any sexual relations involving a woman and a man 'heterosexual.' The label, however, is misleading. First, it encourages the reduction of heterosexuality to reproduction. Second, it frustrates a clear understanding of the way medieval people classified sexual relations. (16)

While reproduction requires a male and a female partner, I do not mean to suggest that such a pairing was the only marker of human sexuality. Rather, the stakes of monstrous sexuality are further pronounced in the reproductive consequences of certain sexual unions. The danger is not that the method of reproduction is so far away from human means, but rather that it is so very familiar. A creature that exceeds the rules of 'kind' in terms of physicality threatens the boundaries of humanity, but one that does so and is also capable of propagation is far worse. To possess a frightening body is terrifying, but to use that body to make more monsters is far more dangerous. However, reproductive monsters are troubling for more reasons than that they can create more scary monsters who might attack the human race. These reproductive monsters cannot be conceived of, reductively, as animals who act on instinct, but instead they seem increasingly human. They no longer exist in isolation, but possess communities and connections, and even social orders – indeed, through reproduction, they have something to protect, nurture, and perpetuate, an impulse that is not just animal but also human. Therefore, it is those monsters whose bodies bear markers of sex and sexuality that most clearly threaten the boundaries of human communities precisely because they are capable of creating their own communities. Even worse, they might invade the boundaries of these human communities, inserting themselves into the economy of reproduction and inheritance. The reproductive monster frightens by both replicating itself and by invoking the specter of miscegenation.[12]

The monster is formulated as originary to human culture, and indeed to Britain, through means of miscegenation. In his monograph, *Of Giants: Sex, Monsters, and the Middle Ages*, Cohen recounts Geoffrey of Monmouth's story about the origins of the naming of the British Isles (Albion), in which the exiled daughters of a nameless Greek King (the eldest of whom is called Albina) arrive at an uninhabited island. The sisters are visited by and copulate with the devil, resulting in the birth of a tribe of giants, who rule 'the land for eight hundred years, until the arrival of Aeneas's great-grandson, who imposes on their primal chaos a

---

[12] For a discussion of the attitudes toward miscegenation operating particularly in Anglo-Saxon England, in and among the various tribes and invaders, see Giacone, 'Woman in a Boat.'

new world order' (49). These giants, he argues, are foundational to British identity, and particularly to British masculinity. The sisters, who are exiled because they plot to kill their unwanted husbands, however, provide a transgressive feminine origin from which springs the giants, products of miscegenation, that precede the masculine order. British masculinity, based on descent from Rome, always opposes the giant, and yet defines itself by means of this opposition. The giant serves simultaneously as enjoyment and prohibition – pleasure and violence, allowing humans the satisfaction of fascination, and yet attacking them. He serves as the origin of masculinity against which human men must measure themselves and to whom they never can measure up, a phallic father, in both the literal and figurative senses: 'if the giant is sometimes made to represent the masculine body's lost prehistory, that is precisely because he figures the dangerous instability of its present integrity' (xv). Therefore the giant both opposes and enables British masculinity, and proceeds from the union of demon and human.

Although Cohen focuses on male monsters, both male and female monsters pose reproductive threats to human society. Barbara Creed, in her study of horror films, claims, 'the reasons why the monstrous-feminine horrifies her audience are quite different from the reasons why the male monster horrifies his audience' (3). For Cohen, the male monster is a creature of excess and violence, a body and masculinity against which men can never compete, and for Creed the female monster is a creature driven by her womb and her need to reproduce. The horrifying bodies of both male and female monsters, though, do share a common marker – sexualized identity. Those monsters against whom humans set themselves most fiercely are monsters who are explicitly gendered and sexualized. The monsters that seek to replicate themselves and in their reproduction mimic human practices are the most threatening of all, and demand a firm human response. This human reaction is spurred by anxiety about both transgressive sexuality and the capacity for reproduction – the idea that bodies are no longer under control. Thus, monsters whose bodies bear signs of human gender identity and reproductive capability are those monsters that spur the most vehement responses of characters and readers. These monstrous bodies require more than killing – they merit the most remarkable acts of erasure, both literal and figurative.

ALWAYS ALREADY: ERASURE AND THE TRACE

In his essay 'Monster Culture,' Cohen's second postulate is 'The Monster Always Escapes,' but perhaps a better formulation might be 'the monster always returns.' The term 'escape' implies only the present circumstance, but the idea of 'return' requires that there be a prior incarnation from which the monster was inadequately expunged. If the monster returns, then it never has been absent, *really*. This study seeks to elucidate the nature of monstrous presence and the myth of monstrous absence. I argue that the sexualized monster never disappears completely from the text after it has been removed or erased; instead the monster haunts the remainder of the text as a trace. The monstrous body is a body that is always already present. Its existence precedes the humans who seek it out – just as Grendel precedes Hrothgar – thus it is 'already.' Similarly, no matter how stridently the characters, authors, or readers of a text try to remove the monster from its pages, the monster 'always' remains. Indeed, what is left behind serves as a trace of the monster. For example, when a viewer scratches out portions of the images from a manuscript, it is obvious to later viewers that something has been removed, whether it is the image's eyes, or, as is the case in *Wonders of the East*, its penis. This visible attempt at removal is a clear trace of that which has been effaced.

In using the terms 'always already' and 'trace,' I borrow from the work of Jacques Derrida. He uses the phrase 'always already' in reference to language and the failure of representation, as in the existence of the thing before and beyond the language we construct to name it.[13] According to Derrida, because the thing always precedes our language for it, language is always fundamentally fractured and faulty in its attempts at representation. I borrow Derrida's terms not to question the intrinsically deconstructive nature of language, but as an attempt to capture the problems inherent in representation, and particularly in representing the monstrous. The rupture between the thing and our representation of that thing invokes the idea of the present absence. Absence and presence are always in play, Derrida suggests. While the reality of the thing cannot be expressed by language, its presence is suggested at the same time that its absence is reaffirmed: 'Being must be conceived as presence or absence on the basis of the possibility of play and not the other way around' ('Structure' 93). In order to capture the nature of the present absence, Derrida introduces the concept of the 'trace.'

The trace occupies the territory between past and present – it physically marks the space of absence. In Derrida's own language, 'The trace is the difference which opens appearance and signification' (*Grammatology* 119). The trace, then, occurs between the thing itself and the act of representation. It is what is left over after the thing is gone; as David Arnason argues, 'We may now define *trace* as the sign left by the absent thing, after it has passed on the scene of its former presence' (5). For Derrida, the trace marks an historical space, an origin that can never be understood or that has probably never existed. This notion can help us to understand the position of the monstrous. Cohen claims that the monstrous is that which precedes man and defines man – the monstrous is foundational to British masculinity. The monster can serve as a kind of origin. But the human attempt to understand and control monstrosity through representation can never reproduce this originary identity; instead, efforts at reproduction and ultimately erasure of the monstrous result in a trace. The trace of the monster in the text declares its presence through its absence, and proclaims the impossibility both of representation and erasure.

Although Derrida investigates the term 'erasure,' my use of the term is

---

13 See Derrida, 'Structure, Sign and Play in the Discourse of Human Sciences,' and *Of Grammatology*, especially chapter two.

informed primarily by Michael Camille's 'Obscenity Under Erasure: Censorship in Medieval Illuminated Manuscripts.' For Derrida, *every* sign has undergone erasure and so all language is intrinsically incomplete. For Camille, erasure is an act of will undertaken purposefully by a viewer of a text: 'works of art become victims of an attack that seeks to destroy all or parts of them' (139). He cites Mary Caputi, who, in her discussion of obscenity, says the obscene is 'the violation of boundaries, the exceeding of subconsciously consensual limits' (5, quoted in Camille 139). The erasure, then, seeks to delimit the violation of these boundaries, to reinstate the boundaries. But Camille argues that the job of the art historian is to look not only at what is pictured, 'but also to what has been obfuscated, effaced, and rejected as overstepping the bounds of what it is permissible to picture' (139). Rough and passionate iconoclasm is not the only method of erasure; rather, he remarks on the 'deliberation' with which some acts of erasure are performed (140).[14] He claims, 'picturing things that should not be seen has resulted in a performative response, which makes them subsequently unseeable' (141). Prime objects for this kind of response are the 'facial and the sexual' (140). Faces were often erased because of 'the power of the face to behold,' which is linked with the 'evil eye' (141). Indeed, Camille notes the power of images to act on observers, recounting multiple injunctions to pregnant women not to look at bestiaries, particularly 'dog-headed apes or monkeys' (143), which might result in the women giving birth to similarly deformed children. Thus, demons and monsters, especially their faces, are often erased from manuscripts (144). Sexual erasures, often the removal of genitals, are also traditionally linked to the 'evil eye' (146), although Camille suggests that these erasures might also result from 'prudery and looking at what should not be seen, the sexual organs' (146). Therefore, the performance of erasure yields as much information about the cultural response of the viewer as it does about the originary state of the image.

Erasure, however, does not necessarily serve as a destructive or diminishing act, but can construct a different kind of knowledge. While erasure is an act of removal, in changing the original image, the eraser actually creates something new: 'We tend to associate creation with construction not destruction, but the selective obliteration of parts of an image surely constitutes not merely editing and expurgation, as with a text, but an embodied response' (140). Camille points out that erasure creates a new possibility for understanding – in fact, he implicitly invokes the idea of the trace: 'for once you rub something away, you tend to draw attention to what was there before the obfuscation ... erasures can tell us a great deal about what kinds of images were considered powerful and dangerous' (146). The blank spot left behind by the erasure then acts as a trace of not only what was there before, but also of the embodied response of an earlier viewer. Therefore, when a monster is not only represented but erased, we can see, through the trace of the monster, that which was most threatening to human viewers or readers. While

---

14 Another possible method of erasure is idolatry and devotion. Images are sometimes rubbed off a page through years of being kissed in adoration (Camille 141).

Camille often breaks these responses into the demonic or the sexual, I have found that erasures occur when the categories are combined, when the object of erasure is not only monstrous but sexualized. The impetus for the erasure, then, can be combined as well; it is not just the obscene body that inspires the erasure, but the dangerous *and* obscene body. If an image of a dog-headed monkey might cause a monstrous birth, a sexualized monster – a two-headed man with an erect penis – could be far more dangerous.

Erasure might take the form of the literal removal of parts of an image, as when the genitals in the manuscript illustrations are scratched out in *Wonders of the East.* But I suggest that erasure can also function more subtly, as when a scribe or artist decides to leave out or change unacceptable parts of a narrative in a new version of a text. Ultimately, however, desire for erasure on the part of the writers, scribes, artists, or viewers is thwarted. When someone attempts to erase the monstrous – from the text or from the body – the reader or viewer can see evidence of the attempted erasure. Traces of that which was erased remain, whether it is the blank spot on the page that results from scratching out part of an image or the void in the narrative left by Grendel and his mother once they have been killed and decapitated.

Erasure is the primary mode of responding to monstrous and sexualized bodies in Old English, but the same cannot be said for sexualized monsters in Middle English texts. In Middle English texts, as I shall demonstrate, the problem of the monster is often solved through the narrative apparatus of transformation, or metamorphosis. The impulse behind erasure remains, but the means of controlling the sexualized monster has shifted. Indeed, while the transformation of the monstrous body in Middle English serves a purpose similar to that of erasure, this method results in an even more frightening prospect. Through transformation, Middle English monsters can be stripped of their monstrosity, usually by magical means – or at least their monstrous attributes are no longer visible. Transformation is a means of controlling the most threatening elements of a sexualized monster – through transformation, the dangerous elements of identity can be removed, or at least seem to disappear. I suggest that most transformations are doomed to be incomplete because of the problem of the trace, for the new body will always be a reminder of that which preceded it. This type of change happens, for example, when the monstrous body of a demon's son in *Sir Gowther* is replaced by the body of a child of God. Gowther is not erased; he remains in the narrative throughout, but his essence changes. But what happens if the monstrous elements only appear to be removed, but really they only appear to be gone? Because the monstrous, through transformation, has the possibility of becoming invisible, monsters become capable of infiltrating human communities and passing as human – as happens in *Mandeville's Travels.* Thus, the author of *Sir Gowther* attempts to overcome the dangers inherent in transformation by linking it with the idea of religious conversion. However, as with the idea of conversion, we continue to see the trace of what was there before the change.

Transformation, however incomplete, allows space for bodies to change; this

16

kind of transformation, however, does not occur for Old English monsters. The only way Old English monsters lose their monstrosity is through erasure, either literal or metaphorical. The bodies of Old English monsters, then, cannot be rescued from their monstrosity – we might think of them as permanently monstrous.[15] Bodies and identities in Anglo-Saxon England are what they are: they are represented as incapable of true metamorphosis. While some scholars might suggest that Anglo-Saxon texts like the riddles feature shape-shifting bodies, I would argue that the riddles, although playing with concepts of the body, are more concerned with linguistic play and cleverness than with the actual capability of bodies to mutate or transform.[16] Perhaps this lack of physical transformation reflects the party line of institutions reliant on the maintenance of essential bodies and identities, as much as it is representative of larger cultural beliefs about the body. However, bodies, as they are represented in Old English literature, do not change, beyond the changes related to natural aging or physical punishment; monstrous bodies remain forever monstrous.[17] Later medieval monsters, however, can and do live as humans; thus, we might see their bodies as more transitive and perhaps even temporary.[18] In Old English literature, the body is immutable. It can be killed or taken apart, but even then it retains its essence. In Middle English, however, the body possesses the potential for change; a body may seem to be one thing, when it is indeed another, or, alternately, a body can in fact be one

15 Bynum, too, notes an Anglo-Saxon focus on the development of an essential identity: 'In the mid-twelfth century, people producing a wide variety of discourses tended to think of change not as replacement but as evolution or development, as alteration of appearance or mode of being ... Behavior revealed character or type; a self was always what it was. The 'end' or goal of development, if there was development, was to achieve the ideal version of the type or self' (23). If, as Bynum claims, change is not truly available for humans, then it is certainly not possible for monsters.

16 Linguistic play can certainly reveal some truths about bodies in coded ways, as scholars like Glenn Davis and Sarah Higley have argued. However, my concern in this text is with the treatment of literal bodies, as they are represented in narrative texts. Like the riddles, the charms might similarly be seen as attempting to change bodies – in terms of illness or health, or even perhaps irritating character traits like talkativeness – however, they are not descriptive of actual changes, particularly in the sense of true physical metamorphosis, like the removal of a tail or the addition of a second eye.

17 Certainly the Old English lawcodes indicate physical punishments – for instance, the loss of a nose or hand in response to law-breaking – but this kind of punishment indicates even more vehemently the permanent nature of the body. To remove these parts is to indicate the effect of crime upon the body that perpetrates it. These changes mark bodies as criminal, just as a tail or a tusk identifies it as monstrous.

18 Bynum also notes this shift, identifying it as a cultural trend toward change: 'Toward the end of the twelfth century, however, a new understanding – a new model – of change emerged ... people were increasingly fascinated by ... radical change, where an entity is replaced by something completely different' (Bynum 25). She explains this fascination with change by changes in society: 'Agricultural, economic, and urban growth in the course of the eleventh and twelfth centuries had led to transformations of familial and social structure that made it increasingly possible (if still not easy) for people – especially privileged people – to change their social roles' (26).

thing, then become another. However, the common trait for both erased and transformed bodies is the trace. In Old English, when a body has been erased, we can see the blank spaces left behind that indicate what it once was. Similarly, Middle English monsters may be transformed into humans, or at least into creatures that seem human, but even then, as I shall demonstrate in chapters three and four, their bodies retain traces of what they once were. The monster, as Cohen suggests in "Monster Theory", always returns.

BRIDGING THE GAP: OLD ENGLISH TO MIDDLE ENGLISH

Old and Middle English literatures present marked contrasts: different languages, different concerns, different dilemmas. However, the periods are of course not completely unconnected.[19] Generalizations about the distinctions abound – as we can see in the facetious title of Hugh Magennis' recent article, 'No Sex, Please, We're Anglo-Saxons.' While it is true that sex and sexuality are much more difficult to locate in the corpus of Old English literature than in Middle English literature, they are not entirely absent. Similarly, while the body seems often to be of less concern in Anglo-Saxon literature as opposed to Middle English, it *does* matter. The bodies of saints are just as tortured in Old English as in Middle English, and characters within the texts do lead embodied lives. While Old English does not provide us with an infinite number of aggressive and outspoken women like the Wife of Bath, it does provide some, including the fascinating and dangerous Thryth, who causes men literally to lose their heads, and the rhetorically powerful Judith. Despite general assumptions to the contrary, questions of gender, sex, and the body are evident in Old English literature, as they are in Middle English literature, although not to the same extent or with the same frequency.

The acts of erasure inflicted on Anglo-Saxon monstrous and sexed bodies, however, do not take place in a cultural vacuum. A more general sort of erasure of the sexed body takes place in the corpus of Anglo-Saxon writing.[20] Through examining the consistent erasure of the sexualized body in the corpus, we can better

---

[19] Wallace, in *Premodern Places*, argues for a shift away from categories of 'medieval' and 'Renaissance,' to avoid 'the peculiar eddying forcefields' (11) of these terms. Although he studies later medieval texts, he claims that Anglo-Saxon England is just as relevant to his topic, recognizing that it is 'further removed from us in time and language, hence more difficult to retrieve' (11).

[20] In fact, throughout the Anglo-Saxon period, canon law forbade sex to even married people for most days of the year: 'Sexual relations with one's spouse were also to be kept within strict bounds, and were prohibited when the wife was menstruating, pregnant, or nursing a child, and during certain periods in the church calendar, such as Sundays and Fridays and most major saints' days, as well as all of Lent and Advent. This left about fifty days a year when a married couple could legitimately have sexual intercourse, and even this was hemmed in by restrictions as to position, time of day, and proper dress' (Weisner-Hanks 37).

understand just how accurately the erasure of the monstrous body in *Wonders* and *Beowulf* reflects the norms and practices of the period. However, because the monsters are reduced only to their bodies, and to the identity that is clearly articulated through their embodiment, we can also recognize how fundamental the body is in constructing medieval identity. In acknowledging these erasures of monstrous sexuality, we can both identify and understand the impulses behind the larger cultural practice of the erasure of sexuality. Magennis argues that '[i]n their treatment of sexuality, most Old English literary texts reflect either ... the lack of concern with sexual themes, characteristic of the Germanic heroic tradition, or the "sexual pessimism" inherited from patristic teaching, an attitude which received expression in particularly acute form in Anglo-Saxon England' (14). In recent years, scholars have considered masculine, feminine, and even, in the case of Clare Lees' and Gillian Overing's *Double Agents*, absent bodies. But Anglo-Saxon culture as we know it does not teem with transgressive bodies. Those bodies that we do see are most often set within a Christian scope. When explicitly sexual bodies are drawn or written, they are meant to give the message that the sexual body is, as with the tusked women of *Wonders*, offensive and disgusting.[21] The naked bodies of Adam and Eve in the Junius 11 manuscript illustrations are normative and indeed modest; the creatures that have penises are the fallen angels, rather than Adam. As Mary Dockray-Miller observes, 'initial differentiation between the figures of Adam and Eve in the drawings is done most easily by reference to their breasts, specifically their nipples, rather than to the more standard gender markers of hair, dress, or naked genitalia' ("Breasts" 221). These images suggest that to possess a sexualized body is to be more transgressive than Adam and Eve. The fallen angels alone are depicted as having bodies with genitals. Archbishop of York Wulfstan's famous *Sermo Lupi ad Anglorum* also attributes explicit sexual acts to a people grown depraved and wicked. The homilist's desire is to horrify listeners and inspire repentance. Thus, he depicts the sexually repugnant men who purchase a woman together and then 'wið þa ane fylþe adreogað, an after anum 7 ælc æfter oðrum' [with that one woman they practice abomination, one after another and each after the next] (Bethurum lines 88–9) in order to inspire the audience's horror and to change their behavior. Even in the lawcodes concerning rape, we hardly have a legal definition of the term. We know what happens to bodies that break the law,[22] but most of these bodies are physically censured and changed as punishment. While sexed bodies, in these examples, are present, they are depicted in order to be corrected, ultimately.

Erasure of sexual bodies also occurs in the kinds of bodies that are represented

---

21 For a discussion of sexual practices in Anglo-Saxon England, see Pasternack and Weston, *Sex and Sexuality in Anglo-Saxon England*.

22 Richards, 'The Body as Text in Early Anglo-Saxon Law' and O'Brien O'Keeffe, 'Body and Law in Late Anglo-Saxon England' both discuss practices of maiming the body as a form of punishment, and the kinds of restitution for criminal maiming of an innocent body.

and the ways in which they are depicted. Scribes might choose never to depict sexed and gendered bodies, or they might 'remove' layers of sexuality from source materials. Along with being a Christian body, the body in most Old English literature is male, be it the hero Beowulf or the monk and prolific homilist, Ælfric. However, this masculinity is almost never displayed in terms of its sexual potential, but rather its superior position in the social or religious hierarchy.[23] Women are not completely erased from this literature, and are in fact present in a variety of genres, from saints' lives to elegies to historical chronicles. We even see a few of these women translated from the Latin hagiographical tradition to the Anglo-Saxon vernacular, like the female saints Juliana and Elene, and the biblical heroine, Judith.[24] Their bodies, however, are considerably revised by Anglo-Saxon writers in order to conceal sexual details that are present in Latin sources. As Mary Clayton argues, concerning Ælfric's *Book of Judith*, these revisions reveal 'a deep-seated anxiety with regard to women using their bodies in ways which had been firmly repressed by centuries of church prescriptions' (225). In the Anglo-Saxon saints' lives of virgin martyrs, despite the fact that sexuality is a matter of consistent concern, Hugh Magennis argues, 'the explicit emphasis on such themes is diminished' (3).[25] Women's sexual bodies in these texts are generally excised, or 'removed' by Anglo-Saxon writers, despite their existence in source materials.

The scenes of sexual intercourse or temptation that occur in Anglo-Saxon literature are generally covert – another means of erasing bodies from the text. In the story of Cynewulf and Cyneheard, contained in the Anglo-Saxon *Chronicle* entry for the year 755, Cynewulf, protected only by a small band of retainers, is caught by Cyneheard while 'on wifcyþþe on Merantune' (Bately 36) [visiting a mistress in Merton]. The language here does not give any explicit sense of the sexual in the scene, although translators and readers alike assume a tryst. Roberta Frank urges caution in such a reading:

> The Chronicle entry as a whole makes clear that Cynewulf was closeted with a woman friend at Merton. But given the reluctance of the vernacular to allow Adam, Cain, and Joseph to 'know' their wives, there is some reason to be

---

23 Most of the figures represented through Old English literatures are upper class. Class above gender seems to be the significant term in power dynamics.

24 Although study of these texts reveals many intricacies and complications to traditional notions of Anglo-Saxon gender, the literal sexed bodies of these women rarely transgress acceptable norms.

25 Some scholars conceive of virginity as a radical sexual identity, but the institution of the convent at least provides a place within the confines of Anglo-Saxon society for people to enact this identity. Even for the transvestite saints' lives, like those of Eugenia and Euphrosyne, 'the theme of transvestitism, however, with its use of subterfuge, cannot be more than a sub-plot in the life of the virgin martyr, since her gaining of glory comes not in the avoidance of conflict, through disguise, but in her open declaration of defiance at her trial and execution' (Magennis 3).

suspicious of readings that take *wifcyþþe* not as 'female companionship' but as 'carnal knowledge of a woman.' (309)

She does not completely disregard the possibility of such an understanding, but asks readers to allow for a more nuanced and subtle reading, where connotations remain connotations and reveal only the modesty of the scribe: 'The twelfth-century chronicler, like his Anglo-Saxon predecessor, only hints, decorously and indirectly, at what Æthelweard and modern translators so explicitly affirm. In the privacy of the Old English vernacular, the half-said thing alone worked wonders' (309).[26] Indeed, much of Old English writing relies on such practices of subtlety, in regards to discussions of sex.

We see this 'half-spoken' sexual scenario again in *Beowulf*, when Hrothgar retires to his bedchambers with his young wife, Wealhtheow – who has already given birth to sons. 'Ða him Hroþgar gewat mid his hæleþa gedryht,/ eodur Scyldinga ut of healle;/ wolde wigfruma Wealhþeo secan,/ cwen to gebeddan' [Then Hrothgar, protector of the Scyldings, went out of the hall with his troop of retainers; the warlord wished to find Wealhtheow, the queen as a bedfellow] (662a–5a). Here, Hrothgar leaves Beowulf to meet Grendel while he retreats to his private nuptial chamber. The phrase, 'to gebeddan,' echoes the connotations of *wifcyþþe*. In other occurrences of this word in the corpus of Old English writing, it refers to such fecund relationships as those between Adam and Eve, and Rebecca and Isaac (*DOE* corpus). We certainly see no explicit sexual behavior, but we cannot ignore the connotations of the King retiring to bed to join his wife as a, in Klaeber's terms, 'bedfellow.' Through the rest of the poem, Wealhtheow's role is largely ceremonial; she carries the meadcup and serves the men in the appropriate hierarchical order. She serves just the kind of function Magennis claims:

> Secular heroic poetry in Old English is highly modest in content and has no overt interest in sexual themes … women are typically gracious and nobly-adorned, but presentations of them lack a sexual dimension. The heroic world is a public rather than a private world and its conflicts do not usually arise from matters of sex. (11)

Wealhtheow embodies the former; she is appropriately garbed and gracious, and, even as her husband joins her in bed, she seems to be without sexual dimension. The 'half-said thing' may, as Frank suggests, work wonders, but it also covers up bodies, keeping readers from knowing precisely how they function in private. As Karma Lochrie suggests, the 'technology of secrecy … structures power relations, including those produced by religious institutions, cultural practices, social idioms, and individual behavior' (*Covert*, 2). In other words, keeping these bodies

---

26 See also Scragg, '*Wifcyþþe*.' He argues that *wifcyþþe*, which he suggests might simply mean 'in the company of his wife' (180), should not be read as 'an opprobrious moral comment' (185) because of the passage's generally positive vision of the King's activities.

private is a means of structuring power in Anglo-Saxon England – particularly in terms of a literary culture largely perpetuated by an institution invested in and populated by celibate people.

Sex, however, is not entirely erased from Anglo-Saxon literature. Where the *Chronicle* and *Beowulf* present a hardly spoken sexuality, the Old English riddles are sometimes more explicit in their use of *double-entendre*. Many scholars have recently turned their attentions to the functions of the sexual valences in these riddles, riddles including 25 (the onion), 44 (the key), 45 (dough), and 61 (churn? helmet?), that all draw attention to sexual states, bodies, and behaviors.[27] The onion riddle invokes the image of an erect penis with lines like 'Staþol min is steapheah, stonde ic on bedde' [I am firm and erect, and I stand up in bed] (4a–b), and a sexual encounter when the churl's daughter 'on mec gripeð, ræseð mec on reodne, reafað min heafod, fegeð mec on fæsten' [grips me, assaults me in my redness, seizes my head, [and] confines me in a tight place] (7b–9a). The key riddle also urges the prurient answer of 'penis,' saying that this object hangs 'bi weres þeo' [by a man's thigh] (1b), and that it 'bið stiþ ond heard' [is stiff and hard] (3a). The same is true of the dough riddle, which uses language that might describe an erection. This thing is 'þindan ond þunian' [rising and swelling] (2a) and it is also a 'banlease' [boneless] (3a) object that 'grapode hygewlonc hondum' [the proud-minded woman gripped with her hands] (3b–4a). Many scholars have recently turned their attentions to the functions of the sexual valences in these riddles, often with very different results. John Tanke argues that the function of a riddle ultimately is to replace a sexual reading with another 'clean' solution: 'Solving a double-entendre riddle involves the concealment of its sexual solution' (30). Mercedes Salvador agrees, arguing that 'In sum, the sequence formed by riddles 42–6 seems to have been conceived as a section focused on the body, ultimately warning a potential audience against the dangers of relying on the carnal/literal dimension of the texts and, by extension, of life' (96). While she sees a cycle including two of the most explicitly sexual riddles as a warning against overt sexual behaviors, Magennis sees these riddles as a signal of real-life acceptance of sexual identity. He says: 'Their attitude is one of good-humoured impudence rather than of hostility to sexuality; and they also proceed on the assumption that the audience accepts that sex is an interesting subject' (17). Sarah Higley echoes this second attitude, arguing that riddle 61 represents not a churn or a helmet, or even a prophylactic, but a dildo, and further, that this 'prurient solution' is in fact 'an item that the sexually experienced were well-acquainted with in A-S England' (49). We see in these examples evidence for the sexual identities of early medieval people, although the majority of the literature tends toward the repression, concealment, or erasure of human sexuality.

---

[27] Tanke lists the riddles that use sexual *double-entendre* (25, 37, 44, 45, 54, 61, 62) and that include sexual subjects (12, 20, 42, 46, 63, 77, 91) (31).

While recent scholarship, including Benjamin Withers and Jonathan Wilcox's 2003 collection *Naked Before God: Uncovering the Body in Anglo-Saxon England* and Carol Pasternack and Lisa Weston's 2005 *Sex and Sexuality in Anglo-Saxon England*, explores questions of gender, sex, and embodiedness in remarkable ways, the contributors in these books seem to draw a stark division between Old English and Middle English visions of sex and the body. Although we have begun to acknowledge the presence and significance of the body in Anglo-Saxon literature, few scholars have connected discussion of the body in Old English literature with the body in Middle English literature. Clearly, sexuality and the body are more prevalent foci in the later literature, but notions of the body did not suddenly and completely change at some arbitrary date dividing the two periods. Certain genres and topics that exist in both periods can help to link what are often perceived as irreparably disparate representations of the body. I use the trope of the monster not only to draw forth those hesitant gendered and sexed Anglo-Saxon bodies, but to connect them to bodies that inhabit Middle English literature. Although Middle English literature appears to be more willing to feature sexed and gendered bodies, it is just as anxious to remove or revise monstrous bodies that demonstrate sex and gender, particularly when they imply reproductive capacity.

As I have argued above, different strategies for removal are available in Old English and Middle English literatures. Monstrous bodies in Old English are permanent, unchanging, and located at a significant distance from human communities. Thus, in Old English literature, monsters are born and not made. To be a monster is to possess permanently a physical body that differs significantly from the norm: the monster's identity is defined by the monstrous form. There can be no hope for inclusion or acceptance by the community because the body marks one as inherently liminal, which quite often (although not always) means dangerous or evil. Indeed, when the monster threatens this distance by getting too close to the community, it is removed. The threat of Old English monstrosity can only be removed by death in the case of Grendel and his mother, or by artistic or narrative erasure in the case of *Wonders of the East*. The monstrous body must either remain remote from human society or it must be removed through dismemberment as well as death. And yet, the trace of the monster remains within the text and on the page, despite the attempt to erase it. For example, although Beowulf has rid the Danes of Grendel and his mother, Beowulf's repetition of the story and his encounters with other monsters invokes them again and again.

In Middle English, however, monsters are capable of changes both spiritual and physical. In an account of his travels, Sir John Mandeville claims that a dragon kissed by the right man can be transformed into a lovely maiden. Similarly, the monsters that inhabit romances, like the half-demon dog-like Sir Gowther, can be redeemed through penance to such a degree that not only their physical appearance, but their paternity can change – although the trace of monstrosity may remain. In Middle English texts, the body is no longer the primary indicator of identity: instead of revealing monstrosity, the transformative body can conceal it in dangerous ways. Caroline Walker Bynum argues for two formulations of change: metamorphosis and hybridity. Metamorphosis is what she calls 'replacement change,' where something literally becomes something else. Hybridity, however, is visible multiplicity, where something has the parts of more than one creature: her example concerns the werewolf, which is hybrid in that it is part man and part wolf (*Metamorphosis*, 29–30). However, I argue that these two categories are not independent of one another, but that hybridity also defines metamorphosis. That is, when a creature transforms from one thing into another, the transformed creature *becomes* hybrid – the former identity is never entirely abandoned and replaced by the new identity. The metamorphic monster is always in some way hybrid. The body that may seem to be human never really is entirely human after its transformation. The monstrous form is always implicated in bodies which can or which have taken on monstrous attributes of excess, lack, or hybridity. So although these transformed monsters may seem to be human, they are in fact only *passing* as human.

Transformation, while seeming to rid the monstrous body of its monstrosity, is actually a far more dangerous proposition. Transformation renders monstrosity no less physical, but instead invisible to the viewer. Even in the most positive of transformations, a trace of monster is left behind; the erasure of the monstrous is always already incomplete. The danger of transformation, of course, is that the hybrid creature is rendered invisible to the larger community – the once-monstrous body presents a myth of unity that the reader recognizes as essentially untrustworthy. Ultimately, then, erasure in its many forms is unsuccessful. Through the presence of the trace – be it a blank space in an illustration or Beowulf's retellings of the fight in the mere – the monster is never truly removed from the text. While transformation seems like a solution to the problem of the monstrous body, that solution too is marked by traces of the prior body. The monster never departs, as I shall demonstrate, but rather reproduces itself infinitely, resisting attempts at both erasure and transformation.

In order to see the relationships between Old English monsters and those in Middle English, I offer four case studies, two drawing on Old English texts and two drawing on Middle English texts.[28] Chapter one, 'The Indecent Bodies of the *Wonders of the East*,' examines the three manuscript versions of the Anglo-Saxon *Wonders of the East*. In this chapter, I demonstrate that monsters with visibly sexed bodies in *Wonders* are erased, dismembered, or revised. *Wonders* is an illustrated catalog (Latin and Old English) of wondrous places and creatures, but its

---

[28] These case studies require a close attention to details in specific texts, rather than attempting to cover every representation of sexed and gendered monsters. Many of the works regarding medieval monsters already offer comprehensive approaches, as in Friedman, *The Monstrous Races in Medieval Art and Thought*. While these works are invaluable in thinking about monstrosity as a category, their overarching structures demand a focus on commonalities rather than moments of inconsistency or incoherence. I would argue that these individual differences, in relation to larger social constructions of the category, allow a deeper exploration of the elements and functions of specific kinds of medieval monsters.

illustrations of the human monsters are surprisingly sexual – seven of the fewer than twenty monsters feature genitals, which are rarely depicted in Anglo-Saxon art. Later viewers, however, have erased the genitals in six of these seven illustrations. This kind of erasure corresponds with the erasure, in many manuscripts, of the eyes of demons, thought to have the power of the 'evil eye.' In this text, however, the element of threat is not a penetrating gaze, but rather a reminder that these creatures are, in part, human, and that they are involved with the processes of reproduction. In *Wonders*, the sexualized bodies of monsters act out against viewers of the text in such a threatening way that their bodies must be either erased or revised. These consistent reactions and interactions with the monstrous and sexualized body by readers, viewers, authors, and artists reveal sexuality as the most threatening element of the monster. In their attempts to control and delimit the sexual capacities of these frightening bodies, however, the erasers instead, through the trace, highlight them.

In chapter two, 'Dismemberment as Erasure: The Monstrous Body in *Beowulf*,' I show that the acts of erasure practiced in *Wonders of the East* are also present in the longest Anglo-Saxon poem, *Beowulf*. The gendered and sexed bodies of both Grendel (the hypermasculine cannibal) and his mother (the threateningly reproductive and gender-transgressive female) highlight Beowulf's own conflicted masculine identity, as well as his inability to participate in the reproductive economy. His response to these bodies is not to transform them, but instead to erase them through acts of dismemberment. However, the acts of dismemberment and erasure also reconstruct and reinscribe these monstrous bodies into the center of the poem, emphasizing the difference between what the poet tells his reading audience (that Beowulf fought one monster at a time) and what Beowulf tells his listeners about the monster fights (that he fought them both together). The monsters survive as a narrative trace through their stories, which are told and retold until the very end of the poem.

As the first of the Middle English chapters, chapter three, 'Circulation and Transformation: The Monstrous Feminine in *Mandeville's Travels*,' takes as its subject one of the most popular travel narratives of the later medieval period. *Mandeville's Travels* is a text concerned with circulation, both that of the narrator, Sir John, and the circulation of reproductive bodies within the marriage economy of various communities. Of the twenty-seven monsters described in *Mandeville's Travels*, four are transformative: a dragon woman, a reproductive dead body, the self-mutilating Amazons, and the virgins whose bodies conceal serpents. I argue that the ability of these transformative monsters to infiltrate human communities and to interrupt their marital and reproductive practices reveals an anxiety about the permeability of English communities and the proximity of the monstrous to the human.

In chapter four, 'Paternity and Monstrosity in the Alliterative *Morte Arthure* and *Sir Gowther*,' I discuss a medieval attempt to dispel the threat of the monstrous body through redemption and salvation. While the threat of the body of the giant of Mont St Michel from the Alliterative *Morte Arthure* can only be removed by a violent killing that includes castration, *Sir Gowther* provides an alternative. Through physical mortification and penance, Sir Gowther, a creature of physical excess who is the son of a demon, is transformed through the power of religious authority into a child of God. Sir Gowther's transformation thus presents a possible solution for anxieties about the disruption of communities and social classes. However, the nature of the trace and the instability of the body may leave readers wondering if, as Cohen suggests in "Monster Culture", the monster will escape this time.

Chapter 1

THE INDECENT BODIES OF
THE *WONDERS OF THE EAST*

THE MONSTROUS IN MEDIEVAL LITERATURE

A MAN STARES out from inside the frame of a picture. His hands clutch the right and left sides of the frame, and his feet – five toes on each plus a dog-like dewclaw – balance him on the base of the frame. He has well defined calves and thighs and strong shoulders. Just below his shoulders, however, are his ears. He has no head, but bears all of his facial features – eyes, nose, mouth, and even eyebrows – in his chest [see image 1]. He is completely naked in this image, but his genitals are partially obscured by a darkened spot on the page. Who is he? What is the meaning behind his strange physical formation? All that the text, written above the picture in the Tiberius manuscript of *Wonders of the East*, reveals about this figure is that there is an island 'on þam beoð menn akende butan heafdum, þa habbaþ on heora breostum heora eagan 7 muð. Hi syndan eahta fota lange 7 eahta fota brade' (Orchard, "*Wonders*" 192) [on which are born men without heads, who have their eyes and mouth in their chests. They are eight feet tall and eight feet wide]. He is clearly monstrous – his body is neither fully animal nor exactly human. His pose seems mildly aggressive, but the text does not mention any dangerous behavior or, indeed, any interaction with humans. How, then, is an audience to respond to this monster? We know the response of one viewer, who covered the figure's groin with a dark ink-splotch. But what is the motivation for this response? Does the desire to remove the genitals from view reflect an aversion to a naked body? A rejection of the monstrous body? I argue that this cover-up does more than conceal nudity or confirm monstrosity; rather, the desire for genital erasure reveals just how human this monstrous body is, and just how dangerous is its sexed body.

The Anglo-Saxon *Wonders of the East* proves a fertile ground for study of the body in Old English literature precisely because it features both illustrations and written descriptions of the bodies of monsters. These representations of the monstrous are all the more intriguing because illustrated versions of *Wonders* survive in three different manuscripts. A conjoint examination of the three manuscript versions reveals a pattern of erasure and revision linked to bodies that are both monstrous and sexed. The sexed body in this text reveals more than biological sex; rather, any body that features genitals or secondary sex characteristics reveals the potential of that body to engage in sexual activity, and therefore to reproduce. It is only the bodies of sexed and therefore sexualized monsters that suffer any kind of erasure. These erasures become apparent in comparisons of images among the manuscripts as well as in contrasts between the words describing certain monsters and the images that illustrate these monsters. Many of these acts of erasure are literal, performed perhaps by a scribe or artist working on the manuscript, or by a later medieval viewer of the text, while others are more figurative: for instance, blank spaces might be left in one illustration where another manuscript provides a detail.

These acts of erasure reveal important beliefs about monsters and their bodies in Anglo-Saxon culture. What is removed from an image reveals what is most powerful, frightening, and unacceptable to artists and viewers.[1] Viewers of the monsters in these manuscripts do not attempt to transform monsters into humans by erasing their strangest or most exaggerated parts – the parts that set them out as monsters in the first place. Rather, the kinds of erasure that occur prohibit the monster from seeming *more* human by removing his or her most human elements – the genitals and secondary sex characteristics. The only way to deal with the monstrous body in *Wonders* is to remove it, or at least the parts of it that seem the most human, most implicated in the human reproductive cycle, and therefore most challenging to human identity. Erasure demonstrates the permanence of monstrous identity, as these monsters have no possibility of becoming human and are not candidates for redemption or acceptance into human communities. The Anglo-Saxon monster is figured as a permanent Other. It is not the monsters' violence against humans that is erased or removed from these texts; the artists freely represent excessive violence against vulnerable human bodies. Instead, what is erased is a more subtle threat: that of monstrous sexuality and reproductive potential. And unlike Middle English writers, as I shall argue, these later viewers do not dispel the threat of the sexualized monstrous body by allowing it to transform into a human one. However, the removal of the sexual elements of these images highlights what is most terrifying in them: monsters are not entirely foreign and strange, but rather, they are all too familiar and human.

In *Wonders*, monstrosity is physically manifested in ways that depart from human physical appearance. These monsters may have bestial body parts, such as the women whose bodies feature boar's tusks and camel's feet, or they may simply possess an excess or lack of normal human body parts, in the case of the men without heads, whose faces are instead located in their chests. I insist particularly that monstrosity has to do with the construction of the body, although monsters

---

[1] It may be that the erasers are later medieval viewers, as Michael Camille argues that most acts of erasure in medieval manuscripts take place late in the Middle Ages (151). The acts of excision that have taken place in the Tiberius manuscript have not been dated, so it is not possible to know, absolutely, whether they are Anglo-Saxon or not. While these potentially later erasures might suggest an anxiety about the body that is not necessarily Anglo-Saxon, these acts of literal excision are only one part of a larger systematic erasure of monstrous and sexed bodies in these manuscripts. They function as part of a pattern that is very much Anglo-Saxon.

do often perform actions that can be deemed monstrous. Lisa Verner argues that monstrosity can be based on appearance or behavior alone, claiming that 'a broad interpretation of "deformed" would include behavior as well as appearance … "ayen kynde" can also mean morally perverted' (5–6).[2] Behaviors, immoral or not, can be changed, where bodies cannot – indeed, according to Verner's injunction, many of the human characters of *Wonders*, including Alexander the Great, might very well be deemed monstrous. While we might consider his violent actions excessive, it does us little good simply to call him a monster, and it provides us little useful information about the 'other' kind of monster – the 'wonders' that are the focus of this text. Action alone is not enough to define a creature as a monster because these actions are not permanent in the way that possession of a tail or a tusk is permanent. Monstrous action only emphasizes monstrosity that is already located in a body that transgresses the rules for human bodies, because monstrous actions can be finite and temporary, where the monstrous elements of these bodies are fixed and permanent. A bodily definition of monstrosity allows us to understand how Anglo-Saxon writers understood human bodies and articulated the cultural rules that governed the body, gender, and sexuality.

If the body makes the monster, and monstrosity is a permanent identity – a monster cannot 'ungrow' a tail or a tusk – then so too must a human's identity be found in his or her body, a body in which biological sex determines gender and sexuality. Through erasure, a monstrous body might be curtailed, but in *Wonders of the East*, it is never transformed into something else. Viewers do not chop off tusks or tails, making a monster more human and less monstrous; what they remove is what is most human in the monster: his or her sexual identifiers. Genitals and female breasts are the most taboo and the most private elements of human bodies in Anglo-Saxon culture, obviously because they are linked to sexuality and reproduction.[3] These physical characteristics are distinctly human; animals' reproductive and secondary sexual attributes are profoundly different. Therefore, when a monster possesses these sex characteristics, the monster exhibits a quality in common with the human, not the animal. The possession of these sexed body parts indicates the monster's potential to reproduce, to do so in human ways, and – perhaps most frightening of all – to do so with a human partner.

Because *Wonders* combines detailed descriptions of monstrous human bodies with visual representations of them, it is a text of obvious importance for understanding late Anglo-Saxon attitudes toward sex, gender, and sexuality. Asa Mittman suggests that 'these wondrous beings were called into existence in order to provide a basis of comparison through which their creators might exercise and exorcise their anxieties about their identities as Anglo-Saxons and as human

---

2 Verner's use of the Mandeville definition is effective; however, her interpretation 'deformed against kind' stretches into something less appropriate for *Wonders*, particularly because it is not a text about morality, but, as I argue, about description.
3 As I discussed in my introduction, sexuality is notably rare in the Anglo-Saxon literary tradition, although not absent.

beings' (6). The gendered bodies of the monstrous both disrupt and reaffirm the social hierarchy – that is, monsters reveal and enforce the standards for appropriate human appearance and behavior. They demonstrate the boundaries beyond which humans should not proceed, and threaten to consume them or incorporate them if they do. If monsters exist only in opposition to humanity, then they confirm its cohesion and stability. However, as Jeffrey Jerome Cohen argues in his essay 'Monster Culture (Seven Theses),' the monster works simultaneously through fear and desire:

> the same creatures who terrify and interdict can evoke potent escapist fantasies; the linking of monstrosity with the forbidden makes the monster all the more appealing as a temporary egress from constraint … we distrust and loathe the monster at the same time we envy its freedom, and perhaps its sublime despair.
>
> (16–17)

Human viewers experience a variety of emotional responses to the textualized monster. As Camille comments, 'Medieval images acted forcefully upon their viewers' (143), especially because of medieval philosophies regarding vision and the active nature of the gaze.[4] Sometimes simultaneously, viewers may be confirmed in their fears, reassured by the textual nature of the monster, and also attracted to the dangerous transgression it embodies. Such strong responses often lead to more than internal reaction; they may lead to physical reactions taken against the manuscript page that contains the monster; for example, the removal of the offending part of an illustration. Because emotional responses to the monster may be so widely varied, it is difficult to determine which emotion drives a visceral response – is it fear or envy or disgust or anxiety that causes a viewer to lash out against an image on the page? Indeed, it may be because these emotions are inextricably intertwined that they lead to such aggressive reactions. Yet patterns of such reactions highlight the elements of the image that provoke response, and therefore indicate which elements seem to hold the most power and inspire the greatest anxiety.

In this chapter, I argue that the sexed and sexualized body of the monster, like the sexual body of man, is controlled through repressive acts of erasure.[5] As

---

4   The power of the gaze is an important element of the erasure of eyes. For more on the gaze in medieval literature, see Akbari, *Seeing through the Veil* and Biernoff, *Sight and Embodiment*. Gaze theory, too, suggests the active power of looking, particularly in relation to the cinema. See Mulvey, *Visual and Other Pleasures*.

5   Psychoanalytic approaches to medieval literature have been widely debated, from Lee Patterson's work on Chaucer's pardoner in *Chaucer and the Subject of History* to Jeffrey Jerome Cohen's body of work with medieval monsters and bodies. I follow Cohen's use of psychoanalytic theory, particularly Lacan, to explain and understand medieval behaviors and relationships. According to both Sigmund Freud and Jacques Lacan, primal repression is that which first causes a break between the conscious and unconscious, or between the Symbolic and the Imaginary, leading to the construction of the ego. The repudiation of the mother and the recognition that one is a discrete human being is the first moment of identity construction and

Jacques Lacan suggests, 'the repressed is always there, insisting, and demanding to be. The fundamental relation of man to this symbolic order is very precisely what founds the symbolic order itself – the relation of non-being to being' (*Seminar* 12). That which is repressed does not disappear, but instead constantly informs the identity of the subject. Man defines himself against what he is not, or what he rejects, but in the act of doing so he incorporates into his psyche that which he has repressed. However, the acts of erasure that occur in *Wonders* demonstrate more than repression, or simple removal. Instead of dispatching the object they erase, they reconstruct it. In psychoanalytic terms, this tendency is more akin to sublimation, a socially constructive form of repression. It is a particularly sexual process, one in which the 'undifferentiated sexual disposition of the child, by being suppressed or by being diverted to higher, asexual aims – by being "sublimated" – [is] destined to provide the energy for a great number of our cultural achievements' (Freud, 'Dora' 198). Sublimation is a kind of repression, then, that is channeled into positive social acts of creation or protection. The motivation behind these behaviors has been directed to the unconscious, and therefore may be unrecognized by the actor, yet the behaviors are purposeful and conscious choices. By erasing the bodies of monsters, the artists or later viewers reshape them into more palatable and less dangerous figures, as their unconscious motivations (repression and sublimation) inform their conscious actions (erasure).[6] In these achievements, however, we can see a trace of that which was sublimated – though the bodies of monsters have been revised, we can still recognize what has been removed, and what once helped to define the body and the threat of the monster. Sublimation does not simply cover up what was unacceptable, but often instead emphasizes it, pointing to what is lacking both in the image and the eraser. Therefore, when the body of the monster is erased, through some prohibitive or protective act of sublimation, the monstrous body is not merely confirmed but, in fact, impacts the identity of he who erases it.

MANUSCRIPTS:
WORD AND IMAGE IN TIBERIUS, BODLEY, AND VITELLIUS

The Old English texts that exhibit monstrous human bodies inhabit, at length, only a few genres, although, as Mittman suggests, they are 'threaded into all of the sources which comprised the fabric of Anglo-Saxon belief' (69). For instance, the *Beowulf* manuscript, Cotton Vitellius A.xv., is rife with monsters, and has been

---

subjectivity. See Freud, 'Repression,' and Lacan, 'The Mirror Stage,' in *Ecrits*. All later acts of repression participate in the further building of the subject, placing just below the surface that which challenges and frightens, and that which one is afraid one might be or become.

6 I do not mean to suggest that the erasers are consciously aware of their repression and therefore enact erasures to manifest the process. Instead, their behaviors demonstrate the fact that repression and sublimation are happening – although the exact motivation behind the erasure may very well remain unclear to the actor or to a later viewer.

called, by Andy Orchard (in *Pride and Prodigies*) and others, a book of monsters. It contains the longest Old English poem, *Beowulf,* famous for its monsters, Grendel and his mother, but it also contains *Alexander's Letter to Aristotle* and *Wonders of the East.* These two texts come to Old English from Greek and Latin tradition, and both concern a traveler's report of the foreign and 'barbarian' East.[7] In their respective tours of the East, both texts expose the native monsters for the reader's or viewer's delectation. *Alexander's Letter* is built around the epistolary premise of the traveler's report back to his teacher, but *Wonders* offers no such explicit narrative structure. Instead, in the style of a bestiary, it shows readers through both prose descriptions and illustrations thirty-seven different wondrous sights, including strange animals, exotic landscapes, foreign communities, and monstrous humans. Readers and viewers of *Wonders* are left to construct the meaning of the monstrous body, without the context of a narrative or even a narrating figure.

The Vitellius manuscript contains one of only three extant versions of *Wonders of the East.* This travel narrative/bestiary survives in Cotton Vitellius A.xv. (Vitellius), Tiberius B.v. (Tiberius), and Bodley 614 (Bodley).[8] Many of the monstrous-human bodies of *Wonders* are presented differently in these three versions; as Patrick McGurk notes, there are two cycles of pictures that circulate in these texts (108), where Tiberius and Bodley represent one, and Vitellius the other, although there are deliberate differences even between Tiberius and Bodley.[9]

---

7 We have no direct source, but *Wonders* derives primarily from a Latin text called *The Letter of Pharasmanes [or Fermes] to Hadrian on the Wonders of the East,* or in another incarnation, *Epistola Premonis regis ad Traianum imperatorem* (McGurk 88, James 9, 34). James dates the former source text from between the fourth and fifth centuries, though the manuscript he locates it in comes from the ninth century (10). Orchard also offers an excellent overview of the sources (*Pride and Prodigies,* 22–6). This source text fits into, and borrows from, an enormously popular Latin and Greek tradition of monsters, but the Anglo-Saxon *Wonders* completely 'discard[s] all the personal touches in Fermes, the prologue, the epilogue, and the passages where he speaks in the first person' (James 25).

8 The three manuscripts are London, British Library ms Cotton Vitellius A.xv., dated approximately at the year 1000; London, British Library ms Cotton Tiberius B.v., from the eleventh century; and Oxford ms Bodley 614, from the twelfth century (James 1). Citations here derive from Orchard's editions in *Pride and Prodigies.* In each of the three manuscripts, Tiberius, Bodley, and Vitellius, the written descriptions of the wonders are accompanied by illustrations. While there is very little variation in the content of the written texts in the three manuscripts, in Latin or Old English – although, as Mittman notes, there is an 'expansion of the text through the inclusion of several additional "marvels" in each subsequent version' (69) as well as some minor changes (77) – the illustrations do vary in significant ways. The Tiberius descriptions are written in both Old English and Latin, while Vitellius uses only Old English, and Bodley, only Latin. I quote hereafter only the Old English, although I occasionally examine the Latin diction in order to clarify or interrogate certain Old English terms. For more on the historical context of the manuscripts, see Mittman, esp. 69–78.

9 McGurk claims: 'the *Marvels* texts and picture cycle are enmeshed in a complex textual and pictorial tradition ... It is likely that a Rheims model lay behind, perhaps directly behind, the

Indeed, most of these differences occur when the monsters possess clearly sexed bodies. In the illustrations, parts of these monsters' bodies may be erased or revised. These changes are often noticeable only after the viewer compares the three manuscript illustrations of the same monster. Similarly, the written description, relatively unchanging among the manuscripts, might be revised through each illustrator's manipulation of its details. Examination of these moments of disjuncture among the three manuscripts reveals anxieties about not only the monstrous forms that they depict, but also about the human sexual body and identity.

Upon opening the Tiberius manuscript of the *Wonders of the East*, one is most immediately struck not by the Latin or Old English writing, but by the pictures that accompany the text. Pictures indicate and elaborate upon what the writing describes: wondrous creatures and strange places. We know before we read a word that the beings presented in the manuscript are anomalies, bodies of interest that cannot be seen in the everyday world of the Anglo-Saxon viewer, although they are ubiquitous in the marvelous East.[10] The organization of the wonders follows neither a conventional narrative nor a logical order. Wondrous animals, wondrous places, and wondrous people are all equally apt to appear at the beginning, middle, and end of *Wonders*. It is difficult to resist the urge to totalize the experience of the text, and to constitute it in some unifying structure, but the text itself resists this impulse.[11] *Wonders* betrays no particular structural

Tiberius *Marvels*, but at what stage in the transmission of the Latin text in England the Old English version was added and what was the relationship of the vernacular Tiberius text to that in the Beowulf-manuscript are difficult to determine. There were two picture cycles of the *Marvels* in England' (107–8). Tiberius is the only manuscript with thirty-seven wonders listed. Vitellius does not have the final five of the Tiberius manuscript, including vineyards, the gryphon, the phoenix, the black inhabitants of the fiery mountain, and Jamnes and Mambres. The Bodley manuscript has twelve more marvels than Tiberius, of which Andy Orchard says, 'all but two ... wonders derive directly from Isidore's *Etymologiae*' (22). The two not from Isidore, both Orchard and James note, derive from popular tradition and even Germanic lore (Orchard 22, James 62).

10 The importance of the pictures is also reflected in the composition of the manuscript page, and in their relationships to one another. In Tiberius, the page is a planned and structured space. McGurk tells us that the text was written after green initials were drawn to guide the text; the drawing and framing of pictures followed the writing, but all this structure was 'guided by underdrawings [of the frames and pictures] done at an earlier stage' (34). Although plenty of space is allotted for each picture, the scribe occasionally struggles to fit both Latin and Old English descriptions in the space preceding them. McGurk comments that this happens in 78v and 85r (31).

11 This resistance to order and hierarchy also makes allegorical readings of the bodies and text as a whole troublesome. Austin argues that: 'the illustrations and text suggest that the *Wonders* views Eastern peoples not with distaste but, rather, with curiosity and an interest in hierarchical order. The *Wonders* has an arrangement different from other related texts. The anonymous compiler re-arranged the order of the texts and images so that the marvels begin with animals, progress to humans with bestial characteristics, and end with humans who enjoy cooked food, clothing, and political organization' (28). While it is true that the text lists seven beasts before it names its first group of human monsters, almost as many beasts are interspersed throughout

or hierarchical control – it is this lack of structure, and indeed of clear boundaries between what is beast, what is monstrous, and what is human, that necessitates the acts of erasure.

Wonders is not a text whose primary focus is religious, despite frequent scholarly attempts to understand it as a text about Christian order and salvation. Scholars tend to look outside of the text itself to determine its stance on monsters and on the order of creation; to do so they often turn to Augustine, who fits rather uncomfortably with the structure (or lack of it) expressed in *Wonders*. Greta Austin, who argues that *Wonders* is organized according to a Christian hierarchy that begins with beasts and culminates with civilized humans, wants to see an Augustinian structure reflected in *Wonders*, claiming that the purpose of the hierarchy is to 'represent, in pictures as in words, the order and diversity of those to whom God offers his salvific grace. The *Wonders* implicitly takes a theological position: that the various peoples of the East were descended from Adam and could be saved' (43–4).[12] This structure is supposed to work in a way similar to God's location in the hierarchy as preeminent to the angels. However, *Wonders* is not explicitly concerned with the possibility of salvation for the races of monstrous men, 'genera hominum monstrosa' (Augustine XVI. 40) in a Christian sense. In this text there is no mention of God or of salvation; only a threat of hell for Mambres in the final entry. Austin unconvincingly claims that the Jamnes–Mambres section, an apocryphal fragment present only in Tiberius, provides 'a Christianizing gloss to a text that was originally pagan' (45). Lisa Verner, too, sees this last entry in *Wonders* as a means for the anonymous author to '[redirect] his audience's perspective onto the true and proper path … Instead of enjoying these tabloid reports for their own sensationalist pleasures, the Christian ought to be contemplating "the middle kingdom of hell" and "eternal punishment" as this

the remainder of *Wonders*, significantly disrupting a supposed development from animal to human. Six other groups of monstrous animals follow in the manuscript, the gold-digging ants (section 9), the *Lertices* (14), the dragons (16), the *Catini* (28), the *Gryphon* (34), and the *Phoenix* (35). Similarly, the final humans in the manuscript are hardly the most civilized: the text ends with the story of the damned Jamnes and his warning to his brother Mambres. These brothers are part of a textual tradition (Mambres inadvertently summons Jamnes' spirit by opening his magic books), and it is fairly obvious that they are of a civilized community that does, as Austin says, eat cooked food, wear clothes, and exist within a political organization. However, the final illustration of the manuscript in Tiberius reveals Jamnes in hell, which is filled with naked bodies and the uncivilized consumption of the bodies by the devil. Austin herself acknowledges this group of people as the last of five moments of 'inconsistency' in her hierarchy (33), a significant problem in itself. In a text that depicts only thirty-seven marvels arranged in a supposedly hierarchical order, five inconsistencies and a decline in the humanity of the final seven wonders suggest a troubled system.

12 Austin's argument grows from her citation of Augustine's claims about the origins of the monstrous human races in *De Civitate Dei*, an oft-repeated rhetorical move in studies of the medieval monster. See discussion pp. 3–5. Lisa Verner, in *Epistemology of the Monstrous in the Middle Ages*, also suggests a Christianizing structure to monster narratives such as *Wonders*.

final entry so abruptly and pointedly reminds us' (75).[13] This last entry, and thus its Christian comment, occurs only in Tiberius. To assume a Christian purpose for all three manuscripts based on a passage present in only one of them is to vastly undervalue Vitellius and Bodley, and also to imply that the texts must possess only one meaning – a meaning provided by the most attractively and expensively illustrated manuscript. *Wonders* is not a single text, but a set of texts that have varied meanings.[14] Yet one meaning remains constant and clear among all the manuscripts: none of the monsters contained in them are saved or redeemed. They exist permanently as monsters and as a foil to humanity. These texts are not about conversion or salvation of the monster; rather, they articulate and attempt to emphasize the monster's undeviating strangeness. All three versions of *Wonders* are about the experience of the strangely fascinating, simultaneously dangerous, and attractive bodies of the monstrous.

While most medieval viewers would witness the monstrous bodies provided by only one manuscript, the relationship between the three extant manuscripts significantly influences our twenty-first century understanding of them.[15] The

---

13 Verner also lists the additional eleven wonders related in Bodley, and examines the 'three tales of the Accursed dancers' (76) that ends *Wonders* in this manuscript. She suggests that this final entry too contains a Christian element, and she acknowledges, following Andy Orchard in *Pride and Prodigies*, that these stories are later additions, meant to 'establish the proper Christian perspective in relation to the marvelous and monstrous in the reader's mind' (78).

14 Mittman argues for important differences among the three manuscripts, claiming that despite the varied nature of the manuscripts, they 'nonetheless have generally been considered all together. Indeed, some scholars have worked to elide the differences, picking and choosing their favorite details from each in order to produce a composite manuscript' (69). Mittman calls for closer attention to be paid to the conditions under which the manuscripts were produced, as well as for acknowledgment of the differences among the manuscripts.

15 The stemma for the three manuscripts is unclear; it is difficult to determine the pattern of descent for both text and image, but none seems to be directly copied from one of the others (McGurk 87). However, Bodley offers a structure very similar to that of Tiberius. Making space for illustrations in Bodley also seems to have been a priority; in fact, outside the text of *Wonders*, the reader finds empty frames that were meant for further illustrations, or that can be accounted for by scribal miscalculation. The text, Latin only, precedes the images consistently, and large, colored capital letters also adorn the beginning of the description of each wonder. Because of the similarities between the images in Tiberius and Bodley, it is clear that both scribes followed similar, if not identical, exemplars (McGurk 87). Paul Gibb suggests that Bodley texts were based on Tiberius (9). The Bodley scribe seems to have been more bound by a reliance on his exemplar, as is evidenced in tiny pinholes around the simple lines of most illustrated bodies, which were used to guide the artist's hand, whereas the Tiberius artist seems to have been more skilled and to have taken more artistic license, as his illustrations are more detailed and he uses color much more consistently. The Bodley artist rarely colors the bodies of his human monsters, though often dogs, ants, or camels are colored in reds or browns. The frames of the illustrations are occasionally colored, as are the backgrounds of most images. Three exceptions to the uncolored human monstrous body exist. These three all feature the same coloring of the human–monster form – pale green. The first is a representative of a people who are called 'Hostes,' a variation of Latin *hostis*, meaning 'stranger' or 'foreigner'

Tiberius and Bodley artists have followed a similar exemplar with a reasonable degree of artistic ability, Tiberius being more sophisticated than Bodley. However, the artist of Vitellius, who demonstrates a lack of artistic skill, seems to have followed a completely different exemplar.[16] Kenneth Sisam dismisses the artistry of the images, saying 'bad draughtmanship gives many of them a ludicrous effect' (78), just as M.R. James remarks that the images are 'often, undesignedly, comic in

(40v). The Latin text tells us that they are big and tall and also that they are of a black color, 'colore nigro' (Orchard, "*Wonders*" 177). Moreover, they eat humans, as we see depicted in the illustration. The monster bends over a human victim. The second group, although not described as man-eaters, is also described as black. We are simply told that there is a mountain where there are black people, 'homines nigri' (181), and that no other people can approach because this mountain is aflame. The illustration does not reflect the flaming mountain, but does show two men above the waist, their lower bodies concealed by a hill (47r). The frame and background are entirely uncolored, but the bodies of these two men are pale green. It seems that this green skin is meant to depict dark skin color. Nowhere else in the text is a race of people described as having black skin. The third illustration that features pale green monstrous human bodies relates to a passage that does not discuss skin color. This picture reflects the story of Jamnes and Mambres (48r). The dead Jamnes warned his brother against the use of his magic books, which has landed Jamnes in hell, where there is great heat and eternal punishment. Neither Jamnes, Mambres, nor the large demon who consumes tortured bodies are colored, but two smaller demons who float around the bodies in torment are shaded this pale green. Sarah L. Higley, in 'The Wanton Hand: Reading and Reaching into Grammars and Bodies in Old English Riddle 12,' claims that medieval people seem to have held biases 'against swarthy images, [which are] often given to the demons who appear in medieval illuminations as tormentors of the white-faced Christ' (30). She continues, '*Sweart* in Old English carries powerfully negative connotations; for instance, in Christ III it is the demons that are black, the angels that are white' (35), which is further supported by the Bosworth–Toller Dictionary's definition of the adverb *swearte* as 'darkly, dismally, evilly' (35). In *The Devil*, Russell states: 'Blackness and darkness are almost always associated with evil, in opposition to the association of whiteness and light with good. This is true even in black Africa … so that negative perceptions of blackness are more causes of, than caused by, racism' (64–5). Byron, in *Symbolic Blackness*, similarly claims that in patristic discourse, '[*melas* (blackness) as an indication of evil] was not necessarily a reference to actual Blacks or Ethiopians, even though these peoples may have been the inspiration for such discourses. Discourses about the Black One and blackness symbolized threats to the respective communities to whom these writings were addressed' (76). I do not argue that the skin color of the first two groups of people makes them monstrous (they seem to have many other problematic qualities), but the fact that they are associated with the demonic in this manuscript cannot be denied.

16 McGurk states that the Vitellius probably comes from a Latin exemplar that is older and different from those of Tiberius and Bodley, and that its illustrations may have come from a different cycle (87). The illustrations are not ordered clearly, and at times it is difficult to determine which picture is meant to accompany which description. Unlike Tiberius and Bodley, Vitellius' text preceded its pictures, and 'limited space left for the artist can explain the simplicity or omission [of illustrations]' (97). On some pages, the art intermingles with the text, completely unframed, while at other times monsters engage with frames that are meant to contain them. Color is used intermittently, though it rarely seems conducive to interpreting the image.

a high degree' (51). These critiques of the artist's ability, however accurate, must not cause us to overlook the power of the images to inform interpretation. For instance, in his edition, Paul Gibb suggests that the lack of skill with which the images are drawn is part of the artist's intent to inspire certain reactions in his audience (5), while Susan Kim admits the artist's crudeness, but argues that the illustrations are meaningful because they 'consistently push at the transgressive relationship between text and image, and between image and viewer which are suggested in the other manuscripts of *Wonder of the East*' ("The Donestre" 170–71). That an artist is unskillful does not mean that he lacks control over what he chooses to include or exclude; rather, he may just do so with less aesthetic ability. We cannot entirely dismiss images that provide fascinating interpretive clues simply because the artist demonstrates less skill: an audience would have seen these images and used them to help understand the text, regardless of the quality of the illustration.

Therefore, despite the differences in skill among their artist, each manuscript contributes to a larger understanding of the body in *Wonders of the East*. Tiberius, the most skilled and probably most expensively produced manuscript, features the most obviously erased, and also the most obviously sexed, bodies. Bodley, which draws from an exemplar very similar to Tiberius', is the most modest manuscript, often concealing its monsters' bodies or erasing their sexuality. Vitellius, frequently seen as an outlier with little to contribute to the conversation, provides very different images, and thus forces readers to think about the kinds of representational and affective choices all of the artists must make. As is evident in the various ways artists choose to depict the monsters in Tiberius, Vitellius, and Bodley, the same words do not result in the same image.[17] The details drawn by the artist are not necessarily present in the scribe's verbal description. While this variation may seem like simple artistic elaboration, patterns of erasure or revision in a text suggest reactions to the dangers implicit in these monstrous bodies. Tiberius, for instance, depicts genitals on several of its monsters, although the text says nothing about these features, and neither Vitellius nor Bodley reflect these details. This difference is something that we would not recognize if we did not examine all three manuscripts. I argue that we can glean significant information about reactions to monstrosity by closely examining acts of erasure and revision that occur within a single manuscript, between two or three manuscripts, and, finally, between each image and its corresponding text.

---

17 While these differences might be due to chronological influences, or variations in audience, for the parameters of my argument I am more concerned with the larger pattern of sexualized erasures that occur, rather than the specific contexts that might drive each manuscript. Because of the lack of a clear stemma, we cannot determine exactly how much each manuscript followed or changed its source. However, the consistent concern with sexuality seems to suggest a larger cultural message that transcends immediate contexts.

THREE TYPES OF ERASURE

In her recent survey of Anglo-Saxon art, Karen Rose Mathews finds only 'sixteen images ... which represented nude figures with genitalia' (146), though the sources she consults span three centuries.[18] From *Wonders*, only the image of the *donestre* is included in Mathews' list. However, I have found that genitals are drawn far more frequently – although they may have been, in part, erased. In my study of the three manuscripts, I have found seven explicitly sexed figures, five of which feature male genitals.[19] I argue that acts of erasure – that is, attempts to delete portions of a monstrous body either through language or art – render these once-virile images impotent. As I shall discuss, artists sometimes pose the creature so as to conceal the groin. In Tiberius, it seems that a penis is either hinted at through faint lines or has been drawn and erased by either the same artist or a later viewer. Whereas Tiberius features monsters with genitals, which, as we shall see, may or may not have been scratched out or erased, Bodley simply leaves these areas completely vacant or poses its creatures in concealing positions. Vitellius addresses the problem of the naked and explicitly sexed body most often by covering it in clothing, although the artist does depict the *donestre*'s genitals (83v) [see image 2]. The differences between these manuscripts reveal an instability in transmission. These monsters' bodies were apparently troubling for the artists who drew them, and, in the case of Tiberius, for the readers who saw and censored them. What is never pictured in the first place in Bodley and Vitellius has been removed from the images in Tiberius.

The reactions of the artists and viewers to sexed bodies in *Wonders* can help us to understand Anglo-Saxon norms and the ways sexuality and sexual bodies contribute to the construction of identity. If the display of sexed parts in a monstrous body (indicating that body as sexual) make the body more terrifying and invite erasure, then how must an overtly sexed and sexual human body be perceived – for example, a human body whose gender or sexuality does not

---

[18] Mathews herself states: 'this survey does not claim to be exhaustive as it is based on analysis of images available in published sources' (146). Whether or not she has found every single appearance of genitalia in manuscript illumination, the larger point, that few images of sexually and genitally explicit bodies exist, remains clear.

[19] Although Michael Camille uses the terms penis and phallus interchangeably in his work, I restrict my use of the term phallus to instances that demonstrate significant symbolic power and authority. The psychoanalytic term phallus derives from the initially anatomical term phallus, which derives from the Greek *phallus*, meaning penis. Lacan indicates the distinction between the two by his use of capitalization. For him, although the word phallus is endowed with the idea of generative power, it remains distinct from the Phallus, which indicates both the effects of the Castration and Oedipus complexes and sexual difference in both physical and social ways. In his works, Freud notably did not distinguish between the penis as a body part and the phallus as a representation of physical and sexual difference. Lacan, however, reserves the term penis for the body part and phallus for what he terms the imaginary and symbolic functions of the penis.

'match' his or her biological sex, or even the pregnant body of a woman? Because these three versions of *Wonders* exist in a manuscript culture that only rarely illustrates bodies that possess genitals or secondary sexual characteristics like breasts, such sexed bodies here are drawn, I argue, to indicate their dangerous potential for sexual behaviors and reproduction. These Anglo-Saxon authors and artists demonstrate that monstrous identity is fixed and located in the body: therefore, we can recognize the danger of monstrosity and transgressive sexuality because it is manifested visibly in the body. Amanda Hopkins and Cory Rushton argue that in the context of medieval culture, most sexuality was deemed transgressive, at least according to the letter of the law, but they also suggest that the law does not necessarily reflect actual sexual practice. Therefore, they ask: 'How is the modern reader to interpret the dynamic between the erotic and the transgressive in texts produced by a culture in which all sexual activity was (supposedly) regulated, and sexual desire was, of its very nature, transgressive?' (5). This consistent pattern of erasure demonstrates precisely what is transgressive in terms of sexuality. Bodies that blur too many categories (for instance, the animal and the human, or the male and the female) are the most dangerous, and must be censured and censored.[20] The response of the eraser is not to take away monstrous qualities, but to remove elements that depict sex and sexuality.

Excision as a kind of erasure is a common enough occurrence in medieval manuscripts, both as a means for correction of errors and of responses to images.[21] Erasures, specifically the purposeful scratching out of a part of an illustration, Camille suggests, 'can tell us a great deal about what kinds of images were considered powerful and dangerous' (146). One of the most commonly excised parts of an image is the face or the eyes, for these body parts are linked with the 'evil eye.' Camille suggests that 'Christians were also fearful of the effects of the evil eye. Someone was clearly so afraid of the eye of the devil ... in a twelfth century scene of Adam and Eve that he carefully cut out just the parchment face of the tempter' (141–2). As he further claims,

> Medieval images acted forcefully upon their viewers. The reasons for this are partly linked to medieval theories of vision itself, which gave an active role to the eye in the process of perception. Vision entailed the eye actually taking an imprint of the thing seen ... vision was a far more active and dangerous sense than it is for us today. (143)

Thus, a demon gazing out from a page was considered a literal threat to the viewer's safety, and by rubbing out his face, the danger was nullified.[22] Suzannah

---

20 As Cohen argues in his seven theses, monsters represent category crisis. They combine elements that do not or should not go together. I argue here that the monsters who are the most dangerous are those that blur the line even further; they are clearly monsters, but they manifest clear signs of humanity.

21 Camille notes that the images most often erased were demonic and/or sexual (144).

22 See note 4 for more on the gaze in medieval literature.

Biernoff, claiming that the evil eye is most frequently affiliated with women, suggests that such a gaze is sexualized, as it 'poisons, penetrates, entraps, seduces or otherwise harms the implicitly male viewer' (53). She further articulates 'the potential of sight to cause physiological change' (96) through the *modus operandi* of the evil eye. The eyes, then, have a powerful effect on viewers, but I suggest they are not the only body parts that can cause such anxiety. If a gaze is so capable of penetrating and changing a viewer, what then can a penis do? If we acknowledge that a viewer cuts off the active and dangerous gaze by scratching out the part that does the gazing, then we must apply a similar logic to the erasure of genitalia.

Just as a reader removes the threat of the evil eye, so does he respond to the sexed elements of the monstrous body in *Wonders* in order to rearticulate his active control over the manuscript page. Acts of erasure of these sexed elements demonstrate that they, like the evil eye, threaten to poison or penetrate the viewer. To be penetrated, by the gaze or by something more transgressive, places the viewer in a passive role, one that in medieval culture is feminized. As Ruth Mazo Karras has argued, medieval gender roles are commonly associated with the active/passive binary: 'a man who took a passive role or a woman who played an active role was not transgressing the boundaries of sexual identities as much as the boundaries of gender' (27). Perhaps one of the most dangerous elements of these monsters is that they refuse to abide by their designated textual and sexual roles; they, who ought to be passive objects on the page, perform an active penetration of the viewer, who ought to hold the active role as the controller of his own gaze. In such a case, the viewer or artist might use erasure to regain his active status and to maintain his proper socially dictated gender role. The viewer thus sublimates the threat of the sexual body of the monster (and perhaps his own) through his erasure of the image.

While erasure literally destroys elements of the text, it also serves as a constructive process. In erasing something, an alternate meaning is created, calling our attention to that which has been erased. This deconstruction is akin to Jacques Derrida's examination of 'sous rature,' translated by Gayatri Spivak as 'under erasure.'[23] When one erases something, a trace of that which was erased remains. Spivak defines the trace: 'this is to write a word, cross it out, and then print both word and deletion. (Since the word is inaccurate, it is crossed out. Since it is

---

23 In *Of Grammatology*, Derrida rethinks the nature of absence as being a kind of presence: he argues that '*differance* makes the opposition of presence and absence possible … *differance* produces what it forbids, makes possible the very thing it makes impossible' (143). Presence, then, is defined by absence, and absence, in turn, is defined by presence; these concepts rely on one another. With monsters and men, human identity is produced by its *differance* from monstrous identity, just as these monstrous bodies are produced by the humans who draw them, create them, and thereby are present in them. According to Derrida, absence and presence are far more complex than simple opposites: they mean through the 'presence-absence of the trace, which one should not even call its ambiguity but rather its play' (71). Seemingly contradictory, one cannot have absence without a kind of intermediate presence in that absence.

 Et alia insula inbrixonte ad meridie
ṃɡ naseantur homines sine capitib: qui
i pectore habent oculos & os alti st pedu
·um · & lati simili modo pedu·um ꞉
Ðonne is ðep ealand rað ppa hpixonte
onþam beoð menn akende butan heap
ðum· þa habbaþ onhpeoptum heopa
eagan ꞇ muð hi pyndan eahta potalange
ꞇ eahta pota bpade ꞉-

ꞇ ascantur &ibi dracones longitudinem
habentes·cl·pedu·uas latitudine colũnaru·
ppᵹ multitudine draconũ nemo facile
adire poteft transflumen ꞉-
Ðæp beoð dpacan kende ða beoð onlenge
hundteontiges pot micla ꞇ pi pæꞇ
lange ꞇ beoð gpeace ppa peanite ꞇ epiaꞝ
micle pondapa· dpacena micelnyrꞇ
næniȝ mann naht eaðelice onþ land
ȝepapian mæȝ ꞉-

Image 1: *Blemmye, Wonders of the East*, London, the British Library,
MS Cotton Tiberius B.v., fol. 82r (© the British Library Board)

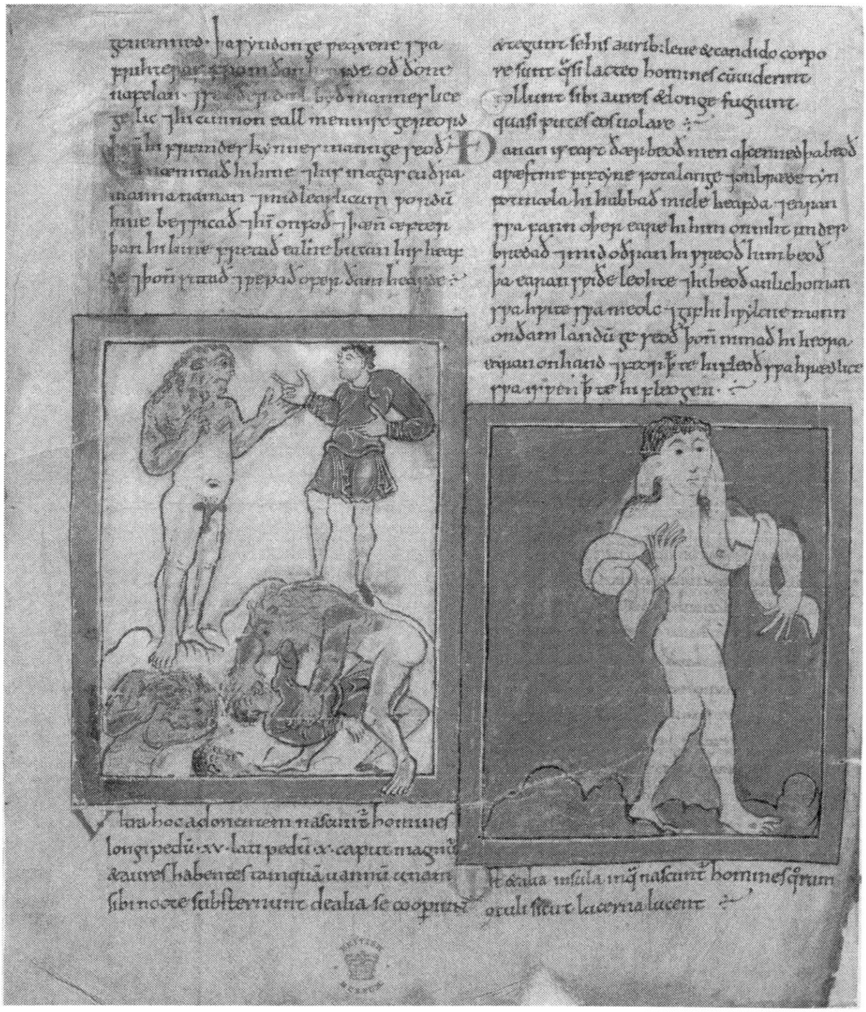

Image 2: *Donestre*, *Wonders of the East*, London, the British Library, MS Cotton Tiberius B.v., fol. 83v (© the British Library Board)

Image 3: *Donestre, The Wonders of the East*, London, British Library,
MS Cotton Vitellius A.xv., fol. 103v (© the British Library Board)

& parentū er & cognātoꝝ noīā in quirūt. blan
dientes sermone:ꝰ ut decipiant eos & ꝓdant. Cūq:
coꝑhendunt eos:ꝰ perdunt eos & comedunt. et ꝑea
coꝑrehendunt capð ipsᵉ hoīmīs quē comederīt:ꝰ
et suꝑ ipsum ploiant.

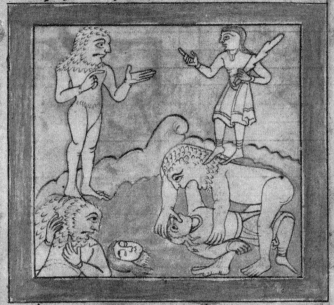

Itᵉ hoc ad ouentem nascuntᵉ hoīes longi pedum
xv. lati pedū.x:ꝰ capud magnū & aures habentes
tangm uannū. quarū unā sibi nocte substernunt.
de alia ū se cooperiunt:ꝰ & tegunt se his aurib;.
Leui autē & candido corꝓe sunt quasi lacteo.

Image 4: *Donestre, Wonders of the East*, Oxford, Bodleian Library,
MS Bodley 614, fol. 43r (© the Bodleian Library, the University of Oxford)

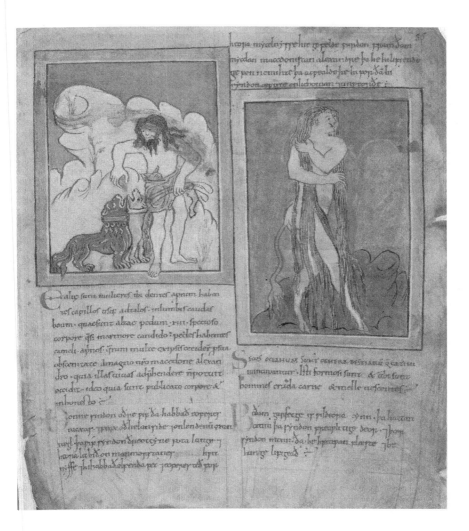

Image 5: Women: huntress and tusked woman, *Wonders of the East*,
London, the British Library, MS Cotton Tiberius B.v., fol. 85r
(© the British Library Board)

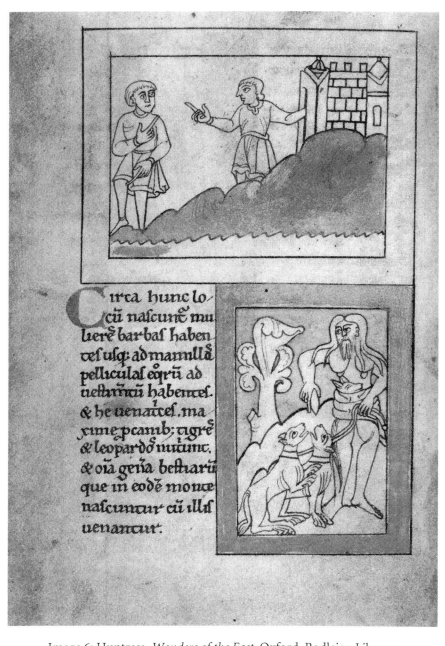

Circa hunc lo-
cū nascunē mu
lierē barbaf haben
tef ufq; ad mamillā
pelliculaf eǫrū ad
ueftitūtū habentef.
& he uenattcef. ma
xime pcamb; tigre
& leopardo nūtūtc.
& oīa gеñа beftiarū
que in eodē monte
nafcuntur cū illif
uenantur.

Image 6: Huntress, *Wonders of the East*, Oxford, Bodleian Library,
MS Bodley 614, fol. 44v (© the Bodleian Library, the University of Oxford)

Image 7: Women: huntress and tusked woman, *The Wonders of the East*,
London, British Library, MS Cotton Vitellius A.xv., fol. 105v
(© the British Library Board)

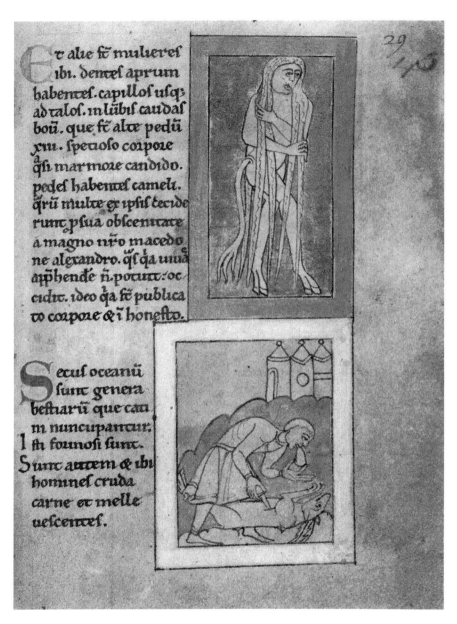

Et alie sunt mulieres ibi. dentes aprum habentes. capillos usqʒ ad talos. in lũbis caudas boũ. que sunt alte pedũ xiii. specioso corpore qsi marmore candido. pedes habentes cameli. qrũ multe ex ipsis cecide runt. psua obscenitate a magno nro macedo ne alexandro. qs qa uiuã apphende ñ potuit ꞏoc cidit. ideo qa sunt publica to corpore & ĩ honesto.

Secus oceanũ sunt genera bestiarũ que catini nuncupantur. sth formosi sunt. Sunt autem & ibi homines cruda carne et melle uescentes.

Image 8: Tusked woman, *Wonders of the East*, Oxford, Bodleian Library, MS Bodley 614, fol. 45r (© the Bodleian Library, the University of Oxford) necessary, it remains legible)' ('Translator's Preface' xiv). In the case of monstrous bodies, the trace is not quite so clearly legible; we cannot be sure of the 'word' which has been 'crossed out.' Instead, we notice that something has been scratched out, and just as we must attempt to determine what has been removed, we continue to construct meaning based on the new, complete-but-incomplete image.

Excision, however, is only one kind of erasure that is possible: three different kinds of erasure seem to be at work in the three manuscripts that feature *Wonders*. The first type is erasure I term 'never drawing.' In erasures of this kind, one manuscript features explicitly sexed bodies, but one or both of the others never draw these bodies as sexed in the first place. Bodley most frequently engages in 'never drawing.' The second type of erasure is a more literal kind, which I call 'removing.' In this second type, parts of images are literally excised by the scribe or a later viewer.[24] Removing happens most frequently in Tiberius. The final type of erasure I refer to as 'revising.' In acts of revision, the artist does not excise certain parts, but rather changes details of the image so that the effect or message of the image shifts. Both Bodley and Tiberius revise images in order to neutralize their threat. While the second type, removal, is most commonly known as erasure, never drawing and revision also function as analogous acts of erasure. We might first note acts of erasure through obvious moments of excision, but the other two categories are just as meaningful, although certainly more subtle and often overlooked. Michael Camille says of acts of excision:

> It is my argument that we must examine such cases not so much as acts of vandalism but as acts of representation. We tend to associate creation with construction, not destruction, but the selective obliteration of parts of an image surely constitutes not merely editing and expurgation, as with a text, but an embodied response. (140)

---

[24] While it is impossible to determine who performed these acts of erasure, it seems unlikely that the person who performed the literal excisions would be the scribe. Camille makes a general argument that most acts of erasure take place late in the Middle Ages: 'It is my contention that such excision happened at the very end of the Middle Ages, during the fifteenth century, and I would date most of the erasures of sexual images to this period and not before ... It is in the fifteenth century that we can see the beginnings of prurience in representing the sexual act and its intentional obfuscation, not by later readers, but by the artists themselves' (Camille 151). Here Camille discusses medieval manuscripts, most of which are dated to the thirteenth and fourteenth centuries, but he also includes some earlier examples, so it is uncertain how applicable his claims are to the Anglo-Saxon manuscript tradition. While Camille suggests that these potential late medieval erasures represent 'the birth of the obscene' (146), the evidence of multiple kinds of erasure offered in this chapter, however, disputes Camille's reasoning. It seems that artists before the fifteenth century, specifically the artists of Vitellius and Bodley, do themselves conceal sexually explicit bodies. We might read this evidence in reverse, that only one artist rebelled against his exemplar and drew in genitalia, but the fact that Vitellius reveals the *donestre*'s genitals suggests that both cycles of illustrations probably did depict genitals in at least this case.

Just as excision works as a kind of creation, so too do the other types of erasure represent the 'embodied response' of an artist.

NEVER DRAWING

The first type of erasure to be considered in *Wonders of the East* involves what was never drawn. In such cases, the artist chooses not to include sexually explicit or explanatory details in the first place, and the viewer – the viewer of the image or the reader of the writing – without knowing the other manuscripts, would never recognize what was missing.[25] We can see this practice in two particular places, one primarily textual, and the other primarily visual. The first occurs in the description of the men with two faces on one head. The reader learns that not only do these people actually reproduce, but that to do so, 'faraŏ hi on scipum to Indeum, 7 þær hyra gecynd on weorold bringaŏ' (Orchard, "*Wonders*" 192) [they travel in ships to India and they bring their offspring into the world there]. This description is repeated in all three manuscripts. But upon consideration of the *Fermes* source, we learn that this language has been changed, whether through purposeful revision or, as seems more likely, through scribal error. James says, 'In *Marvels* this is strangely obscured: "suis manibus transferunter" is corrupted out of "in anibus caeli transformantur" ' (27). Essentially, rather than changing into storks and flying across the sea to hatch their children, the two-faced people in the Anglo-Saxon version build and board ships and travel across the sea to give birth to their children. This act of revision, purposeful or otherwise, reinforces my claim that Anglo-Saxon artists and scribes did not depict monstrous bodies capable of change. These monsters cannot willfully transform themselves into storks anymore than they can make themselves appear human. A scribe, at some point in transmission, has simply written out significant details, and all of the remaining manuscripts reflect this same choice. The stork men, in all three Anglo-Saxon versions of *Wonders*, then, are metaphorically 'never drawn,' and thus readers' understandings of these monsters' identities and practices of reproduction are absolutely changed.

The second example of this particular practice of erasure is represented through the most obviously sexed body in *Wonders*: the *donestre*. Despite identical written descriptions, the manuscript images demonstrate significant differences. Although the *donestre*'s body is clearly sexed in both Tiberius [see image 2] and Vitellius [see image 3], its sexed elements are 'never drawn' in Bodley [see image 4]. This comparison is particularly striking because Bodley features images that are usually very similar to those in Tiberius, while the Vitellius images almost never

---

[25] I do not mean to suggest that, for instance, the Bodley artist viewed the Tiberius manuscript and chose not to draw what that artist did. However, at some point in the transmission history of *Wonders*, an artist chose to add or subtract certain elements.

share commonalities with the images in the other two manuscripts. The *donestre*, shown in a three-part action illustration, is revealed as completely naked and, in Tiberius, anatomically correct [see image 2] (83v). In the first part of the Tiberius frame, he is drawn with a lion-like head and bright red testicles and penis. Cohen, in a discussion of this frame, even categorizes this monster as having a 'hypermasculine body' in comparison to the weak 'ill proportioned' form of the traveler (*Of Giants* 2). This unabashedly male monster is shown in conversation with a civilized man, who is fully dressed and neatly coiffed. The written description tells us that these creatures 'hig cunnon eall mennisc gereord' (Orchard, "*Wonders*" 196) [know all human languages], and that they speak to any passerby in his own language, and 'næmnað hi hine 7 his magas cuðra manna naman, 7 mid leaslicum wordum hine beswicað' (196) [(call out) his name and the names of people he knows, and deceive him with dishonest words]. These actions are reflected in the first part of the picture, while in the second, to the right side of the frame, we see the monster's attack, where he 'him onfoð, 7 þænne æfter þan hi hine fretað ealne butan his heafde' (196) [seizes him and then afterwards consumes him, all except for his head]. Finally, in the bottom left corner of the frame, we see the distraught monster, hands on either side of his own face, weeping, just as we are told, 'þonne sittað 7 wepað ofer ðam heafde' (196) [then he sits and weeps over the head]. The written description of this monster thus accurately narrates the events of the illustration for the reader.

In the frame of the Tiberius, nothing has been edited out, although something not represented in the language of the description is present in the illustration: the red penis. We might expect such an obvious representation of a sexual body to be erased, but here it not only remains, it is also highlighted. Under the orange-red paint, the original penis is drawn with the same red-brown paint used to highlight the rest of the body. The layer of orange-red paint emphasizes the penis and adds testicles. Where Tiberius contains the most consistent and obvious acts of removal, the presence of this penis can help us to understand the motivations of the later erasers – they are clearly not driven by prudery if they allow such an overt sexual organ to remain in the illustration, or indeed, they may be the ones to have added the orange-red paint. The illustration reveals both the body of the creature and the way in which he terrorizes a human victim; the behavior demonstrates just how dangerous the body and its appetites are, but the viewer is warned of the danger by the highlighted penis. Indeed, there is little possibility of mitigating his threat to the viewer because he enacts his violence to the human body in each portion of the image: there is no reason to subdue the monster by erasing his penis. This is a body so obviously out of control that the Tiberius eraser cannot delimit its danger by removing its 'other' evil eye. Moreover, because of its position in the middle of the text, with acts of removal both preceding and following it, it seems even clearer that the *donestre* did not escape the scraping tool merely out of luck. Instead, this penis, human in its shape but monstrous in its color, does not make the monster seem more human, but instead confirms his monstrosity. Therefore, the red penis does not need to be erased to confirm the creature's monstrosity, but demonstrates a different kind of response and reconstruction of the text – indeed, the red penis here acts as a moment of revision.

Aside from the genitals, the illustration does the best it can to follow the bizarre physical description written into the text, a goal that is certainly challenging. We are told that the *donestre* 'syndon geweaxene swa frihteras fram ðan heafde oð ðone nafelan, 7 se oðer dæl byð mannes gelic' (Orchard, "*Wonders*" 196) [have grown like soothsayers from the head to the navel, and the other part is like a man's body].[26] The Tiberius artist depicts his departure from the human as 'leonine' (Cohen, *Of Giants* 2). He has a wild mane, and in the second and third parts of the picture, an extended snout, though in the first his face looks far more human. In this first part, a reader might identify his more human appearance with the monster's use of human language; he clearly uses this language to create a bond of trust and identification and thus lure in travelers. It is also only in this part of the illustration that the penis is visible. This portion of the image highlights his humanity through its display of both his sexed body and his possession of language. After all, the monster seems most bestial in the second part of the illustration; in the first and third parts, he exhibits human behaviors, speaking, weeping, and (seemingly) feeling regret. However, even though his actions in the second part are violent, they are also sexualized. The posture for consumption is very sexual; the *donestre* straddles his victim and holds him almost tenderly by the waist with one arm, while his other hand grasps his victim's head. The victim is bent backwards, reclining as if he lies on a bed, with his right arm lying beside his body rather than dangling toward the ground. The *donestre* takes his victim's left arm into his mouth almost softly – no teeth or blood are visible.

As the first part of the image indicates, through its linkage between language and the sexed body, it is precisely these human qualities that make the monster most dangerous. His facility with all languages is certainly an impressive and humanizing ability, but ultimately, as the red penis warns, it is in the service of an excessive and sexualized appetite. Similarly, the genitals, not bestial[27] but human, take on qualities of the monstrous in their extreme visibility in both size and color. If the viewer is to think of this monster as more human when he makes use of

---

26 The term *frihteras* as a description of the non-human part of this monster is bizarre. No other occurrence of this word can be found in the corpus of the *Dictionary of Old English*. In fact, the only other form of this word that appears in the corpus is *frihtrung*, which appears twice in Latin–Old English glossaries as the equivalent of *Ariolatus*, 'divine; foretell, prophesy; use divination' (*DOE*). The Latin description that precedes the Old English in Tiberius, however, uses the word *diuini*, meaning 'of the gods,' or, also, soothsayer. Orchard, in his edition in *Pride and Prodigies*, notes that the Vitellius form is *frifteras*, a word that has no notation in the *Dictionary of Old English*, and Rypins notes possibilities for *frifteras, frefteras,* and *frehteras* (61). James' only comment is an exclamation point following the word divine: 'men called "donestre," i.e. divine (!)' (56), denoting the inexplicable nature of this description.

27 Some might be tempted to associate the phallus with base animal behavior and thus to regard it as a symptom of the animal rather than the human. Such readings are out of context here, as the penis appears to be a clearly human appendage – nothing like that of an animal. However, its coloring suggests something that is not quite human, too.

human language, then that humanity is also defined by his possession of the plainly visible, engorged penis, but that humanity is simultaneously undercut by the fact that the penis is exaggerated as well as a distressing shade of red. Thus, as the painted penis suggests, the monster's aggressively naked body should be a warning to the traveler of his menace, and his excessive desire to consume, and therefore to penetrate and possess the bodies of humans. He is a particularly dangerous monster because his initial appeal is very human: he speaks human language and knows human things – he is able to collapse the boundaries between the human and monster in many ways, but the monstrous difference of his body, manifested in the horrifying penis, consigns him to a life of consuming the human but never becoming it. His horrible actions, as depicted in both description and illustration, only serve to highlight the terror of the body.

Neither Tiberius nor Vitellius enact the erasure of 'never drawing' in this image, but the artist of Bodley does. As in Tiberius, the Vitellius artist chooses to depict this creature in a sexed way, despite the fact that it derives from a different illustration cycle. Here the soothsayer appears to have taken on the appearance of a dog, instead of a lion (103v) [see image 3]. The artist does depict a penis and testicles, although here they are depicted as a strange triangular shape below the bent arm and between the thighs, and is not as conspicuous as the red coloring and clear shape in Tiberius; this element is particularly offset by the presence of a woman, whom he chases. Only Bodley, in the case of this illustration, refuses to draw the genitals. Neither the leonine look nor the red penis is visible in the Bodley manuscript (43r) [see image 4]. Instead, the figure has a clearly human head draped with a head-covering, although his head is much larger than the visitor's. Despite being naked and placed in a revealing pose, the body is not depicted as possessing a penis. Excess remains a marker of this creature's monstrosity, but here it is merely in terms of physical size rather than sexual excess. Because both Tiberius and Vitellius offer explicitly sexed illustrations, it seems unlikely that both artists added the genitals of their own voli- tion. Because the penis is present in both illustrations, it seems likely that an exem- plar common to both cycles of illustration featured a sexed monster, and only the artist of the later manuscript, Bodley, refused to draw it.

In depicting a visibly sexed monster, both Tiberius and Vitellius also suggest a sexually potent monster. Susan Kim remarks, 'In the Tiberius illustration, the genitalia are emphatically clear, not only clearly marked, but also red … The Vitellius illustration, moreover, pairs the monster with a female figure unmen- tioned by the text, thus providing a context of sexual difference to underscore the exposure of the clearly male monster race' ("The Donestre" 163). Kim claims that in this odd illustration, the woman on the right side of the frame is moving to pull up her skirt, simultaneously concealing and revealing her clearest mark of sexual difference (164).[28] While I agree with Kim that this figure is female, according to

---

28 Of this illustration, James only says, 'on r. full face, a person with masses of long hair, and some drapery' (56). He assigns no clear gender or action.

the length of her tunic and her head-covering, I remain unconvinced about the movement she attributes to the woman. The woman does seem to be holding her skirt with both hands, but her right foot seems to be touching the ground, while her left foot is raised. Rather than performing a lascivious show-and-tell that distinguishes the male from the female, it seems to me that this woman is depicted in the act of running from this monster. After all, he stands on her right side, waving what is clearly a human leg in the air, scaring her off. Although this image does not depict the monster's actions in a three-part narrative, it does seem to represent monstrous behavior as well as appearance. The opposition, then, is not between the monster's unconcealed genitals and the woman's soon-to-be revealed nether half; instead, the opposition here is between the appearance of the sexually potent and consuming monster, and the response of the weak and frightened human victim. That the visitor is female does emphasize the sex of the monster as male, particularly because this is the only image of a penis in Vitellius. Therefore, Bodley's act of never drawing the sexed body of this monster is particularly pronounced because of the glaring nature of his penis in both Tiberius and Vitellius. This moment of erasure in Bodley does not transform the monster into a human, or make him less monstrous; it merely removes the obvious connection between consumption, sex, and reproduction that he presents in the other manuscripts. Bodley performs its erasure of the sexed elements because it does not draw them – but even as it removes these threatening features, the acts of consumption performed by the neutered monster exhibit a trace of his potency and his desire to incorporate and thereby, perhaps, become human. Through the exaggerated figure in Tiberius and Vitellius, the artists emphasize the danger of excessive masculinity and desire, qualities which result in destruction for the desired object and unsatisfied despair for the subject. This creature's lonely desire for human community, present in all versions, leads to his consumption of its representative. This desire for connection with the human inevitably leads to its destruction, as the monstrous desire and the monstrous appetite are at odds. Thus, the *donestre* serves as a clear warning about miscegenation: possession of human and civilized language does not make him human, as his body attests. The authors and artists warn: he is not like us, and he must not mix with us.

Despite the fact that almost all of the monstrous humans of *Wonders* are naked in the three manuscripts, we see genitals depicted clearly in only this instance. In most cases, the artist has carefully posed the figures so that we cannot see them, as is the case with the Tiberius representative of the *hostes*, who bends modestly over a tiny clothed man he is clearly about to consume (81v and Orchard, "*Wonders*" 192). In Tiberius, not all monsters are given sexual organs, but several are; in Vitellius, only one, the *donestre*, is drawn sexually, while in Bodley, every monster is completely neutered. The Vitellius artist, despite a lack of skill, at least conceals the groin area of most monsters with clothing; the Bodley artist makes it obvious in the completely naked, revealed bodies of his monsters that they have no sexual dimension. While the concealed posing and coverage by clothing in Tiberius and Vitellius might indicate a kind of erasure, this completely asexual approach to the naked body in Bodley is the clearest signal of the erasure of 'never drawing' that occurs in *Wonders*.

Never drawing is the most consistent and yet the most invisible kind of erasure performed on *Wonders*. Unless one considers the texts in tandem, this kind of erasure is undetectable. The trace exists not on the individual page, but on the meta-page of the über-manuscript – a text that can only exist in heavily edited combined editions as in Orchard, in *Pride and Prodigies*. The sexual elements that are never drawn by the later manuscript, Bodley, seem intrinsic to the threat contained in the bodies of these monsters in Tiberius and often in Vitellius. However, I do not mean to suggest an origin that all texts should strive to replicate or achieve. Mittman, using Giles Deleuze's concept of the simulacrum, argues that 'while each [manuscript] is a monstrous duplicate of the last, they are not identical triplets. Rather each is the monstrous progeny of other monstrous manuscripts and circumstances that, in their coupling, never duplicate themselves precisely' (80). As Derrida claims, 'The trace is not only the disappearance of origin, … it means that the origin did not even disappear, that it was never constituted except reciprocally by a non-origin, the trace, which thus becomes the origin of the origin' (*Of Grammatology* 61). Derrida's thinking about the instability and unattainability of origins is particularly relevant for thinking about acts of erasure in *Wonders*, and especially so in regards to practices of 'never drawing,' which only reluctantly exhibits the trace. While I can and shall examine what has been erased from the images of monsters, at a larger level I point to this pattern of erasure as constructing a new kind of meaning for the text, but also indicating a larger cultural pattern of the erasure of sexuality, as demonstrated in the corpus of Anglo-Saxon literature.[29] As Derrida suggests, we cannot reach the origin of the image; we do not know precisely what was there before the erasures, or in their exemplars. However, acts of never drawing in *Wonders* provide a limited access not only to the lost original text, but also to the artistic and personal processes that led to each version of it. Of all the types of erasure, never drawing provides the most consistent vision of the individual artist and his responses to both his exemplar and his culture. As viewers, then, we must construct a new meaning, one that leaves room for the possible nature of the erased origin, hinted at by the trace, and the new meaning created by never drawing.

REMOVAL

The second type of erasure I shall discuss, removal, is the one most traditionally recognized as erasure. Someone, most likely a later viewer, literally scratches or rubs out a part of an illustration because of the power that the image holds. Camille claims that:

---

[29] I have demonstrated this paucity of sexual reference in my introduction. As Hopkins and Rushton note, 'Medieval England appears to be a particular problem for the historian of sexuality: as Bernard O'Donoghue notes, the language itself seems uncomfortable with sex' (7).

> There are countless places in medieval manuscripts where images have been obliterated … purposefully, in a negative reaction. These sites of censure have an obvious relation to a notion of the obscene. Clearly they have offended someone. Picturing things that should not be seen has resulted in a performative response, which makes them subsequently unseeable. (141)

This kind of erasure takes place only in the Tiberius manuscript, and in one general scenario: the genitals of four different male monsters in the manuscript are erased. While we cannot determine the identities of the erasers, or even if they are or are not Anglo-Saxon themselves, what they erase remains as a trace of the power and potential of the image, both as it existed before the erasure and as it now exists. Therefore, these moments of erasure point to what is always already both present and missing in all three. These erasures seek not to make the monsters less monstrous or to transform them into something other than what they are, but instead to render them impotent. If the penis is removed, then the immediate threats of sex and reproduction are thereby interrupted and perhaps prevented. The impulse here is to sublimate an uncomfortable element. These monstrous bodies are permanently monstrous; the elements that are most threatening are removed, not transformed. These elements do not entirely disappear, but rather continue to exist in the trace. Thus, the monster's fundamental identity remains unchanged – only the obviousness of his sexed and sexual identity has been interdicted.

While the violent and sexual threat of the *donestre* is evident, the first example of erasure by removal is less obviously dangerous to human populations. In Tiberius, the *conopoena*, or half dog (80r), stands beside a tree, eating a leaf. This rather calm image is meant to depict an aggressive monster who breathes fire: 'heora oruð byð swylce fyres lig' (Orchard, "*Wonders*" 188) [their breath is like a fiery flame], something we do not see in the illustration. We do see the hybrid body, made up of parts of various animals, as we are told 'Hi habbað horses mana 7 eoferes tucxas 7 hunda heafda' (188) [they have horse's manes and boar's tusks and dog's heads]. The description seems fairly straightforward, and the pictures, for the most part, reflect it accurately. In Tiberius, this very human figure is naked. He reaches across his body toward a tree, so the arm mostly conceals his pectoral muscles, but a navel is clearly drawn. He has a short mane of hair, but is bald between horse-like ears, which rise alertly from his head. We see two tiny black horns, set in front of the ears, that are slightly smaller than the single tusk visible coming from his lower lip, but are the same size as the tiny row of pointed black teeth in his mouth. As compared with this strange head, the body is quite human, with expressive hands that mirror the eloquence of his human-like eyes and eyebrows. The background of the picture is a bright orange, and most of the coloring is done in very neat strokes. However, over his genital area is a strange red smudge that might be overlooked as a brush mistake from the orange background, but instead is clearly an attempt at concealment.

Upon closer inspection, the viewer notices that this spot is an entirely different color from the background, and is a color used nowhere else in the image. This mark is no mistake. One notices two round smudges at the junction of the thighs and one longer smudge that hangs between the legs. Seven small red lines radiate upward from the round smudges onto the flesh-color of the pelvis. The *conopoena* has a penis and testicles, and though it is not so clear as that of the *donestre*, both are this same striking shade of red. Similarly, upon closer inspection, one observes, largely obscured by the red paint, a small black circle bisected by a horizontal black line, perhaps meant to depict testicles as part of the original image; the precision of this circle compared with the crude paint demonstrates that the original artist may have depicted a penis, but the later viewer has covered it up with something only marginally recognizable as genitals. The color of the paint and the covering of the original part of the image suggest a similarity between these two monstrous men, although their actions are quite different. Indeed, both the text and the image depict the *donestre* as a threat to humans; the *conopoena*'s textual description grants him fiery breath, but this is not specifically directed at humans, and the image does not even bother to depict this action. Unlike the *donestre*'s violent consumption, the *conopoena*'s calm demeanor as he eats cannot be conceived of as threatening. The problem of this body is its physical monstrosity, which can be controlled through removal. Where the *donestre*'s sexualized violence pervades the entirety of his image and description, so that erasure could not easily resolve the problems of his body, the *conopoena*'s danger can be neatly managed through subtle intervention. The sexual organ here embodies the threat of the monster, as is doubly reflected in the kind of erasure that takes place in the other manuscripts' depiction of the *conopoena*.

Both Bodley and Vitellius do not draw genitals, rather than removing and/or obscuring them. The Bodley artist poses the figure in exactly the same way as Tiberius, so that we should see the genitals, but this area is obviously blank (38v). Moreover, he has neither horns, teeth, nor tusks. He simply looks far less exotic and far less threatening. Vitellius offers a very different picture, in which this strange body is not only clothed but seemingly richly garbed, with a red cape, blue tunic, and even shoes (100r). We can see one tusk and two horse ears, with a strange third ear coming from the back of the head. In some ways, the bestial features are even more striking in the context of the clothed body. In all three manuscripts, the artist or the viewer has attempted to remove or occlude the threat of this body by erasure of its sexual features.

While the genitals of the fire-breather are obfuscated, the image of the man with two faces, as he is presented in Tiberius (81r), suffers a more traditional form of erasure. His genitals are literally removed in the illustration. Where the *conopoena*'s genitals are covered with red paint, his seem to be scratched out, noticeable in the white splotch against the pink background and his pale skin. He is totally naked and posed in a profiled walking position, with his audience-side right leg crossed over his left, which could easily explain a lack of visible genitals. In this case, however, a light brown spot remains on his lower belly that seems to have denoted pubic hair, as well as a white blotch that points outward from the junction of his legs in a vague erection. This white spot results not from an added layer of paint, but rather from this part of the image being scratched out. In addition to the portion of the dark circular mark left behind is the beginning of a familiar orange-red splotch of paint, and in the midst of the erasure is a tiny dot of the same color. It seems that this color was used in the genital area prior to erasure. Therefore, most likely the original artist drew some sort of penis, a later viewer added his tell-tale, impossible to ignore, red-orange paint to it, and then this final act of erasure took place. Indeed, this creature's genitals warranted a great deal of attention in Tiberius.

Alternately, in Bodley, the figure is posed to conceal the groin (40r), while in Vitellius, he is clothed in a tunic that covers him to the knee (101v); once again, only Tiberius figures its monster as a sexed being. He does not eat humans or breathe fire, but he is, like many of the monstrous people in this text, unusually tall, 'fiftyne fote lange' (Orchard, "*Wonders*" 190) [fifteen feet tall], and his body is described as being white, *hwit*. In terms of appearance, he is also a creature of excess in that he has not one but two faces on a single head: 'tu neb on anum heafde' (190). His appearance is clearly monstrous, but does anything in his behavior indicate a threat to humanity? He does not have fiery breath or a penchant for human flesh, true. He holds a drinking horn, which Mittman posits 'suggests a certain lonely, drunken violence about the Two-Faced Men, which would have increased their apparent threat' (79).[30] If he does indeed present the fear of a lonely drunk, then he must also imply a significant level of civilization: not only does he drink using a crafted vessel, but his culture possesses the ability to make alcohol. Whether or not this monster is drunken, his use of the vessel implies that he is civilized, to some degree, and that his community knows how to craft or trade for such an object, and that he knows how to use it. Like this vessel, his penis and its correlation to reproduction link him to participation in human civilization. The reader learns that not only do these people reproduce but that, to do so, 'farað hi on scipum to Indeum, 7 þær hyra gecynd on weorold bringað' (Orchard, "*Wonders*" 192) [they travel in ships to India and they bring their offspring into the world there]. I have discussed this passage previously to indicate a moment of 'never drawing,' when the original ability of these creatures to transform and fly away was scaled back to an ability to build ships. Despite this move away from transformative ability, this community of monsters is quite remarkable. To no other monster in this text is ascribed so explicitly the power of reproduction, although many descriptions begin with some variation on the formulation 'beoð men akenned' [people are born there]. Moreover, that reproduction is linked to powers of civilized people – the ability not only to travel, but to construct ships capable of a reasonably extended journey. These people possess abilities of human civilized culture, but they also have the very real possibility of entering into these communities. The threat of these monsters is thus not in their violence against

---

[30] Mittman notes, too, the omission in all three manuscripts of the red, possibly bloody knees that these monsters are said to possess (78).

humans, but in the potential of their bodies to *act* in a human manner, while remaining and reproducing as monsters. While in *Wonders* this exogamous threat remains implicit, in later Middle English texts monsters infiltrate human communities precisely because their bodies, through transformation, pass as human.

Like the travelers, the representative of the three-colored men undergoes erasure through the scraping away of a portion of the image. Here, the line from belly to thigh near the groin is removed below the navel, although very faint traces of a pale red penis remain, as well as small marks of orange-red paint on his upper thigh, just below the erasure. This is the only area of his body that appears unpainted, though it manifests clear traces of the same orange-red color used and erased in the other images I have discussed. In Bodley, again, the body is posed in such a way as to conceal the groin (40v). The Vitellius artist, probably because of a lack of ability to draw pectoral markings rather than a desire to feminize the figure, depicts him with exaggerated breasts (102r). The physical description of his community of monsters is far more frightening than that of the men with two heads: we are told that these men are born with skin of three colors, 'þreosellices hiwes,' manes like lions' heads, 'gemona swa leona heafdo,' and are twenty feet tall 'twentiges fota lange,' with a mouth shaped like a fan, 'fann' (Orchard, "*Wonders*" 192).[31] However, we are told that they are shy; if anyone sees or follows them, 'feorriað hi 7 fleoð 7 blode þæt hi swætað' (192) [they take flight and flee, and sweat blood]. The monstrosity here is based almost completely in the appearance and form of the hybrid body; the only act attributed to them is their flight from 'anyone' who sees them. Thus, the appearance of the monstrous sexed body motivates the erasure of the genitals. The monster's action, flight from the humans, is simply not threatening enough to require self-preservation through erasure on the part of the viewer in Tiberius, or the artist in Vitellius and Bodley.

I finish my discussion of erasure through removal by returning to the monster with whom I began this chapter: the *blemmye*, a man with no head. Also possessed of an erased penis, these men have eyes and mouths in their chests, 'þa habbað on heora breostum heora eagan 7 muð' (Orchard, "*Wonders*" 192). His pose is the same in all three illustrations, but in Bodley his groin is blank (41r) and in Vitellius he is clothed below the waist (102v). In Tiberius, it seems that he does have something on his groin – the pubic hair is black, drawn with detail and precision that suggest the original artist, but another strange blotch obscures what might be a penis (82r) [see image 1].[32] Even through the blotch, the viewer can vaguely see its outlines. Inside the large curve of pubic hair seems to be another ring of shorter lines drawn with a lighter ink, which surround a small, flaccid penis drawn with what seems to be brown ink. This is no massive, erect, red phallus, but instead a rather vulnerable human appendage that is covered over. These men may be

31 James notes another case of corruption in the Anglo-Saxon from the *Fermes* source: 'F. has "bestiae colore simile equorum," M. of "homines tripertito colore" ' (77).
32 While there is significant bleed-through on this page from the image on its other side, that bleed-through is distinct from the blotch that appears over the genital area.

'butan heafdum' [without heads], but they are excessive in both height and width, being 'eahta fota lange 7 eahta fota brade' (Orchard, "*Wonders*" 192) [eight feet tall and eight feet wide].[33] We are told nothing of their behavior. The only key to the behavior of these monsters is in the visual representation. In both Bodley and Tiberius, this man curls his fingers around the right and left sides of the frame while standing on it, rather than on the background with which he is provided, 'literally stepping out of it into the real world of the spectator' (Broderick 35). In order to reveal the *blemmye*'s particular brand of monstrosity, the artist is forced to pose him directly facing the viewer, but it is his interaction with his frame that makes him particularly aggressive. As Austin suggests:

> the violation of the frame suggests that the man is too large, perhaps even too 'real,' to be contained by the frame. The *blemmya* exists in a space very close to the reader. The frame is used here as a common denominator between reader and marvel. It collapses much of the distance between reader and headless man and, perhaps, between East and West. (34)

The *blemmye* is uncomfortably close to the reader, and although we know of no actions these monstrous humans make, their appearance here perhaps can communicate the real problem with the monstrous body. His aggression in stepping out of his environment, onto the page, and out toward the viewer communicates a dangerous transgression of space. Like the boat-building monsters, the *blemmye* threatens to enter into the human world, and his possession of an all-too-human penis indicates his potential to reproduce in it. Thus, the unknown viewer, in Tiberius, removes his genitals, as he has with the other three monsters, and the artists of Vitellius and Bodley never draw him as sexed at all. By removing the genitals, the viewers who perform the erasure attempt to remove the sexual threat of a monstrous body that refuses to stay in its proper place, but instead spills over into the human world. The removal of the penis would not permit this monster to pass as human – he is invariably a monster; thus, the alteration to his textual body via the removal of his penis does not transform him into something new. Instead, it confirms his uncanny *differance* from the human.[34] That is, the erasure posits that the monster is not really so human but instead entirely monstrous and Other, but the trace that erasure leaves behind makes him both strangely familiar and human, and simultaneously unfamiliar and different.

We might be tempted to think that the removal of genitals from these monsters has only to do with modesty and a sense of propriety, and this may certainly be a

---

[33] Mittman performs a very interesting reading of the *blemmye*, suggesting that the lack of body parts might suggest either mutilation – a common enough punishment in Anglo-Saxon England – or disease, which he claims is fair basis for 'moral contempt' by viewers (91–2).

[34] I use Derrida's term *differance* to denote the particular difference between the monster and the human, a difference that Derrida posits as 'that sameness which is not identical' ('*Differance*' 932). Similarly, I employ Sigmund Freud's term, uncanny from his essay, "The Uncanny", a term that implies the simultaneity of familiar/unfamiliar in a single event or relationship.

part of the impetus. Camille seems to think this might be the case in general for acts of erasure, as seen in his discussion of the removed genitals in a picture of an idol:

> Here it is not the face that has been removed, but the 'other face,' for the word *fascinum* was sometimes used to describe the phallus ... Has someone removed the genitals not so much from fear of the dangerous evil eye but from prudery and looking at what should not be seen, the sexual organs? (146)

Anglo-Saxon reticence to depict sexual bodies can be interpreted as just this kind of habitual prudery, but more complex motivations seem to be at work in *Wonders*. In Tiberius, not all of the genitals are erased. In fact, probably the most obvious, and the most threatening to humans of all the monsters, the *donestre*, retains his not only excessive, but also red, penis and testicles. If a prudish reader intervened in the text and erased all the genitals that offended his polite sensibilities, then why leave this all-too-obvious example? The erasure of genitals seems to be a means of warning a viewer against the dangerous excess of not only the monstrous body, but also his own. Upon looking at a creature with the head of a lion who towers above a weak human, the viewer might find little to link him to the monster. But the genitalia serve as a marker of humanity and of commonality as well as a reminder of these monsters' reproductive potential. It is both familiar and terrifying. Just as the blank spaces left behind in these other images are traces of the penises that have been removed, so too does the *donestre* act as a trace of their potential and their threat. Perhaps he escapes erasure because to castrate him would not make his image any less terrifying – after all, he lures, consumes, and mourns a human man while we watch. Regardless of the reason, the fact that his penis remains proves that prudery cannot be the primary motivation for erasure in this manuscript. Something else, then, in the removed elements of these images and in their erasers, required repression. These monsters seem to share a potential for reproduction and invasion of the human sphere; it is this fear, the fear of being replaced by the visibly monstrous Other, that seems to have necessitated such a pattern of removal, set against images that erase these same elements of the image in alternative ways. After all, as Karras argues in her discussion of miscegenation, 'Penetration symbolizes power. For men of one group to have sex with women of another is an assertion of power over the entire group' (25). If these erasers remove the means by which the Other can penetrate, then they retain control, and instead assert their own power over the monster.

REVISION

The final type of erasure, revision, is the most difficult to pin down and identify, perhaps because it most clearly manifests a kind of sublimation. Instead of seeing one thing, the person who revises the image directs us to something else, something that amends the most unacceptable elements of the image or monster. It is easy to miss the traces of what was there before because they are buried under and perhaps even incorporated into the newly constructed and censored meaning. In revision, the artist himself responds to the power of an image or description by adapting in such a way that the body appears whole, complete, and original. However, in revising the image in such subtle ways, the artist effectively disguises or removes the most troubling elements of the body. The whole body of the monster is not, then, transformed into something new, but rather the sexed and sexual overtones of the images are sublimated, reinterpreted in such a way that the body seems less perilous, although they are not entirely removed. Recognizing moments of revision in *Wonders* requires readers to examine all three manuscripts, and also to pay close attention to the diction of the descriptive texts. Because so much effort goes into the process of revising a monster or image, we must acknowledge that the body in question demands an especially strong response. Therefore, bodies that are revised are the most dangerous and the most socially and sexually transgressive in the manuscript. Most interesting, the only bodies that are revised in *Wonders* are the bodies of the only two female monsters present in all three manuscripts. Unlike the clearly male and phallic monsters, these women's transgressive bodies are harder to manage through acts of removal or of never drawing. Their monstrosity is too closely aligned with sex and gender hybridity for removal to resolve the threat of their bodies without turning them into humans.

The first moment of revision is one that looks very much like a moment of erasure. Although the text informs us that these monsters are women: 'Ymb þa stowe beoð wif akenned' (Orchard, "*Wonders*" 198) [around those places women are born], the image presents a less clearly female body. A facsimile of the image shows no drawn details on the naked chest of the first female monster in the Tiberius manuscript (85r) [see image 5, figure on left]. I conjectured that these details had been scraped away by a later viewer – or perhaps that they had never been drawn. Upon looking at the picture alone, the viewer has no way of knowing that she is indeed female. The figure, unlike the others in the manuscript, has a beard, dark and unkempt like the shoulder-length hair on its head. Furthermore, although the figure is only half-clothed, the naked chest appears unmarked, having neither breasts nor nipples. The blank appearance of the chest seemed unusual, as most, although not all, of the naked male figures in Tiberius are drawn with detail lines on their naked chests meant to show ribs, pectoral muscles, nipples, and navels. The woman's chest, however, seemed to show no marking at all. However, upon examining the manuscript at the British Library, I discovered that the painting on this particular monster is indeed detailed, delicate, and nearly, though not completely, invisible. The artist has painted her body an extremely pale shade of pink, a color used only sparingly in other parts of the manuscript, and never on another monstrous human's body. The ink used for the detail lines of her body, unlike the brown found in most of the other images, is white. The artist has used the white on top of the pink to mark definition in her forearms, hands, elbows, biceps, nose, cheeks, upper lip, underarms, kneecaps, quadriceps, shin bones, calves, ankles, tops of her feet, individual fingers, and, not least, her belly and breasts. A great deal of attention and energy has gone into detailing the body of this female monster – she is the only human figure to merit such energy and artistry. Therefore, her secondary sex characteristics, her breasts, have not been erased or never drawn. And yet, despite all of this subtle detail, the body remains masculine in form and size – indeed, a reader not as interested in this image as I am might not even notice the pale paint on her torso.[35]

Several elements of this image in Tiberius help to conceal her sex as female. The image and text tell us that these women have beards, *beardas*, which fall down onto their chests, 'swa side oð heora breost' (Orchard, "*Wonders*" 198). The beard in question is scraggly, black, and forked, and accompanied by a long mustache, as well as a similarly unkempt head of brown hair.[36] Most of the male monsters in the manuscript exhibit shorter hair than hers, which is clumpy and shoulder-length. However, a comparison to other women's hair in the manuscript is impossible, as they wear cloth head-coverings. She seems to exist somewhere between categories: not the same as men, but certainly not the same as the demure and covered-up women. Similarly, unlike the male monsters in the manuscript, this woman is actually clothed, according to both the picture and the prose description. She does not wear the long gowns the other women in the manuscript sport, but rather has something wrapped around her hips. The fact that she wears clothing at all reflects a mark of civilization not seen in most of the monsters, who remain completely naked. Still, the skin worn is not only that of a horse, but it has clearly not been thoroughly processed into finished clothing: the horse's head remains visibly attached and the hem is rough and uneven. The clothing clearly does not suit any sort of appropriate social norms for women, as established by the civilized and fully covered women in the manuscript.[37] Furthermore, the clothing renders any anxiety over depicting her genitals as moot. Since we cannot look to this area for confirmation of her sex, we must turn to other elements of her body in order to attempt identification. To a casual viewer, her form does not appear recognizably

---

[35] The paint on this image seems purposely pale and subtle – the color of the paint does not seem to have been affected by age or exposure.

[36] Allen Frantzen, in his discussion of bearded women saints in *Before the Closet*, states, 'the breast is the marker of the female, the beard of the male' (76). In the case of Galla from Gregory the Great's *Dialogues*, Frantzen argues that her beard grows because she is so chaste: her 'unfulfilled sexual nature increases her bodily heat; this is a mannish quality and it takes the form of a beard' (77). Interestingly, Frantzen identifies her as a creature of excess: 'the excess of Galla's feminine nature, denied the release of intercourse with a man, produced a beard, both a sign of manly identity and of womanly disgrace' (77).

[37] In *Wonders* in Tiberius, there is only one human woman, who is being given as a gift. She is modestly clothed in a gown that covers her to the feet and a head-covering that conceals her hair. Women, however, are also drawn in other parts of the manuscript for other texts, and these women are dressed in much the same way. There are no unclothed human women in this manuscript.

female:[38] she is stocky, with a wide torso and shoulders, no waist to speak of, strong arms and legs that are indistinguishable from those of the male monsters in the manuscript, large hands and feet, and broad facial features, especially notable in comparison to the more delicate features of the other female monster with whom she shares the manuscript page. If an illiterate viewer does not notice her pale pink and white breasts, she might not be identified as female – and therefore, she might not be categorized as monstrous.

Just as these women combine both masculine and feminine physical features, in being bearded women, so too do they exhibit behaviors that are an amalgamation of traditionally male and female activities. We learn that they make their tunics from horse's hide: 'horses hyda hi habbað him to hrægle gedon' (Orchard, "*Wonders*" 198) suggesting the feminine labor of making clothing.[39] Their skill as huntresses is emphasized by their reputation to the surrounding peoples, as we are told that they are called great huntresses, 'Þa syndon huntigystran swiðe genemde.'[40] The masculine and feminine are once again contrasted when we read that 'fore hundum tigras 7 leopardos þæt hi fedað þæt synda ða kenestan deor. 7 ealra ðæra wildeora kynn, 7 ealra ðæra wildeora kynn, þæra þe on þære dune akenda beoð, þæt gehuntigað' (198) [instead of dogs, they bring up tigers and leopards, that are the fiercest beasts, and they hunt all kinds of wild beasts that are born on the mountain]. While these women enact the medieval male skill of the hunt and thus the kill, they also have the ability to *fedan*, which carries the meaning of 'to feed' but also to 'nourish, sustain, foster, bring up' and even 'bear, bring forth, produce' (Bosworth and Toller). It seems reasonably clear that these women are not giving birth to the tigers and leopards, but they do more than simply feed them – they nurture and raise them. Even though medieval men probably raised their hunting dogs in the way these women raise their tigers, the use of a word that is so bound to women's work is striking in this context.[41] These women take on masculine habits and carry them to excess, in that they work with animals fiercer

---

[38] I do not mean to suggest that there exists only one phenotype for women, or that only a stereotypically feminine body can be female. Rather, I want to think about this body in comparison to the other bodies as they are drawn in the manuscript. She obviously *is* female, but the fact that she does not initially appear to be is fascinating, and, I suggest, purposeful.

[39] The images in Tiberius and Bodley show us that their tanning and sewing skills leave much to be desired, as the heads are still attached to their skirts and the hems appear uneven and unfinished.

[40] There is no other feminine form of the word *huntigystran* that I have found that appears anywhere else in the corpus of Old English according to the *Dictionary of Old English*. These women seem to be the only actual huntresses featured in Old English literature, a fact that should emphasize both their singularity and their gender transgression. The word mimics their state of being, because it imposes the feminine ending on a masculine word, just as masculinity is imposed on a female body.

[41] Trained hunting dogs were of greater value, as is evident in the Anglo-Saxon lawcodes of Alfred, which list a higher penalty for harming a trained dog than for an untrained one. Moreover, hunting dogs often lived more luxurious lives than peasants. For more information, see Almond, *Medieval Hunting*, and Cummins, *The Hound and the Hawk*.

and hunt animals more exotic than those pursued by most medieval men. The stereotypically feminine ability to raise or nurture young is not erased – a quality that implies the possibility of motherhood and reproduction, and that is emphasized by the possibly productive and nurturing function of the breasts.

These women seem to distort all things civilized, especially in terms of the hunt: women replace men, beasts replace dogs, horses are used as clothing instead of mounts.[42] However, the huntresses are not monstrous simply because they disrupt those traditions. They are frightening less because of their monstrous behavior (usurping masculine work), than because of the place from which this work grows: their monstrous bodies (usurping masculine physical features). As the descriptions and images of these women attest, the anonymous narrator, and even the artists, cannot seem to determine where feminine qualities should end and masculine ones begin. The threat of these women is in their ability to bear the identities of both men and women. Thus, their actions follow the precedents set forth by their bodies; their actions logically follow from their appearances. And in Tiberius, the artist manages to both depict and disguise the female sex of this woman. While he does not remove the clearest marker of her sex, her naked breasts, he invests a great deal of interest in depicting them while simultaneously making them hardly visible.[43]

The subtle revision of the huntress's body is most clear in comparison to her depiction in the other manuscripts. The other artists do not seem as troubled by the dual nature of these women's bodies. The illustration in Bodley shows a bearded figure posed in almost the same posture as in Tiberius, but her chest is neither pale nor subtle (44v) [see image 6]. Instead, she has exaggerated breasts and nipples, accentuating her female attributes in relation to her masculine features and beard. The Tiberius artist, who seemed to have no problem depicting male genitals, chose to emphasize her masculinity by giving her such a masculine figure. However, his approach to her female qualities serves as a kind of revision, not in content, but in style. He emphasizes her femininity by drawing her breasts in a color used nowhere else in the manuscript, but he downplays it by making these breasts barely visible in a frame characterized by typically masculine traits. Regardless, comparing the images confirms the nature of this woman's monstrosity: she possesses both male and female attributes. Animal–human

---

42 The killing of horses for meat would have been a particularly taboo practice in late Christian Anglo-Saxon England, as the eating of horseflesh was associated with paganism (although there is evidence for the consumption of horseflesh at least until the eighth century). For more on horses in Anglo-Saxon culture, see Bond, 'Burnt Offerings.'

43 Scholars have argued about the sexualized perception of breasts in the Middle Ages. Karras says, 'The female breast as depicted in medieval art may not have had the same sexual meanings as the breast today does, since it was used mainly to represent nurturing ..., but motherhood in terms of the nurturing of children was inseparable from the proves of their conception. In all cases except the Virgin Mary, that process involved sexual intercourse' (152).

hybrid creatures fill the pages of *Wonders*, but this kind of gender hybrid must be more taboo and threatening, because it invites special handling and a subtle level of revision. The Vitellius artist too draws a figure that combines masculine and feminine features. Here we see a traditionally dressed woman, in a long and modest robe, who also wears a beard (105v) [see image 7, top figure].[44] Like the Bodley figure, she is clearly a woman, as is indicated by her dress, if not by naked breasts. Even though this artist depicts her as far more civilized because clothed, he does not hesitate to give her both masculine and feminine attributes. Indeed, he seems to play with the irony of her proper female dress and her beard, one of the only parts of her that remains unconcealed by clothing. Although in Vitellius and Bodley both male and female attributes are illustrated clearly, in Tiberius these women are allowed only a limited sexual duality; they bear the markers primarily of the male, hiding in subtlety the elements of the female. Like the men with erased genitals, here a potentially dangerous body, a body that features both human markers and a monstrous appearance, is censored and controlled. The censoring takes place not in largely invisible 'never drawing,' nor in removal by a later viewer, but rather in a careful revision, necessitated by the sublimation of the troubling image in Tiberius.

While readers can attribute transgressive actions to these women, it is not their behavior but their hybrid bodies that are revealed to be monstrous. Like the *donestre*, the hunting women are drawn in conjunction with their monstrous actions. Their hunting, raising of beasts, and identity as a community of women separate from and not reliant upon men is evident in each of these pictures. They do not dress or act as befits proper women, but these irregularities in conduct are merely symptoms of a bodily monstrosity. Their bodies may not be constituted from animal parts, but they are still hybrid creatures. The revision of femininity in the Tiberius illustration reveals to readers the danger of these bodies as well as this particular quality. The barely visible breasts here function like the erased genitals of the male monsters; once they are revised, the dangerous familiarity of the monstrous and potent body is curtailed. The genitals and the breasts are sexualized body parts that reveal a possibility of reproduction that is all too similar to human reproduction. These monstrous human bodies presume too much; their sexualized embodiment inspires viewers' reactions of erasure.

The final figure I shall discuss is the second of the two monstrous women present in *Wonders of the East*. A viewer can easily determine the sex of this creature upon looking at her image in Tiberius (85v), unlike the image of the huntress [see image 5, figure on right, and cover]. She is an appealing and decidedly more

---

44 The Vitellius illustrations are drawn with much less skill and detail than the Tiberius and Bodley illustrations. It is occasionally difficult to understand what they are meant to depict. Here the robed woman holds out a bizarre figure-eight-shaped object that, with the interpretive help of the other manuscripts, might be food. An animal crawls up the side of the frame, right beside this object, suggesting it might be one of her beasts.

feminine figure, but her monstrosity is clearly written on her body by the presence of tusk, tail, and hooves. Rather than facing the viewer, she stands in a sort of profile. Her lower body turns to the right edge of her frame, while her shoulders are squared to the viewer, and her face is shown in a three-quarters' view.[45] The artist seems to be at pains to simultaneously conceal and reveal this body, as is implicit in its odd twisting. Though the woman's chest faces us, she crosses her arms across it, curling her fingers around locks of hair on either side of her torso. The hair cascades over her rotated hips, flowing around her exposed buttocks and between the cross of her legs. Her pubic region is shielded both by her posture of right leg striding across left, and by her hair. Her hair snakes down, in at least six different sections, to her hooves. The tail that protrudes from her posterior also brushes her ankles. While this body in itself is fascinating to observe, her face is equally strange. The features on it are far more delicate than those of the huntress. The three-quarters' view reveals two small, hooded eyes with slender eyebrows arched above. Her nose is just a tiny bit crooked, although still small, and her chin is pointed. Her hair is tucked behind one small ear. The face is certainly lovely compared with the huntress's, but her monstrosity is revealed here in the single dainty tusk that curves from her lower lip up towards her cheek.[46] The whiteness of her body, the only one in the manuscript that remains completely unpainted, is emphasized by the very dark background of the hill on which she stands and the slightly lighter background of the open sky behind her. While such background coloring is not unusual, the depth of the color highlights her form.

This woman does not seem to be threatening, except that her body comprises both human and animal parts. To the non-reading viewer, she does not act out any threat; in fact, the only actions we can attribute to this picture are the covering of the body, the grasping of the hair, and walking. The viewer is meant to understand a monstrosity based completely in the animal–human hybridity of the body, especially in comparison with the non-animalized human body of the huntress.[47] The image in Bodley is very similar to that in Tiberius, also featuring the three perspectives: three-quarters' view of the face, square positioning of the torso, and profile of the lower extremities, including a tail that seems to come through the skin at the spine (45r) [see image 8]. The only major difference here is the erasure of the top of her lip, which excises (through scraping) the tusk. This is a particularly striking moment, as it is the only act of removal obvious in the Bodley manuscript. This erasure is doubly ironic, because it removes a protrusion, like the genitals of the male monsters in Tiberius, but in this image, her tail, a far more phallic object than

---

45 Knock, contributor and co-editor of the McGurk text, claims that in the Tiberius manuscript, only *Wonders* uses 'three-quarters' views' (37).
46 There seems to be a sort of scratch or erasure where we should see her second tusk in the three-quarters' view.
47 I mean 'wholly human' here in that she is not an animal–human hybrid, not that she is not a monster. She is, as discussed above, a male–female hybrid.

the tusk, might have been chosen for erasure. The tusk is also not clearly visible in the Vitellius illustration, though darkened areas around the face make it difficult to determine if the tusk might not have been relocated (folio 105v) [see image 7, bottom figure]. She stands with one arm across her chest, the other holding a short staff. Her hair conceals nothing, but is wavy rather than sleek, and reaches her hooves. This body is overtly female, with exaggerated body parts. Her lips are extremely full, and perhaps even red, unlike any other figure in that manuscript. Her breasts are bulbous and reach down to the split of her legs, all of her sexual parts thus seeming to incorporate one another.

The written text of all three manuscripts offers a judgment against this troubling body, something it refuses to do in any other description. The sexualized combination of animal and human parts results in a body so offensive that it must be exterminated. We are told that Alexander the Great kills these women because of their 'unclennesse' or possibly '*micelnesse,*' either their uncleanness or their greatness, their excess, and furthermore, because they are 'æwisce on lichoman 7 unweorðe' (Orchard, "*Wonders*" 200) [offensive and disgusting in body].[48] Just what about these women's bodies is so terrifying that they must be eliminated? The written description reveals no violent action or horrifying habit that these women perform. Verner, too, remarks that 'these women do not appear to have performed any unclean or offensive action that warrants Alexander's hostility' (70). She sees this condemnation as the author having 'made yet another ethical mistake, although one that is perfectly understandable if one relies on superficialities and lacks the benefit of Christian teaching' (70–71). The elimination of these women, however, has less to do with the questionable pagan status of the narrator (which Verner suggests), and more to do with the 'offensive and disgusting' bodies that they possess. Their bodies imply a threat that is far more transgressive than just exceeding human norms, a threat communicated through the possession of a tail, but even more explicitly through the rupture between the artists' rendering of the tail and the writers' words describing it.

Like the hunting women with their beards, the tusked women's bodies take on a masculine physical signifier: their tails, evident in all three images, as well as in the written description.[49] The reader is told that 'ða habbað eoferes tucxas 7 feax oð

---

[48] Following the description of her hybrid parts, the text states: 'For heora unclennesse hie gefelde wurdon fram ðam mycclan macedoniscan Alexandre. Þa he hi lifiende gefon ne mihte, þa acwealde he hi for þam hi syndon æswisce on lichoman 7 unweorðe' (Orchard, "*Wonders*" 200) [Because of their uncleanness they were killed by Alexander the Great of Macedon. He killed them because he could not capture them alive, because they are offensive and disgusting in body]. Orchard's text uses the emendation 'unclennesse,' which seems to derive from Gordon's 1924 article 'Old English Studies,' despite the fact that Vitellius and Tiberius read 'micelnesse' and 'mycelnysse' respectively. The Latin text reads 'obscenitate' [impurity, indecency] (Orchard 180), which seems to explain the emendation.

[49] The equivalent of tail in the Latin description is 'caudas,' a term that can also be used as a euphemism for the phallus (*Oxford Latin Dictionary*).

helan side, 7 on lendenum oxan tægl. Þa wif syndon ðreotyne fota lange 7 heora lic bið on marmorstanes hwitnysse. 7 hi habbað olfenda fet 7 eoferes teð' (Orchard, "*Wonders*" 200) [They have boar's tusks and hair down to their heels, and ox-tails on their loins. These women are thirteen feet tall and their bodies are in the whiteness of marble, and they have camel's feet and boar's teeth]. While this is mainly a list of parts taken from various animals and applied to the body of a woman, it is not the bestial nature of the woman's body that creates the problem for the viewer. Instead, the danger of her body is revealed in the relationship between the physiological term *lendenu*, given as the location of the tail, and the illuminations of this figure, which reveal artists seemingly anxious about this feature. The revision here is not removal but relocation: the text tells us that the ox-tail comes not from the posterior, but from the loins, in Old English, *lendenu* and in Latin, *lumbi*.

Both the Clark-Hall and the Bosworth–Toller Old English dictionaries define *lendenu* as 'loins.' A *Thesaurus of Old English* similarly defines *lendenu* as 'loins' (53), but the *Oxford Latin Dictionary* defines *lumbus* as 'the part of the body about the hips, the loins; the seat of sexual excitement' (1049). Although this is a reasonably common term in Latin, it occurs rarely in Old English and is, moreover, an odd word to find in this sort of travel narrative. No other such narrative uses this particular word – indeed, no other Old English fiction employs it. *Lendenu*, in a search of the *Dictionary of Old English* corpus, appears primarily in religious texts: Ælfric's homilies, a few passages of Scripture, and one saint's life. It appears only twice in lawcodes, but is used repeatedly in medical texts. While these medical texts can give us a certain amount of help in understanding the word, in other ways they simply compound the problem. But the medical texts certainly do not help us to clarify precisely what 'loins' are.[50]

In most of Ælfric's homilies, the Old English word *lendenu* is linked with the Latin *renes*, the kidneys (*OLD* 1614), as well as with *lumbi*. Ælfric uses the word *lendenu* in four homilies, two pastoral letters (Wulfstan and Sigefyrth), and glosses it in his grammar as *renes*. Despite this gloss, he translates *lumbi* as *lendenu* in two of the four homilies, both in the second series of the Catholic Homilies: the second

---

[50] The medical texts that use this term are *Leechbooks* I and II, usually in a listing of various body parts. The references in *Leechbook* I only imply the proximity of the loins to the thighs: 'Wið lendenece and wið þeona sare' [For loin-ache and for the ache of the thighs] (423). More extended passages in *Leechbook* II list loin pain in the company of liver, spleen, womb, and bladder problems: 'lifer wærc, miltes sar, micgean forhæfednes, wambe ablawung, lendenwærc, sond 7 stanas on blædran weaxað' [liver pain, spleen pain, urine abstinence, womb swelling, loin pain, sand and stones in the bladder grow] (33). A similar passage from *Leechbook* II gives us more body parts to distinguish from the *lendenu*: '7 eft fram þam nafolan oð þone milte 7 on þa winestran rægereosan 7 gecymð æt þam bæc þearme 7 æt þam neweseoðan 7 þa lendenu beoð mid micle sare begyrdedu' [also from the navel or the spleen and in the left spinal muscle and comes at the rear bowel and at the front bowel and the loins are girded with much soreness] (241). While it is difficult to determine what exactly *lendenu* is in anatomical terms, it is clear that it represents something in the area of the groin.

part of the Mid-Lent homily, and Common of Virgins. In the former, *lendenu* occurs in a paraphrase of Ephesians 6:14: 'Standað eornostlice mid begyrdum lendenum on soðfæstnysse and ymscrydde mid rihtwisnysse byrnan and nymað þæs geleafan scyld and þæs hihtes helm and þæs halgan gastes swurd. Þæt is godes word' (469) [They stand earnestly with loins girded in truth and clothed with the corslet of righteousness and take the shield of belief and the helm of hope and the sword of the Holy Ghost. That is God's word]. Here we see the first evidence of loins being girded as an exercise of truth and virtue. *Lumbus* is the source word in Latin, invoking the possibility of sexual connotation. Similarly, in the Common of Virgins homily, *lendenum* is the Old English for *lumbi* in its two occurrences. The first use is in a paraphrase of Luke 12:35: 'Beon eower lendena ymbgyrde and eower leohtfatu byrnende' (61) [Let your loins be girded about and your lantern burning]. The second appears immediately after, in a moment of exegesis. Ælfric informs his audience about how they are to interpret the injunction in Luke: 'On þam ymbgyrdum lendenum is se mægðhad and on þam byrnendum leohtfatum sind þa godan weorc to understandenne' (62) [In the girded about loins is virginity and in the burning lantern, the good work is to be understood]. If girded loins are linked with virginity, ungirded loins are representative of lust.[51]

Similarly, the Easter homily from the second series of the Catholic Homilies makes just this connection. The word appears three times in this text, the first as a paraphrase of Exodus 12:11: 'Begyrdað eower lendenu and beoð gesceode' (19) [Gird your loins and be shod]. The second and the final occurrences of the word find their source in Gregory's Homily 22: 'Hi æton þæt lamb mid begyrdum lendenum' (303) [They ate that lamb with girded loins], and 'On lendenum is seo galnys þæs lichaman and se þe wile þæt husel þicgan he sceal gewriðan þa galnysse and mid clænnysse þa halgan þigene onfon' (303) [In the loins is the lust of the body and he who wishes to take that Eucharist, he shall bind the lust and accept holy food with purity]. This final citation offers us a clear link between lust and loins. The metaphor of loin binding as a restriction of lust is explicit here. Such a connection is echoed in both of Ælfric's pastoral letters that include the word *lendenu*. To Wulfstan, he writes: 'On þam lendenum is, swaswa we leornigað on bocum, seo fule galnys and we sceolan fæstlice þa gewriðan and gewealdan us to clænnysse' (28) [In the loins is, just as we study in books, the foul lust and we shall certainly bind them fast and bring ourselves to purity]. While he here speaks primarily of the celibate religious, the connection is not just between loins and lust, but between loins and *foul* lust.

Thus, although *lendenu* might very well be a reference, in the sense of the medical texts, to a specific body part, it seems more likely that *lendenu* is meant, in

---

51 While 'girding' implies some kind of 'encircling,' my focus here falls on the question not of what is encircled, but of what is closed off or controlled by girding one's loins. Therefore, girding might suggest the entire lower torso, but *lendenu* still seems to refer quite securely to the genital region.

Wonders, as a general reference to that part of the body in order to invoke lust. While Ælfric urges his readers to gird their loins, the female monsters have 'on lendenum oxan tægl' [ox-tails on their loins]. Rather than being carefully contained, these supposedly female loins take on the form of ox-tails, a strangely bestialized and non-productive protrusion. No artist draws the tail in the phallic position that the text suggests. Like Tiberius, Bodley locates the tail at the base of the spine, and makes few adjustments to the Tiberius arrangement [see images 5 and 8]. In Vitellius, we can see the curve of her buttock in a kind of profile, but the tail seems to be coming out of the side of her leg, perilously close to her groin [see image 7]. This figure's torso seems to be an amalgamation of sexual and animal parts. Whatever lack of skill viewers might attribute to the Vitellius artist, perhaps this image with its oddly placed tail is truer to the spirit of the description. She looks like a body of excess in both the human and the animal, not like a lovely human body that merely has supplementary animal parts. It is not just the animal elements that make this woman monstrous, but the combination of her excesses. These bodies, both feminine and masculine via their phallic tail, act out through their 'indecency' against the viewer within their narrative, Alexander, and against the viewer of the text. Alexander solves the problem of these women by killing them for possessing bodies that exceed the boundaries of social and sexual decency, whereas artists neutralize them by revising the images. The authors and artists warn women to stay in their place, a place that, according to Karras, is characterized by passivity: 'one thing we can say with some certainty … is that medieval people would have understood marital sex as something the husband did to the wife' (85). The woman does not act, but instead is the passive recipient of the sexual actions of the man. If a woman were to be the actor and the man, the recipient, this would be a reversal of gender roles, and would effectively gender the man feminine (23). As Karras argues, 'women's sexuality threatened medieval men in many ways: they might be temptresses and lure men into fornication or worse sins, they might behave in masculine ways with each other and so usurp male gender privilege, or they might use sexuality in other ways to control men' (116). These monstrous women embody all three of these qualities: they lure Alexander and direct his behavior (he must either have them or destroy them), but they threaten to do even more than act in masculine ways with one another: they threaten to act in masculine ways with Alexander, who desires them. If the erasers were concerned about their communities being penetrated by male monsters, where penetration was perceived as power, then being penetrated by a female monster could only be seen as far worse – it would be a position humiliating, emasculating, and powerless. The revised image of this monster secures women in their (passive) position, but the traces of their sexual monstrosity reveal to the reading audience the threat to social and sexual phallic order that these women, and perhaps even all women, might embody.

CONCLUSIONS

The erasure of sexed bodies is not a problem only in *Wonders of the East*, but more generally in the corpus of Anglo-Saxon writing, as I have demonstrated in the introduction to this book. Writers enact various kinds of erasure: they might 'remove' descriptions of bodies that are represented as sexual in the source materials, as is the case with *Judith*. They might move toward the eradication of sexual behavior with literal reproofs against especially violent sex, as in *Sermo Lupi*, or figurative castigations, as in the sexed bodies of the fallen angels in the illustrations for *Genesis*. By shielding readers from explicit sexual acts, as in the bedroom scenes in 'Cynewulf and Cyneheard' or *Beowulf*, writers also effectively perform an act of erasure of sex from the text. And yet, sexed bodies do remain, despite these kinds of erasure. The riddles present sexed bodies, despite many scholars' protestations that the sexual solutions are meant to be rejected for other solutions. Indeed, sexual bodies are visible behind the 'clean' solutions to the riddles, much like the modified illustrations of the Tiberius manuscript. Although the possible prescriptive message of the riddles is far less moralistic than the reproofs against sexuality seen in penitentials, laws, or sermons, it is impossible to escape the monastic textual impulse in Anglo-Saxon literature, even in secular texts. But texts like the riddles and *Wonders of the East* allow readers to see evidence of sexed and sexual bodies, despite attempts at erasure meant to render these bodies impotent. To remove the potency of the monster through erasure of sexed elements of the body is not to transform it, but to confirm the fact that while its virility can be changed, its monstrosity cannot.

The sexed bodies present in *Wonders of the East* offer us a rare opportunity to witness the sexual when linked with the monstrous, and to think about the function of erasure in relation to specific bodies. Although the Tiberius, Vitellius, and Bodley manuscripts present different contexts and possibilities of interpretation, each incorporates a kind of textual resistance to bodies that are both monstrous and sexed. Monstrous bodies that are also sexed exceed boundaries and endanger onlookers – so much so that sexual parts are frequently censored or even literally erased. As we can see in the bodies of the tusked women, who must be killed by Alexander the Great, excessive and sexed bodies are considered not only unclean and indecent, but also so threatening that they must be exterminated or expunged. The body, and particularly the sexed body, defines human identity through both an unwelcome genital familiarity and Derridean *différance*.

Because the sexed monstrous body defines monstrous identity, the same might be true for sexed human bodies, particularly because Anglo-Saxon literature resists depicting them. A body compromised by animal parts is indeed monstrous, but does not inspire the visceral reaction of the viewer as does the sexualized monstrous body. A body that exposes sex and reproductive potential, as is the case with each of the monstrous bodies discussed here, must necessarily be one that acts out, in *Wonders*, against the viewer, and in Anglo-Saxon literature, against the constrictions of monastic textual practices. Sexuality, then, is a part of human physicality that inspires prohibitive reaction – and more specifically, acts of erasure, inspired not by prudery, but by more complex processes of repression and sublimation.

Wonders suggests that bodies are fundamental to monstrous identity, and that these bodies are unchanging. Indeed, the only possible responses to sexed, and subsequently humanized, monstrous bodies are acts of erasure, the literal removal of parts of the dangerous body. This removal might require killing, as Alexander kills the tusked women, or might mean simply eliminating those threatening sexualized body parts. The red penis of the *donestre* remains not because it is not threatening, but because it is more monstrous than human. The construction of the sexed body in *Wonders* does not seem to be an anomaly in Anglo-Saxon literature, because of the consistent erasure of the sexed and sexual body throughout the corpus of Old English literature. Rather, these formulations of identity through the essence of the body reflect the Anglo-Saxon understanding of the body as unchanging and inflexible. This does not necessarily imply an allegorical reading of the body, although such interpretations are available. Instead, it reassures its contemporary audience that the most dangerous bodies will be clearly marked and identified; they will not be capable of change, but instead will be controlled through the will of the actor (in the case of Alexander), the viewer, or the scribe/artist. As opposed to later medieval monstrous bodies, these monsters cannot be transformed and redeemed. Therefore, to erase a sexed body is not to change that body or that identity – after all, traces remain – but to attempt to remove its ideological and reproductive threats.

Chapter 2

DISMEMBERMENT AS ERASURE:
THE MONSTROUS BODY IN *BEOWULF*

E RASURES MARK a curious boundary in Old English texts. They manage a precarious balance between securing and sanitizing the monstrous body for viewers and articulating a clear division between the monstrous and the human. Artistic erasure works not to transform a body from monster to human, but rather to eliminate its most threatening elements while maintaining its monstrous essence. Like the monsters, called 'micle mearcstapan' (1348a) [great border-wanderers], of *Beowulf*, erasures exist in the figurative margins of artistic creation but construct the central meaning of the text in significant ways. In *Wonders of the East*, the removal of a monster's penis demonstrates its importance and therefore emphasizes, rather than simply removes, the monster's masculinity as well as his reproductive potential. Like artistic erasure, which is often visible if not always obvious, literary erasure calls attention to important features in a text's subject matter: for instance, if readers recognize a narrative moment in which a character leaves out a particular detail, they learn something about what that character wishes to highlight or to disguise. Similarly, readers can observe moments of revision or of what I term 'never drawing' in literary texts, moments which serve to reveal elements of anxiety or tension in the narrative. In working with medieval literary texts, scholars examine such moments of erasure when they determine which elements one manuscript includes that another does not. However, with a text like *Beowulf*, which exists in only one manuscript, Cotton Vitellius A.xv., erasures take place within the body of the narrative. In fact, the patterns of erasure in this poem point consistently to the bodies of Grendel and his mother, the border-wanderers. They literally wander the borders of Hrothgar's kingdom, living at the outskirts of the community both spatially and socially. But Grendel and Grendel's mother wander other kinds of borders. They tread the borders of humanity because they possess hybrid bodies; their forms exist precariously on the boundaries of the monstrous and the human, and, in Grendel's mother's case, as I shall demonstrate, on the boundaries of the female and the male. In *Wonders*, the possession of a monstrous and sexed body threatens the integrity of the human community and the human body, inviting the literal erasure of and revision to the body. In *Beowulf*, a similar response to the dangerous monstrous body is carried out by the poet, by Beowulf himself, and even by modern critics.

For many years, the monsters were the last aspect of *Beowulf* that critics wanted to discuss; they were deemed too ridiculous, too folkloristic to be worthy of serious scholarly attention. J.R.R. Tolkien, in his foundational 1936 essay '*Beowulf:* The Monsters and the Critics,' addresses this concern directly; he asserts emphatically that 'the monsters are not an inexplicable blunder of taste; they are essential, fundamentally allied to the underlying ideas of the poem' (68). Contemporary scholars, from Jeffrey Cohen to Jane Chance, have acknowledged the import of the monster in their scholarship. Monsters are a part of the landscape of Old English literature and culture just as they are a part of the landscape of *Beowulf.* They embody social and socio-sexual concerns and anxieties, while they simultaneously represent illicit desires and prohibited practices.

Beowulf's monsters are victims of erasure, controlled and delimited by both author and characters. I contend that Grendel and his mother are victims of all three types of erasure: never drawing, removal and revision. As is the case with sexuality in the corpus of Old English literature and with sexualized monsters in *Wonders*, moments of sexual anxiety seem to motivate the strongest efforts of erasure in *Beowulf.* Specifically, the erasures of Grendel and his mother through dismemberment and revision indicate a deep discomfort with the sexualized and monstrous body on the part of those who have the ability to erase, most notably Beowulf and the poet. Erasure of visual images is, to be certain, a different process from the narrative erasures we see in *Beowulf.* In some of the cases of removal and revision, a later viewer, rather than the author or artist of the text, participates in the deconstruction and resulting construction of the image. In the poem, the poet alone manipulates and directs the reader's perception of the monster's body. While erasures highlight moments of anxiety particularly related to the body in both *Wonders* and *Beowulf*, the literary representation of the sexed and sexualized body offers contextualized motivation for its consistent erasure.

It is the physical body of the monster, a body that is simultaneously sexed and sexual, that motivates erasure. In *Wonders*, a reader's primary understanding of monsters comes from their appearance: they are literally drawn for the reader's inspection. In *Beowulf*, the opposite is true. Given the descriptions of the monsters, an artist would be unable to offer a textually accurate illustration. What little detail we can extract about the appearance of the Grendelkin transgresses normal human boundaries; these details act as traces of the monstrous body, visible to Beowulf and, on occasion, to the audience within the text, but never to the reading audience. The reading audience witnesses not the monstrous body itself, but rather the destruction and chaos caused by and originating in the bodies of Grendel, and ultimately, his mother.

Although Grendel is the more savage killer, Grendel's mother is the genesis for Grendel – without her, Heorot would not have suffered Grendel's constant attacks. She acts as an origin in this poem, an archaic mother in whose body we find 'the desirable and terrifying, nourishing and murderous, fascinating and abject' (Kristeva 54). Beowulf reacts to the powerful figure of this archaic mother by covering her up, in the mere and with the reports he offers. However, in attempting to erase her from his stories, Beowulf signals to the reading audience just how important she is. Grendel's mother *matters* in this poem, but she matters in a way that the poet both urges us to remember and helps us to forget, primarily through Beowulf's retellings of his fights. His desire to erase the monster, particularly through the act of dismemberment, is motivated by more than his status as a warrior and protector. I argue that the ways in which Beowulf approaches the bodies of both Grendel and his mother reveal his unconscious need to repress and remember threats to both his body and his masculine identity.

NARRATIVE STRUCTURE AND AUDIENCE

Memory and remembering are integral elements of *Beowulf*, particularly in the ways the poet employs *mise en abyme* – the story within the story. In this poem, identity is largely structured through story-telling. A significant portion of the poem comes to us as *mise en abyme*: through these stories, the reading audience learns about the social and cultural context of the poem, but also about the characters who tell the stories.[1] Through his boasting, we come to understand Beowulf's background and his monster-fighting qualifications; however, we also learn about how he positions himself rhetorically. We see how he counters opposition in his responses to Unferth, and his ability to balance flattery, obligation, and self-aggrandizement without alienating his audience in the poem. Indeed, in these moments of story-telling, the reader's experience of Beowulf's stories is often very different from the experience of the audience within the poem, particularly when the character recounts the story of an event the poet has already described. In order to emphasize the differences between the event and the retellings, the poet constructs two levels of audience for the poem: the audience within the text who sees Grendel's arm and who hears and believes Beowulf's stories, and the audience reading the text who sees what the textual audience cannot.

This strategy enables the reading audience to recognize what Beowulf does and does not reveal about his fights when he reports them to Hrothgar and Hygelac, and recollects them in his death speech. Like comparing images of monsters in *Wonders* from the different manuscripts, placing these descriptions of the monster fights side by side reveals distinct and important differences among them. The audience within the text comprises both Geats and Danes; the Geats witness Beowulf's fight with Grendel and remain at the mere, interpreting the changes in its surface. However, they do not witness the actual fight with Grendel's mother. Beowulf fights her alone, and no one else knows what happens in the mere. Therefore, he can tell any version of the story he likes – his immediate audience must take Beowulf's word for it. The reading audience, however, knows exactly what happens in this fight. We recognize when Beowulf adapts his material to suit his audiences of Danes and Geats, and we also can see when Beowulf omits details, details that he might not wish to revisit because of the strange and erotic tension he

---

[1]   See Harris, "'Double Scene.'' '

experiences in his fight with Grendel's mother. These moments of erasure demonstrate the power of Grendel's mother's status as abjected origin as well as Beowulf's precarious masculine and heroic identity.

Beowulf's story of his fight with Grendel undergoes little erasure because both the reading audience and the Geats and Danes witness this battle directly. This fight takes place in plain sight – in the middle of Heorot. Because the location of the fight is in the center of the hall, we recognize the witnesses' active involvement, although they do not actually engage in the fight: 'Þær genehost brægd/ eorl Beowulfes ealde lafe, wolde freadrihtnes feorh ealgian,/ mæres þeodnes, ðær hie meahton swa' (794b–7b) [There, most earnestly, Beowulf's men drew their swords, wished to protect the life of their lord, the famous prince, as they might]. In this passage, which directly follows Beowulf's initial grasping of Grendel's hand, it is clear that Beowulf's men are watching the battle, swords ready. They witness this fight; thus more than one person can and will report the details of the battle. Because of these witnesses, Beowulf is less able to change the details of the story he tells to Hygelac, though he does amplify elements of the narrative.

But the fight with Grendel's mother is not public: it takes place not in Hrothgar's hall under the gaze of the Danes and the Geats, but in Grendel's mother's mere, where neither Beowulf's nor Hrothgar's men can see the battle. After Beowulf claims that he will take Hrothgar's revenge and commands the dispersal of his property should he not return, Beowulf jumps into the mere alone, and 'brimwylm onfeng/ hilderice' (1494b–5a) [the surge of sea grasped the warrior]. At this moment, the narratorial gaze follows Beowulf, as he swims to the mere and fights Grendel's mother. Beowulf's isolation is emphasized when the poet abruptly shifts his gaze to the warriors waiting at the edge of the mere just after Beowulf cuts off Grendel's head. The poet calls attention to their ignorance when they misinterpret the blood they see in the water. Assuming Beowulf is dead, they say:

> Þæt hig þæs æðelinges   eft ne wendon,
> þæt he sigehreðig   secean come
> mærne þeoden;   þa ðæs monige gewearð,
> þæt hine seo brimwylf   abroten hæfde. (1596a–9b)

[That they did not expect that this man would ever again come victorious to seek their famous lord; because many agreed that the sea-wolf had destroyed him.]

This gloomy misinterpretation – that Beowulf has been defeated – leads the Scyldings, including Hrothgar, eventually to give up and return home (1600b–1602a). Only Beowulf's retainers remain, hopelessly wishing, but, the poet makes clear, not expecting – 'wiston ond ne wendon' (1604a) [they wished, and did not expect] – to see Beowulf again. Although the troops of Danes and Geats watch the water from above, hoping to understand what is going on under the surface of the mere, none of them witnesses what actually happens. Indeed, what they do witness, the staining of the water with blood, they misinterpret as Beowulf's defeat. It is only the reading audience that witnesses what happens in the mere.

In the culture of this poem, a warrior's value depends not only upon the deeds he performs and what he says about them, but also upon the stories circulated by witnesses and listeners. Reputation is established both by words and works, a common paradigm that is reiterated by the coastguard (289a). The stories a warrior tells about himself will be repeated, and affect the ways in which he and his community are perceived. Stories act doubly in this poem – they remember and re-member Beowulf and his monstrous foes time and time again: Grendel's head and arm and his mother's head return to their bodies each time the story is retold. They are reconstituted through language in each retelling, even if parts of their stories are (perhaps conveniently) forgotten. The *mise en abyme* structure of the narrative acts as a net to capture the elements of the stories that are forgotten or purposely left out. It is only through the means of this structure that we can recognize the acts of erasure of the monstrous body performed by both poet and hero.

THE BODY OF GRENDEL

Although both the reading audience and the audience within the poem can determine Grendel's social status as a border-wanderer, it is impossible for either audience to understand entirely his uncanny physical presence. Just as socially he exists on the borderlands, so too does his body occupy the murky boundaries between the human and non-human. Grendel seems to be larger than a normal man; he is called *eoten*, a giant (Klaeber 761a). Moreover, we are told by Hrothgar, who has heard this from his bondsmen, that Grendel was larger than any other man, ' "he wæs mara þonne ænig man oðer" ' (1353a–b). Even more telling is the heft of his head: four men struggle when carrying his dismembered head from the mere (1637b–9b).[2] Michael Lapidge suggests that the *Beowulf* poet 'carefully avoided giving his readers any descriptive details concerning Grendel that would enable

---

[2]   While this description might be hyperbole, the excessive nature of the body is clear. For more on this kind of exaggeration, particularly in reference to Beowulf's own excessiveness, see Robinson, 'Elements of the Marvellous.' Additionally, although we cannot describe Grendel's appearance, we do know his social role. There is no shortage of nouns pointing to Grendel's status as an outsider – he is called 'ellengæst,' bold guest or spirit (86a); 'mearcstapa,' a walker on the border (103a); 'manscaða,' wicked ravager (737b); repeatedly 'feond,' enemy (101b, 725b, 748a, 970a, etc.); and even more explicitly, 'feond mancynnes,' enemy of mankind (164b). Grendel is also called 'gæst,' which can mean either 'guest' or 'ghost.' Lionarons comments on the standard edition of the text, saying that Klaeber's glosses betray a personal, rather than textually accurate, glossing of these words. 'An examination of Klaeber's lexical decisions in his edition of Beowulf shows that in general he prefers the reading "ghost, spirit, or demon" for usages of gæst referring to Grendel and Grendel's mother, and "stranger, visitor, guest" for gæst references to Beowulf and the dragon. His choices tend to reinforce a particular interpretation of the monsters as well as the hero: Grendel and his mother are consistently regarded as supernatural rather than natural (i.e. human or bestial) creatures and thus as "demons" or "spirits," while the supernatural qualities of the hero and dragon are deemphasized in the neutral term "guest" ' (Lionarons 10).

them to visualize him within categories familiar from their external world' in order to emphasize the 'instinctual human fear of the unknown' ("*Beowulf*" 401–2). The fact is, as Lapidge quite rightly indicates, readers cannot put together a coherent picture of Grendel – at least not one based on the evidence of the text. By 'never drawing' Grendel in the text, the poet emphasizes Grendel's monstrosity, not his humanity. As with the male monsters of *Wonders*, this act of erasure does not transform the monster's body into something new; rather, it accentuates his strangeness and the dangers that his excessive body presents. Although certain critics and translators see him as bestial, his form seems to be that of a man, not an animal. We can surmise some basic facts in support of his humanoid form from the action of the text: Grendel must walk on two legs, rather than going on all four as a beast. The nature of his tracks, the way he grabs his enemies, and his ability to flee with only one arm all suggest that he must be upright and walk like a man. But little evidence of his appearance actually resides in the poem.

Grendel's body receives only two explicit, descriptive passages in the poem: we see directly only his glowing eyes and his dismembered arm, the first of which makes him seem more alien, and the second of which makes his body more understandable, but also more uncanny. No one but Beowulf, presumably, sees the light in Grendel's eyes, because everyone else is asleep in the hall when he arrives. Nevertheless, first we learn that 'him of eagum stod/ ligge gelicost leoht unfæger' (726b–7b) [from his eyes shone a horrible light most like a flame]. Glowing eyes seem to be a standard among monsters, belonging not only to the Germanic nightmare creatures that Lapidge compares to Grendel, but also to monsters in *Wonders*.[3] Secondly, after Beowulf has ripped Grendel's arm off, the audience is allowed to view it. Though many translators like to take their liberty with this particular noun – Seamus Heaney even calls it a 'claw' – Grendel's hand is only called initially a 'grape' (836a) [grip]. Later, when the people look at the hand, it is described for the reader: 'feondes fingras; foran æghwylc wæs,/ stiðra nægla gehwylc style gelicost,/ hæþenes handsporu hilderinces/ eglu unheoru' (984a–7a) [the enemy's fingers; on the end of each, each of the hard nails, was most like steel; the heathen warrior's hateful awful handspurs]. 'Handspur,' at least according to the glossary of Klaeber's third edition, may be a possible reference to a claw, which would explain Heaney's bold interpretive choice. What is most surprising here is not that the nails are frightening, or even that they might be claw-like. No, most amazing is the fact that the formation of the hand itself seems quite human.

Grendel's hand is simultaneously familiar and unfamiliar – like Grendel, it is both human, and more than human. It has fingers and so cannot be an animal paw. On the hand, only the super-strong nails seem remarkable – and even these

---

[3] Lapidge says that these nightmare creatures feature 'a large head and uncanny bulging eyes' ("*Beowulf*" 384). In *Wonders*, the monsters live on an island 'in ðam beoð men akend þara eagan scinað swa leohte swa man micel blacern onæle on þystre nihte' (Orchard 198) [on which people are born whose eyes shine with a light just as if one had lit a great lantern in a dark night].

71

are described in human terms, as steel is a man-made metal. True, we are told in the next lines that no iron tool could hurt this bloody hand; nevertheless, we are not told that its skin is scaly or green or even rough. What is most shocking about the hand is how it can (or rather cannot) be damaged, not how it looks. In many ways, this hand is just a familiar appendage whose appearance signals Grendel's status as a shamed and defeated criminal,[4] but also as a creature whose body is both like but not like those of its onlookers. The hand looks much like theirs, but it also exceeds theirs in strength and resilience; it possesses its own built-in armor. It is reassuring and terrifying, familiar and unfamiliar: it is uncanny. As Freud suggests of the uncanny or *unheimlich*:

> we are reminded that the word '*heimlich*' is not unambiguous, but belongs to two sets of ideas, which, without being contradictory, are yet very different: on the one hand it means what is familiar and agreeable, and on the other, what is concealed and kept out of sight … on the other hand, we notice that Schelling says something which throws quite a new light on the concept of the *Unheimlich* … everything is *unheimlich* that ought to have remained secret and hidden but has come to light. ("The *Uncanny*" 517)

The hand, as I have suggested above, seems familiar and comforting as it reassures the audience of Grendel's demise, but it also reveals the Derridean *différance* that characterizes his body, a body that both before and after remains hidden and mysterious – a body that perhaps ought to have remained hidden, but which, to the pleasure and terror of the onlookers, has come to light. Thus, Grendel's body, uncannily human and monstrous, appears only in fragments to the audience within the poem.

Like his hand, Grendel's head is uncanny by the very fact of its dismemberment, as well as in its specific physical qualities and excess. It is very much like a human head, but it is also profoundly unfamiliar because of its sheer size, and the fact that it is no longer attached to a body. We are told that 'þa wæs be feaxe on flet boren/ Grendles heafod, þær guman druncon,/ egeslic for eorlum ond þære idese mid,/ wliteseon wrætlic; weras on sawon' (1647a–50b) [then Grendel's head was carried onto the floor by the hair to where men drank, a terrible thing for the earls and the women with them, a wondrous spectacle; the men looked on it]. We learn that Grendel has hair, which tells us he does not have animal fur, as few hunted animals were carried into the hall by their hair. Hair also signifies as a marker between the civilized and the uncivilized, particularly in illustrations. For example, in *Wonders* civilized men have short caps of neatly coifed hair, while monstrous humans have long, shaggy, messy hair. Being carried by the hair suggests that Grendel's hair is probably not trimmed and combed, but wild and uncivilized. He is not animal, but he is also not entirely human.

---

4 The removal of hands is linked to a criminal tradition discussed by Katherine O'Brien O'Keeffe in 'Body and Law in Late Anglo-Saxon England,' and Leslie Lockett in 'Grendel's Arm as "Clear Sign" in Feud, Law, and the Narrative Structure of Beowulf.'

In the description of this moment, the poet concentrates not on what the head looks like, but rather its effect upon the crowd of onlookers, which serves as another kind of erasure for the reading audience. The head is 'egeslic' [terrible], but also 'wrætlic' [wondrous] to these viewers. The experience of the head seems to be sublime – the men cannot seem to look away. The effect of the head is also uncanny by virtue of its disembodied status. Freud particularly addresses the experience of the dismembered limb, saying:

> Dismembered limbs, a severed head, a hand cut off at the wrist … feet which dance by themselves … all these have something peculiarly uncanny about them, especially when, as in the last instance, they prove capable of independent activity in addition. As we already know, this kind of uncanniness springs from its proximity to the castration complex. ("The *Uncanny*" 527)

Thus, what is so strange about the head is indeed that it continues to function after it has been removed. Although there is no will left to operate it, still it inspires fear and awe in its audience. Freud suggests that what is really troubling about the dismembered limb is its connection to castration; this is particularly so in the case of decapitation, an act connected to removing both intellect and authority. Therefore, although Grendel's body is erased through its lack of description, its danger is simultaneously exaggerated and nullified through decapitation. Notably, the head is not made familiar to the reading audience. While the audience within the poem experiences the terror of the head directly, the reading audience's curiosity is deferred and directed away from the monster's body. In this way, the reader's experience of the body of Grendel is far different from the viewing audience inside the text. By removing the head from the reader's visual inspection, its actual physical status is, in effect, erased from the reader's experience of the poem. In *Wonders*, viewers can only recognize moments of 'never drawing' when the manuscript images are set side by side, revealing what an artist has chosen to leave out, an experience unavailable to its contemporary audiences. However, in *Beowulf* such an act of erasure simultaneously piques the reader's interest and leaves it unsatisfied. Therefore, readers cannot respond to the body itself, but instead only recognize the impact of the body upon those who witness it. However, unlike the moments of 'never drawing' in *Wonders*, here the reader may understand that the body of Grendel is concealed.

What the readers know that the characters do not, however, is Grendel's genealogy – nor would the pagan characters in the poem understand the import of his ultimate patriarch. The poet tells us, 'fifelcynnes eard/ wonsæli wer weardode hwile,/ siþðan him Scyppend forscrifen hæfde/ in Caines cynne' (104b–7a) [that unhappy man occupied the land of the monster-kin for a time, after God had condemned them as Cain's kin].[5] Grendel is said to *live* in the land designated for banished kin of Cain, the infamous brother-killer. Only a few lines later, Cain's

---

5   For an allegorical reading of the Cain connection, see Williams, *Cain and Beowulf.*

banishment and his offspring are described: 'Þanon untydras ealle onwocon,/ eotenas ond ylfe ond orcneas,/ swylce gigantas; þa wið Gode wunnon/ lange þrage; he him ðæs lean forgeald' (111a–14b) [All evil progeny were born from him [Cain], the giants and elves and evil spirits, also the giants who fought against God for a long time; He repaid them for that]. The poet suggests but does not state explicitly here that Grendel is part of Cain's evil progeny, for he lives in that land, and he suffers, like those who are being repaid for their fight against God.

It is not until Grendel's mother enters the picture, over a thousand lines after the poet's first reference to Cain, that Grendel's kinship to him, and thus to giants, elves, and evil spirits, is confirmed: 'Þanon woc fela/ geosceaftgasta; wæs þæra Grendel sum,/ heorowearh hetelic' (1265b–7a) [from him [Cain] were born many fated spirits; Grendel was one of them, the hateful cursed foe]. So it seems that Grendel has a dual lineage based both in the monstrous and the human.[6] He is both the progeny of the human Cain and the progeny of those monsters born of Cain. Clare Lees claims that: 'The poem opens with the patrilineal family of the Scyldings – the ruling family of motherless Danes – and the ruling dynasties, whether Danish or Geatish, form one of its fundamental preoccupations' (141). As the warriors' lineages define them, so too does Grendel's. However, Grendel's lineage is strangely incomplete, despite his connection to his many-times-removed progenitor: the poet does not identify any particular father for him. Thus, the Danes are 'motherless' while Grendel is 'fatherless.' The Danes, however, are only nominally 'motherless' in the patriarchal terms of their family tree as it is written into the poem. Grendel's 'fatherless-ness' is a much bigger problem.

We know only that Grendel has a mother; whether his father is human, monstrous, or even necessary to Grendel's mother's ability to reproduce is unclear. However immediately 'fatherless' Grendel is, the figure of Cain stands in as a patriarch to define Grendel's truly monstrous but also tragically human lineage. Most importantly, this mythological and biblical vision of monsters as Cain's offspring affirms their status as inborn. Cain, as the utterly human child of the first couple, Adam and Eve, performs a horrible action: killing his brother, Abel. Neither in *Genesis* nor in *Beowulf* does his physical body transform in any way: he does not suddenly sprout a tail or grow to excessive size.[7] Instead, when he

---

6 The idea of lineage is very important within the logic of the poem: it is Beowulf's lineage that leads him to his battle with Grendel: he comes to, and is allowed to help, Hrothgar because of debts owed by his father; even brother-killing Unferth's sword has a powerful lineage.

7 Cain is cursed by God in *Genesis*, but the curse is not primarily physical, although 'God him sealde tacn þæt nan þæra ðe hine gemette hine ne ofsloge' (4.15) [God gave him a mark so that no one that met him would kill him]. In Ælfric's version of *Genesis*, the curse is rendered thus: 'Nu þu bist awyrged ofer eorþan þeo þe oponode hire muð ond underfeng þines broðor blod of þinne handa. Þonne þu tilast ðin on eorðan, ne sylð heo ðe nane wæstmas; woriende ond flyma þu bist ofer eorþan' (4.11–12) [Now you are cursed over the earth, she who opened her mouth and received your brother's blood from your hands. When you till the earth, she will give you no produce; you will be roaming and an exile over the earth]. While the mark of Cain

reproduces, he begets monsters who appear as something other than, or more than, human: he produces 'giants and elves and evil spirits' as well as Grendel. Grendel's monstrous form descends from the human Cain, whose performance of the most taboo act in Anglo-Saxon wergild culture, fratricide, is enough to pervert his progeny. While Grendel is not a beast, he is also clearly not entirely human, although it is his human qualities that are often erased or covered up by the poet.

Despite his monstrous and excessive inheritance and body, dangled in tanta-lizing pieces before the reading audience, Grendel has human motivations and responses, no doubt inherited from his originally human patriarch. He hears the happy noises of the hall from the dark place in which he lives, and they cause him suffering: 'Ða se ellengæst/ earfoðlice/ þrage geþolode,/ se þe in þystrum bad,/ þæt he dogora gehwam/ dream gehyrde/ hludne in healle;/ þær wæs hearpan sweg,/ swutol sang scopes' (86a–90a) [then the bold spirit painfully suffered hardship, he who lived in darkness, for each day he heard the noise in the hall; there was the sound of the harp, the clear song of the poet]. In this passage, Grendel longs for the light and warmth of this happy hall, while he suffers through the time of hardship. This suffering seems to be more than physical; instead, it is brought on by the contrast of the light and fellowship of the hall to his life of darkness and loneliness.

Moreover, Grendel is capable of weeping, a human physical ability and emotional response. The Danes witness Grendel's despair at his defeat by Beowulf: 'Norð-Denum stod/ atelic egesa, anra gehwylcum/ þara þe of wealle wop gehyrdon,/ gryreleoð galan godes andsacan' (783b–6b) [For the North-Danes, horrible fear rose up, for each one of those who heard his weeping surge, God's enemy singing his terrible song]. Grendel's weeping, however terrifying to the Danes, is expressed in human terms, as a response to physical and emotional anguish. Like his body, it is uncanny – it is not an animal howl, but rather a 'ter-rible song,' that horrifies listeners because of its eerie resonance with the many other songs that are sung in Heorot. It is not merely a roar of pain, but both 'gryreleoð' [a terrible song] and 'wop' [weeping].[8] Whether or not we can picture Grendel as entirely human, we cannot imagine him as completely bestial. His lineage as the kin of Cain and his behavior point to a hybrid monstrous–human

---

does seem to be physical, it is meant as a protection, not a disfigurement. The curse, rather, is that Cain will be an outcast, in fact, a border-wanderer like Grendel. The curse is similar in the poetic *Genesis B*: 'þu þæs cwealmas scealt/ wite winnan and on wræc hweorfan,/ awyrged to widan aldre' (1013b–15a) [for this killing you will endure punishment and wander in exile, cursed for eternity]. Strikingly, intermarriage with Cain's descendants, in the poetic *Genesis*, ultimately results in giants. We are told that God, through the flood, wants to strike down 'gigantmæcgas, gode unleofe,/ micle mansceaðan, metode laðe' (1268a–9b) [the sons of a giant, hated by God, the great evil-doers, loathed by the Creator]. In *Genesis B*, then, the descendants of Cain physically manifest their curse when they intermarry – although this is never attributed to the 'mark of Cain.'

8   'Wop' is defined by the Bosworth–Toller and Clark-Hall dictionaries as 'weeping, lamenta-tion.' It seems to be a primarily human ability, in a scan of the 370 entries in the *Dictionary of Old English* corpus.

identity that springs from an all-too-human origin. The original monstrous action of brother-killing results in monstrous bodies, which again and again perform monstrous actions – despite the very human motivation, at least in Grendel, of envy. Grendel is therefore more than just a narrative trope to elevate Beowulf's heroic status. He is both a monster and a man – a creature characterized by an excess of masculinity in terms of size and strength, but also by clear human needs and desires. It is the lack of satisfaction for these desires that drives Grendel to act with such excess, attempting again and again to consume that which he cannot become.

Grendel's consumption is indeed violent and excessive in its scope, capacity, and haste. Through Beowulf's eyes we first see the way that Grendel kills. He watches Grendel's techniques, having already decided his strategy for defeating the invader.

> þryðswyð beheold
> mæg Higelaces,   hu se manscaða
> under færgripum   gefaran wolde.
> Ne þæt se aglæca   yldan þohte,
> ac he gefeng hraðe   forman siðe
> slæpendne rinc,   slat unwearnum,
> bat banlocan,   blod edrum dranc,
> synsnædum swealh;   sona hæfde
> unlyfigendes   eal geferemod,
> fet ond folma. (736b–45a)

[the kinsman of Hygelac, the mighty one observed how the enemy of man wished to proceed in his sudden attack. Nor did the enemy think to delay, but he quickly seized, at the first opportunity, a sleeping warrior, eagerly tore into him, bit into his body, drank blood from his veins, swallowed huge morsels; very quickly had he consumed all of the dead man, feet and hands.]

Grendel is not just here to kill but to consume; this is a hall for feasting, and he does just that. But Grendel's eating is more than ravenous, and even more than bestial. He devours every part of this body, as the poet tells us, even the hands and feet – such excess reveals indiscriminate consumption. This is not the work of any familiar predator. In fact, the only animals that compare with Grendel's ability to consume are the hippopotami in *Alexander's Letter to Aristotle*,[9] which swallow whole Alexander's guides. The differences between these two creatures, however, are significant: the hippopotami live in the dangerous 'East,' and even there do not

---

[9] 'Þæt wæs þonne nicra mengeo on onsione maran 7 unhyrlicran þonne ða elpendas in ðone grund þære ea 7 betweoh ða yða þæs wæteres þa men besencte 7 mid heora muðe hie sliton 7 bodgodon 7 hie ealle swa fornamon' (Orchard, *Pride*, 234) [Then there was a host of water monsters in appearance larger and more terrible than the elephants, who took the men to the ground (river bottom) and between the waves of the waters dragged the men and slit them and bloodied them with their mouths and snatched them all up].

venture into human habitation; rather, the men travel to them and invade their territory. Grendel, on the other hand, is an invader of civilized human space, and he is much closer to home for the reader as a more local monster.[10] More significant is the matter of motivation for consumption: the hippopotami are simply beasts acting on instinct; they lack the forethought of Grendel, who eats with such glee, and who has waited, longing for companionship, outside the hall for many years. His inability to be a part of the halls moves him to 'eat the Other,' an inherently sexual act. In psychoanalytic terms: 'the subject takes possession of the object by inserting it into its body, by imitating it in its ego, by incorporating it' (Kear 256). Once incorporated, however, 'the foreign body remains foreign within the body' (257) – the desire remains unsatisfied, and so Grendel must return again and again, hungry to possess the bodies of men with whom he cannot connect. Grendel's excessive consumption only reinforces Beowulf's initial assumptions about Grendel: he cannot be approached like any being Beowulf has fought before. The excesses of his body, extreme consumption, and nightly usurpation of the human hall reflect the lineage of his uncanny and monstrous form: his heritage and his body are also both human and some indescribable monstrous other.

GRENDEL'S MOTHER

Although Grendel's sexual excess is manifested through his 'eating of the Other,' Grendel's mother's is demonstrated in the very existence of her son. She has conceived and borne the monster; her fecundity, then, is her most monstrous and most dangerous trait. She appears, in some critical opinions, as ancillary to her son, but in fact she precedes and exceeds him as a sexual and reproductive threat. For many years, scholars, even Tolkien, ignored her presence in this text.[11] In response to this critical erasure of Grendel's mother from the poem, contemporary scholars have sought to highlight her position and importance, but in doing so continued to understand her body through her son's identity. They struggle to manage her dichotomous position as monster and woman, a creature subject both to no rules and to a multitude of social restrictions. Some scholars attempt to remove her feminine or human identity: Jane Chance sees Grendel's mother as an 'inversion of the Anglo-Saxon ideal of woman as both monstrous and masculine' (288), while Gwendolyn Morgan refers to her as an 'ogress,' saying readers should

---

10 Although *Beowulf* is set in a distant past for its contemporary readers, its setting is not the monster-infested and dangerous 'East,' but rather north of England in a more familiar landscape.

11 Tolkien's essay, 'The Monsters and the Critics,' fundamentally redirected the future of *Beowulf* scholarship to envision the poem as a poem, not just an historical document. However, he quite obviously excludes Grendel's mother from any discussion of the monsters. As Lees has observed, 'Tolkien's monsters are Grendel (the monstrous son) and the dragon; Grendel's mother and other female characters are not mentioned' (133).

'equate Grendel's dam to the negative aspect of the Feminine' (65). Keith Taylor and Christine Alfano use the term *ides* [lady] to reclaim Grendel's mother from 'feminine monster imagery' (Alfano 12),[12] attempting to rescue her from her status as a monster – the only status that might free her from the confines of her sex. It seems that these feminist arguments seek to simplify her hybrid nature: either she is all monster/masculine, or she is no monster/feminine. But what makes her interesting and troubling is that she resists these binaries: she is a woman, she is a mother, and she is a monster.

The poet suggests to us that she is, indeed, monstrous, whether we follow Klaeber's gloss of *aglaecwif* as 'monster of a woman,' or Alfano's.[13] In addition to calling her an *ides* [lady], he calls her a 'merewif mihtig' [mighty mere-woman] (1518a–19a), 'brimwylf' [water-wolf] (1506, 1599), and a 'grundwyrgenne' (1518), glossed by Mitchell and Robinson as '(female) monster of the deep' (*Beowulf* 265), but which seems to mean more literally 'female outlaw from [under?] the ground.'[14] In writing about the word *aglaeca*, Stanley suggests it is 'a word which we do not understand' (75); the same might be said for most of these names, as the debate over their meaning and translation continues. Our uncertainty about these names reveals a perhaps purposeful instability in understanding or categorizing Grendel's mother. What the names do reveal is a contested and hybrid identity for Grendel's mother, emphasized by the poet's pairing of descriptors: she is both a lady (*ides*) and a warrior woman (*aglaecwif*); she is a woman, but she is of the water not the land (*merewif*); she is water-wolf and a female outlaw (*brimwylf* and *grundwyrgenne*). Grendel's mother is neither just a woman nor merely a monster. She is both, and therefore has been doubly removed from the center of social power and authority.

Grendel's mother is liminal but also central. We cannot ignore her place in the narrative of *Beowulf*: she is in the center. Beowulf swims down to her mere around line 1500, halfway through a poem of approximately 3000 lines. She is the last foe we see him fight in his youth, and participates in the first moment when we see his vulnerability. And yet, she does not even have her own name, but is identified only

---

12 Taylor argues that the poet's use of the word *ides* [lady] 'commends Grendel's mother for performing a brave deed' (22).

13 Kuhn and Stanley also opposed Klaeber's gloss of *aglaeca*. Kuhn argues that Grendel's mother was an 'aglaec-wif,' 'a female warrior.' '… There is no more need to introduce the idea of monstrosity or of misery here than there is in line 1519 where she is called merewif, defined simply as "water-woman," "woman of the mere" ' (218).

14 Fascinatingly, Skeat links the term 'wyrgen' to the term 'wolf.' In his *Etymological Dictionary*, he initially connects this term with the verb 'worry.' He says 'these verbs were closely allied to the sb. which appears as AS wearg, wearh, werg, a wolf, an outlaw … the vowel change from ea to y being well exhibited in the derivative wyrgen, a female wolf, occurring in the comp. grund-wyrgen, a female wolf dwelling in a cave' (719). However, this association has been corrected by Klaeber in his 1912 *Anglia* essay. Dobbie also notes that the Old Icelandic cognate, 'vargr, "wolf," may also mean "outlaw" ' (197).

through her maternal identity[15] – a fact that has led many critics to see her fight only as an addendum to the story about her son. The reductive naming by critics and translators – Grendel's dam, the 'she-wolf' (Bradley 451), 'the brawny water-hag' (451) and the like – functions as a kind of erasure outside the poem, making Grendel's mother into a recognizable, and therefore easier to overlook, female monster – a reproductive beast or a witch. Grendel's mother undeniably occupies a troubling middle ground in the poem that is constantly being revised and erased, but, as I shall demonstrate, her body and her story ultimately leave a residue on the troubling conclusion of the poem, as Beowulf continually relives, revises, and erases his sexually charged encounter with Grendel's mother.

The fact of the matter is that Grendel's mother is simply less visible, less witnessed, than her son. Her arm does not hang above the mantle for the entire hall to see, and her head does not serve as proof of the defeat of the grendelkin when Beowulf returns from the mere. Indeed, her existence is not even referenced by Hrothgar until *after* she kills Æschere to avenge the death of her son. She is, in many ways, invisible. Though Beowulf looks on her, 'ongeat þa se goda grundwyrgenne,/ merewif mihtig' (1518a–19a) [then the good one saw the accursed monster of the deep, the mighty mere-woman], the audiences within and outside the poem never do. Even in the very physical struggle that takes place between Grendel's mother and Beowulf, we receive little description. Nevertheless, as with Grendel, body positions can suggest some basic information about her form. Beowulf grabs Grendel's mother by her shoulder, 'gefeng þa be eaxle' (1537a).[16] Like Grendel, she walks and moves like a human, and uses her arms, shoulders, and hands in battle. Like Grendel, she is not described, but unlike Grendel, her dismembered body parts are not turned into trophies: her body remains a mystery to all but Beowulf.

Upon first observation, it almost seems that Grendel's mother is a weaker reflection of her son.[17] In one of the most complicated comparisons of the poem,

---

15 Overing notes that 'often the women in the poem are not identified other than as daughters, wives or mothers. Of the eleven women in the poem we know the names of five…these are, notably, all queens, with some titular power of rule' ('Women' 223).

16 Bammesberger argues that 'eaxle' should be amended to 'feaxe,' thus having Beowulf throw Grendel's mother to the ground by her hair. His argument relies on metrical motivation: 'metrically the change of <eaxle> to <feaxe> in line 1537a eliminates an irregularity. Palaeographically it is defensible. Contextually it would be a major improvement … Seizing her by the hair … was most effective. The legal term feaxfeng occurs only once in our corpus of Old English, namely in Æthelberht's laws … [it is] no doubt a legal term' ("The Half-line" 4). Despite the metrical problem posed by eaxle, I choose to keep it. Though Beowulf throwing Grendel's mother by her hair to the floor has obvious and interesting echoes of domestic violence, and also links to the carrying of Grendel's head to Heorot, the connections with Grendel's fight through the word eaxle, mentioned above, are more convincing than Bammesberger's arguments for emendation.

17 Irving, who sees Grendel as a representation of 'Other,' 'Darkness,' and 'Death' (*A Reading* 111) suggests that 'the encounter with Grendel's mother represents a continuation of the

her might is compared to his: 'Wæs se gryre læssa/ efne swa micle, swa bið mægþa cræft,/ wiggryre wifes be wæpnedmen,/ þonne heoru bunden, hamere geþruren,/ sweord swate fah swin ofer helme/ ecgum dyhtig andweard scireð' (1282b–7b) [the terror was lesser by even so much as is women's skill, the war-terror of a woman, in comparison with an armed man, when a bound sword, forged by hammer, a sword decorated by blood cuts the boar on the opposite helmet, with strong edges].[18] This is perhaps one of the most important lines for understanding Grendel's mother, yet it has been either ignored or handled only briefly (and often simplistically) by most scholars, who tend to suggest that she is simply weaker than her son.[19] However, the poet does not compare her strength to her son's, but rather he suggests that her *gryre* [horror, terror, dread] (Bosworth and Toller 492) is less than Grendel's by as much as a woman's war-terror is less than the war-terror of an armed man as he participates in a fight against another armed man.[20] We must first determine how much less a woman's war-terror is than an

symbolic conflict with Grendel ... From the first point of view, Grendel's mother is merely Grendel brought back to life' (112). He goes on to acknowledge that her motivations are distinct from her son's. In his later *Rereading*, Irving acknowledges his own 'unconscious' biases in this reading (70).

18 Klaeber explains the line in a note, saying that her characterization as less dangerous 'is evidently to be explained as an endeavor to discredit the unbiblical notion of a woman's superiority' (181). Mitchell and Robinson, in their edition, say of this line only that 'The narrator's account of the fight against Grendel's mother does not bear out this statement, unless it is taken to refer to the fact that the female kills only one thane whereas the male kills thirty' (91). Hala leads me to focus on terror as the object of the comparison. He says, 'the subject of the sentence is "terror" ("gryre") – as being less fearsome by only so much as is the strength of women or "battle-wives" is less than that of male warriors' (40). Irving, notably, does not even mention this comparison in his reading of Grendel's mother. Instead, he simply allies her with the mere (*A Rereading*, 114). Orchard in his *Critical Companion* only includes the line in a description of Grendel's mother's approach, but does not examine it (193). It is remarkable that few of the feminist responses to the poem investigate this fascinating comparison. Although Alfano does not read this line, she wants to claim that Grendel's mother is actually just a human woman whose perceived monstrosity derives from the ways in which 'her character and actions defy gender assumptions' (12). She sees Grendel's mother's monstrosity as only being implicated through her relationship to her son. In opposition, Overing does not discuss this line because she does not see Grendel's mother to be exactly human: 'she is not quite human, or rather she has her own particular brand of otherness; her inhuman affiliation and propensities make it hard to distinguish between what is monstrous and what is female' (*Language* 81).

19 Rogers reads the line simply as 'the female monster is said to be weaker than her son' (246). Chance Nitzsche says only that she 'is weaker than a man' ("Anglo-Saxon Woman" 288), but adds to this claim in *Woman as Hero*, 'In their eyes recognizably female, she threatens them physically less than her son' (101). Puhvel makes much of this line, saying, 'the author makes it emphatically clear that she is as a fighter vastly inferior to Grendel' (81). Cohen comments ironically that she is 'supposedly less fierce than her son' (*Of Giants* 27).

20 Donaldson translates it thus: 'The attack was the less terrible by just so much as is the strength of women, the war-terror of a wife, less than an armed man's when a hard blade, forge-hammered, a sword shining with blood, good of its edges, cuts the stout boar on a

armed man's. In Anglo-Saxon literature, we have virtually no examples of a woman's war-terror; women might invoke battles, as does Judith, but they do not fight them.[21] In *Beowulf*, no other women engage in physical warfare; even Thryth has warriors do her killing for her. For an Anglo-Saxon woman to engage in 'war-terror' would be significant; thus, I would suggest that the fear inflicted by a battle-mad woman is rather different from an armed man's. Therefore, when the poet suggests that the horror that Grendel's mother inspires is less than that inspired by Grendel by as much as a warrior-woman's is less than a warrior's, it seems none too certain to me that he disparages the fear or strength Grendel's mother might inspire and possess. What we can tease out of this difficult comparison is that she invokes a different kind of fear, and is less aggressively frightening than her son, although, as Mitchell and Robinson suggest, the truth of this statement is not borne out in the violent fight between Grendel's mother and Beowulf (*Beowulf* 91). While this comparison might attempt to minimize the physical threat of this woman, it also indicates that Grendel's mother is indeed a woman to be reckoned with.

Strangely, though, Grendel's mother is not even mentioned until after her attack. In Hrothgar's speech following her attack on Heorot, he links her with her son as a border-wanderer and finally shares with Beowulf and the reading audience what he and the Danes know about her:

> 'Ic þæt londbuend,   leode mine,
> selerædende   secgan hyrde,

helmet opposite' (23). Rogers translates it as: 'The terror was less by even so much as is the strength of maidens, the terrible power in war of a woman in comparison with a weaponed-man' (246). Orchard translates the line as: 'The terror was less, even as much as the power of females, the war-terror of women in contrast to armed men' (*Critical Companion* 193). Heaney's translation is: 'Her onslaught was less/ only by as much as an amazon warrior's/ strength is less than an armed man's/ when the hefted sword, its hammered edge/ and gleaming blade slathered in blood, razes the sturdy boar-ridge off a helmet' (1282–7). This translation is particularly troubling in Heaney's comparison of Grendel's mother to an Amazon, a warrior woman. In no sense in this poem is she portrayed as a true warrior woman, experienced in warfare. This term weakens the point of the comparison. I translate the term 'wæpnedman' here as 'armed man,' although its semantic sense is most often simply 'man.' The choice of this term is necessary for the poetic line to work metrically, but I shall later argue that the choice is significant in that it carries the force of a warrior-masculinity in this comparison. Multiple translators, including Donaldson, Orchard, and Rogers above, seem to feel that the term signifies a particular kind of masculinity, as they also choose to translate it as 'armed man.'

21 Even Judith, who chops off her enemy's head, does so when he is unconscious. Juliana's fight with the dragon is similarly impressive, but it is first a spiritual engagement, punctuated with physical moments. This is not to suggest that Anglo-Saxon women did not engage in war; rather, their participation in fighting is not reflected in the literature, which, I would suggest, is a fairly powerful kind of erasure. Æþelflæd, daughter of Alfred the Great, who ruled the Mercians both with and without her husband and brother, is not depicted in the Anglo-Saxon *Chronicle* as leading troops to battle, although she well might have. William of Malmesbury said of her that she was 'a woman, who protected men at home and intimidated them abroad' (quoted in De Pauw 83).

þæt hie gesawon   swylce twegen
micle mearcstapan   moras healdan,
ellorgæstas.   Ðæra oðer wæs,
þæs þe hie gewislicost   gewitan meahton,
idese onlicnes;   oðer earmsceapen
on weres wæstmum   wræclastas træd,
næfne he wæs mara   þonne ænig man oðer;
þone on geardagum   Grendel nemdon
foldbuende;   no hie fæder cunnon,
hwæþer him ænig wæs   ær acenned
dyrnra gasta.' (1345a–57a).[22]

['I have heard land-dwellers, my people, hall-counselors say this, that they have seen two such large border-wanderers holding the moors, alien spirits. The first, as far as they could ascertain for a certainty, was in the likeness of a woman; the other, miserable in the form of a man, traversed the tracks of exile, except he was greater than any other man. Land-dwellers in days of old named him Grendel; they did not know of a father, whether to him was previously born any of secret spirits [they did not know whether for him there was any father, earlier born of secret spirits.']]

Hrothgar's somewhat belated revelation, then, figures her as an appendix to Grendel, something not worth knowing until now, likely because he assumed she, as a woman, would not be a threat. Her form seems to be human, like Grendel's, though apparently there is some doubt on the part of the witnesses as to what they have actually seen. They do not observe her up close, and, more significantly, they do not say she is a woman. They say she has the likeness, *onlicnes*, of a woman. This phrase can be interpreted in two ways: (1) her physical categorization is called into question because of her social practice or her relation to the monstrous Grendel; or (2) although she has some of the features of a woman, she is significantly physically different from human women. If Grendel is 'greater than any other man,' we might wonder if his mother is likewise larger than normal women, but we are not told that she is.

Most interesting in this passage, though, is the insinuation about Grendel's parentage. No one supposes that this woman-figure is his wife. She is clearly understood by the poet and the people within the poem to be his mother. Furthermore, no one has observed a third giant, a father: ' "no hie fæder cunnon,/ hwæþer him ænig wæs ær acenned/ dyrnra gasta" ' (1355b–7a) [they did not know whether for him there was any father, earlier born of secret spirits]. As Gwendolyn Morgan suggests, the poet emphasizes 'the lack of a Grendel senior' (59).[23] Most scholars

---

[22] Klaeber's commentary refers to Earle's rendering of the line: 'whether they [i.e. the two demons] had any in pedigree before them of mysterious goblins' (182). This privileges a reading of him as plural rather than the singular I choose above.

[23] Morgan's reading of the significance of this is perhaps overstated: 'Whether because the Great Mother here, as in her most basic character, requires no mate to procreate or, as in some later

comment on this passage only to remark on Grendel's own troubled status: Gillian Overing claims that Grendel is a 'doubtful male' because 'the human community don't know who his father is' ("The Women" 223). Cohen argues more broadly that, 'This inability to name a progenitor from which to trace descent condenses all the problems of origin the giant embodies' (*Of Giants* 26). These critics assume that there *is* a father who is simply not named. But the text suggests that the community does not know if there is a father for Grendel *at all*. The problem, then, is more than that Grendel is the product of a broken home, or that his father is simply absent. The true concern is that Grendel is simultaneously the kin of Cain – the original monstrous patriarch – and fatherless.

In a poem obsessed with lineage, Grendel's generation is never fully explained and thus it stands as an example of the 'never drawing' kind of erasure; the poet simply refuses to depict this monstrous moment for us. Perhaps this mystery, like actual descriptions of the monsters, is more frightening than an explicit answer. Cain is not Grendel's father – nor can we be certain that anyone is. What must be most feared about Grendel's mother is that she might not need a father in order to bear children. The trace of this erasure, the gap in Grendel's genealogy, draws the audience's attention to it, and thus to the reproductive potential of Grendel's mother. Rather than obscuring a disturbing moment, the poet's omission makes Grendel's mother's body *more* transgressive, not less.

Grendel's mother acts as an origin in this poem; she is troubling not because she is uncanny, like Grendel, but rather because she possesses a body that is hybrid; neither woman nor man, but somehow, at least in terms of procreation, both. She moves beyond the problem of the unfamiliar/familiar, but presents another paradox – that of the desirable grotesque: she is both obscene and appealing. The greatest threat provided by Grendel's mother is her identity as mother; it is through her offspring, but more centrally through her autonomous fertility that she threatens the patriarchal order. She is the only parent of Grendel, an archaic mother who, as Barbara Creed says, 'is the parthenogenetic mother, the mother as primordial abyss, the point of origin and of end' (17). She need not function as male – she acts instead as a single point of origin, a female one. As Julia Kristeva argues, 'fear of the archaic mother turns out to be essentially fear of her generative power. It is this power, a dreaded one, that patrilineal filiation has the burden of subduing' (77). She serves as an abject figure; a woman, especially a mother, whose body must be rejected and excluded in order to establish patriarchal and patrilineal identity. Grendel's mother must be defeated here not simply because she is a physical threat to Heorot like her son, but because she, as a singular origin, disturbs the patriarchal social order through her excessively sexual and reproductive body.

---

manifestations, he is sacrificed to her fertility, the absence of a husband-father suggests that the male principle cannot endure the suffocating embrace of the female, either as mate or offspring' (59).

ARMS AND THE MAN:
BEOWULF IN THE FIGHT AGAINST GRENDEL

Beowulf's fights with Grendel and his mother reveal the differences not only between these two opponents – the uncanny and the archaic mother – but, most significantly, between Beowulf's responses to their sexed (and sexualized) bodies. While his fight with Grendel, as I have noted above, takes place in the public arena of Heorot, witnessed by Geats and Danes, his fight with Grendel's mother remains hidden, as it happens deep under the waters of her mere. Beowulf's response to Grendel is, unsurprisingly, above board, abounding in socially admirable masculine traits, while his reaction to Grendel's mother is more troubling. In the second fight, he displays signs of sexual engagement, followed by actions that imply shame and disavowal. While both fights result in the destruction of the monster, significantly they both also end with the dismemberment of that monster. When Beowulf defeats Grendel by dismembering him, Beowulf seems to absorb some of Grendel's excessive masculinity. However, once Beowulf attacks Grendel's mother, his assumed masculinity fails, forcing him to take up a phallus that belongs not to men, but to giants. I will show that it is this ephemeral and external excess that demonstrates his own profound impotence, sparking his need for erasure and revision.

Beowulf's very presence in Heorot is a kind of personal revision and a repression of his younger, less heroic self. Beowulf's motivation, through most of the poem, seems to be for the preservation and defense of communities. He performs heroic deeds for the benefit of friend, as with Breca, and community, as with Hrothgar and later with Hygelac and Heardred. He is also happy to accumulate treasure and reputation, as is appropriate for his culture. However, much later in the poem, buried in a tiny seven-line sentence, we learn of another kind of motivation for Beowulf's extreme acts of heroism: his youthful reputation was not only poor, but, perhaps worse, inconsequential. More than two-thirds of the way through the poem, after Beowulf has fought both of the grendelkin, the poet finally tells us:

> Hean wæs lange
> Swa hyne Geata bearn   godne ne tealdon
> Ne hyne on medobence   micles wyrðne
> Drihten wereda   gedon wolde
> Swyðe sægdon   Þæt he sleac wære
> Æðeling unfrom   edwenden cwom
> Tireadigum menn   torna gehwylces. (2183b–9b)

[He had long been humiliated, so the sons of the Geats did not consider him good, nor would the commander of the troop do him much honor on the meadbench; they very much said that he was slack, an unbold nobleman; a change came to the glorious man for each of his afflictions.]

Beowulf's early reputation is as a hesitant, 'unbold' warrior, one who is poorly thought of by his countrymen, peers, and leader. He earns little on the meadbench, either in terms of respect or, we might expect, gifts. Beowulf is described as a 'slack' young man – lacking in bravery and, as the word signifies, masculinity. He has begun to develop a better reputation among the Geats, and now, here in Heorot, hopes to establish a fame so strong that his origins cannot be questioned. Beowulf's ignominious youth seems to be something both he and the poet attempt to repress, covering it over with the trappings of honor and victory, of swimming matches and battles won. When Beowulf comes to Heorot, it is as a burgeoning hero seeking to repress his youthful 'humiliation,' and establish his reputation for boldness.

Beowulf fights against Grendel using irreproachable tactics – tactics meant to demonstrate and perhaps overperform his own infallible masculinity. All others have fought against Grendel using swords, a strategy that the reading audience is constantly cued to know must fail by the poet's reminders that Grendel is charmed against weapons.[24] However, Beowulf does not undertake this approach because he knows of the charm; rather, he has determined that Grendel 'wæpna ne recceð' (434b) [cares not about weapons], a phrase that seems to indicate the monster's lack of weapons, not his immunity to them, as Beowulf notes this behavior is 'wonhydum' (434a) [rash]. Therefore, when Beowulf decides to forego his armor and weapons, he does so to up the stakes of the fight and the reputation he stands to gain by winning it:

> 'No ic me an herewæsmun   hnagran talige
> guþgeweorca   þonne Grendel hine;
> forþan ic hine sweorde   swebban nelle,
> aldre beneotan   þeah ice eal mæge
> nat he þara god   þæt he me ongean slea,
> rand geheawe   þeah ðe he rof sie
> niðgeweorca;   ac wit on niht sculon
> secge ofersittan   gif he gesecean dear
> wig ofer wæpen   ond siþðan witig god
> on swa hwæþere hond   halig dryten
> mærðo deme   swa him gemet þince.'   (677–87)

['I consider myself no poorer in war-skills, in war-works than Grendel himself; therefore I will not kill him with a sword, deprive him of life, although I entirely could. He does not know of those good [weapons] with which he might strike against me, hew my shield, though he might be strong in hostile battle; but we two shall forego the sword in the night, if he dares to seek war without weapon, and then wise god, holy lord may assign glory on whichever hand seems fitting.']

Beowulf wants to establish himself as Grendel's equal, having clearly articulated that he believes himself to be a match for the monster in his fighting ability. He

---

24   See especially line 798.

denigrates Grendel as uncivilized and inhuman by pointing out that Grendel does not use weapons, nor does he even know of them. Although the speech is rhetorically savvy, the battle strategy seems somewhat cavalier and perhaps reckless. If indeed this is a monster who consumes thirty trained warriors, 'þritig þegna' (123a) [thirty thanes], during one nightly visit to Heorot, we must assume that Grendel is truly superhuman: stronger, larger, and infinitely hungrier. In this approach, Beowulf seems willing to wager his life in exchange for incontrovertible proof of his über-masculinity.

Beowulf's decision to forego weapons helps develop the significance of arms in this portion of the poem. In a poem filled with metonymy where a leader is both literally and figuratively the shield, *scyld*, of his people, the arm stands for something much more intimate. The arm is equated with masculinity, and acts as a symbolic phallus – thus, the battle with Grendel is all about demonstrating whose prowess and authority are greater. First, Beowulf's arm is set against Grendel's appetite as soon as he enters Heorot, when Hrothgar notes 'þæt he þritiges/ manna mægencræft on his mundgripe' (379b–80b) [that he had the strength of thirty men in his handgrip]. If Grendel's desire to consume represents his will to incorporate the identities of his victims, then the parallel with Beowulf's arm establishes it as that which can stop Grendel's consumption, but also that which will assume its function. If Beowulf's fantastically strong arm can defeat Grendel's emasculating appetite, then Beowulf's masculinity is increased; his victory over Grendel renders him superior to both Grendel and the men he protects from future consumption. Hrothgar's articulation of the relationship between arms and masculinity is confirmed by Beowulf in his speech regarding his strategy for defeating Grendel. In the final part of his speech quoted above, Beowulf claims that victory will be bestowed ' "on swa hwæþere hond halig dryten/ mærðo deme swa him gemet þince" ' (686–7) [the holy lord may assign glory on whichever hand seems fitting]. Therefore, the glory attained by victory goes not to the man, but to his hand, that which assures him victory.[25] Metonymically, the hand becomes the man. More specifically, the hand becomes the man when he engages in acts of violence. The arm, then, functions as a phallus, and the contest between Beowulf and Grendel will decide whose authority, masculinity, and potency are greater.

Beowulf's method of battle with Grendel, however, fuses the two of them,

---

[25] The importance of the hand is confirmed in a further exchange with Hrothgar, in which Hrothgar compares his coming of age as a leader and a man to 'raising his hand:' ' "Næfre ic ænigum men ær alyfde,/ siþðan ic hond and rond hebban mihte/ ðryÞærn Dena buton Þe nu ða" ' (655a–7b) [Never have I granted the stronghall of the Danes to any man before since I was able to raise hand and shield]. Hrothgar has retained authority over Heorot and not turned it over to another since he came into his own as a warrior and leader. His authority over the hall lies in his ability to raise hand and shield in battle, but in this moment when he gives the hall over to Beowulf, he indicates the inadequacy of his hand. He can no longer act as the shield of his people; it is Beowulf's hand and not his that will be raised in defense of Heorot and the Danes.

through their hands, in a strange unity, a sort of *assemblage*, whereby their masculinities become contingent and intertwined through the grip of their hands. As individuals both are in the process of performing their identities, or as Gilles Deleuze and Felix Guattari suggest, they are in the process of becoming – becoming animal, becoming man, becoming any of the infinite number of permutations of self, none of which are merely 'resemblance' or 'imitation' (262). Elements in a system, they explain, are not discrete, but 'are bound up with one another, even cross over into each other, changing according to the point of view' (230). Thus, we might think of Beowulf and Grendel's connection as the kind of hybridity discussed by Cohen in *Medieval Identity Machines*, whereby 'In medieval culture, the horse, its rider, the bridle and saddle and armor form a Deleuzian "circuit" or "assemblage," a dispersive network of identity that admixes the inanimate and the inhuman' (xxiv–xxv). According to Cohen, the rider's identity is a composite of all of these elements, rather than being something separate and individual; so too do the monster's and the hero's identities become interdependent in their circuit. In this case, however, Grendel and Beowulf lack the inanimate elements of the connection Cohen discusses, particularly because Beowulf strips himself of armor and weapons: 'ða he him of dyde iserbyrnan/ helm of hafelan, sealde his hyrsted sweord/ irena cyst ombihtþegne/ ond gehealdan het hildegeatwe' (671–4) [then he took off his shirt of armor, the helmet from his head, gave his ornamented sword, the best of irons, to his attendant and commanded him to guard the battle-gear]. This moment of stripping frees Beowulf of machinery, and makes the connection between his body and Grendel's all the more intimate, emphasizing the homosocial and queer undertones. He even seems to anticipate this strange *assemblage* in his strategy speech, declaring ' "ac wit on niht sculon/secge ofersittan" ' (683–4) [' "but we two shall forego the sword in the night" ']. He uses the dual here, a form that is rare in *Beowulf*.[26] While the dual allows for a more poetic line, the fact that Beowulf does not separate himself from his enemy, maintaining a clear 'ic/þu' or 'ic/he' division, indicates a connection that is both grammatical and physical. The dual, in one of its most familiar occurrences, links separated lovers in 'Wulf and Eadwacer'; here, it unites the bodies of two males in a moment that is both intimate and violent. In using the dual, Beowulf reduces the distinction between the self and the Other, uniting them in an identity of violent hybridity.

Beowulf and Grendel come together in a way that is strangely mutual, as

---

26 Both uses of the dual in *Beowulf* denote similar rhetorical and physical connections. In the first, Beowulf uses the dual to connect his body with Breca's as he defends himself against Unferth's accusation. The connection here has potential queer implications as well as the rhetorical purpose of indicating that Breca must rely on Beowulf to survive the swimming match (537–44). The second occurrence is when Wealhtheow cautiously rejects Hrothgar's adoption of Beowulf; she uses it to unite herself and Hrothgar, granting herself a rhetorical position of authority as well as emphasizing their union and Beowulf's position as an outsider (1186).

Grendel reaches for the warrior, and Beowulf responds. Beowulf waits and watches while Grendel seizes and eats one of his companions, and does not act until Grendel actively seeks him. Beowulf has engineered the situation, whereas Grendel remains ignorant – so much so that when he reaches out expecting to grasp, *onfeng* (748b), another tasty warrior, he is unpleasantly surprised by what latches on: 'Sona þæt onfunde fyrena hyrde/ þæt he ne mette middangeardes/ eorþan sceatta on elran men/ mundgripe maran' (750a–53a) [Immediately he found, the guardian of crimes, that he had not met in the middle-earth, in the regions of the earth, a greater hand-grip in another man]. In this moment, Beowulf's passivity recedes and Grendel, who has 'rixode' (144a) [ruled] the hall nightly in Hrothgar's place, struggles for mastery in the hall with a man whose hand-grip exceeds those of all other men. If, as Karras has claimed, in the medieval sexual act, 'to be active was to be masculine, regardless of the gender of one's partner, and to be passive was to be feminine' (23), Beowulf's early passivity marks him as feminine, but when he meets Grendel's arm with his own impressive grip, both he and Grendel remain active and engaged, exhibiting their masculinity through their shared hand-grip.

The masculinity apparent in this hybrid *assemblage* is extreme, excessive, perverse, and violently dangerous. Once their hands are united, Beowulf and Grendel very nearly topple Heorot, heretofore the signifier of ultimate authority and potency for the Danes and for Hrothgar.[27]

> Þa wæs wundor micel   þæt se winsele
> wiðhæfde heaþodeorum   þæt he on hrusan ne feol
> fæger foldbold   ac he þæs fæste wæs
> innan ond utan   irenbendum
> searoþoncum besmiþod.   þær fram sylle abeag
> medubenc monig   mine gefræge
> golde geregnad   þær þa graman wunnon
> þæs ne wendon ær   witan Scyldinga
> þæt hit a mid gemete   manna ænig
> betlic ond banfag   tobrecan meahte,
> listum tolucan   nymþe liges fæþm
> swulge on swaþule. (771a–82a)

[Then it was a great wonder that the wine-hall withstood the brave ones in battle, that it did not fall to the ground, the fair building, but it was so firm inside and out, from iron bands, skillfully smithied. There from the floor many mead-benches were torn away, I have been told, adorned with gold, where the hostile ones fought. It was not thought before, among the wise ones of the Scyldings, that any man ever by any means might break it, magnificent and bone-adorned, destroy it with skills, not unless the embrace of fire [might] swallow it with flames.]

---

27 Heorot is called the best of halls (78) and its size and reputation are emphasized in lines 81–2.

The power of each is magnified by his connection with the other. Grendel, once capable of ripping the door off the hinges (721–3), now, enclosed in this circuit with Beowulf, almost completely destroys the hall. Meadbenches are torn up and only the iron skeleton of the building keeps it from collapse. The unit that Beowulf and Grendel have become presents a danger akin to the most destructive force in a culture whose very word for building suggests wood as its primary construction material (*getimbred*, betimbered): their fight almost brings about the destruction of the hall and the community it represents.

This most dangerous union only appears to end when Grendel tears himself away from Beowulf, leaving behind his arm. However, the doubled masculinity produced in this circuit transfers to Beowulf, about whom the poet now declares, 'se þe mann wæs mægene strengest/ on þæm dæge þysses lifes' (789–90) [he was the strongest in might of men on that day of this life]. The poet iterates Beowulf's strength in this temporal manner, indicating a shift that comes through his contact with and defeat of Grendel: *now* Beowulf possesses the greatest strength, on this particular day in this moment. However, this claim simultaneously reveals that this status is temporary – lasting perhaps only for this day – just as the circuit is dynamic and in flux. As Deleuze and Guattari suggest, 'a multiplicity is defined not by the elements that compose it in extension, not by the characteristics that compose it in comprehension, but by the lines and dimensions it encompasses in "intension." If you change dimensions, if you add or subtract one, you change multiplicity' (270). When the *assemblage* of Grendel–Beowulf breaks apart, the dimensions of it and each of them are changed. Subtracted from Grendel is his arm, the metonymic symbol of his masculinity, and added to Beowulf is the value of this arm. It is through the connection of hands that Beowulf retains this inflated masculinity, created through the circuit of violence: Beowulf 'hæfde be honda' (814) [had [him] by the hand], which ultimately leads to the splintering of this doubled identity, as Grendel's arm tears away: 'him on eaxle wearð/ syndolh sweotol seonowe onsprungon/ burston banlocan' (816b–18a) [on his shoulder, a lasting wound became visible, sinews sprang apart, bonelocks burst]. Grendel's life-force is lost along with his arm, as he 'feorhseoc fleon' (820a) [flees, sick unto death], a strength that Beowulf assumes symbolically as he retains the arm and absorbs what Grendel has left behind. When he places Grendel's arm under Heorot's roof, the poet tell us it acts as a 'tacen sweotol' (833b) [clear sign], but he never specifically states what it signifies. I argue that it functions as a phallus – a sign of the defeat of the Father of Prohibition, placing Beowulf in the position of ultimate authority and masculinity.[28] The arm acts as a signifier of that excess masculine identity and potency created by the circuit of Beowulf and Grendel's

---

28 See Cohen, *Of Giants*: 'The Father of Prohibition initiates the law through the prohibition of incest and therefore stands at the mythic origin of culture. His primal "NO" hurls the child into language, the system that orders the wilderness of experience' (14). Linked also to the Father of Enjoyment, the giant exists as the origin of language, and access to the enjoyment lost by prohibition and language.

hand, and transferred to Beowulf as the victor. Indeed this dismembering of the other acts to sublimate the queer overtones of the fight, removing masculinity from one (now passive) participant and relocating it into the active body of Beowulf.[29] Grendel's arm is not merely a sign of victory or relief for the Danes, but rather a sign of Beowulf's inflated masculine prowess – an identity that is not wholly human, and also not solely his own.

Through the mechanics of the grasp, Beowulf takes on elements of Grendel's excess, but Grendel's body remains monstrous: enormous, superhuman, and mysterious. The only effective way of neutralizing the monster is through dismemberment – a method consistent with the acts of erasure performed in *Wonders of the East*. By taking away Grendel's arm, an appendage that performs the function of the phallus – a maneuver akin to erasing the penises of the monstrous men in *Wonders* – the poet affirms the danger of his monstrous and sexualized body. By removing this phallus, the poet points our attention to the gaping wound left behind by its lack, just as the erasure in *Wonders* makes us all the more aware of what was once a part of the image. Just as the eraser gains power over the sexed body of the *Wonders* monsters through the act of removal, so too does Beowulf's removal of the arm endow him with authority over, and indeed through, the body of Grendel. The power of the phallus is conferred upon Beowulf, who assumes the masculinity and authority embodied by the monster who has nightly ruled Heorot. But this status is fleeting because the poet locates it firmly in the body. Beowulf can possess it while he also possesses the arm, but he cannot maintain it. As Cohen suggests, 'subjectivity is always enfleshed; that human identity is – despite the best efforts of those who possess it to assert otherwise – unstable, contingent, hybrid, discontinuous' (*Machines* xxiii). In the connection of the Deleuzian circuit, Beowulf's identity becomes hybrid with Grendel's, but that hybridity does not transform his body; instead, it is manifested in, and dependent on the flesh of the arm he possesses and displays as a token of his inflated masculinity. Therefore, in this battle to determine, as I suggested above, who has more masculine authority, Beowulf proves not that he does, but rather that he is capable of removing the symbol of his opponent's masculinity, and wielding it as his own.

---

[29] I do not suggest that queer was a category for Anglo-Saxons. Scholars like Lochrie, in *Heterosyncrasies*; Bennett, in *History Matters*; and Schultz, in "Heterosexuality", argue that we cannot make heteronormative presumptions about the Middle Ages by suggesting that most sexuality is conceived of as negative. However, I would argue that certain cultural heteronormative expectations exist in this period, and in *Beowulf* men who become kings are expected to marry and reproduce. Battle, as a primarily masculine activity, certainly demonstrates the value of homosocial relations in the culture. However, in this battle the poet emphasizes elements of desire, positing both participants as trading back and forth between passive and active positions more than in a normal battle. Beowulf, after all, begins the battle stripped and in bed.

WÆPNEDMEN, WÆPENWIFESTRE, AND
THE FAILURE OF THE SWORD

If Beowulf's masculinity and reputation rely on his possession of the arm, then his credibility and identity are significantly threatened when Grendel's mother takes it back. The poet tells us she attacks the hall 'sunu deoð wrecan' (1278b) [to avenge her son's death], even though she is inexperienced in the art of invasion which her son had so clearly mastered. Since she ventures to the hall to achieve some kind of justice, taking one important life for the life of her son, it is unsurprising that she also might wish to retrieve the trophy they have made of her son's arm. Yet her attack on the hall is both hurried and frightening to her: 'heo wæs on ofste, wolde ut þanon, feore beorgan, þa heo onfunden wæs/ hraðe heo æþelinga anne hæfde/ fæste befangen, þa heo to fenne gang' (1292–5) [she was in haste, wished to be out of there, to protect her life; when she was discovered, immediately she had seized tightly one noble, then she went to the fen]. She comes in not like Grendel, greedy and perhaps even reckless, but fearful and rushed, taking only one man in clear exchange for the loss of her son. Since the poet notes her haste in grabbing a warrior and leaving immediately, it is especially interesting that she manages to take Grendel's arm from underneath Heorot's high roof: 'heo under heolfre genam/ cuþe folme; cearu wæs geniwod/ geworden in wicun. Ne wæs þæt gewrixle til' (1302b–4b) [she seized from its gore the well-known hand; sorrow was renewed, had [returned] to the dwelling places, that was no good exchange]. She snatches Grendel's hand, to the grief of the Danes. The importance of the dismembered limb overrides her fears of detection and retribution, revealing the significance of this action and the symbolic value of the limb. The poet comments that this is a bad exchange: Æschere for Grendel. Because the comment directly follows her retrieval of the hand, however, we might also notice the ways in which the arm serves as a bad exchange: for her, the living arm of her son is exchanged for the dead arm that was removed; for Beowulf, the symbol of his victory and masculinity is exchanged for absence, a blank space on the wall of Heorot that can serve only as a trace of what was once present. In retrieving this symbol, his mother reveals to Beowulf, to Hrothgar, and to the audience the extent of the arm's value. As Hrothgar states, 'nu seo hand ligeð/ se þe eow welhwylcra wilna dohte' (1343b–4b) [now the hand has fallen away, in which all of you placed your desires].[30] The arm is a locus for the desires of the people, for safety, and for reassurance of the human control over the rapacious and consuming monstrous body. When Grendel's mother takes it back, she removes Beowulf's assumed phallus, and indicates her own ability to castrate as well as to reproduce. Beowulf has no choice but to fight

---

[30] Mitchell and Robinson suggest these as possible translations for this line in the glossary under dugan: 'had power with respect to your every desire/was willing to give you whatever you desired' (*Beowulf* 253).

her. In doing so, he must reclaim and reiterate both his victory and his masculinity.

If Beowulf's masculinity is endangered when he loses the arm, that does not mean that Grendel's mother becomes male when she comes to possess it. However, when she reclaims the arm and in her fight with Beowulf, she transcends her status as archaic mother and becomes something even more frightening, like Barbara Creed's monstrous women from horror films, for whom 'the horrific nature of the monstrous-feminine results from the merging of all aspects of the maternal figure into one – the horrifying image of woman as archaic mother, phallic woman, castrated body and castrating parent represented as a single figure' (27). Grendel's mother becomes a phallic and castrating woman – a creature whose danger is based on her status as a female – who takes on a phallic object in order to penetrate her attacker. Marcia Ian states that the phallic mother, 'a grown woman with breasts and a penis' (1), 'represents the absolute power of the female as autonomous and self-sufficient; at the same time she is woman reduced to the function of giving suck. She is neither hermaphrodite nor androgyne, human nor monster, because she is emphatically Mother' (8). The phallic mother's central identity is her role as mother, just as Grendel's mother's sole identification and motivation in the poem is her status as the monster's mother. She does not sacrifice her female nature in taking up the phallus – as either arm or weapon – but instead threatens the patriarchal order as well as the integrity of the male body by maintaining a body that is at once feminine and phallic.[31]

Grendel's mother's phallic nature is evident in both her possession and use of phallic objects as well as in the language of the poem. The poet continually points to her conflicted status through his use of ambiguous and conflicting language. As Andy Orchard notes:

> despite being identified as female three times in rapid succession as soon as she is introduced *modor, ides, aglæcwif* (lines 1258b–1259a), the first time a pronoun is used of Grendel's mother it is grammatically masculine (line 1260a; cf. lines 1392b, 1394b; 1479b) ... the poet's ambivalent depiction of Grendel's mother seems confirmed by the implicitly masculine designation of her as a *felasinnigne secg* ... the confusion is compounded further when Grendel's mother is seen in action. (*Critical Companion* 189)

The poet designates her throughout the poem as grammatically both masculine and feminine. As Orchard suggests, the grammatical confusion points to her troubling and dangerous body and behaviors; in particular, I would argue, to her appropriation of arms. The fact that she is referred to, grammatically, by both masculine and feminine referents can perhaps be understood through a brief return to the language of her vexed comparison to Grendel, discussed earlier in this chapter:

---

[31] Ian seeks to deconstruct the concept of the phallic mother as one that is culturally and socially constructed, not merely based on a naturalized vision of women's bodies.

'Wæs se gryre læssa/ efne swa micle, swa bið mægþa cræft,/ wiggryre wifes be wæpnedmen,/ þonne heoru bunden, hamere geþruren,/ sweord swate fah swin ofer helme/ ecgum dyhtig andweard sireð' (1282b–7b) [the terror was lesser by even so much as is women's skill, the war-terror of a woman, in comparison with an armed man, when a bound sword, forged by hammer, a sword decorated by blood cuts the boar on the opposite helmet, with strong edges]. A significant question raised by this comparison is that of weaponry. Are we meant to assume that the woman in the comparison is armed, as is the man to whom she is compared – the *wæpnedman*? If we attempt to create the same kind of compound for an armed woman, we get the word *wæpenwifestre*. The Old English vocabularies, however, designate *wæpenwifestre* as actually meaning 'hermaphrodite' (Clark-Hall 394).[32] According to a search of the *DOE* corpus online, this definition results from its gloss of the word 'hermafroditus' in a glossary copied at Abingdon Abbey in the first half of the eleventh century.[33] The term *wæpnedman* carries the meaning of 'man,' not necessarily the literal translation of 'armed man' that seems suggested by the conjunction of the compound terms *wæpned* and *man*.[34] However, glosses can provide insight into the semantic force of such conjoined terms. For the glossator of *hermafroditus*, *wæpned* does seem to have carried the semantic force of the masculine, that, when combined with *wifestre*, provided a suitable translation for a person of two sexes. In this sense, then, a woman who takes up a weapon is figured as taking on masculine characteristics. If *wæpnedman* holds the same meaning as 'man,' then the possession of weapons seems to signify masculinity. David Rosen claims that 'arming as role and *techne* becomes the definitive feature of masculinity' (14). Similarly, Overing, in *Language, Sign, and Gender*, argues, 'the sword may metonymically share human attributes, or the sword or other war gear may replace the warrior,' remarking also that 'historical evidence shows that the sword was an important heirloom, passed on from one generation to another, given, in some cases at birth along with a name, or later as a token of manhood' (46). Indeed, the possession of weapons is closely related to one's gender and identity – and particularly to masculine identity. Grendel's mother takes up Grendel's arm and other weapons, thus appropriating and revising masculine identity and acting as phallic mother, which demands a response similarly laden with sexual overtones.

When Beowulf meets Grendel's mother in her mere, the fight is not only more dangerous and the description more detailed than the fight with Grendel, but the

---

32 This word does not appear in the Bosworth–Toller dictionary, but it is featured in both Clark-Hall and the *Dictionary of Old English*.

33 This gloss occurs in Antwerp Plantin-Moretus manuscript 32, a grammar which includes a copy of *Excerpts from Priscian*, as cited in the *DOE*.

34 However, it is interesting to note that the term *wæpnedman* is used in the comparison of the terror of Grendel's mother, and that most translators use the term 'armed man' in their translations, as I have noted previously.

language used to describe it is sexually charged.[35] Chance remarks, 'the poet exploits the basic resemblance between sexual intercourse and battle' (102). As Shari Horner suggests, 'the ensuing struggle plays out anxieties about female sexuality' (485), while it also illustrates anxieties about Beowulf's own sexual identity. Beowulf seizes Grendel's mother by the shoulder, 'Gefeng þa be eaxle' (1537a), pulls her to the floor, 'brægd ... þæt heo on flet gebeah' (1539a, 1540b), and she grasps him, from her position on the floor, 'ond him togeanes feng' (1542b).[36] In the process of this rolling around on the floor of her cave, Beowulf is described as battle-hard 'beadwe heard' (1539a) and that he was swollen (or enraged) by the life-enemy 'þa he gebolgen wæs, feorhgeniðlan' (1539b–40a). *Gebolgen* is a form of the word *belgan*, 'to swell with anger' (Bosworth and Toller 81), connected with *belg*, 'bulge' (82). *Gebolgen* shows up repeatedly in non-sexualized accounts of anger in the *Dictionary of Old English Corpus*. However, the connotation of 'swollen' and 'hard' as masculine sexual traits is reinforced by their opposition to 'soft' as feminine and feminized. In his chapter, 'Kiss and Tell: Anglo-Saxon Tales of Manly Men and Women' in *Before the Closet*, Allen Frantzen discusses the feminized figure of Sardanapallus in *Historiarum adversum Paganos Libri Septem*. Here he claims that 'another word that characterizes Sardanapallus is "hnesclice," which means "soft," "wanton," or "weak." It is a term also used in an Anglo-Saxon penitential to describe men who have sex with other men' (91). If to be soft is to be feminine and to play a traditionally female role in sex acts, then to be hard suggests just the opposite.

Although terms like 'battle-hard' and 'swollen' work as combat metaphors, these *double-entendres* are employed purposefully to paint Beowulf as full of a very masculine vigor, but also as a sexually engaged combatant. His response to Grendel's mother is a sexual one; she is an abjected figure, a taboo, who is simultaneously repulsive and fascinating, an uncanny embodiment of what the hero both rejects and desires. Phallic *double-entendres* abound in the Old English riddles of the Exeter book, particularly in riddle 44 (the key) and riddle 45 (dough). As Glenn Davis argues, 'no other poem or group of poems in the verse corpus addresses sex as openly as the erotic riddles do' (49). These riddles notably invite the prurient solution of an erect penis in the midst of a sex act, but have 'clean' answers. In the key riddle, we are told that 'þonne se esne his agen hrægl/ ofer cneo hefeð, wile þæt cuþe hol/ mid his hangellan heafde gretan' (4a–6b) (when the man pulls up his own robe over his knee, he wishes to greet that well-known hole with the head of his hanging thing). The key is depicted as 'stiþ ond heard' (3a) (stiff and hard), just as Beowulf is 'heard.' We are told later in this riddle that a good sword, another *double-entendre*, should also be hard: 'heard sweord' (2509) (hard blade). Similarly, the dough riddle's *double-entendre* emphasizes the terms of erection through swelling. The dough is 'weaxan' (1b) (growing), 'þindan ond

---

[35] Some elements present in this chapter have also been published as an article, 'Wigge Under Wætere: Beowulf's Revision of the Fight with Grendel's Mother,' in *Exemplaria* 21.1 (2009), 63–82.

[36] See n. 16.

þunian' (2a) (swelling and standing out), and 'hebban' (2b) (heaving or rising). Indeed, Davis considers this entire section of the poem 'a lengthy erotic *double entendre* riddle fused into a longer narrative poem' (50). The poet thus emphasizes Beowulf's sexual and masculine engagement in the fight by using the *double-entendres* 'hard' and 'swelling.'

However, Beowulf's masculine authority in battle, and particularly in this sexually charged battle, is called into question by his near-defeat by Grendel's mother. After he has pulled her to the floor and she has grabbed him, he falls on his back on the floor while Grendel's mother sits astride him, having pulled her short sword: 'Ofsæt þa þone selegyst, ond hyre seaxe geteah,/ brad ond brunecg, wolde hire bearn wrecan,/ angan eaferan' (1545a–7a) [Then she sat upon the hall-guest and drew her short sword, broad and with a shining blade, she wished to avenge her child, her only son]. This is a dangerous position for Beowulf, one that makes not only him, but scholars and students alike, as Fred Robinson claims, uncomfortable. In the title of his 1994 article, Robinson asks the question, 'Did Grendel's Mother Sit on Beowulf?' He reconsiders the Old English word *ofsittan*, determining ultimately that the meaning should be 'set upon,' as in Grendel's mother attacked Beowulf. His motivation for this reconsideration is that, 'like the students in our classes, the translators of the poem ... are often uncomfortable with the meaning which the glossaries stipulate for *ofsittan*. To avoid the comic indignity of Beowulf's being sat upon, they fudge the verb's meaning in artful ways' (2). Robinson's essay aims to determine the 'diverse meanings' of the derivatives of the verb 'sittan,' but he also acknowledges that 'the central meaning of the simplex *sittan* is indeed "sit"' (3). While Robinson makes a fine point that in most other contexts, *ofsittan* does not seem to mean 'sit upon,' this translation for the *Beowulf* passage remains viable and perhaps preferable. In her close reading of this passage, Rosemary Huisman investigates the power dynamics of the fight, saying 'Not only is he [Beowulf] the Goal of process, but the monster *sits* on him! The clause ... is the high point of the monster's success in the encounter' (223). If the term simply meant 'set upon,' Beowulf's reversal of the situation could not be so dramatic. Grendel's mother does not use a sword to attack Beowulf – she uses a 'seaxe' (1546a) [dagger]. In order to use this weapon effectively, Grendel's mother must be on the same level as Beowulf. She would have a very difficult time impaling him with her short blade while standing, as he is clearly lying on the ground: he has stumbled, 'oferwearp' (1543a) and fallen to the ground himself, 'þæt he on fylle wearð' (1544b) [so that he became fallen]. In order to reach him with her dagger, she must be on top of him.

Furthermore, Beowulf reverses his submissive posture – that is, being sat upon on the ground – when he rises to his feet.[37] Huisman, too, notes this reversal: 'In line 1556b Beowulf himself has the Actor role: he stands up' (224). This line in the

---

37 This moment parallels the beginning of Beowulf's match with Grendel. He begins this match lying in a passive position, and waits for Grendel to approach, performing another reversal much like this one.

poem serves as a turning point as well, which the manuscript's scribe marks in an emphatic way. Here, Beowulf 'eft astod' (1556b) [stood up again], and the battle takes a crucial turn. Significantly, this line also serves as the end of section XXII of the poem. In the beginning of section XXIII, marked in the manuscript with this number as well as with a large initial 'G,' Beowulf seizes the giant sword and begins his successful attack on Grendel's mother.[38] Such a radical section break in the poem suggests a meaningful reversal in the action. It is not just that Beowulf goes from being 'set upon' to attacking; rather, he goes from a passive and perhaps even submissive posture to an active and aggressive one, from being 'sat upon,' with Grendel's mother's dagger at his chest, to rising up and beheading her. Horner suggests that 'she again tries to penetrate his armor, this time with her blade, and she again fails … Her failure is mandated by the principles of female enclosure which do not permit women to breach boundaries … Beowulf's armor acts as both a literal and a social barrier that she cannot cross' (485). According to Horner's explanation, Grendel's mother is incapable of exceeding her role as a woman, and therefore Beowulf's masculinity, like his armor, remains unbreached. And yet, she has appropriated both her son's arm, hard-won by Beowulf and affiliated with intensified masculinity, and now, as a kind of *wæpenwifestre*, the *seax*, as she takes the masculine position of active penetrator. Beowulf's passive posture, although temporary, is alarming, and it is the resulting gender instability that makes students and translators uncomfortable. This response results not because Beowulf being topped is truly comic, as Robinson suggests, but more precisely, because it is not comic at all. The discomfort for reader and fighter alike illustrates the impact of this fight and this moment. Beowulf is at the mercy of a phallic woman who does indeed exceed the boundaries of gender, and of sexuality, in this fight. In claiming and employing these phalli, she symbolically castrates Beowulf, removing from him the excess masculinity gained by his fight with and defeat of Grendel, even if her blade never pierces his body. While in *Wonders* acts of removal remain static because all that remains of them is the trace, in *Beowulf* the limb that has been removed, as well as its symbolic function, remains in play throughout the narrative structure.

Because of the language and body positions described, this scene figures as one of the most suggestive narratives available in Old English: a (monstrous) woman sits astride a man, who lies prone on the floor; she threatens to penetrate him after his sword has proved to be ineffective and must be replaced by a sword not his own – a giant sword. Hugh Magennis argues that in their treatment of sexuality, most Old English literary texts 'reflect either … the lack of concern with sexual themes, characteristic of the Germanic heroic tradition, or the "sexual pessimism"

---

[38] Mitchell and Robinson suggest that these fitt-divisions were inserted by the poet, rather than by another copyist, noting that 'most scholars have thought that the fitts represent the poet's conception of how the narrative is segmented, and if this is the case, then they are important structural markers' (*Beowulf* 6).

inherited from patristic teaching, an attitude which received expression in particularly acute form in Anglo-Saxon England' (14).[39] Indeed, *Beowulf* is a poem whose only other possible reference to sex is the moment when Hrothgar retires to his bed chamber with his wife, Wealhtheow: 'wolde wigfruma Wealhþeo secan,/ cwen to gebeddan' (664b–5a) [the warlord wished to find Wealhtheow, the queen as a bedfellow].[40] These two scenes provide a striking contrast: the prim exit to the bedroom, versus the wrestling match in which Grendel's mother and Beowulf take turns being on top. The poet, who consistently invites readers to compare Beowulf and Hrothgar, must also be calling for a comparison here; Hrothgar is to the bedchamber and Wealhtheow as Beowulf is to the mere and Grendel's mother. And because Hrothgar engenders tenuous heirs in this bedchamber – as a king should – we must question just how potent Beowulf's masculinity is in the mere.

If the trouble with Grendel's mother is that she possesses and uses phallic items she ought not to have, we must also wonder about the state of Beowulf's phallic authority.[41] Beowulf seems to have consistent trouble with swords. If to possess a weapon is to possess masculine attributes, then what happens to masculinity when a sword fails? The answer must be that masculinity is also diminished. Although Beowulf is the only man brave enough to fight against these monsters, he is also the only man in the poem whose sword fails not once, but repeatedly.[42] Beowulf's sword fails him at multiple points in this narrative, the last of which is in his final fight with the dragon. The poet not only remarks on the tragedy of Beowulf's loss, but on what should be expected of the sword: 'Hreðsigora ne gealp/ goldwine Geata; guðbill geswac/ nacod æt niðe, swa hyt no sceolde,/ iren ærgod' (2583b–6a) [The gold-friend of the Geats did not boast of great victories; the war-sword failed, naked at battle, as it should not have, the iron, good from old times].[43] We are assured that this is no newly minted weapon, but rather an old and tested blade, a

---

39 For a more comprehensive discussion of sexual practices in Anglo-Saxon England, see Pasternack and Weston, *Sex and Sexuality*.

40 The phrase, 'to gebeddan,' has sexual connotations, but no explicit sexual meaning. In other occurrences of this word in the corpus of Old English writing, it refers to such fecund relationships as those between Adam and Eve, and Rebecca and Isaac (*DOE* online). We certainly see no actual sexual behavior, but we cannot ignore the connotations of the King retiring to bed to join his wife as, in Klaeber's terms, a 'bedfellow.'

41 I suggest that the weaponry is an essential part of Grendel's mother's identity, and indeed her gender and sexual identity. In *Medieval Identity Machines*, Cohen argues for conjoined identity for a knight and his horse, 'the composite body formed by the passionate union of a knight with his horse' (xxiii) – a cyborg identity. This notion of the cyborg derives from Haraway who, in *Simians, Cyborgs and Women*, states that a cyborg is 'a hybrid of machine and organism' (150).

42 The connection between the phallus and the sword is made most explicitly by Freud in *Psychopathology*.

43 For a discussion of the sword in Beowulf, see Lerer, 'Hrothgar's Hilt' in *Literacy*. See also Cronan, 'Origin' and 'Rescuing Sword'; Koeberl, 'Magic Sword'; Overing, 'Swords and Signs'; and Frantzen, 'Writing the Unreadable Beowulf' in *Desire for Origins*. Cooke's 'Three Notes' provides material evidence about descriptions of the swords in the poem.

sword that should not have failed. The lack of victory here seems related intimately to the failure of a weapon that should have been up to the task. And yet, this experience is nothing new to Beowulf, nor to the reader: indeed, we never see Beowulf with a sword that *does not* fail or melt. He successfully fights Grendel hand-to-hand, deciding to deliberately forego the sword (677a–87b). In his fight with Grendel's mother, two swords do not act as they should. The first sword problem occurs when he moves to strike against Grendel's mother, and it completely fails him – it is simply unable to penetrate her flesh: 'Ða se gist onfand,/ þæt se beadoleoma bitan nolde,/ aldre sceþðan, ac seo ecg geswac/ ðeodne æt þearfe; ðolode ær fela/ hondgemota, helm oft gescær,/ fæges fyrdhrægl; ða wæs forma sið/ deorum madme, þæt his dom alæg' (1522b–8b) [Then the guest discovered that the battle-gleamer would not bite, harm her life, but the blade failed the noble at his need; it had endured many a hand-battle, often sheared a helmet, the war- garment of one fated to die. That was the first time for the dear treasure that it laid down its glory]. Despite its reputation and history as a valuable and experienced weapon, the sword is of no use here.[44] In fact, the diction in this last phrase reinforces the symbolic function of the sword, as Klaeber's glossary notes that *dom*, translated above as 'glory,' can also mean 'authority,' a term clearly connected to the Lacanian sense of the phallus, which signifies the law of the Father. Thus, as the sword fails, Beowulf loses his authority, and is pinned by Grendel's mother. The human sword, no matter how prestigious, is inadequate, especially in comparison to the excessive masculinity generated by Beowulf and Grendel's Deleuzian circuit and carried over into Grendel's stolen arm.

Beowulf attempts to bolster his masculinity and authority when he takes up a second sword, the sword of giants found in the mere, but this masculinity, like that located in Grendel's arm, is temporary because it resides solely in the sword. After reversing his passive posture, 'Geseah ða on searwum sigeeadig bil,/ ealdsweord eotenisc ecgum þyhtig,/ wigena weorðmynd; þæt wæs wæpna cyst,/ buton hit wæs mare ðonne ænig mon oðer/ to beadulace ætberan meahte,/ god ond geatolic, giganta geweorc' (1557a–62b) [Then he saw among the armor a victory-blessed blade, the ancient sword with strong edges made by giants, the honor of warriors; that was the best of weapons, except it was greater than any other man could bear out to battle, good and adorned, the work of giants]. This is a sword of immense reputation and size, one whose accrued victories and origins lend it superhuman value and power. That Beowulf is able to carry and

---

[44] It is, of course, noteworthy that the sword is Unferth's, given to Beowulf as a means of signaling Unferth's reconciliation with and support of Beowulf as a champion. Beowulf had bested Unferth in *flyting* prior to his fight with Grendel by reminding the court of Unferth's status as a brother-killer (see especially Clover, 'The Unferþ Episode'). Whatever connotations the sword has as the fratricidal sword, these seem to be less significant than the illustrious history of the blade. Although this is Unferth's sword, the true owner of the human sword is less significant. Beowulf accepts the weapon knowing Unferth's history, and fully expects it to be successful in battle. Were it his own sword, it would have also failed because, whatever else it might be, it is a sword made by and for human men.

use this sword of giants is to his credit – after all, the poet assures us that no other man could put it to use because of its heft.[45] James Hala, too, notes the phallic nature of the giant sword, saying that the 'stalemate' between Grendel's mother and Beowulf, who struggle for 'phallic' authority, can only be broken by a 'third term': 'the *eotenisc* magic (and phallic) sword. This sword, in as much as it succeeds where Hunlaving failed, represents the Phallic/Signifier' (46). Therefore, the masculine authority by which Beowulf ends his fight with Grendel's mother is not his own, but rather is external, imbued in the sword, not the man. In taking up this item, Beowulf is bound to succeed, but it is the sword's virility, not his own, that grants him victory.

Once Beowulf takes up the excessive masculinity of the sword, he not only uses it to defeat, but to castrate the bodies of Grendel and his mother, an act tantamount to the moments of erasure that take place in *Wonders*. Like the artists and later viewers who manifest control over the monstrous form through never drawing, removing, and revising its sexed elements, Beowulf removes the heads of his foes to rearticulate his mastery over their bodies. As we cannot in *Wonders*, here we see the motivation for such vehement acts of erasure: the sexed bodies of these monsters serve as a real threat to humankind, as well as to masculine authority. As Grendel's mother continues her attack, Beowulf decapitates her: 'yrringa sloh/ þæt hire wið halse heard grapode,/ banhringas bræc; bil eal ðurhwod/ fægne flæschoman' (1565b–8a) [he angrily struck so that it cut hard against her neck, broke the bone-rings; the sword went all through the body that was fated to die]. This action repays her for her figurative castration in retrieving her son's disembodied arm – it is invested specifically with Beowulf's anger as well as his strength. The complete penetration of the giant sword emphasizes the fullness of the size and authority of the monstrous sword, and locates its authority firmly over the phallic body of the monstrous mother, as it penetrates and castrates her. In removing her head, he affirms her authority and potency – her potential for harm against him and his masculinity – and her head becomes another phallus, an object like Grendel's arm that affirms both the threat she presented and Beowulf's victory over her. However, Beowulf turns his attention from the foe who nearly took his life and threatened the integrity of his body and his identity, and displaces his rage into decapitating the already dead, 'aldorleasne' (1587a) [lifeless], body of Grendel: 'hra wide sprong/ syþðam he æfter deaðe drepe þrowade/ heorosweng heardne – ond hine þa heafde becearf'

45 It is this ability, in fact, that makes us question his human status. He is greater than any man because he can carry the sword, because he has the hand-strength of thirty men, and he is so supernaturally able to beat monsters. Beowulf's form, however, remains all too human and is ultimately mortal and imperfect in battle. However, up until he locates the sword, Beowulf is not particularly effective against Grendel's mother; as Huisman suggests about Beowulf seizing the sword, 'Because he has the mental attitude of a hero, Beowulf can still be given the lexical description yrre oretta, "angry champion" (l. 1532), though so far in this encounter he has scarcely functioned as a grammatical hero' (221).

(1588b–90b) [the corpse sprang open widely, since after death it suffered a blow, a hard sword stroke – and he cut off his head]. The poet emphasizes the fact that Grendel is dead in this passage in order to emphasize the strangeness of Beowulf's action. He has come to the mere, knowing full well Grendel is already dead; he has defeated and decapitated Grendel's mother, who is his stated objective for this venture; and he has decapitated the corpse of his already defeated enemy. This final choice seems dictated not just by rage, but perhaps by shame, and certainly by the desire to re-assume his enemy's excessive power and masculinity. Just as the penises of the male monsters in *Wonders* are scratched away by a viewer to remove the threat of the monster, as evidence of their human and reproductive characteristics, so too are the heads of Grendel and his mother removed. In removing the parts that are most human – the heads – of his victims, Beowulf castrates them and attempts to negate the threat to his authority presented by their monstrous and sexualized bodies.

Although Beowulf is the castrater, he suffers another kind of castration: the audience never sees him hold a sword that doesn't fail. The sword of giants is no exception: the blade of the sword melts before it ever reaches the surface of the mere. The waning of the sword is so striking that the poet describes not once but twice its melting, even subjecting it to simile: 'þa þæt sweord ongan/ æfter heaþoswate hildegicelum,/ wigbil wanian; þæt wæs wundra sum,/ þæt hit eal gemealt ise gelicost,/ ðonne forstes bend Fæder onlæteð,/ onwindeð wælrapas' (1605b–10a) [then the sword began to waste away after battle-sweat, the war-blade into battle-icicles; that was a wondrous thing, that it all melted, most like ice when the Father releases frost's bonds, unwinds the water-fetters]. The metaphor of ice-melting equates the dissolution of the sword to a natural cyclical process, except in this case it is the blood of Grendel's mother, and of Grendel, that causes the sword to fail. In overcoming his foes by taking on the phallic power made by and for giants, Beowulf's own puny human masculinity can only come up short; it simply does not possess the potential of the monstrous bodies of his foes, or of the makers of the sword. The poet's second reference to the melting of the sword emphasizes the strange and hostile nature of the monstrous bodies. We are reminded that 'sweord ær gemealt,/ forbarn brodenmæl; wæs þæt blod to þæs hat,/ ættren ellorgæst, se þær inne swealt' (1615b–17b) [the sword had melted earlier, the wavy-patterned sword burned up; that blood was too hot for it, the poisonous alien spirit who had died in there]. The blood – called 'battle-sweat' in the first description, recalling the physical labor and conjoined bodies of the fight – literally is 'too hot' for the sword, thus melting it.

Beowulf's own sword-might fails in his battle with Grendel's mother; he can only be successful when he attains a sword of excess, which is not his own, and is not, in fact, human. In picking up the monstrous sword, he becomes more than human, and in its melting, he becomes less of a man.[46] Both Beowulf's life and his

---

[46] Many scholars discuss problems of masculinity in this poem; see Frantzen, *Before the Closet*; Rosen, *Changing Fictions*; and Lees, 'Men and *Beowulf*.' Masculinity can be considered in

masculinity are at stake in the battle against Grendel's mother. Although he protects his life and defeats his enemy, his human masculinity and sword-might fail him in the process. Not monstrous himself, although he is the strongest possible human, he cannot maintain the monstrous sword as a phallus. His assumed and excess masculinity melts away, leaving behind only a trace in Beowulf's debased human masculinity. When the fight is over and this borrowed masculine authority has dismembered both Grendel's mother and Grendel, then Beowulf returns to the surface, carrying his failed sword, the melted hilt of the monster sword and the head of Grendel.[47] What has been left in the mere, the body of Grendel's mother, serves as a reminder of Beowulf's own failed masculinity, resuscitated briefly by the borrowed sword of creatures of excess masculinity. He has been successful in battle, but in the process of the battle he has lost something: Grendel's arm, once the phallus, transfers its authority to Grendel's mother when she takes it from Heorot. In defeating her, Beowulf should take the trophy of her head which he affirms as a phallus when he castrates her through decapitation. His taking of Grendel's head is an attempt to assert masculine authority over the body of the phallic woman, but taking the head of Grendel's limp corpse signifies instead his own 'sleac' (2187) [slack] nature. In leaving her head behind, he turns his back on the real symbol of his success, valor, and potency, and instead presents Hrothgar and the Danes with signs of his inadequacy, impotence, and cowardice that only the reading audience can recognize.

DISMEMBERING, REMEMBERING, AND REPRODUCTION: ERASURE, REVISION, AND THE TRACE

The bodies of Grendel and his mother are, as I have demonstrated above, monstrous bodies that are defined through excesses of both gender and sexuality. Grendel's excessive masculinity, supplemented, fetishized, and pursued by Beowulf, sets forth an unattainable but strangely desirable level of masculinity that is both feared and admired in Anglo-Saxon culture. The multiple castrations Grendel undergoes foreclose his masculine authority and ability to penetrate and consume, but also act as

---

various ways, relating to vigor in battle and/or to sexual identity. I suggest that the two are inherently related in Beowulf's body, especially because of his contact with the dangerous excess gender and sexuality of Grendel's mother.

[47] Cohen argues that there is a relationship between scenes of beheading and 'political, sexual, and social coming of age' ('Decapitation' 174). The moment Grendel's head is revealed 'unambiguously announces Beowulf's full status as a hero, as a man to be revered as a vehicle of cultural ethic' (173). Building on this claim, I argue that while the revealing of the head may announce him as a hero and a man to the community, Beowulf's revision of the story is noticeable to the textual audience, who recall his unrecounted wrestling match with Grendel's mother and the nature of his failed and melted swords. He is a victorious hero, but a hero who revises the details of his glory.

attempts to usurp and possess these characteristics. However, the hybrid body of Grendel's mother undergoes castration to end both her attacks on culture and her function as an avenging and productive mother. These are not traits Beowulf wishes to procure, so instead he must disavow them. Dismemberment in this poem is, as I have suggested, akin to the erasures performed on the images in *Wonders of the East*. The severed body parts of monsters demonstrate the need to remove the gendered and sexualized monster from the culture within the text, as well as from the text itself. However, these phallic remnants of monstrous bodies continue to haunt the rest of the poem. The arm and heads loom and reappear each time Beowulf must tell and retell the story of his exploits in Denmark: they serve as a trace of those bodies which Beowulf attempts to erase through dismemberment. In particular, the continued erasure of Grendel's mother demonstrates again and again the danger presented by her body, dangerously hybrid, both phallic and reproductive, and points to the failures of Beowulf's own inadequate masculinity.

The taking of Grendel's arm by Beowulf is a means of controlling the monstrous body and removing its potency, although it does not in any way diminish the monstrous status of that body. Precisely as the erased bodies of *Wonders* remain monstrous, so too do the bodies of Grendel and his mother; similarly, signs of absence and removal serve to emphasize rather than delimit the powerful nature of their monstrous bodies. The arm, displayed on the wall of Heorot, stands as a trace of the defeated body of Grendel. However, the significance of the arm becomes most clear when it is no longer present; its absence marks its presence (Derrida, *Of Grammatology*, 61). The trace is 'the mark of the absence of a presence, an always-already absent present', of the 'originary lack' (Macksey and Donato 254). All in the hall notice the missing trophy: 'Hream wearð in Heorote; heo under heolfre genam/ cuþe folme' (1302a–3a) [An outcry arose in Heorot; she had taken the well-known hand, covered in blood]. The people's reaction is to the removal of the hand, as much as to the loss of Æschere. The hand represented a kind of victory over the monstrous, an ability to quantify, to interpret, and to understand a body that cannot even be described.[48] The hand is a representation of the body and serves as a thing 'for the delectation or interpretation of the viewer' (Lerer, "Grendel's Glove", 740). Seth Lerer says of the dismembered parts of the monsters, 'they survive within the poem's telling as tame representations of former horror' (741). Thus, through dismemberment, the body of the monster, and the horror presented by that body, can be tamed and experienced as a kind of pleasure.

Therefore, when the arm is removed, the people no longer have an assurance of Grendel's taming, or of Beowulf's mastery of his excess masculinity. In losing the arm they lose a sense of security in both the knowledge of the form of the monster,

---

[48] For a legal reading of the hand, see Day, 'Hands Across the Hall,' and Bremmer, 'Grendel's Arm.' See also Lerer, 'Grendel's Glove'; Godfrey, '*Beowulf* and *Judith*'; and Lockett, 'Grendel's Arm.'

and of their control over that monster. Because they have possessed the arm, they have come to understand the nature of the terrifying body that threatened them. As Lerer claims, 'Grendel's left-behind and returned body parts ... become the tokens of this purification ... the killing of the monster necessarily requires the display of body parts, their communal beholding, and their understanding as the signs and tokens of the creature's death' (738–9). The arm, and, later, the head act as traces of the monster's body; although Beowulf attempts to remove the monster from the hall through dismemberment, the very act of dismembering results in the trace – the arm or the head – thereby unraveling the process of erasure.

By this logic, however, Grendel's mother's body is never clearly understood or absolutely tamed, because it is never brought to the surface as evidence. Although she, too, is decapitated, her head remains in the mere and is never put on display or witnessed by any human other than Beowulf. Thus, only Grendel's body serves as confirmation of the death and defeat of the monster within this text. His body is the only material sign of what happens to the grendelkin. In taking the head of Grendel rather than his mother, Beowulf perpetuates the erasure of sexualized and transgressively gendered monsters already at work in the poem. In the traditional paradigm of *Beowulf* studies, this maneuver might be dismissed easily by noting the primacy of Beowulf's fight with Grendel. Grendel is, after all, larger than his mother, has been the source of Heorot's misery for twelve years, and is Beowulf's explicit reason for coming to Denmark. However, as Paul Acker claims, 'The combat with Grendel's mother is central to the poem not just as the second of three combats but as arguably the most mysterious and compelling' (708). She comes closer to defeating the hero than does her son. Moreover, Grendel's mother is the genesis for Grendel – without her, Heorot would not have suffered Grendel's constant attacks. Beowulf reacts to the powerful figure of this archaic mother by covering her up, literally, in the mere, and figuratively, with the reports he offers. However, in attempting to erase her from his stories to the audience within the poem, Beowulf's revisions signal to the reading audience just how important she is, just as Grendel's head reminds the reading audience that Grendel's mother's head remains in the mere.

Beowulf's desire to elide and erase the sexual nature of the fight, as I shall demonstrate, iterates his own troubled identity. Just as the final weapon of the battle never makes it to the surface of the water, neither does evidence of the most threatening body – the monstrous feminine body of Grendel's mother. The hilt stands as a trace of the monster weapon, much as Grendel's head serves as a trace of his mother's body, reminding the reading audience and Beowulf that Grendel's head stands in for, but is not, hers. Although Hrothgar and his men make their own interpretation of these objects, it is Beowulf who provides and contextualizes the object for interpretation.[49] Thus, the reading audience alone witnesses Beowulf's process of erasure.

---

[49] Lerer compares the headless bodies of Grendel and his mother to the now bladeless sword, calling both 'impotent' and saying 'those monsters now are like the hilt itself. Both come as a

However, Beowulf is not the only man to erase Grendel's mother from the narrative; she is strangely absent from the story until her attack. Grendel, on the other hand, is a constant topic of dialogue from the poet and in Heorot, mentioned in at least three places before his battle with Beowulf (lines 86–188, 405–90, 702b–36a). As he is the marauder Beowulf has come to defeat, these mentions are unsurprising – but the fact that no one thinks to tell Beowulf about Grendel's community of monsters is striking. In fact, Grendel's mother is not mentioned until after she makes her single foray into Heorot. Then Hrothgar seems to remember having heard of her before, saying 'Ic þæt londbuend, leode mine,/ selerædende secgan hyrde,/ þæt hie gesawon swylce twegen/ micle mearcstapan' (1345a–8a) [I have heard landsmen, my people, hall counselors, say that they saw two such great border-steppers]. In the poet's, and Hrothgar's, neglect to mention Grendel's mother to the audience, and to Beowulf, we see the first act of erasure. This is the erasure of never drawing: Grendel's mother is simply never mentioned, either as a conscious maneuver to elide her presence, or as a manifestation of the unconscious process of repression – regardless, she seems to make men uncomfortable, and that discomfort results in her early erasure from the poem. However, as Cohen suggests, the monster always returns; thus, it is only after she appears in the hall that the poet offers, through Hrothgar, the first confounding description of Grendel's mother, discussed earlier in this chapter. Most intriguing about this passage, though, is who reports to Hrothgar: two, and perhaps even three groups claim witness of two monsters: landsmen – workers and owners of land outside Heorot – report to Hrothgar, but also his own hall counselors, *selerædende*, claim to have seen the pair. The third possible group, his 'people,' might just be metonymically referring to either of these two groups, but it also might refer to a larger, less specific group of Hrothgar's people. These multiple accounts of Grendel having a companion are meaningful because Hrothgar seems to disregard not one but many reports. In any other feud, the hall would be prepared for vengeance at the loss of a member; Hrothgar's erasure of Grendel's mother from the early narratives about Grendel results in the loss of his beloved counselor Æschere.

In addition to the obvious necessity of narrative suspense, one might presume that Hrothgar's erasure results from a conjecture about the differences between monster culture and human culture, or that because of her supposed sex, he assumes Grendel's mother is not capable of the revenge required by the human social system. His speech in the wake of her attack proves another, perhaps retrospective, kind of understanding. He twice construes her action as an appropriate human response: 'Heo þa fæhðe wræc' (1333b) [she has avenged the feud] and 'ond nu oþer cwom mihtig manscaða, wolde hyre mæg wrecan' (1338b–9b) [and now the other has come, the mighty harm-worker, has wished to avenge her

---

written tale, able to enter the hall and hurt no one, to sit silently like a souvenir of an alien kingdom' ("Grendel's Glove" 179). But Grendel's mother's head is not disempowered entirely because it never serves as a souvenir.

kinsman]. According to these statements, her response is not entirely unexpected by Hrothgar, although he has never mentioned her before. It is only after her attack that he challenges Beowulf to seek her and to end the feud by killing her. However monstrous her body and actions might seem to the Danes, Hrothgar still endows her with clear human motivation, but a motivation that exceeds the sex roles set by Germanic society. This ineffective erasure is particularly ironic but also revealing about the assumptions regarding sex and gender in this social context: Hrothgar knows Grendel to be a creature of excessive violence, one bound neither by the rules of society nor the constraints of human physiognomy (how else could Grendel eat so many men, including their hands and feet?), but he seems to expect that Grendel's mother, because she is a woman, would not transgress her gender station and enact any form of revenge. It is his false assumptions about the boundaries of sex and gender that lead to a moment of profound strategic loss: the death of a trusted counselor, who seems to be worth any number of eaten warriors. That this act of erasure has drastic consequences, however, is a lesson that no one seems to learn.

Yet just as Hrothgar left Grendel's mother out of the picture in Heorot, so too does Beowulf attempt to erase her in his various reports regarding the events in the mere. While Beowulf defeats Grendel without real peril to his own life, Beowulf nearly dies in his encounter with Grendel's mother. Because this battle is more difficult, we might expect Beowulf to boast afterwards of his success in it, as he has when speaking of previous exploits. And yet Beowulf has less to say about this fight than conventions might dictate. After his fight with Grendel, witnessed by both Danes and Geats, Beowulf spends twenty-two lines (958a–79b) recounting precisely what has just happened for Hrothgar's benefit. He spends only twenty-five lines (1652a–76b) recounting what went on in the mere with Grendel's mother. While these lengths are similar, the situations are quite different. First, as I have shown, neither Danes nor Geats witness Beowulf's fight with Grendel's mother; while they can repeat the story of his fight with Grendel from their personal experiences, they can offer only the paltry details provided by Beowulf about his fight with Grendel's mother. Secondly, the poet allots this second monster-fight twice the space he designated for the first. That is, since the fight with Grendel's mother is twice as long and difficult as the fight with Grendel, Beowulf should similarly emphasize this more challenging battle. If these fights are, indeed, Beowulf's means of advancing his reputation as a hero and a warrior, he should speak as well as he fights. And while Beowulf gives a blow-by-blow account of his fight with Grendel, providing the difficulty and the means by which he succeeds – that is, removing Grendel's arm – he fails to give much detail regarding his fight with Grendel's mother. In his report to Hrothgar, he merely says that he escaped with his life through God's protection (1658b), and that he used an 'ealdsweord' (1663a) [ancient sword] found in the mere. He employs litotes only once in the speech, saying 'Ic þæt unsofte/ ealdre gedigde' (1655) [With difficulty, I survived with my life], a contrast with his earlier speeches about Breca and the sea monsters. Thus, Beowulf seems to understate the nature of his fight with Grendel's mother, offering very little detail and using the rhetorical strategy of litotes only sparingly. The literal level of the speech also remains unclear: we do not learn where he struck his enemy or even what weapons the enemy used. Beowulf's speech regarding the fight is suspiciously short and vague, especially since it is here that Beowulf must assure Hrothgar and the Danes that they are safe from Grendel's mother, and that he has avenged Æschere's death.

In offering only paltry details of his fight with Grendel's mother, particularly in comparison to his willingness to boast and redundantly recount the details of his fight with Grendel, Beowulf begins his strategy of replacing her body with Grendel's – a kind of revisioning of her body and her story. He does not lie, precisely, by suggesting that his fight against Grendel's mother was easy; rather, he overstates the number of opponents he faced. He admits the challenge when he gives his victory speech to Hrothgar, saying that he won the fight *unsofte* (1655a) [not easily] and *earforðlice* (1657a) [with difficulty] – both terms necessary to emphasize the value of his victory. However, he skirts the exact details of the fight, never explaining that it was Grendel's mother *alone* who challenged him so effectively. Instead, Beowulf amplifies the number of opponents in describing the fight to Hrothgar, when he claims that he fought both Grendel and his mother in the mere:

> 'Ofsloh ða æt þære sæcce,   þa me sæl ageald,
> huses hyrdas.   Þa þæt hildebil
> forbarn brogdenmæl,   swa þæt blod gesprang,
> hatost heaþoswata.   Ic þæt hilt þanan
> feondum ætferede.' (1665a–9a)

[Then I struck the house's guardians, at the battle, when I had the opportunity. Then that battle-sword, that wavy-patterned sword, burned up, as that blood sprang forth, the hottest of battle-sweats. I have brought the hilt thence from the enemies.]

Both *hyrdas* and *feondum*, 'guardians' and 'enemies,' are clearly plural forms. This battle, Beowulf claims, was so difficult because he fought not one, but two enemies. If only one of these terms was plural, we might search for a metrical explanation.[50] Instead, I suggest that the grammatical form Beowulf uses is his first

---

50   Similarly unsatisfying is Klaeber's suggestion that, despite objections about consistency with the facts, it 'could be vindicated as "generic plural" ... it has sometimes been regarded as evidence of an earlier, different version of the story' (189). I would suggest that often editors and scholars act as apologists for Beowulf, trying to preserve his perfection. While a generic plural is possible, there are only two occurrences of this sort in *Beowulf*, which Klaeber notes occur at 565 and 1074, referring to a sword (*mecum*) and to Hildeburh's son and brother (*bearnum* and *broðrum*). In these cases, the context clarifies the numerical confusion: we don't imagine that Beowulf wields two swords, or that Hildeburh loses more than one son and one brother. However, the plurals *hyrdas* and *feondum* are conveniently unclear. Unlike the paired terms, *bearnum* and *broðrum*, *hyrdas* and *feondum* do not occur in the same lines, but several

rhetorical strategy designed to mask the exact identity of his actual opponent. This is not the only time Beowulf links Grendel and his mother as a 'them'; as I shall discuss later, Beowulf uses the plural again in lines 2353a–4a. This later use of the plural further confirms this plural as a part of Beowulf's defensive strategy. Beowulf does not use the traditional ironic understatement to underscore his strength and glory; instead, he revises the story by inflating the number of opponents he faced, thereby removing any uncomfortable details about the private grappling he did with his lone female opponent. Thus, he begins his attempt to cover up and replace the body of Grendel's mother with that of her dead son.

In bringing up Grendel's head, rather than Grendel's mother's head, Beowulf confirms the details of his revised story to his listening audience; however, the reading audience knows better. In addition to shifting his noun forms from singular to plural, Beowulf also implies through this second rhetorical strategy that he fought both Grendel and his mother. The poet tells us clearly that Beowulf decapitates an already dead Grendel after having dispatched his mother: Beowulf sees 'guðwerigne Grendel licgan,/ aldorleasne, swa him ær gescod/ hild æt Heorote' (1586a–8a) [war-weary Grendel lying, lifeless because he was injured earlier in the battle at Heorot]. Grendel is undeniably dead, but Beowulf decapitates him anyway: 'þa heafde becearf' (1590b) [then he cut off the head]. John Edward Damon, too, notes that 'this beheading is gratuitous … this act is necessary symbolically or ritually, but not literally' (430). Although he has already chopped off Grendel's mother's head, the head he brings back to Hrothgar is Grendel's. Damon argues that 'the carrying back of the head supersedes any attempt to bring back treasure and wealth; the head of his enemy appears to have been the most valuable object Beowulf could recover' (427). While the reading audience knows that Grendel was dead when Beowulf beheaded him, the audience within the poem must believe that the enemy of greatest threat was Grendel. Otherwise, why would Beowulf, who entered the mere to avenge Æschere's death by pursuing Grendel's mother, bring back Grendel's head?

When Beowulf replaces Grendel's mother's head with Grendel's, he does so to confirm his fictional construction of events in the mere. In effect, he inscribes Grendel's body over the top of his mother's and thereby turns his head into a trace of hers, and of the true events in the mere. Damon argues that 'the poet represents the decapitation as a repayment for Grendel's actions, but from our argument we can see that it precisely balances the beheading of Æschere' (430). To take her (dead) son's head as a trophy is perhaps similar to her abduction of Hrothgar's most trusted advisor, but it is not a 'balanced' response – Æschere was alive and died when he lost his head, while Grendel was dead already; Grendel's mother left Æschere's head behind for the Danes to find, while Beowulf removed Grendel's head from the mere only after Grendel's mother was no longer alive to mourn

---

lines apart. Because Beowulf uses the plural twice, and three lines distant, an error seems extremely unlikely.

him. Indeed, to compare Grendel's head to Æschere's is to compare Grendel's mother to Hrothgar. But because she is dead before her son is decapitated, the parallel fails. The trophy of Grendel's head, then, points exactly to the lack of balance in the situation, rather than affirming it. As with the conflicting details offered about the women's tails in *Wonders* (the text suggests their position is on the loins, while the image depicts them on the posterior), the revision of these bodies is not disguised for an audience reading carefully. However, the distraction of the visual representation – be it the fascinating drawing of a pretty female monster or the presentation of an enormous monster head – allows the audience to accept and overlook the revision of the moment. For Beowulf, both the reading audience and the audience within the text are distracted by the new details provided by the experience of his decapitated head.

Damon further argues that Grendel's head 'symbolically sever[s] the bonds that held them in mutual antagonism, terminating through enacted ritual the monsters' claim of sovereignty' (430–31), using as evidence Hrothgar's appreciative exclamation upon seeing Grendel's head (1778–81). The head is so enormous that it requires four men to carry it – it is a spectacle, even if it is the wrong one, so of course Hrothgar remarks upon it. However, in bringing this head, Beowulf lends support to his story about fighting two monsters, thus encouraging just such a response from Hrothgar. Perhaps Beowulf asserts Grendel's mother's loss of control over her son's body by bringing Grendel's head to the surface, but this seems rather a stretch. Instead, by bringing Grendel's head to Hrothgar, Beowulf supports his story that he fought two foes, leaving the audience to suppose (a little ludicrously, perhaps) that Grendel, still alive but possessing only one arm, presented the greater threat in the fight in the mere. Thus, by leaving Grendel's mother's head behind but bringing back her son's, Beowulf suggests that Grendel's mother was not all that dangerous. By leaving her head in the mere, Beowulf has implied that Grendel's mother is not as threatening, or as important, as her son. But in truth, the phallus he has brought back is hollow and does not hold the power or authority he suggests that it does. Rather, Grendel's head is merely a trace of the masculinity removed from Beowulf by Grendel's mother. In choosing her son's head rather than hers, Beowulf chooses the lie over the truth, the fiction of masculinity and authority over actual potency.

In erasing Grendel's mother, Beowulf simultaneously denies and confirms her power and importance. By bringing back the decapitated head of a corpse rather than hers, he does not show her to be unworthy; instead, he demonstrates to the reading audience the effect she has had on him. In telling a story that replaces her sexualized threat with the bodies of two monsters, he reveals how very powerful she was. There is no rhetorical need for Beowulf to relate the sexual nature of the fight to the Danes, but the very fact that he completely covers up the one-on-one nature of it shows his discomfort and his unsuccessful attempts to revise and repress it. She has the power to make him cover his tracks, to force him to lie about what happened in the mere. His anxieties about her body and its effect on his own are laid bare. While he attempts to erase her from the poem by leaving her head behind and revising her story, through Grendel's head and the reconfigurations he must construct for Hrothgar, her body is both remembered, and re-membered. By leaving her head behind and changing the story, Beowulf unravels the significance of her decapitation, and thus the empowerment of dismemberment, along with her erasure, is rendered incomplete. Grendel's head, and the story that Beowulf must tell and retell, different every time, serve as traces of the exchange in the mere: like Grendel's head, Beowulf is no longer what he says he is.

The particular problem of the fight with Grendel's mother is that it is a story that must be repeated again and again – therefore, in each repetition of the story, Grendel's and his mother's monstrous and sexually transgressive bodies invade the narrative, requiring Beowulf to continually erase and revise. Beowulf's revision of his fight for Hrothgar is especially striking in light of the way in which he tailors his story for Hygelac upon his return to Geatland. In this context, Beowulf does not suggest that he fought both Grendel and his mother in the mere, and he makes no mention of the material evidence he provided for Hrothgar. Instead, he distracts his audience from the nature of the fight with Grendel's mother by de-emphasizing it in comparison to his detailed discussion of Grendel, and by providing another kind of material evidence of his success – his gifts. Beowulf replaces his words with another misleading sign of his works, substituting the approbation of Hrothgar for the real story of his valor.

Upon his return to Hygelac, Beowulf must promote his foreign success and demonstrate that he achieved his original goal of freeing Heorot from Grendel's malice. The sheer amount of treasure he brings back speaks of his value at Heorot: when Beowulf shares his gifts of jewelry and armor, he provides material evidence of his triumph. Using almost the same language to describe the dangerous nature of the fight, Beowulf, using litotes, claims that 'unsofte þonan/ feorh oðferede' (2140b–41a) [I bore away my life from there with difficulty]. However, this time he acknowledges his struggle with Grendel's mother, saying 'þær unc hwile wæs hand gemæne' (2137) [for a while, there for the two of us was a common hand-grip]. Interestingly, here, again, he uses the dual *unc*, that rare form that implies a kind of united two-ness. That the term surfaces here demonstrates a strange, reflexive openness regarding the nature of the fight; he does not use the term in this instance to describe his fight with Grendel, with whom he did in fact share a hand-grip. He reveals that 'ic heafde becearf/ on ðam [guð]sele/ Grendeles modor/ eacnum ecgum' (2138b–40a) [I cut off Grendel's mother's head in the war-hall with a great sword], but says nothing about decapitating Grendel's corpse. Moreover, he mentions nothing about bringing Grendel's head to Hrothgar.

While this account is certainly closer to the actual events in the mere, it, too, restricts and restructures the information provided. Beowulf only reveals a select portion of the fight, and notably leaves out compromising information, which suggests more than a poetic impulse not to bore readers with a redundant story. Specifically, Beowulf imports a detail from his fight with Grendel when he claims that he and Grendel's mother had a shared hand-grip.[51] Beowulf may have grasped Grendel's mother's shoulder in order to throw her to the ground, but never do the two grasp hands; rather, they wrestle on the ground, rolling one over the other. This detail stands as a deliberate revision of the actual nature of the fight. He also neglects to mention that he left Grendel's mother at the bottom of the mere, choosing instead to decapitate Grendel's corpse as evidence for Hrothgar. As Horner suggests, 'He then cuts off Grendel's head, bringing both it and the sword hilt back to Hrothgar as his battle-spoils. Both of these prizes can be read as the "texts" of Grendel's Mother, subsuming her into the peace-weaving paradigm. The "texts" woven by the peace-weavers in *Beowulf* are their sons' (485–6). Grendel's body, then, like all sons in the poem, takes the place of his mother's body, reconfiguring her meaning and function. His body distracts the attention of readers and viewers from the centrality and significance of his mother and origin. Although Beowulf does not deny the fight with Grendel's mother, he erases the sexualized nature of the struggle, and replaces it, literally, with a detail from the fight with Grendel. Grendel's body, once again, stands in for that of his mother; her fight remains unseen by the audience within the text.

Scholarly attention to Beowulf's speech to Hygelac turns only superficially to the section concerning Grendel's mother – few scholars even notice the differences between this telling and Beowulf's earlier story. As the only scholar to focus on these speeches, Huisman examines the rhetorical situation of each telling, remarking that 'The difficulty of the task is not, however, Beowulf's primary emphasis here, as it was for Hrothgar' (230). Instead, she claims that to honor Hygelac best, Beowulf must focus on his rewards: 'in the immediate social context of this telling is that Hygelac can realize that his hero/retainer has performed a difficult deed, which brings glory to Hygelac' (230). While the rhetorical situation of the report to Hygelac dictates the nature of the retelling, it remains significant that Beowulf in this second retelling reveals both more about the fight (that it was against Grendel's mother), and less (that he brought Grendel's head back). Lerer claims that 'Beowulf offers a revision of the tale and a potential recasting of its central themes' (*Literacy* 183). However, he focuses on the naming of Hondscio and the description of Grendel's glove as revised elements. Like Lerer, Orchard notes these specific additions:

> The most noticeable feature of Beowulf's own account of his battles with Grendel and his mother (lines 2069b–2143) is the extent to which it offers additional details to those already presented: for example, here we learn for the first time the name of the Geat killed by Grendel – Hondscio (line 207a) – and the fact that in his predations Grendel carried a 'glove' made of 'the skins of dragons' … Aside from these details, which are seemingly linked (the common noun *hondscio*

---

[51] The phrase 'hand gemæne' may also be translated, more liberally, as 'hand-to-hand fighting,' as Heaney and others have done.

would seem to mean 'glove'), however, we are – most importantly – presented with Beowulf's own perspective. (*Critical Companion* 224)

It is revealing that these scholars note the rhetorical differences in the speeches but focus primarily on the additions to Beowulf's fight with Grendel.[52] Perhaps it is because Beowulf spends nearly twice as much time speaking about his fight with Grendel. Perhaps it also relates back to the old attitude that the fight with Grendel's mother serves simply as an addendum to the fight with Grendel. More tellingly, this diverted attention reveals the trick that Beowulf and the *Beowulf* poet play on their audiences. The new information highlights the fact that Beowulf offers a revision of the story; through this means, the poet asks us to compare this version of the story with Beowulf's previous version. Thus, the poet subtly reminds his audience of Beowulf's revision of the fight, but also distracts us from the troubling nature of this revision through Beowulf's provision of new and intriguing information. While Beowulf should amplify these details, as they are pertinent to Hygelac, there is little need for him to restrict his discussion of Grendel's mother, unless there is something troubling about the nature of this very challenging battle.

The battle with Grendel's mother is elided one final time by Beowulf in the poem's last mention of the monsters: while he invokes Grendel before he battles the dragon, it is the poet who remembers Grendel's mother. Beowulf, in his rally before the fight with the dragon, recalls aloud his fight with Grendel, saying that, if he thought it could work, he would fight the dragon without a sword, 'swa ic gio wið Grendle dyde' (2521b) [as I long ago did against Grendel]. Beowulf draws his inspiration from his fight with Grendel, but the poet reminds us that Beowulf also fought Grendel's mother, even if only the reading audience really knows what happened: 'æt guðe forgrap Grendeles mægum,/ laðan cynnes' (2353a–4a) [in battle he crushed Grendel's kin, the hated race]. Alfred Bammesberger suggests that the plural form of the word *mæg* in line 2353b means 'Grendel and Grendel's mother,' rather than offering a bizarre form of the singular ("Half-line" 3). This use of the plural recalls Beowulf's use of the plurals *hyrdum* and *feondum* when, in his first telling of the fight, he implies that he fought both Grendel and his mother in the mere. The poet consequently points the reader back to both fights and their consequences: that not just Grendel is exterminated, but that his whole 'race,' his family is too. The feud can only be ended when the audience is absolutely assured that no grendelkin remain. The stakes of his retelling and retooling of the narrative are high; the retelling emphasizes the importance of the fight in the mere, while the retooling demonstrates Beowulf's discomfort with the events that took place there. Because Beowulf repeats the story the reading audience cannot help but notice the ways in which he both conceals the details of the fight, and changes them entirely.

---

52 Schwetman too focuses on the additions, noting only that 'After briefly telling of his victory over Grendel's mother, he ends his speech with an account of the rewards he received for his heroic deeds' (145).

Even as he turns to his death, Beowulf returns the audience's attention to Grendel, while he simultaneously deflects it away from Grendel's mother. And yet, when he gives the necklace to Wiglaf, lamenting his lack of an heir, he implicitly invokes her fecund body as a balance to his own impotence. Although Beowulf wants his listeners to remember the former, the poet clearly wants his readers to consider the latter.

CONCLUSIONS

Because Grendel's mother draws Beowulf into perhaps the most violent and sexually suggestive encounter in Old English literature, it is no surprise that Beowulf seems compelled to revise what happened in the mere. I have suggested that Beowulf, out of discomfort over the sexualized nature of the fight, revises the events that took place in the mere when he reports to Hrothgar and Hygelac. Beowulf's attempts at erasure simultaneously cover up and reveal the bodies of Grendel and his mother. While parts of Grendel's body surface and resurface in the poem, it is only through the trace of her son's body that Grendel's mother's body is remembered. Beowulf's decapitations and revisions to his story continue the pattern of erasure of the sexualized monster revealed in *Wonders of the East*. While Grendel's body, too, is a monstrous and sexually excessive body, Beowulf's victory over it through its dismemberment is meant to affirm and demonstrate his masculine prowess. However, each time Grendel's body and story are revisited, so too are the power and potency of the erased body of Grendel's mother confirmed. The structure of the text both enables and resists the erasure of Grendel's mother. She is featured in the center of this poem, and is, in fact, central to it, just as she is both named (as Grendel's mother) and never named (in having no name of her own). She necessitates Beowulf's most complicated and only unwitnessed fight. Because of the location of the fight in the middle of this text, however, it can be read doubly. Instead of being seen as central, Grendel's mother can be seen, and has often been, merely as a follow-up to Beowulf's fight with Grendel – a loose end to be tied up. The poem ends with the death of Beowulf, but even in his death by his final monstrous foe, the dragon, we are reminded of his earlier fights. In each of his retellings of the fight, traces of the dangerous body of Grendel's mother remain.

The poet reveals Grendel's mother's centrality in the poem by showing her to be a lost object, but also an origin. Specifically, Grendel's mother maintains her primary position in Grendel's family tree. As Mary Dockray-Miller claims,

> In Anglo-Saxon culture at large, both during and after Bede, patrilineage was the focus of most extant genealogy; such a patrilineal focus was also coupled with a usual exclusion of women's roles and names at all, erasing and eliding the biologically crucial maternal body from both the family tree and the historical focus. ("Breasts" xiii)

Grendel's mother reconstructs genealogy because she replaces his father in the lineage, making herself a singular kind of origin – albeit one named only in relation to her son. This is a culture that is obsessed with 'sustaining the patriarchal and patrilineal agenda,' as Gayle Margherita has argued in reference to Morgan le Faye, but in order to do so, the patriarchy must posit the feminine as an origin 'of both sin and signification' (13). She argues that 'the mother's lack of discursive potency unveils the symbolic castration of the male subject, and threatens to silence him altogether' (148). In their underwater battle, Grendel's mother very nearly kills Beowulf, and thus silences him in particular ways. He cannot tell the story as it really happened because to do so would reveal the symbolic castration Beowulf suffered in the mere. After all, in his possession, not one but two swords melt, when they come into contact with Grendel's mother. As Kristeva argues, 'it is always to be noticed that the attempt to establish a male, phallic power is vigorously threatened by the no less virulent power of the other sex, which is oppressed … That other sex, the feminine, becomes synonymous with a radical evil that is to be suppressed' (70). Despite her near mastery in the mere, Grendel's mother is not a speaking subject; she lacks this 'discursive potency' that Beowulf performs in his ability to boast. When he takes off her head, Beowulf removes what Mary Flavia Godfrey posits as 'the source of intellection and creation' (10), the locus of speech and of the power to report. Beowulf forecloses her ability to speak – an ability already hindered by her status as a woman and as a monster – by slicing off her head, and he silences her yet again when he leaves her head at the bottom of the mere, replaced as a sign above ground by her son's head. And yet, oddly, it is Beowulf whose voice is manipulated by the female monster in the mere. She acts as both a castrated symbol of absence and as an origin – of Grendel, but also of Beowulf's own frightening chasm of lack.

THE ANGLO-SAXON BODY

The body and its permanent status as monstrous characterize the monsters of Old English literature. Like the monsters of *Wonders of the East*, Grendel and his mother are defined by the bodies they possess, bodies that are both excessive and hybrid in terms of their physical form and their sex and gender characteristics. However, these excessive bodies transgress codes of gender and merit acts of erasure designed to delimit their threats to established social patterns of sex, gender, and sexuality. Ironically, it is the acts intended to remove or revise the most troubling sexed elements of these bodies that instead emphasize them and simultaneously demonstrate their power. The very permanence of these monstrous bodies reveals Anglo-Saxon notions of the body and its status as permanent and unchanging, in the most basic of ways. As Bynum suggests,

> In the mid-twelfth century, people producing a wide variety of discourses tended to think of change not as replacement but as evolution or development, as alteration of appearance or mode of being … Behavior revealed character or type; a

self was always what it was. The 'end' or goal of development, if there was development, was to achieve the ideal version of the type or self. (*Metamorphosis* 23)

In such a paradigm, although a person might develop – age, grow, decline, and die – the basic truths about that person and his or her body would never change. The body reveals the essential self inside, and that is a self that is permanent. Since bodies and identities are not capable of transformation, then, monsters must be controlled not through reformation, but rather through erasure.

All in all, this philosophy of the static body is reassuring. People's bodies represent what they are; monstrosity is visible and unmistakable. Sexual excess and transgression, too, are clearly visible under this paradigm. The permanence of these bodies in the literature does not necessarily reflect historical truths about bodies, but rather these fictional bodies may be thought to reflect beliefs or ideas about the body – beliefs that are meant to circumscribe behavior as much as to describe it. Thus, if one's body is permanent and reliably so, then threats from the outside – which are many, in Anglo-Saxon England – can be clearly identified. These fictions about the body also serve the purpose of articulating who is on the inside, socially speaking.[53] The obvious difference of monstrous forms exhibits the dangers of exogamy, and particularly of miscegenation. These Anglo-Saxon texts demonstrate the appeal of exogamous sex, but curtail it through acts of erasure of the sexualized elements of the image or narrative. In doing so, they attempt to persuade readers and viewers of the dangers inherent in miscegenative practices. England is an island, isolated from other cultures in certain ways – although it is also an island populated by multiple populations and distinct Germanic tribes who were themselves invaders.[54] The history of the island is a history of invasions and then of settlement and integration. Bodies as markers of identities not only demonstrate who is a member of which group, but also indicate that identity is stable, unchanging, and a reliable indicator of lineage, function, and desire.

To make monstrosity indelibly visible is to assure people that they will know a monster when they see one; it also assures the people that they themselves are not monstrous. Their bodies, equally permanent, should thus serve unchanging purposes. The system of beliefs presented by *Wonders* and *Beowulf* expands outward to propound beliefs about social structure and functions. It keeps people in their places, with little room for variation and advancement. Its appearance in

[53] I do not mean to suggest that there are no threats from inside the nation or the tribe in Anglo-Saxon culture and literature. Beowulf all too clearly indicates that problems are just as likely to come from inside a culture as from outside it, in the figure of Hrothulf. Rather, the threats of miscegenation carry a broader social significance, one relevant to the island as a whole, rather than just to individual nations that suffer under greedy or flawed leaders.

[54] As Howe asserts, Anglo-Saxons held complex and troubled relations with their neighbors, particularly those to the north: they 'feared the incursions of outsiders from a north that lay beyond. If north was the compass point from which Anglo-Saxons learned to expect danger, it was also the region in which they would experience the peril of falling into sin and thus of violating their covenant with God' (*Writing* 136). See also Giacone, 'Woman in a Boat.'

this literature marks attempts to represent and to persuade people of the unchanging nature of the human body and its function in society. It clearly says: stay away from monsters, from those who do not look like you, no matter how appealing, and no matter how fascinating. But it also says: you are who you are, and you are here to serve a defined purpose, whether that is fighting, farming, praying, or giving birth to children. It indicates that social roles must be maintained because the body's function and status possess a clear and unchanging essence. Whether or not this is true – and the frightening and fascinating bodies of monsters suggest that it is not – this ideology permeates texts about monsters, and thus about bodies in Old English literature. The monster provides an outlet for the strange things bodies might do or be.

Chapter 3

CIRCULATION AND TRANSFORMATION:
THE MONSTROUS FEMININE IN
MANDEVILLE'S TRAVELS

Toward the end of the twelfth century, however, a new understanding – a new model – of change emerged ... people were increasingly fascinated by ... radical change, where an entity is replaced by something completely different.
(Bynum, *Metamorphosis* 25)

Women are more essential to reproduction than men – a society could not survive with a few women of child-bearing age; but it could survive if most men were eliminated and a few kept in a cage somewhere. Again, women have to be circumscribed: the whole system can be seen as built upon womb envy on the part of the inessential male. (Craib 51)

IF OLD ENGLISH narratives figure the body as permanent, then in Middle English literature the body begins to look profoundly flexible, plastic, and, perhaps, unstable. The shift between the literatures of these two periods is often seen as being cataclysmic: the concerns of Anglo-Saxon authors might seem to be washed away by the voices of Norman and later Middle English writers, but 1066 is not a neat cultural dividing line, as has been long acknowledged. Some Old English writing bleeds past this famous date, and early Middle English literature sometimes reflects Old English poetic practices and concerns. However, the shift that takes place, writ large, between these two periods, does offer readers a different vision of the monster, and of sex, gender, and sexuality. Middle English literature is rich with monsters, particularly in its exploration of more Continental genres like romance as well as travel narratives and visions of the exotic East. The bodies of both monsters and people seem far less taboo in Middle English; however, that is not to suggest that these bodies are any less dangerous, either physically or culturally. The gendered monsters of one of the most popular travel narratives of the period, *Mandeville's Travels*, represent a new kind of threat to English identity and to the body: the danger of transformation, invisibility, and the miscegenation that results from these new bodily states.

The permanent bodies of Old English monsters mark them as Other, as outsiders; these monsters also dwell outside of human society in their own communities. Their status as monstrous is both physical and unchanging; they can never become a part of human civilization because their difference is written visibly on their bodies. The human response to the monstrous body is a desire for

116

its erasure or its death, not for its transformation or redemption. If they enter human communities, it is only briefly, and for a clearly delineated purpose. For instance, Grendel enters the Danes' hall, Heorot, in order to consume the men whose camaraderie and 'hall joy' he seems to envy, while Grendel's mother comes to Heorot to avenge the death of her son. Each monster retreats after achieving these goals and returns home, to the monstrous mere. The separation of monstrous and human society is even more pronounced in the *Wonders of the East*, discussed in chapter one, where human society is located at a significant distance from groups of monsters. Only wayward travelers, who frequently get eaten, or adventurers, like Alexander or the anonymous narrator of *Wonders*, come into contact with these monsters; the wayward travelers seem to be profoundly lost, while the adventurers seem to have come for the precise purpose of seeing these monsters. In *Wonders*, only tales of the monsters are brought home, while Beowulf brings back trophies of the monstrous: Grendel's arm and his head. Yet in both of these Old English texts, the communities exist in very different spaces with intercourse occurring only between individual members for limited periods of time and for very specific purposes.

The same, however, is not true in Middle English: monsters not only affect but also enter human communities. Whereas Old English monstrous bodies, and therefore monstrous identities, are permanent,[1] many monstrous bodies in Middle English literature are capable of transformation. They pass into and out of these communities, at times with a kind of ease that signals a distinct change in visions of monstrosity between the two periods. It is not only a different understanding of a physically monstrous body that permits monsters to enter communities; rather, monsters are able to disguise, to cover up, or to transform their monstrous bodies (we might think of Bertilak, who doubles as the Green Knight, or the Wife of Bath's hag, who becomes a beautiful woman). In some cases, the monstrous body, against the individual's will, covers up an identity that is human, through a curse or some such narrative device. In other cases, the monstrous identity of the body is invisible to onlookers because it resides inside the human-appearing body, waiting for private and intimate moments to make itself known. Regardless of the individual situations, we see in Middle English literature, and in *Mandeville's Travels* specifically, the ability of a monstrous body to transform or be transformed – something evidently not possible for monsters in Old English literature. In *Mandeville's Travels*, four monsters possess bodies that physically transform from one thing to another – be it from woman to dragon, death to life, wife to Amazon, or potentially lethal virgin to carefully kept wife. Significantly, these monsters are geographically dispersed and are not confined to a single area of the mysterious or exoticized East. For the Mandeville author, monsters are not stable and permanent either in their physical formation or in their geographic location.

---

[1] This is not a comprehensive study of *all* Old English monsters, but the majority of the monsters have permanently monstrous bodies and identities, as I have shown of the monsters in *Wonders* and *Beowulf*. I have not yet come across a transformative Old English monster.

Monsters, whose bodies had been unchanging and easily identifiable as monstrous, and who could thus be identified and kept outside the community, enter human communities and can even remain unrecognized because of their ability to transform themselves. While monsters could be erased by authors, artists, viewers, and even characters in Old English literature, they persistently disrupt communities in *Mandeville's Travels* because they are not located away from civilization. Each of the four narratives of transformative monstrosity in *Mandeville's Travels* makes less secure the notion that the monstrous is elsewhere.

BODIES AND THE COMMUNITY

The new interest in the possibility for physical transformation is figured in well-known Middle English texts, both original and translated (from local tales of werewolves to romances to Ovid), and represents a distinct shift from the focus of Old English texts. Caroline Walker Bynum, in *Metamorphosis and Identity*, explores concepts and representations of change in Middle English texts. Just as I suggest a lack of transformative bodies in Old English literature, so too Bynum notes that,

> metamorphosis stories, popular in Antiquity but not in the early Middle Ages, revived. The proliferation of tales of vampires, fairies, and werewolves testifies not merely to an enthusiasm for alterity and escapism but also to a fascination with, and horror at, the possibility that persons might, actually or symbolically, become beasts or angels, suddenly possessed by demons or inspired to prophecy.
> (25–6)

Stories of physical change and transformation are not prominent in Old English literature. Instead, narratives concerned with valor in battle, either literal or spiritual and often biblical, form the cornerstones of the literature. However, in the later Middle Ages, classical texts gain increasing popularity, and authors including Ovid, whose *Metamorphosis* primarily focuses on the problems and potentials of transformation, become implicated in understandings of the body and identity.[2]

---

[2]   As McKinley suggests, 'Ovid has long been considered one of the most popular classical authors in the high and later Middle Ages ... While copies of the Roman poet's works were produced in the greatest abundance on the continent ... from the twelfth century onward, they gradually made their way into medieval England. Geoffrey Chaucer and John Gower drew extensively from Ovid' (41). Ovid's *Metamorphosis*, a book whose main concern is the transformation of bodies, becomes a text both widely read and widely referenced in the later Middle Ages. I do not want to insinuate that Anglo-Saxon readers had no knowledge or exposure to classical texts. Lapidge, in *Library*, claims that classical poets seem to have been known in Anglo-Saxon England, even if few manuscripts survive: 'But of the classical poets unrepresented by any surviving Anglo-Saxon manuscript, there is no doubt that both Lucan and Claudian were studied in Anglo-Saxon England ... Arguments could also be mounted for

This new interest in changing bodies reflects a significant shift in social structure that takes place between 1100 and 1400. Bynum explains this emerging interest in the idea of change by suggesting that changing bodies are reflective of significant social changes:

> Changing social circumstances provided the context for such relevance. Agricultural, economic, and urban growth in the course of the eleventh and twelfth centuries had led to transformations of familial and social structure that made it increasingly possible (if still not easy) for people – especially privileged people – to change their social roles ... Thus we find, in the years around 1200, a new fascination with the other and with images of change in which one thing is, for better or worse, really replaced by something else. (*Metamorphosis* 26–7)

The changes she discusses here are relatively early, and are not limited to England. I would suggest that similar changes do happen in England: the Norman Invasion and the shifts it brings to the language of court and culture is only the first of many changes over the next several hundred years. While pilgrimage and crusade influence changes in the ways in which the English see themselves as individuals as well as part of the larger Christian community, another widespread event also informs the transition. The Black Death, which devastated England in the fourteenth century, affected the ways in which people functioned socially as well as their perceptions of the body and its integrity.[3] As Richard Haddlesey suggests, 'Though the Black Death occurred over a relatively short period in England (c.1348–50), its influence on subsequent generations cannot be ignored ... It is estimated that in excess of fifty percent of the population was wiped out by the epidemic and did not replenish fully, until well into the eighteenth century' (par. 3). Although his concern is primarily with how social changes affect architecture, he notes that the events surrounding the plague changed the ways people treated death and burial. It reasonably follows that people must perceive the body in radically different ways after having witnessed the death of over half of the population. With social change providing the arena, the changing bodies in Middle English literature reflect notions of a no longer stable personal identity. When a body becomes so permeable and so vulnerable to forces outside of itself, as happens not only through the ravages of the plague, but also through social instability in the form of war and famine (par. 11), it seems that one might perceive it as being not under one's own

---

Anglo-Saxon poets' knowledge of Ovid (especially the *Metamorphoseis*)' (67). While some readers may have been acquainted with these poets, such scant knowledge and such rare appearances do not suggest popularity.

3 Pilgrimage and crusade are certainly important practices that change the ways in which the English perceive of themselves and their bodies. I do not mean to assert that a single cause existed for social change in the Black Death, but rather to focus particularly on the ways in which the Black Death challenges notions of the integrity of even the healthiest of bodies. Of course, issues of conversion too have much to do with ideas of transformation, but I am here particularly interested in changes that are physical, as well as spiritual.

control. The body, then, no longer appears permanent in the literature of the period, but rather is susceptible to change, either for the better or for the worse.

The changes in perceptions of the body and its stability also present a likely climate for concerns about sex, gender, and sexuality. We might expect laws and practices to reflect and mediate, or perhaps even to control, sexed and gendered bodies; however, it seems that legal changes in relation to sex after the Black Death are relatively few. James Brundage remarks,

> The period between the demographic disaster of the Black Death and the religious revolution of the sixteenth century saw surprisingly little change in the law and theology of sex and marriage. This relative stability is unexpected, since one might suppose that the disappearance of between a quarter and a third of Europe's population during the mid-fourteenth century epidemics would have produced drastic changes in the ways society dealt with sex, marriage, and reproduction. (*Law* 487)

We might note, instead, that legal changes in this period are more concerned with issues of social class and control, including religious and sumptuary laws. However, as Brundage does note, one of the developments that does occur following the Black Death is 'greatly increased activism of royal and especially municipal governments in regulating sexual behavior' (487). In other words, the state has a greater stake in delimiting and controlling sex, particularly in light of a significantly diminished population.[4] Sex, then, has a new place in the political arena. As either result or reflection of these new attitudes and regulations, gender, sex and sexuality, too, become more prominent concerns in Middle English texts. Therefore, not only are sexual bodies increasingly important, they are also unstable; the literature of this period both constructs and reflects these timely concerns with the body, and especially with issues of sexual circulation and reproduction.

Mandeville's Travels, likely written between 1357 and 1360 (Tzanaki 15), is a text deeply concerned with issues of circulation, both literal and sexual. The titular narrator transverses not only the Holy Land, but also the marvelous East, in his desire to have the world laid open before him. He lists more than twenty different kinds of human monsters in his pilgrimage. Of these monsters, four are transformative: the daughter of Hippocrates, who turns from a woman into a dragon; the impregnated dead woman who gives birth to a monstrous head; the Amazons; and the poison virgins.[5] Although drawn from a number of sources,

---

4   See Platt, *King Death*, which discusses the economic and social results of the Black Death and the subsequent loss in population. He particularly notes the shift toward later marriage and smaller families that seems to result from the plagues themselves and the social changes that follow them.

5   Two other people might be considered monstrous transformations: two men, in different parts of the narrative, are raised from the dead by contact with Christ or with a relic. The living dead, also, certainly comprise a category of monstrosity. For more on the living dead, see

these transformative monsters bear some significant similarities. First, in each case the monstrous and transformative body is female. Secondly, each case raises questions of marital and reproductive circulation for these monstrous bodies. The monsters I study here are often not only monsters of hybridity, but they undergo literal metamorphosis: changing from one thing to another. Thus, the quality they all share is a lack of permanence. The problem with the transformative body is that at times it appears to be completely human, while at others it is clearly monstrous. When the body appears human, it can participate in the marital economy; however, this situation becomes complicated when the body is transformed. Whereas truly and permanently monstrous bodies do not exist in human communities, those that are transformative are able to enter and to participate in these communities. In Middle English literature, and especially in *Mandeville's Travels*, the monster has infiltrated the human community of readers, forcing readers to reconsider the nature of monstrosity and the permanence of human identity, as well as the stability of their communities.

MONSTERS AND TRANSFORMATION

A widely circulated medieval text, *Mandeville's Travels* gained popularity because of its ability to entertain the concerns of many audiences, from those looking for a practical travel guide to those desiring to envision strange and interesting people and places.[6] The text is both typical in its depictions of the marvelous and unique

---

Gade, 'The Naked and the Dead'; Stern, 'Legends of the Dead'; and Smith, 'Death and Desire.' I would argue, however, that these two figures are not truly monstrous, as they are brought back to their living forms and are not corpses continuing to live unnaturally. They are miracles rather than monsters.

6   The narrative's popularity has led to its many variations; although most of the manuscripts offer the same general story, the details vary, and we have no 'original' form against which to compare the various redactions. 'The *Book*'s archetype, written c. 1357–60, is no longer in existence, so far as is known. It can only be postulated from the two versions directly descended from it, the Continental and the Insular' (Tzanaki 15). Here, I study the Insular or Insular-derived versions written in English rather than the Continental (primarily written in French) because there seems to have been very little correspondence for this book between England and France after the original text came to England: 'None of the versions made outside England is known to have crossed the sea before the sixteenth century except the archetype of the Insular Version (an Anglo-French copy of the original French text, from which all extant versions of *Mandeville's Travels* derive) and a degenerate and unfinished French manuscript' (Seymour, *Metrical* 1). The Insular version seems to be particularly English, because 'most of the c. 25 manuscripts extant circulated in England' (Tzanaki 16). The Insular version, however, gave rise to other redactions in England like the Defective Version, which 'proved the most popular English text; about 38 manuscript copies remain and all the English editions stem from it' (16). In total, forty-four English copies are extant; of these copies, one copy of the Bodley, dated between 1390 and 1450; two copies of the Cotton, dated at 1400; thirty-eight copies of the Defective, dated after 1400; and one copy each of the

in its particular collection and description of monstrous humans. Recently, *Mandeville's Travels* has enjoyed a revival in scholarly interest. Book-length studies by Iain Macleod Higgins and Rosemary Tzanaki have approached the text through various theoretical lenses.[7] In *Writing East: The 'Travels' of Sir John Mandeville*, Higgins is primarily concerned with the shape of the world, as presented by the text's titular fictional narrator, Sir John Mandeville. In *Mandeville's Medieval Audiences*, Tzanaki considers the text's multiple functions for its multiple audiences, claiming that it participates in five genres: pilgrimage, geography, romance, history, and theology (xi). Both of these recent studies discuss the monstrous, most often as a subset of the larger category of the 'marvelous.' Although both recognize the marvelous as a significant part of *Mandeville's Travels*, they seem to speak of it as functioning in opposition to, or separately from, the more serious aspects of the text. In her preface, Tzanaki assures us that 'the author's own intentions were rarely understood and his religious syncretism was often ignored, with audiences preferring the more marvelous aspects of his work' (xi). For her, willful audiences, translators, and redactors have focused inappropriately on these 'marvelous aspects,' often ignoring or revising the larger arguments of the text's 'original' author. Higgins, however, suggests multivalent reading practices rather than readerly error. He refers to the marvelous aspect of the text as 'a marvelous mélange that may remind us of the culturally and historically shifting boundary between the imaginary and the real, as it serves to provide a kind of aesthetic pleasure in counterpoint to *The Book*'s historical, moral, and religious lore and lessons' (*Writing East* 85). According to both Tzanaki and Higgins, the marvelous is secondary to, not complicit in, the most important and serious purposes of the

Egerton, 1400–1430; the Metrical, fifteenth century; and the Stanzaic fragment, fifteenth century, remain (Higgins, *Writing East* 22, table 1). Both Higgins and Tzanaki consider multiple versions of *Mandeville's Travels*, because, in Tzanaki's words, 'it is impossible to read the *Book* as a single text due to its multiplicity of incarnations and reincarnations across Europe. This intertextual richness has been largely ignored by modern scholarship, with each commentator choosing a single text as the basis of his or her reading. This has resulted in the *Book* being read in very limited ways, at least partly due to the version studied' (19). While it is Tzanaki's goal to consider all of the manuscripts dated before 1500, Higgins focuses on the Bodley, Cotton, Defective, Egerton, and Metrical versions in English, using other language versions for comparative purposes (*Writing East* viii). Although the Cotton version has been used by most scholars for primary reference, I consider the Defective version as my primary text. Seymour states that the 'text of the Defective Version established itself as the dominant form of the book in England' (*Defective* xi–xii). Not only was it the most popular English version of the text, extant in over thirty different manuscripts, it is the 'oldest English translation of the Insular Version' (xi), and served as the base text for both the Cotton and Egerton versions (xii). Although I cite the Defective version as primary, I follow Higgins in considering the Cotton, Egerton, Bodley, and Metrical versions.

7   Both scholars address the problem of the many varying manuscripts of the text, and both call the text *The Travels of Sir John Mandeville*, in order to more clearly assert the distinction between the fictional narrator, Sir John Mandeville, and the anonymous author of the text, who is most likely *not* Sir John Mandeville.

text. However, the reception history and continued focus on the marvelous by readers, translators, and redactors suggest that these elements held significance for medieval readers that should not be ignored. The monsters of this text are not ancillary to its fundamental purposes, nor are they to be conflated with the miraculous; they are a fundamental part of the meaning and message of *Mandeville*.[8]

Indeed, medieval readers, translators, redactors, and artists often focus on the marvelous, although not necessarily exclusively, as Tzanaki indicates in her study of the many manuscript versions. Early in its reception history it was read most often as a pilgrimage narrative, a function that remained important even after illustrators began to focus more predominantly on the marvelous elements. Tzanaki sets the new emphasis on the wonders against what she considers to be 'the more serious religious aspects of the *Book*' (77). Those who illustrated and compiled the manuscripts, then, focused on the wonders, but readers also expressed an interest in these same marvelous creatures:

> But it was the strange peoples who captured the reader's eye most often, particularly the Plinian Races; almost every annotated manuscript draws attention to the extraordinary aspect and customs of the inhabitants of countries beyond the Holy Land. Even the remarkable animals, ranging from parrots to griffins, did not impress as much as the weird and wonderful human or semi-human races found in the Orient. (124)

While the narrative of pilgrimage and the idea of travel drive the narrative, it was the monsters, and specifically the human monsters, that garnered the greatest amount of attention in a text noted for its own popularity. The frequency of focus on these elements, however, does not make them necessarily less 'serious' than other components of the book. Rather, it demonstrates that the new interest in the wild potential of bodies was a fundamental part of the ways people might think about their place in the orders of nature, religion, and civilization.

Given its popularity, the material included in *Mandeville's Travels*, especially its most celebrated element, the monsters, must have held special resonance for its audience. Many texts offered similar travel narratives – several even serve as sources[9] for the author – but something about this particular narrative drew

---

8 In this chapter, I refer to the text as *Mandeville's Travels*, following the lead of the most recent published editions of the text although I recognize the important differentiation between author and speaker. Notably, Seymour, editor of the 2002 *Defective Version of Mandeville's Travels* (EETS), retains the title as *Mandeville's Travels*, in accordance with most of the previously published editions of the various manuscript versions. I refer to the anonymous author as the Mandeville author and I occasionally refer to moments of the text as Mandeville's story; by this I mean the fictional story presented by the fictional Mandeville character.

9 The two main sources were William of Boldensele's *Liber de quibusdam ultramarines partibus* (1336) and Odoric of Pordenone's *Relatio* (1330); both were translated into French in 1351 by Jean le Long (Higgins, *Writing East* 9). Higgins, along with others, suggests the author's reliance on the French translations above the original Latin versions, although he seems to have used the Latin at times. According to Lisa Verner, he also relied on 'the works of Jacques de

audiences.[10] While many of these texts and sources include monsters, it is not just the fact of the monstrous, but the way in which it is employed that is so appealing. The monsters in *Mandeville* are, in fact, not merely curiosities by the wayside, but rather, I argue, they provide the context by which we can construct the larger meaning of the text. *Mandeville's Travels* is a text about the role of the Christian in the world; the monsters represent the diversity that comprises the world outside of the familiar boundaries of European geography and culture. Although many scholars, including John Block Friedman and Andrew Fleck, argue that monsters were not conceived of as truly human, many of the monsters in *Mandeville* live in communities whose behaviors reflect the practices of European Christians.[11] Mary Campbell asserts that the Mandeville author attempts to naturalize the monsters, saying 'The Elsewhere of sub- or supernature, into which the West had so long projected the other halves of its divided self, is *not* accessible to the earthly traveler, and Mandeville has rendered the places and peoples that once belonged to it as "part of nature, part of us" ' (160–61). Therefore, this narrative, especially through its monsters, unearths repressed elements and desires of the Western self, making

Vitry, Vincent of Beauvais, John of Plano Carpini, Odoric of Pordenone, Hetoum (or Hayton) of Armenia, and the anonymous (and ubiquitous) *Letter of Prester John*' (124). For more on source materials, see both Higgins and Tzanaki. A great deal of scholarship has focused on the author's use of source material. Some scholars have seen the author as a plagiarist because of his extensive borrowing. Mezciems has shown that such a designation would have been meaningless for medieval readers. In addition, it is important to note that the author frequently reworks his borrowed material in significant ways.

10 As Tzanaki claims, 'it was one of the most popular works of the late medieval period, being read by a wide range of audiences from its inception in the 1350s or early 1360s until the seventeenth and even eighteenth centuries. The huge number of surviving manuscripts – around three hundred – and early editions across Europe attest to its importance. By the 1420s there were versions of the *Book* in French, Anglo-Norman French, English, German, Flemish, Czech, Castilian, Aragonese and Latin, and within another fifty years it had also been translated into Italian, Danish and Gaelic' (1).

11 In the chapter 'The Human Status of the Monstrous Races,' Friedman recounts medieval scholastic arguments concerning these monsters and concludes that 'it was not possible to grant full and equal humanity to an alien race … As long as the definition of "man" was based upon a Western model, the monstrous races could only be assigned a subordinate place in the Chain of Being' (196). He claims that the medieval learned vision of monsters remains largely unchanged from Greek and Roman thought, which held that 'the sense of the alien or 'other' in the marvelous races of the East was so great as to disqualify them … from the epithet "men" ' (34). This same argument is repeated by Kim Hall, who claims that monsters' 'fantastically grotesque bodies serve to create "absolute difference between the reader and the subject" ' (27, quoted in Fleck 383), and by Fleck, who argues that monsters 'are included in Christian cosmography because they provide an aesthetic contrast, as a clearly sub-human other, to the reader's sense of self' (385). Verner includes a chapter on *Mandeville's Travels* in which she concludes, somewhat unhelpfully, that monsters 'are, sometimes simultaneously, pious and secular, informative and diverting, symbolic and arbitrary. In the *Travels*, meaning has become fluid and dependent on perspective or situation' (153). She offers readings of some specific monsters, including the Cynocephali, the Pygmies, the Cannibals, and the Blemmyae, but mentions none of the monsters that are the focus of this chapter.

them available to an audience that both requires and rejects them. The monsters of *Mandeville* are not distractions from its central purpose; they are intrinsic to it. They ask humans to consider what it means to be Western, what it means to be Christian, and, indeed, what it means to be human.

These questions regarding basic human identity are questions intrinsically embodied by the monster. As Cohen claims in 'Seven Theses,' monsters are the 'harbingers of category crisis' (6); the bodies of monsters demonstrate the ways in which boundaries of identity or culture might be breached. For example, hybrid monsters possess the characteristics of multiple beings. If, as I have suggested before, a monster possesses a human body with an animal attribute, like tusks, then that monster belongs to both categories – the human and the animal simultaneously, despite the fact that these categories are constructed in opposition to one another. A monster that embodies both the human and the animal deconstructs each category, for how can they exist exclusively if they co-exist in a single body? In previous chapters I have demonstrated the difficulty of these particular categories, and the ways in which people have responded to the crises presented by the bodies of monsters. However, most of these crises have been merely physical, not temporal. In other words, in Old English a monstrous body always is, always has been, and always will be, monstrous. But in Middle English, a new kind of monster presents a different crisis of category: a monster whose body can transform or change blurs the line between human and monster because that monstrous body is no longer stable and permanent. As Bynum argues, change exists in two formulations: metamorphosis and hybridity. Metamorphosis is what she calls 'replacement change,' or a series of replacement changes, where something literally becomes something else. Hybridity, however, is visible multiplicity, where something has the parts of more than one creature: her example concerns the werewolf, which is hybrid in that it is part man and part wolf (*Metamorphosis* 29–30). She clarifies by denoting that hybridity is about a dual (or more) nature that exists simultaneously while metamorphosis is about mutation – a temporal change (30). This new possibility, of monstrous bodies to transform, and to be at times one thing and at others something entirely different, destabilizes both individual identity and cultural certainty. If one cannot identify a monster by looking – and indeed, if a monster can appear as a man, temporarily – then anyone might be a monster. Furthermore, if monsters are no longer clearly marked as Other, then there is no fundamental reason they should have to live apart in their own communities. And thus, if monsters no longer live only in distant and discrete communities, then there is no telling how many monsters live in human communities. Thus, it is when the monstrous becomes less visible, or less permanent, that the relation of the monstrous to the human must change. If a monster can pass as a human, then that changes what it means to be human.

CIRCULATION AND EXOGAMY

If a monster can pass as human, that alters what it means to be human, but it also demonstrates an adjustment in the perception of the integrity of communities. In fact, the circulation of bodies within communities is of profound concern in late medieval England. People's bodies circulate literally as they engage in pilgrimage and crusade, but they also circulate in terms of marriage, sex, and reproduction. Because so many lives were lost in the plagues of the late fourteenth century, the country both needed to repopulate itself and to regulate reproduction to maintain the social order. Yet, as Colin Platt notes in *King Death*, depleted communities and parallel birth and death rates resulted in zero growth for England in the late medieval period (15). Bodies, it seems, were not circulating as they needed to in either the upper or lower classes: village women were able to 'follow work,' which allowed them to 'marry late or not at all' (41), and the governing classes faced failures of succession, and were confronted with the real possibility of the 'complete failure of a gentry line,' often because they were 'starved [for] heiresses' (76).[12] Particularly at stake in this economy are the bodies of women, who, as Ian Craib notes,

> are more essential to reproduction than men – a society could not survive with a few women of child-bearing age; but it could survive if most men were eliminated and a few kept in a cage somewhere. Again, women have to be circumscribed: the whole system can be seen as built upon womb envy on the part of the inessential male. (51)

Thus, controlling the ways in which women circulate is crucial for population growth; their bodies must be directed in particular courses for marriage to ensure both reproduction and social stability.

This system, identified by Gayle Rubin in "The Traffic in Women" as the 'trafficking of women,' relies on the subordination of women to men, so that their exchange may forge bonds between men. When women are subjected to the kind of trafficking that Rubin discusses, they are therefore reduced to their bodies and valuable primarily through their ability to procreate and extend their husbands'

---

12 Platt notes that these threats became less severe after 1500, when family sizes began to increase again. However, he states that 'clearly one of the more important consequences of the post-plague recession was a re-shaping of the English governing classes at county level. The new pattern was partly owed to long-standing endogenous factors: to economic and social changes that had originated before the Black Death. Nevertheless, the real imperative was the post-plague phenomenon of repeated family failures; for while landed families everywhere could usually ride out a recession with some success, they could not protect themselves against the slow attrition of low fertility or the sudden fatal onslaught of a pestilence ... Biology – more than war, economic recession or the everlasting folly of politicians – was what caused the continuing "unstablenesse" of their world' (77).

lineage. Rarely in control of the exchange of their own bodies, women are subordinated to the men who exchange them, namely their fathers, brothers, and husbands. However, when women begin to choose their own directions – as they did in late medieval England – they threaten the stability of the entire system. Thus, because of its own concerns with population and social striation, the Mandeville author's cultural milieu was concerned with practices of marriage, and especially with the ways in which women's bodies functioned as commodities in the marriage market.

In *Mandeville's Travels*, the bodies of monstrous and transformative women do not abide by the forms of proper circulation. Often, they disseminate themselves, disrupting patriarchal order, as well as the order of humanity. They may also, by passing as human, infiltrate human communities, fundamentally affecting the ways in which the traffic of women can be safely implemented. These monstrous women's bodies reflect anxieties about the bodies of real women in medieval culture, but they also demonstrate the flaws of the system of marital and sexual circulation. These problems are also inherent in Sir John's own body, which is both under- and over-circulated in a variety of ways.

Mandeville's Travels narrates the circulation of its titular fictional narrator, Sir John Mandeville through Rome, Constantinople, the Holy Land, India, and the marvelous East. Although the text was first written between 1357 and 1360, Sir John leaves his home in England in 1332, beginning this pilgrimage with the attitude that though Christians of the West are sinners (guilty of 'pruyde, enuye, and couetise' (Defective 4) [pride, envy, and covetousness], it is their duty to reclaim the Holy Land from the undeserving: 'we owe to calenge þe heritage [þat] oure fader left to vs and do it out of straunge men hondis' (4) [we owe it to the heritage that our father left to us to take it out of strange men's hands]. Sir John, however, is less a crusader than an observer, as scholars including Stephen Greenblatt, Donald Howard, Iain Higgins, and Rosemary Tzanaki have noted. Greenblatt claims in *Marvelous Possessions* that *Mandeville's Travels* is 'about what it means not to take possession, about circulation or wandering as an alternative to ownership, about a refusal to occupy' (27).[13] Ultimately, as Greenblatt suggests, Sir John seems persuaded that Christian men should address their own problems at home before they can properly convert the non-Christians of the East. After the Sultan lectures him about Christian law and how Christian men do not abide by it, Sir John comments:

> And þanne hadde Y grete merueyl of þis grete sclaundre of [oure faith], for þei þat schulde be yturned þurʒ oure good ensample to þe feiþ of Ihesu Crist, þei beþ ydrawe awey þurʒ oure wickide lyuyng. And þerfore it is no wonder þouʒ þei clepe vs wicked. But þe Sarasyns beþ trewe, for þei kepiþ wel þe comaundementis of here *Alkaron* … (Defective 61)

---

13 This quotation refers explicitly to what Greenblatt says his chapter will address, but it also
refers to the work done by *Mandeville's Travels.*

[And then I marveled at this great slander of our faith, because they that should be converted by our good example to the faith of Jesus Christ are drawn away by our wicked living. And therefore it is no wonder that they call us wicked. But the Saracens are true, because they keep well the commandments of their *Alkaron* ...]

Sir John's ambulation through the Holy Land and beyond, then, provides a lesson about the desire for crusade and conversion, as the narrator implicitly asks those who would crusade and convert to first improve their own adherence to Christian tenets, and to pay attention to the function of their own communities.[14]

While *Mandeville's Travels* is a text concerned with the journeys of Sir John and the spread of Christianity, it is also a text concerned with the circulation of bodies. The experience of the monstrous is an important part of his book. Sir John brings forth a number of such fascinating 'dyuersiteez' (209) [diversities] and 'meruaylles' (209) [marvels] in his narrative for an audience of medieval readers at home, providing an encounter with these monstrous bodies for the gratification of curious onlookers as well as a warning for the well-being of potential travelers. However, *Mandeville's Travels* is interested in an even more specific kind of circulation: that of reproductive bodies.[15] Sir John limits his own engagement in this particular sphere. He writes the book when he is old and infirm, without mentioning a family of his own: 'and now am come to rest, as man discomfited fro age and travail and feebleness of body that constrain me thereto' (Egerton 222) [and now I am come to rest as a man overcome by age and physical labor and feebleness of body that keep me at home].[16] We have no way of knowing what has

---

[14] For further discussion on the problems of pilgrimage and crusading, see Tzanaki.

[15] Shoaf, in *Chaucer's Body*, also uses the term 'circulation' in a figurative and abstract sense. He notes that the term 'circulation' would have been a word familiar to Chaucer from his reading in alchemy (3). He further notes the definition of the term from the *Middle English Dictionary*: 'circulacioun n. [L] Alch. The operation or process of changing the "body" (by heating or cooling) from one 'element' into another, or an instance of it' (MED C: 276). Circulation, in alchemical terms, means the transformation of a body from one thing into something else entirely, thus corresponding with Caroline Bynum's discussion of metamorphosis, to be discussed later. Shoaf himself uses the phrase 'anxiety of circulation' to denote a number of upheavals in the fourteenth century in England, from the Black Death to the mobility of the lower classes (4). He comments: 'All these phenomena, and many others, can usefully be understood as instances of greater, more fluid, and finally more mysterious circulation – of goods and people as well as signs' (4). Thus, the term 'circulation' functions economically as well as geographically. In a search of the Middle English corpus through the *Middle English Dictionary*, more than 100 forms of 'circulation' appeared. These occurrences concerned topics from alchemy, potion-making, the circulation of liquids through the body, circulations in the heavens (particularly of the planets or the sun), and the circulation of the four elements.

[16] For this portion of the chapter, I cite the versions of *Mandeville's Travels* that most clearly express a common idea. Each version carries a section making a similar point, although the Defective version has a significantly truncated version of the final section. For example, this is the Cotton rendition of this passage: 'And now I am comen hom mawgree myself to reste for gowtes Artetykes þat me distreynen þat deffynen the ende of my labour ...' (210) [And now, in

passed in the thirty-four years between pilgrimage and the composition of his narrative for this fictional character, but we do know that he shuns a marriage while he travels. Sir John brings back only the story of his travels rather than a nuptial and familial and thus enduring bond to the East, choosing to forego a marriage to a Babylonian princess: 'And he wolde haue maryed me full highly to a gret Princes doughter 3if I wolde han forsaken my lawe & my beleue' (Cotton 21) [And he [the Sultan] would have married me full highly to a great Prince's daughter if I would have forsaken my law and my belief].[17] Greenblatt regards this refusal as 'his own version of renunciation in the service of the Christian faith' (27), and sees it as a part of his larger project to travel without 'taking possession.' Sir John's circulation is, in a sense, finite and clear: although he has conversations with some of the most powerful men in the East, and even serves them militarily, he does not foster connections. Although he is a knight, he maintains a kind of religious purity, in that he will not marry outside of his faith. This articulation of his physically circulating but sexually restricted body attempts to set him up as impervious to the Other, and thus also to the monstrous.

Where Sir John's reproductive circulation is carefully guarded, that of the Eastern peoples is laid open before him and his readers, as he regularly accounts for the marital and reproductive practices of the communities he visits. Usually at stake in these accounts is the way in which women are exchanged, thereby creating connections between and among communities. Because Sir John himself is 'off the market,' he does not participate in the reproductive economies of the places he visits; he is able to maintain a kind of distance and avoid particular kinds of social obligation. As Gayle Rubin, in her influential essay, 'The Traffic in Women: Notes on the 'Political Economy' of Sex,' writes:

> Kinship systems do not merely exchange women. They exchange sexual access, genealogical statuses, lineage names and ancestors, rights and people – men, women, and children – in concrete systems of social relationships. These relationships always include certain rights for men, others for women. 'Exchange of women' is a shorthand for expressing that the social relations of a kinship system specify that men have certain rights in their female kin, and that women do not have the same rights either to themselves or to their male kin. (177)

These practices of exchange form the basis of society, denoting to whom one is related, and thus to whom one owes loyalty or property. Particularly important here is the lack of control women possess over their own bodies and choices, as we can see in the Sultan's offer of a Prince's daughter for Sir John. Although men and

---

spite of everything, I have come home to rest because of gout and arthritis that restrain and mark the end of my labor …].

17 The Defective version states this just a little less clearly: 'he wolde þat I hadde weddid a grete princes dou3ter and riche of his londe, so þat I wolde haue forsake my treuþe' (21–2) [he [the Sultan] wished that I had married the daughter of a great prince, rich in lands, so that I would have forsaken my faith].

children exist as part of the transaction in the system, women are the commodity given by men to other men. Therefore, when Sir John removes his own body from circulation, he makes a choice not available to the women who are exchanged within these cultures. He is exogamous to these communities, like the monsters who will infiltrate them; however, unlike the monsters, Sir John maintains the binary of us/them in remaining out of circulation, and therefore avoiding miscegenation.

Miscegenation – a circulation of bodies that is too exogamous – is a practice deserving of serious censure by medieval communities. To marry too far away, either geographically or socially, means the kin group will be able to collect less consistent favors or rewards for the new relationship they have formed. Therefore, medieval women's sexual and reproductive circulation is controlled not only by their parents' financial interests, but also by the interests of their local authorities.[18] Exogamous marriages – even those that are geographical rather than religious or racial – demand particular social and legal responses.[19] However, responses to religious or racial exogamy are severe: Cohen, in *Medieval Identity Machines*, points out that laws forbade unions between Christian men and Jewish and Moslem women, remarking that 'such miscegenation was associated with bestiality and sodomy, and was likewise punishable by death' (201–2).[20] Miscegenation disrupts the proper flow of inheritance; these other prohibitions – which invoke the crossing of physical boundaries of sex, gender, and even humanity – act to control and delimit men's and women's sexual choices, behavior, and reproduction.

It is by equating miscegenation with qualities of hybrid identity that these acts are meant to be proscribed. However, the anxieties about, and laws regarding, such sexual practices demonstrate that they very likely occur. The fact that moments of miscegenation are visible in literature shows that communities are not as impermeable as might be hoped. Miscegenation, however, seems to be visible and recognizable in many of the representations explored by Cohen.

---

18 While families may police the ways children marry, larger social forces could also dictate to people whom they should or should not marry: 'Feudal lords demanded that widows and heiresses who controlled property for which they owed military service must marry men who were capable of making good the obligation' (Brundage, *Law* 438). Thus, municipal authorities could intervene in individual affairs, and punish women who did not make what they deemed to be appropriate (read: financially beneficial to the local area) matches. In fact, 'some towns penalized women who chose to marry men who lived outside the city limits' (499).

19 Brundage claims that miscegenation, 'sexual relations between a Latin Christian and a non-Christian partner who was also non-European,' could result in harsh punishments: 'a Latin man found guilty of miscegenation with a Saracen woman was to be castrated, while the woman was to have her nose removed' (*Law* 207).

20 He also notes, however, that characters like Bevis of Hampton and Guillaume d'Orange marry Saracen women, who ultimately convert to Christianity. One might argue that these conversions echo larger cultural desires to convert and gain control over Moslem lands. It is interesting that such a desire might be achieved through cross-cultural exchange of these converted women.

However, *Mandeville's Travels* demonstrates a much more frightening prospect. Many of the monsters in Sir John's narrative are not confined strictly to monstrous communities. They have intercourse with humans, and may even be part of human communities. As I shall demonstrate, the dispersal of these monstrous bodies is of profound concern for human communities because the division between the monstrous body and the human body in *Mandeville's Travels* is at times invisible, particularly because of the possibility of transformation of these bodies. The exchange and circulation of women's bodies, then, becomes a far more socially and individually perilous system. When bodies become trans-formative, monstrosity becomes illegible: in Middle English literature, one no longer is precisely what one seems. The gendered bodies of transformative monsters in *Mandeville's Travels*, then, challenge and disrupt the cultural exchange and circulation of women's bodies.

THE DRAGON WOMAN:
OUT OF CIRCULATION

Despite the fact that monsters appear throughout Sir John's narrative, critics often split it into two halves: the religious first half, and the marvelous second. In the first, he journeys through the Holy Land, speaks with the Sultan about the prob-lems of Christianity, and rejects marriage to a prince's daughter. In the second half, he moves past the Holy Land into the marvelous East. Here he encounters the communities of the Great Khan and Prester John, two powerful leaders, and he sees unfamiliar and fascinating parts of the world before journeying home. Donald Howard argues that these two halves of the text are set against each other structur-ally and purposefully: 'The book, for all its digressiveness, is remarkably struc-tured; its two parts are set against each other so as to reveal a common truth from different perspectives' (67).[21] However, I argue that these structural categories are not absolute. The first half is not devoid of monsters, just as the second half is not devoid of Christianity. In fact, of the four transformative monsters that are the concern of this chapter, two appear in the first half and two appear in the second half – and those in the first half do not mirror those of the second half. Instead, the dispersion of these monsters indicates that they are not geographically limited to a single and exotic space – they are everywhere. Therefore, a witness cannot simply ride away and safely distance himself from these monsters. They are implicated in, not simply extracted from, civilization.

The first two transformative monsters of the text are, in some ways, historically removed from the narrator. Rather than being monsters he claims to witness, they are described to him as parts of the history of the geography he encounters. They

---

21 For Howard, the first half is a journey through biblical time while the second half is a journey through a time *before* biblical time.

are fundamentally linked to the places in which they exist – the dragon woman because she is the heir to a kingdom, and the monstrous head because it causes the destruction of the city of Satalia. In each case, the women are part of a particular economic and cultural situation, one that is disrupted, changing their status and their abilities to circulate properly. In both situations, women's monstrous bodies challenge the system that is meant to circulate them. As Rubin claims,

> If it is women who are being transacted, then it is the men who give and take them who are linked, the woman being a conduit of a relationship rather than a partner to it … [This] does imply a distinction between gift and giver. If women are the gifts, then it is men who are the exchange partners. ("Traffic" 174)

In neither case do men participate properly in exchange because the women seem to exist independently of families and fathers. They, in a sense, become partners in their own exchange – an adaptation of the system that is not only unproductive, but also dangerous for entire communities. This is certainly true for the dragon-shaped daughter of Hippocrates, whose father and community have long been absent when, just outside of Constantinople, Sir John learns of her story.[22] She functions as a danger to the community precisely because she is trans-formative, and cannot circulate or be properly exchanged.

In his description of this first transformative monster, Sir John indicates a divi-sion between the monstrous form and the human trapped inside, one that is not entirely borne out through the narrative. Although he does not actually witness this creature, he explains its nature to his audience: 'And somme seiþ þat in þat yle of Lango is Ypocras douȝter in schap of a dragoun þat is an hundred feet long, as men seiþ, for Y haue not yseye it' (Defective 15) [And some say that in the isle of Cos is Hippocrates' daughter in the shape of a dragon that is a hundred feet long, as men say, because I have not seen it]. The monster here is clearly identified as human: she is the daughter of a known man who has only assumed the 'schap,' or in the Cotton version, 'forme and lykness' (14) [form and likeness], of a dragon – she is not really a dragon at heart. Therefore, her appearance – her shape or her form – is monstrous but, the author seems to suggest, her essence as well as her

---

[22] Although discussed cursorily by recent scholars, her significance has historically been over-looked; for instance, Bennett, in *Rediscovery*, remarks on the dragon woman only because the Mandeville author changes the location of the tale from the location in his source material, and she never comments on the details of the story itself (50). More recently, Higgins has noted the tale's early placement in the narrative, 'coming as it does right after the apology for digressing into "choses estranges," this local legend … both reinforces and supplements the already established expectations about *The Book*'s heterogeneous nature and capacious extent – incidentally disproving the common recent view that the *Mandeville* author's "taste for romancing" grew as he went and took "bolder flight" only when the text passes beyond the biblical East' (*Writing East* 85). The significance of this story, however, lies not only in the fact that its location suggests another geographical possibility for marvels, but also in the geographical and social proximity of such a marvel to recognizable and civilized human communities like Constantinople.

lineage are quite human. Not only is this identity human, but it is also, as Tzanaki suggests, noble: 'Thus we are dealing with a person of noble birth; her noble nature is at least partly retained while she is externally a monster' (153). Despite the outward form of dragon, he describes her inward reality as both human and noble.

It is precisely because she is noble that the transformation of this girl is so troubling. She has not set the spell on herself; instead she has been enchanted, by Diana in most versions, but by a cruel 'stepmoodire' (673) [stepmother] in the Metrical: 'And heo was þus chaungid fro a feire damysel to a dragoun þur a goddess þat men clepiþ Deane' (Defective 15) [And she was thus changed from a fair damsel to a dragon by a goddess that men call Diana]. While Diana's classical association with female chastity lends her motivation to maintain the young woman's virginity, we can only suppose that the stepmother's desire to keep her out of circulation stems from the stereotypical dynastic impulse of most fairytale stepmothers.[23] The stepmother wants to replace the rightful daughter with her own children, thus subverting the uppermost level of the class structure by effectually neutralizing or neutering the heir to the throne. The only way for this enchantment to be broken is through the kiss of a man both appropriately classed and brave, a knight: 'And men seiþ þat heo schal dwelle so to þe tyme þat a kny3t come þat is so hardy þat dar go to here and kisse here mouþ, and þan schal heo turne a3en to here owne kynde and be a woman, and aftir þat heo schal not lyue longe' (15) [And men say that she shall dwell in this way until the time that a knight comes that is so hardy that he dares to go to her and kiss her mouth, and then shall she turn again into her own kind and be a woman, and after that she shall not live long]. This kind of spell may seem very familiar to modern readers; however, it is not the frog that is transformed into a handsome man but the body of the woman that is transformed upon the arrival and success of a worthy contender from the proper social class. Her status as inwardly human is reaffirmed here, when the author declares not only that she will be a woman again but that this transformation will enact a return 'to here owne kynde.'

Her imminent death upon the transformation, however, shows both the danger of her body and the disruption of the system of sexual circulation. If transformation means death, does the young woman truly seek to be transformed? Her actions and reactions are certainly complicated by the ultimate outcome of her transformation. A fundamental element of the traffic of women is the notion that women are the objects of trade, although they are not complicit in the act of trading, as Rubin notes ("Traffic" 174). Thus, neither do women trade themselves, nor do the most significant profits of the transaction benefit them. However, no one is left to trade the dragon woman but herself, and it seems clear that she will see little real benefit in re-entering the system of commerce. She will be dead, having provided her husband with no progeny, although she will endow him with

---

23 The Bodley version says that Diana transforms her because she is envious (426), so the impulse for the maintenance of her virginity is not emphasized in quite the same way.

her land. Similarly we must question the impulses of the knights who come to offer the transformative kiss. What is the reward for the knight if his betrothed will soon be dead? The inheritance of the kingdom seems more likely than either the promise of a lovely wife or the satisfaction of saving a damsel from her own body. If such a financial and social boon is the primary motivation for the knight, then the knight is a fundamentally flawed representative of this ideal class. Marriage for him should be a means of establishing a proper lineage, and no children can be gotten from a dead wife. Just as her body would be out of circulation, so too would his be.

Her contact with the first knight to visit her, 'the knight of Rhodes,' reveals both his inadequacy and her own internalized monstrous behavior. He is clearly flawed, lacking both bravery and the ability to uphold his boasts to win her. When he does approach, with the intention of kissing the dragon, he sees her and flees because he 'sau3 it so [hydous]' (Defective 15) [saw it was so (hideous)]. Among the variations of the Defective version, the description of her repulsive form is augmented in other ways, one manuscript saying 'meruelous' instead of hideous, another adding 'hydous and so horrible' [hideous and so horrible], and yet another declaring that he ran when he saw 'the huge beest' (15, note) [the huge beast]. While the text emphasizes the horrors of the dragon's form, it also suggests that any knight worthy of winning her hand and her kingdom must be brave enough to face such a monster. The Defective, Cotton, Bodley, and Egerton versions attribute the knight's death directly to the dragon's actions, as a direct and angry response to his cowardice and failure.[24] After he flees, 'þe dragoun folewid after and toke þe kni3t and bare hym mawgre his teeþ on a roche, and of þat roche heo caste hym into þe see, and so was þe kni3t lost' (15) [the dragon followed after and took the knight and bore him in (her) teeth onto a rock, and from that rock she cast him into the sea, and so the knight was lost]. The Cotton lends her act just a little more violence, because she carries him by 'his hede' (15) [his head] to fling him into the sea. The knight is clearly a failed representative of his class, unfit to marry her and to rule a kingdom because of his inability to perform as a proper knight should. Her monstrous form, in a sense, prevents upward mobility for a knight who is clearly undeserving.

While deserved, the punishment of the knight also raises concerns about the woman who enacts it – the gentlewoman trapped inside the hideous body of the monster. The dragon form preserves her life, but does it preserve her humanity? While we have been assured early on that the dragon 'doþ no man harm but yf ony

---

[24] In the Metrical version, we do not even have a chance to hear about the knight's reaction, because his horse is so violent: the horse takes one look at the dragon and 'He fledde for feere and wolde naught bide/ Til he come to the see side,/ And into the see lepe the hors than,/ And so was lost both hors and man' (693–6) [he fled for fear and would not stay until he came to the seaside, and the horse leapt into the sea, and so both the horse and the man were lost]. The death of the knight cannot be blamed on his own desire to run, or on the dragon's response to his running; instead, 'his failure is explained as the result of the dragon's great ugliness rather than his own lack of courage' (Tzanaki 157).

man do here harm' (Defective 15) [will do no man harm unless any man should do her harm], this story offers an intriguing glimpse of human motivation and dragonish action. Even if we consider the knight's cowardice to be deserving of death, the audience should be shocked that the damsel in distress functions as the agent of his demise. Her female human reaction to the insult and rejection by the knight leads to her dragonish murder of him. However much we are told she is only dragon on the outside, she seems to have assimilated some of the behaviors inherent in the physical form of a dragon. The transformation of her body serves as more than a disguise of the real girl inside. Bynum argues that in the act of transformation, 'something perdures, carried by the changing shape that never completely loses physical or behavioral traces of what it was' (*Metamorphosis* 32). Although the human resides inside the dragon, the physical possibilities of the dragon body change the abilities and identity of the human inside. Just as traces of the human remain, so must traces of the dragon.

The dragon body that informs the human identity, however, is not entirely permanent. Because of this transformative ability, the woman's human body is misleading and open to misinterpretation. Somehow the young woman is able to transform back and forth, for a young man who does not know about the curse comes upon her castle after a shipwreck and finds her in human form. He sees 'a damysel þat kembid here heed and lokid in a myrrour, and heo hadde myche tresour aboute here, and he trowid þat heo hadde be a comyne woman þat dwelled þere to kepe men' (Defective 15–16) [a damsel that combed her hair and looked in a mirror, and she had much treasure around her, and he thought that she was a common woman (a prostitute) that dwelled there to keep men]. This man, who is notably *not* a knight, considerably misreads her situation. Instead of recognizing her as being *out* of circulation, he sees her as a much-traded object, a prostitute. He assumes that she has earned the treasure lying around through the exchange of her body. Readers, however, recognize that she, like the money and castle, is an economic asset that is not being properly transferred because of her monstrous form. The treasure may also serve to remind us that she is a dragon that does what dragons do: sit on treasure. The image functions multivalently to suggest the same truth that the man misunderstands: she is an unusable commodity. Moreover, the mirror that she gazes into serves as a reminder of the problem of her physicality. The mirror, often a symbol of female vanity, duplicity, and falseness, asks us to decide upon her true identity. Higgins suggests that, 'Perhaps the mirror into which the damsel gazes is a symbol less of vanity than of self-knowledge: powerless to help herself, the passive figure understands her situation and motives far better than the two lecherous suitors do their own' (*Writing East* 88). Does the mirror reflect her true form, the human one, or does it suggest a trick that the unsuspecting young man will soon suffer? Upon considering the mirror, readers are asked to decide which is the true identity of the maiden: her original form or the monstrous one imposed upon her? Perhaps the unsettling answer to such a question is that, because traces of the dragon will always remain, the maiden and the dragon are truly inextricable.

While the audience might feel pity for the trapped woman, it must also recall her violent response to the knight of Rhodes. If we recognize that a real (although cowardly) knight failed, then we can only expect worse for this poor sailor who has so grievously misread her situation. We must see her as at least a little dangerous – a little more dragon and a little less human than the simple spell suggests. The woman tells the man to make his shipmates knight him and to return to her the next morning; however, this transition seems less than convincing because class status simply cannot be that easily changed. She also warns him not to fear what he might find and assures him that he will be repaid for his efforts:

> And heo bade hym haue no drede, for heo schulde do hym non harm yf al hym þou3t þat heo were [hidous] to se. Heo seide it was don by enchauntement, for heo seide þat heo was siche as he sau3 here þanne. And heo seide 3if he kissed here, he schulde haue al þe tresour and be lord of here and of þese yles.
>
> (Defective 16)

> [And she bade him have no fear, for she would do him no harm, if all he thought that she was (hideous) to see. She said it was done by enchantment, for she said that she was such as he saw her then. And she said if he kissed her, he would have all the treasure and be lord of her and of these isles.]

Her promises of what he will gain by kissing her further suggest her anticipated return to economic circulation. However, according to Rubin, she should not be responsible for her own exchange: 'To enter into a gift exchange as a partner, one must have something to give. If women are for men to dispose of, they are in no position to give themselves away' ("Traffic" 175). In this way, the dragon woman steps outside of the structure of the traffic in women, just as she tries to uphold it. The assets of the castle have been removed from the community by her transformation, and they must be restored for the community to regain function. Yet the system has been corrupted by her participation in it as a partner; the patriarchy cannot be adequately restored by a woman exchanging her own body, a body that is and will remain exogamous by its monstrous nature.

Indeed, the new knight is destined to fail, in part because the dragon woman fails to establish a proper exchange for herself: he is neither 'hardy' nor really a nobleman. His knighthood, bestowed by his shipmates, is neither valiantly won nor validly granted. He is less of a knight than the knight of Rhodes, a fact that seems to be noted by the dragon, as she reacts less violently to him:

> And when he sau3 here come out of þe caue in likenes of a dragoun, he hadde so grete drede þat he fli3 to þe schip. And heo folewid hym, and when heo sau3 he turned no a3en, heo bigan to crie as a þing þat hadde grete sorwe, and heo turned a3en. And als soone þe kni3t deide. (16)

> [And when he saw her come out of the cave in the likeness of a dragon, he had such great fear that he flew to the ship. And she followed him, and when she saw he did not turn back again, she began to cry like a thing that had great sorrow, and she turned back again. And also soon the knight died.]

136

This time she does not kill the man so recently made a knight. Like the dragon, the audience should note his cowardice but criticize it less, as he is not truly a knight. In most of the versions he dies not from her violence but later from fear, as the Bodley version clarifies: he 'soone deide for feredness that he had whenne he saw3 hir come after him' (427) [soon died because of the fear that he had when he saw her come after him].[25] His attempt to change social class is not only futile but also fatal. He is killed not by an outside source, like the first knight who fails to live up to the standards of his class, but by an inherent weakness. The dragon woman simply does not hold the same expectations for him as she did for a real knight, and so does not punish him herself; her attempt to exchange herself has failed.

In this second interaction, the monster's dual nature and geographical location become clearly linked with danger to the community. Here the dragon woman's human emotions overpower any dragonish action. Higgins argues that the audience feels sympathy for the monster, saying 'one can hardly deny that the erotic legend is told in a manner that evokes pity for the transformed, trapped, and desperately human damsel rather than awe or terror at the power of pagan magic, as one might expect in a pilgrim's guide' (*Writing East* 88). We are invited to feel pity at the conclusion of the tale when the final lines inform us that no knight has yet met with success. While we cannot help but critique a class of knights that fails at a task requiring no real fight with the monster, we also cannot ignore the hybrid nature of the dragon woman. This narrative therefore figures the men participating in the exchange as nearly as problematic as the body that cannot and should not be exchanged. Her person and situation remain an alluring attraction and have enticed a number of knights, members of the elite class who are responsible for propagating their bloodlines, to very unproductive deaths. The human body that drew the ignorant sailor in through its attractiveness and (false) availability continues to lead men astray with its promises of plenty: 'But when a kni3t comeþ þat is so hardy to kisse here, he schal not dei3e but he schale turne þat damysele into here ri3te schap, and he schal be lord of here and þe yles biforeseid' (Defective 16) [But when a knight comes that is so hardy to kiss her, he shall not die but he shall turn that damsel into her right shape, and he shall be lord of her and the isles mentioned before]. Higgins comments that this is a '(mocking?) challenge to chivalric readers' (*Writing East* 88); they are invited to prove their worth in view of clear evidence of their failure.

The dragon woman remains a danger to communities precisely because her body is transformative. Monstrosity removes her from the social role she ought to occupy – it interrupts the processes of both reproduction and inheritance. Although the story is often seen as a less-than-serious diversion, the consequences for a knightly community seem serious. Because the fictional Sir John, the aged

---

25 In the Metrical version, he does not die at all; he flees in line 745 and in line 746 the author begins talking about the geography of Rhodes.

knight as a narrator, is painted somewhat ironically, the comment on knighthood here is often taken to be similarly satirical, as Tzanaki indicates:

> And it is true that an episode which could have been no more than a frightening monster story has been transformed into a tale where the 'knight' unexpectedly proves to be an anti-hero and the dragon is the wronged victim. This reversal of the expectations of romance, while preserving its attributes, is a humorous development ... Mandevillian irony is used here to parody romance as well as to make a more serious point. (155)

But what is this serious point? Higgins suggests that 'the legend can be read as an indirect critique of the knightly estate partly resembling the more open attack in the exordium, which reproaches those involved in divisive quarrels at home when there is a divine inheritance to be won overseas' (*Writing East* 86). While this claim reflects the primary set of concerns of *Mandeville's Travels*, it also ignores another serious comment made about communities at home. Marital circulation is a part of this economic equation, and women's bodies are the basis for this circulation, as is all too evident in the dangerously remote transformative body of Hippocrates' daughter, the dragon woman. The woman's body, in this episode, is bound to the monstrous one. Because she is monstrous, she is capable of taking lives, but because she is transformative, she presents the tempting possibility of reintegration. The latter makes her most dangerous.

NECROPHILIA AND THE REPRODUCTIVE BODY

Community and women's bodies also figure significantly in the following story about the fall of the city of Satalia.[26] The story of the dragon woman of Cos and the story of Satalia both center on problems of marital and sexual commerce. The dragon woman's transformative body prevents her from circulating as she ought to, but it also demonstrates the danger of placing a monstrous body into the system of sexual exchange. Like the dragon woman's story, the tale of Satalia is one about the conjunction between desire and monstrosity. It is a story frequently overlooked by scholars, who do not take its point to be serious, read, as it often is, as a kind of counterpoint to the preceding story of Hippocrates' daughter. As Tzanaki notes, 'Coming as it does so soon after the dragon-woman tale, this story shows certain thematic similarities: a lady, a love, a wrongful deed, a horrible monster and vengeance wreaked on the perpetrator of the act' (158). While these

---

26 While many critics discuss Hippocrates' daughter, they pay much less attention to the fall of Satalia. Most often, the two stories are linked both structurally and thematically by scholars. Howard argues that the stories of Hippocrates' daughter and the fall of Satalia, which he sees as paired together purposely, reflect the corresponding structure of *Mandeville's Travels* as a whole. However, he ultimately fails to comment at any length or with any detail on the meaning of the stories.

thematic similarities are fair, the more important elements to notice in both stories are the ways that desiring and monstrous bodies destroy communities. The monstrous bodies in this tale, however, are very different from the barren body of the tragic dragon woman. The story of the fall of Satalia offers two quite complicated kinds of transformative bodies not present in the story of Hippocrates' daughter: the reproductive body and the dead body.

At the center of this story is a young man who transgresses the sexual boundary between living and dead bodies. Mandeville recounts the narrative of the destroyed city of Satalia that has been lost 'þurȝ þe foly of a ȝong man' (Defective 17) [through the folly of a young man]. This young man has lost his beloved: 'þer was a faire damysele þat he loued wele, and heo deide sodenly and was [put] in a graue of marbel' (17) [there was a fair damsel that he loved well and she died suddenly and was put in a grave of marble]. Like the knight killed by the dragon woman, he is a man of some status according to the Metrical version, which claims he was 'a burgeis sone of grete renoun' (763) [a burgess' son of great renown]. Despite his good reputation, he engages in a behavior that is not only ignoble, but also perverse: 'And for þe grete loue þat he hadde to here, he went on a nyȝt to here graue and openyd it and went yn and lay by here and ȝeode his way' (Defective 17) [And because of the great love that he had for her, he went at night to her grave and opened it and went in and lay by her and went his way]. The Cotton version attributes his act to 'lust' rather than love (16). His necrophilic act is problematic because he transgresses the boundary between living and dead bodies, and in doing so he does not perpetuate his line with a woman who can bear children. He has closed off his own genetic transmission in the community, much like Hippocrates' daughter, whose ability to circulate has been foreclosed by her enchanted and transformed body.

While he is the one acting perversely, it is the dead body of his lover that becomes transformed. Just as he crossed the boundary between living and dead by engaging in sexual relations with a dead woman, so does her body transgress this boundary by performing the functions of a living body. Nine months later,[27] the young man hears a voice that tells him to return to her grave and to open it 'and behold what þou hast gete of here, and if þou go nouȝt, þou schalt haue grete harm' (Defective 17) [and behold what you have gotten by her, and if you do not go, you shall have great harm]. The man returns to the grave as he is directed, and upon opening the tomb, he releases the monstrous birth of his dead lover – a hideous head: 'þer flowe out an hede riȝt [hidous] to se, þe whiche alsoone flowe aboute þe cite and þe cuntre, and als soone þe cite sank doun' (17) [there flew out a head right (hideous) to see, which immediately flew about the city and the country, and immediately the city sank down]. The Egerton adds 'horrible' to 'hideous' (19), while the Bodley offers even more description: 'Thenne anon flewe out of the towmbe as it had ben in manere of an heede of a foule forshapen

---

[27] The length of time in the Metrical and Bodley versions is twelve months, while Egerton, Cotton, and Defective go by the natal nine.

horrible beest' (428) [Then at once flew out of the tomb something in the manner of the head of a foul transformed horrible beast]. In the Metrical version, the head, along with its eye and countenance, are 'brennynge' (784) [burning], and they catch the city aflame and 'brent it clene vnto þe grounde' (786) [burned it clean unto the ground]. When the young man turns away from proper exchange, he disrupts the system of marriage by which communities reproduce themselves: 'Kinship rules enabling the circulation of women also ensure that if there is a shortage of women of child-bearing age, then those available are enabled to bear children, since they are assigned to a husband' (Craib 50–51). Although he performs the office of a husband, he does not do so with a living woman with whom he could produce an heir. As an heir himself, it is his duty to marry and reproduce, but he does not abide by the rules of circulation. He traffics not in the body of a woman who can yield heirs, but rather one who can only produce death. Therefore, it is the young man's desire, a desire for a body which can no longer circulate because it is no longer living, that results in the destruction of the entire community.

The crime in this story is not so much the necrophilia – although it is obviously punished – but the young man's inability to integrate himself into the economy of marriage and community. We never witness the supposed birth of this horrifying head, but both the length of time of its gestation (nine months) and the fact that the voice claims that the young man 'gets' it by his dead lover suggest that the head is the monstrous progeny of the perverse union. Instead of reproducing his wealthy line within a sanctioned union, the young man reproduces death and destruction in the form of an incomplete and horrifying monster. Only in the Bodley version is the head described as being that of a beast; the absence of description in the other texts suggests that it takes a more human shape, as it is the (monstrous) product of human bodies. The feminine processes of pregnancy and birth imply a natural kind of transformation of the human form; the processes of death and decay are similarly natural. However, by combining the properties of both birth and death, the author offers a new kind of monster – one not associated with the more recognizable living dead. The dead lover here does not perambulate or even function as more than a plot device; she is the means through which the young man enacts his perversion. And yet it is her body, inappropriately placed by her lover into an exogamous transaction (because she is dead and he is living), that exceeds the boundaries of humanity. While the flaming head is clearly monstrous, the more dangerous monster is the living dead body of his lover, a hybrid female body that operates productively and destructively, which lures him even after death. The young man's union with the monstrous – a thing that looks like his lover but is transformed by death – results not only in the horrifying head, but in the literal destruction of the entire city of Satalia.

The Mandeville author emphasizes ideas about dangerous unions, monstrous bodies, and destroyed communities by linking the story of the dragon woman with the story of the fall of Satalia. In one, a proper knight is required to relieve the dragon of her 'hideous' form, while in the other the son of a prominent figure in the community engages in an unsanctioned and exogamous union. In both, whole communities are punished: Cos waits indefinitely for Hippocrates' daughter to marry, providing a new leader, and Satalia is destroyed because the burgess' son fathers a monster with his dead lover. Howard argues that their pairing reflects two sides of the same coin: 'one is about the possible and hopeful, the other about the forbidden and dreadful; in one death may be overcome, in the other death is hideously reproduced. It would not be impossible to see in them a suggestion of salvation and damnation, spiritual life and spiritual death' (66). While the fall of Satalia is certainly representative of spiritual death, I argue that the story of the dragon woman seems more reflective of futility and the crisis of the transformative body that is hopelessly dual. Although she might still be rescued from her dragon form by a kiss, the result of such 'salvation' is ultimately death for her. Once transformed, the body cannot be truly redeemed; it carries with it lasting traces of the other identity. Campbell, too, remarks on the paradox represented by both stories, as well as by *Mandeville's Travels* as a whole. For her, the East through which Mandeville travels is a paradox because it simultaneously represents biblical history and the marvelous. The tales of Satalia and Hippocrates' daughter reflect just such a paradox, in their representation of a series of images that she claims carry through the text as a whole: 'tomb/ditch/pit/well/breast/flood: earth and water, body and spirit, fecundity and carnality and necrophilia. Paradox is the major arrangement …' (152). The recurrence of such images noted by Campbell reflects larger concerns not only with birth and death, but with marriage and reproduction – concerns necessary for the perpetuation of communities. These paradoxical images are excessive; they appear continually throughout the text, but, more importantly, they represent bodies that are excessively changeable and thus untrustworthy.

These two tales represent very similar anxieties about the proper transmission of bodies and the ways that too much or too little circulation can destroy communities. Tzanaki argues that the 'two tales are versions, or rather inversions, of the romance theme of courtly love, taken to unpleasant extremes' (159). They reflect punishments for misbehavior, as 'those who do not live according to the rules of virtue, particularly members of the nobility, are punished accordingly through supernatural means' (160). While the first knight and the young man are clearly punished for behavior inappropriate for nobles, the fact that more innocent characters are also punished complicates the moral lesson. The initially innocent young daughter of Hippocrates is trapped indefinitely in the form of a dragon, alternately killing or weeping over the men who flee her horrifying 'schap,' while the entire city of Satalia suffers for the young man's moral failings. The two tales do function as moral exempla, but the moral is about something less idealistic than virtue. Instead, both tales urge the socially appropriate circulation of stable and human bodies, while they simultaneously suggest that the bodies of women – not just dead women – teeter terrifyingly close to the possibility of monstrous transformation. Most significantly, these women's bodies are affiliated with named and recognizable communities; they are no longer curiosities to be stared at from afar, but are implicated in the processes by which civilized communities live and die.

SELF-INFLICTED MONSTROSITY

The Amazons are the only monsters in *Mandeville's Travels* who transform them-selves, and therefore turn themselves into monsters purposefully. Neither the dragon woman of Cos nor the reproductive dead woman of Satalia manifest control over their own bodies or the transformation of those bodies. While the dragon attempts, unsuccessfully, to exchange herself in the marriage market, the Amazons eschew marriage and construct their own form of sexual circulation, making over not only their bodies but their entire society. In taking possession of their own bodies, they disrupt the patriarchy, but maintain social hierarchy and order in their community and in the surrounding area. However, the connections among these stories are stronger than they might seem. Although the stories of Hippocrates' daughter and the Head of Satalia are told before Sir John reaches Jerusalem, and reflect the distant past of their respective locations,[28] the next two transformative monsters, the Amazons and the poison virgins, are reported after Sir John visits Jerusalem, and as he makes his way through the marvelous East and the lands of the Great Khan and Prester John.[29] While most critics see a strong division between the two halves of *Mandeville's Travels*,[30] I argue that the concerns reflected in the bodies of all of these transformative women show a sustained interest in the boundaries of communities and in the potential of bodies in circula-tion. All of these stories reflect a similar concern about the narrative proximity and reproductive circulation of monstrous bodies. Most significantly, the bodies of the Amazons are associated not with biblical history, as Howard suggests, but with Christian continuity. In their position as guards, they protect humanity from the

[28] The city of Satalia has been completely destroyed by the fiery head, and no new communities have come to exist in its place. Similarly, the community at Cos is also one that exists only in the past, because it has no heir after the King's daughter is turned into the dragon.

[29] They are not a part of what Higgins calls the 'famous set-piece list of monsters' (*Writing East* 150), a list of the traditional Plinian races that shows up in all but the Metrical version. While the list is fascinating, it offers no transformative bodies; moreover, as Tzanaki notes, it 'is a simple listing of attributes, with none of the sociological commentary accorded other strange peoples such as the Cynocephali' (95). These monsters, including the single-footed men, the men with faces in their chests, and the hermaphrodites – derived from Pliny and the *Speculum historiale* (95) – are the monsters most commonly identified with the post-Jerusalem portion of the narrative.

[30] Howard designates the post-Jerusalem portion of the narrative as the 'second half,' and claims that it works as a journey backward in time. Howard claims, 'In this world of the distant past lies the dispersal of individuals, peoples, and languages; at the root of all, the expulsion from Paradise. We pass through the leavings of the *first* age of the world, the age before the law of Moses, the Age of Nature. It is, however, *fallen* nature, nature in decline from its primeval state – a world of grotesques, sports and freaks of nature, of anthropophagi and men whose heads do grow beneath their shoulders ...' (72). This is a fairly limited and unproductive conception of monsters, particularly of the Amazons and poison virgins, who have such great effects on the communities around them.

coming of the next age, which will be hastened by the Jews – the coming of the Antichrist. However, in their authority over their own community and in the configurations of their physical bodies, they remain liminal to 'normal' human society. While most of the non-Christian societies in *Mandeville's Travels* can be considered liminal to some extent, the community of Amazons is differentiated through the marked and monstrous bodies of its members as well as its transgressive social practices.

The Amazons are human women who become monstrous when they mark their bodies as physically different. Rather than a magical transformation by a cruel stepmother or a jealous god, these women effect their own transformation. They cut off one breast of all female children: 'And ʒif it be a female þei don awey þat on pappe with an hote hiren' (Cotton 103) [and if it is a female, they do away with one breast with a hot iron]. This is not mere butchery; it functions practically while simultaneously serving as a marker of social status within the community itself: 'And yf þei be of gentel blood, þei brenne of þe lyft pap for beryng of a schild; and yf þei be of oþer blood, þei brenne of þe riʒt pap for scheotyng of a bowe. For wymmen þere beþ goode werriouris' (Defective 69) [And if they are of gentle blood, they burn off the left breast for the bearing of a shield, and if they are of other blood, they burn off the right breast for the shooting of a bow, because women there are good warriors]. While the process by which the breasts are removed differs among the manuscripts, some suggesting that the breast is burned off, others that it is cut off, the designation of the breast removed according to social class remains unchanged in all manuscripts.[31] Thus, the removal of the breast distinguishes the women not only from external societies, but also within the internal social order. That upper-class women bear shields while lower-class women shoot bows raises interesting questions about this specific division of labor. The fact that certain classes perform certain battle functions is less significant than the fact that such class distinctions are articulated through the form of the body. Single-breastedness, then, not only identifies these women as Amazons, but also declares their class identities within their community. In this case, the transformation serves a social and delineating purpose, as well as constituting a kind of hybrid gender identity. In taking off a breast, these women declare themselves independent of men, and take on the social roles men used to occupy in their community. Their bodies, then, serve as a warning of their *differance*.[32] Through the act of transformation, they declare themselves indelibly Other, and therefore monstrous.[33]

---

31 The Egerton and Bodley versions have female children's breasts being shorn away rather than burned off, although the breasts are said to be burned after they are removed (111, 458).

32 I refer here to the Derridean concept of identity through differentiation, which indicates similarity, but not sameness – a principle that can distinguish the monstrous body from the human one.

33 I would not suggest that single-breastedness in contemporary culture is in any way the same thing. I am speaking specifically here about purposeful and not medical interventions in the

Through their single-breasted, and therefore monstrous, bodies, the Amazons transform themselves in much the same way that this community's female-only identity developed: through physical actions in response to troubling social circumstances. The Amazons, who 'wole suffre no man among hem noþer to haue lordschipe of hem' (Defective 68) [will suffer no man to (live) among them nor to have lordship of them], were once defined by their roles as wives and mothers left behind in war. Their King, Solapence,[34] 'was sleiȝe in bateil and al þe good blood of his lond wiþ hym' (68) [was slain in battle and all the good blood of his land with him]. The women, instead of becoming prisoners or settling for lesser men, band together and kill the rest of the men left among them: 'þei gedrid hem togedir and armed hem wel and þei slowe al þe men þat were yleft in here lond' (68) [they gathered together and armed themselves well and they slew all the men that were left in their land].[35] In this moment, the women take charge of the circulation of their own bodies: they decide with whom they will procreate. Although the Defective, Egerton, and Bodley manuscripts make no moral judgments about this action, Cotton comments that when they kill these men the women are 'creatures out of wytt' (102) [creatures out of their minds]. The slaying is troubling, as is evident in Cotton's comment upon their insanity when performing it, but it is not so troubling that the community is shunned by others or condemned by Sir John.[36] It is the action, however, that defines them as a community of women actively without men; as they cut the men from their community, so too do they cut off a breast to enable their performance of the traditionally masculine practice of war. Here it is the arguably monstrous murder of men of 'low blood' that leads to the marking of the body as monstrous. This is quite different from the case of the dragon woman, where the monstrous body informs the monstrous acts that the dragon undertakes. By excising men from their culture, the Amazons remove a version of their femininity, reconstituting how sex, gender, and sexuality function. The removing of the breast visibly marks this shift.

While the excision of men and breasts seems to be antithetical to the continuance of community, it actually protects proper reproductive circulation. It is

body meant to be functional both socially and practically speaking. Ideas of the body and of normality function differently in twenty-first century communities, as is discussed by Warner in *The Trouble with Normal.*

34 He is Colopeus in Cotton, Egerton, and Bodley, while he is Tholopeus in Metrical.

35 Metrical has them fighting and killing the enemy army, as 'alle thaire lordis oolde and yonge' (1804) [all their lords old and young] have been killed. This move makes the women's violence less troubling because it is directed at an enemy army out of vengeance, but still reiterates class issues: while the husbands in the other texts are of 'good blood,' here they are all 'lords,' suggesting a similar class status.

36 Sir John notably refuses to make judgments upon the practices of other cultures, except the Jews, who are painted as completely evil throughout. For a discussion of his unbiased treatment of many communities, see Fleck and Sobecki in addition to Higgins in *Writing East*, Tzanaki, Howard, and Greenblatt.

preferable that these women kill rather than be led by, marry, or have children with men who are not of 'good blood.' This does not mean that they will not continue to circulate with acceptable men: the Amazons do not give up their identities as mothers or even as sexual beings simply because they have banned men from their community, just as they do not lose their identities as women because they cut off a breast and take up the weapons of war. The location of sex acts, however, is not in the center of the community, but is instead liminal to it:

> And whanne þei wole haue ony man to lye by hem, þei sende for hem into a cuntre þat is nere to here lond, and þe men beþ þere viii dayes oþer as longe as þe wymmen wole and þenne þei goþ ayen. (Defective 68–9)

> [And when they wish to have any man lie by them, they send for them into a country that is near to their land and the man is there eight days or as long as the women wish and then they go again.]

Here it is unclear whether the relationship takes place in the Amazons' country, with the man departing after this short period of time, but this issue is clarified by Bodley and Egerton. Bodley says, 'they drawe hem to the side of the londe where her lemannes arn dwellynge, and be with hem ix or x dayes' (457) [they draw themselves to the side of the land where their lovers are dwelling and are with them nine or ten days]. These relationships are external to both countries; they take place instead on the borders between. Seemingly, then, these women disrupt the traffic of their own bodies: they do not marry, or use their bodies as commodities by which they build relations with their neighbors. As Rubin suggests, 'As long as the relations specify that men exchange women, it is men who are the beneficiaries of the product of such exchanges – social organization' ("Traffic" 174). Therefore, because women are now the ones who make the decisions about exchange, they stand to benefit from their own bodies.[37] By controlling the circulation of their own bodies, they control the social organization of their community. If the women bear female children, they become Amazons, and if they have male children, they 'sende hem to here fadris when þei kunne goo and ete' (Defective 69) [send them to their fathers when they can walk and eat].[38] By killing low-class men, the

---

[37] Lochrie argues that Amazons possess a kind of 'queer virginity' (*Heterosyncrasies*, 104), wherein the Amazon 'eschews sexual concourse with men except at scheduled annual times and exclusively for the purpose of creating more females' (104). She also notes that 'this virginity is sexual and martial, but as a virtue it is problematic because it neither excludes desire nor makes itself available to male exchange' (105). While Lochrie uses the figure of the Amazon to challenge notions of heteronormativity, she pays little attention to the specific details of the Amazons in *Mandeville*, whose initial heteronormative context is disrupted by war and its resulting discrepancies in terms of social class. However, she does mark the ways in which the Amazons' control over their own bodies and exchange marks them as perpetually Other.

[38] Cotton, Egerton, and Bodley all say that they may also kill male children, but Defective and

Amazons protect their social structure; this protection of the social order is perpetuated through the class-based removal of the right or the left breast from young girls. Proper circulation is thus ensured through the murder of inappropriate partners, the selection of fathers from nearby lands, and the marking of bodies so that class status cannot be transgressed.

The Amazons are worthy of notice for their effective governance, even as this is affected by their physical forms and social structure. Sir John and members of most surrounding communities marvel at the social structure of the Amazons. In *Mandeville*, they are not merely inversions of femininity as they are elsewhere in medieval literature, as noted by Tzanaki:

> The legend of the Amazons is also transformed into something rather different from its originals. In the *Roman d'Alexandre* and the *Letter of Prester John*, the Amazons are seen as an inversion of normal customs: instead of the knights returning from warfare to their ladies, it is stressed, sometimes comically, that the roles are reversed by the warrior-women. Mandeville's approach is not the same. The Amazons, no longer historical legend but contemporary exoticism, are remarkable more for their admirable political system than their sexual roles. (44)

They are significant for more than their transgressive and fascinating physical forms, or for the ways in which they deploy their sexuality. All the manuscripts say that the Queen 'gouerneþ þat londe wel' (Defective 69) [governs that land well], and all but the Defective manuscript elaborate on the manner of her election and the prowess of the women in general. The women 'maken here queen by electioun þat is most worthy in armes' (Cotton 103) [make her, who is most worthy in arms, queen by election]. Their martial identity is paramount to their ability not only to retain a group identity, but to support themselves financially, for 'þei gon often tyme in sowd to help of oþer kynges in here werres for gold & syluer as othere sowydoures don' (Cotton 103) [they often go as soldiers to help other kings in their wars for gold and silver as other soldiers do]. Quite unlike the dragon woman of Cos, they circulate reproductively and financially, even if they do not marry, nor is their reproduction inherently monstrous and destructive, like the product of the reproductive dead woman of Satalia. The Amazons do destabilize notions of gender by taking on the social roles of both men and women. Rubin argues that gender is socially constructed through the ways in which the sexes divide their labor: 'The division of labor by sex can therefore be seen as a "taboo": a taboo against the sameness of men and women, a taboo dividing the two sexes into two mutually exclusive categories, a taboo which exacerbates the biological differences between the sexes and thereby *creates* gender' ("Traffic" 178). In the community of Amazons, while there are social divisions, there is no sexual division of labor

Metrical erase this more unpleasant possibility. The most popular text, then, the Defective, makes the women less violent and more understandable as human mothers.

146

because there are no men. Women do everything, from parenting, to fighting, to ruling. Therefore, the Amazons upset traditional social systems by taking over the circulation of their own bodies and through the performing of tasks typically belonging to men. However, their behavior also confirms the difference between the sexes by removing all men from their community. The Amazons do not merely break traditional notions of gender; they uphold socially constructed boundaries of class and race, and thus are not entirely disruptive figures. Although they might initially seem to elide the boundaries between the sexes, in actuality they confirm and perpetuate these boundaries through the ways they circulate their bodies only outside their community.

While they themselves circulate sexually, part of their narrative function is to keep undesirables *out* of circulation. They kill off the men of their community who are not of 'good blood,' but, more importantly, they use their physical location and martial prowess to keep the most loathed of groups – the Jews – from circulating freely. Thus, the Amazons, while monstrous and socially disruptive, ultimately serve the good society at large, unlike the rest of the monstrous transformative women in *Mandeville*. The Amazons may be preferable to the Jews, but they still remain external to 'normal' human society. While Sir John is notably tolerant of the many strange cultures he encounters, his attitude toward the Jews is harsh.[39] The Jews here are the twenty-two tribes enclosed, legendarily, by Alexander the Great.[40] They are surrounded on three sides by hills and on the fourth, by the Caspian Sea, and are forced to pay tribute to the Amazons:[41] 'And ȝe schal vndirstonde þat þe Iewis haueþ no lond of here owne to dwelle ynne but among

---

[39] Greenblatt notes: 'And now I turn to the second shadow that falls across *Mandeville's Travels* and darkens the generous accounts of Brahmin mystics, Tibetan cannibals, and Chinese idolators. Such peoples were, of course, completely fantastic for a fourteenth-century European audience, but there was a strange people, an other, actually living in their midst. I am referring to the Jews, and toward them Mandeville is surprisingly ungenerous. The Jews of his own time scarcely figure into his account of the Holy Land ... But when Mandeville turns away from the Dome of the Rock to the sphere beyond, the Jews make several peculiar and highly charged appearances' (50).

[40] Westrem remarks on the author's association of the Jews with Gog and Magog, 'which we have seen literalists in western Europe already doing in the twelfth century' (69). Gog and Magog, he explains, have been adopted 'as a pseudonym for political threats from the Goth under Alaric to the Soviets under Brezhnev' (55). See this article for a study of the historical tradition of Gog and Magog and their geographical representations.

[41] In all but the Defective, it is clearly the Amazons to whom the Jews must pay tribute. In the Defective, the Jews pay tribute to the 'queene of Ermonye' [queen of Armenia] (112). The Index of Places for the Defective version says that Damazyn is another name for Ermonye (231). Perhaps the scribe of this text misread his original referring to the Amazons and thus made this transition. The error on the part of the Defective scribe is borne out by evidence from the later German version, the Von Diemeringen version. The editor of the Egerton text says, 'Von Diemeringen expands the story about the Queen of the Amazons. She was called Pencesolya and she penetrated into the mountain fastness and reached and subdued the enclosed people. He gives a fine picture of the lady seated in conference with two Jews in their

þe[se] hullis, and ȝit þerfore þei paieþ tribute to þe queen of Ermonye' (Defective 112) [and you shall understand that the Jews have no land of their own to dwell in but that between these hills, and yet therefore they pay tribute to the queen of Ermonye]. The Cotton expands on the Jews' inability to leave this land: 'And ȝit þei ȝelden tribute for þat lond to the queen of AMAZOINE the whiche þat maketh hem to ben kept in cloos full diligently tat þei schull not gon out on no side but be the cost of hire lond' (175) [And yet they yield tribute for that land to the queen of the Amazons, who makes them be kept in close full diligently, so that they shall not go out on any side, but by the coast of their land]. The Metrical version makes the relationship the clearest: 'And sho with strength holdith ham in/ That thei may not thens wyn' (2223–4) [And she holds them in with strength so that they may not wend from there]. The Amazons function as guards of the Jews – these monstrous women constitute the boundary between a community completely reviled and the community that reviles them.[42] Once again, the Amazons exist in a liminal space, this time between the Christian and Jewish communities.[43]

Although the Jews function as the most loathed Other in *Mandeville*, the

characteristic medieval hats' (185, note 1). While most other versions do use the term 'Amazon,' this text expands the story so that the name cannot be mistaken in any way.

[42] DiMarco discusses the place of *Mandeville*'s Amazons within the Amazon tradition. He traces two traditions that seem to inform the depiction of the Amazons as the killers of men and the guards set against the Jews, noting that the episode describing their community and practices – particularly their killing of the men of their community – is not meant to comment on their later appearance as guardians (70). He suggests that 'the contradictory conception of her that develops – as the defender against the Jewish Gog/Magog or as convert of the Jewish Antichrist – reflects both the hopes and anxieties latent in Christianity's struggle for hegemony' (81).

[43] *Mandeville*'s treatment of the Jews, while not unusual for medieval literature, is, as Greenblatt has observed, surprising. They are guarded by the Amazons because they are a threat to Christian communities. *Mandeville* sets up a kind of conspiracy theory, one that Scott Westrem claims is the 'most direct claim I know of that European Jews were complicit in a plot against Christians' (68): that Jews around the world maintain the Hebrew language so that they can communicate with the enclosed Jews when they are finally freed by the Antichrist through the form of a fox (Defective 112). When they are free, they will go forth to 'destruye christen men' (Defective 112) [destroy Christian men]. The Jews are clearly a significant threat in the Christian imagination – and certainly in the author of *Mandeville*. In *Mandeville's Travels*, they alone are enclosed and guarded, while creatures with tails and faces in their chests are simply marveled at. Greenblatt argues that this response results from the fact that Jews are not only or necessarily real, but more significantly, present within Christian and European communities, and that they directly compete with Christians for control over the Holy Land: 'they are located, in a way Mandeville evidently finds intolerable, between the realms of the secular and the sacred, metonymy and metaphor, because they embody the estrangement that continually threatens to surface in relation to his own beliefs, because they are at once rivals in the dream of repossession and rivals in the dream of wandering' (Greenblatt 50–51). While Sir John and the readers of his narrative marvel at the strangeness of the faraway Amazons, the dragons, and the men with faces in their chests, the Jews are dangerous in a different and more immediate way because they are present in Christian Europe. Jews are by no means to be tolerated, and clearly exist as an antithesis to Christians, while other more distant human communities, like

monstrous women offer us an even deeper understanding of the anxieties surrounding difference and community. While the Jews will never be mistaken for Christians because they fundamentally differentiate themselves through language and their own kind of exclusive community, monsters can, and do, pass as 'normal' humans.[44] These monstrous bodies infiltrate human communities, and exist within them. Monsters like the Amazons present a threat that differs significantly from the threat of the Jews, one that is less obvious and clearly stated. They are dangerous not because they one day will take over the world, like the Jews, but because they contaminate and change communities through transgressive reproductive practices. Whereas the other transformative monsters are negative figures, the Amazons embody a kind of social wish-fulfillment; they are human women who declare their monstrosity through their transformation of their 'normal' physical forms so that no one can mistake them. Their transformation does not conceal, it reveals.

The Amazons' choice to construct such insurmountable class boundaries is what makes them eligible to protect Christendom from the Jews. The social structure of the Amazons is, as I have noted above, much admired by Mandeville. He seems to approve of their means for electing a queen, of their obedience to her commands, and even of their sexual moderation.[45] As Higgins comments, 'Despite its manlessness, then, "la terre de Femynie" looks very much like a model secular society in a world where war was considered a heroic necessity: disciplined, practical, hierarchical, monarchical, meritocratic, and democratic, Amazonia is almost everything that the exordium says Christendom was not' (*Writing East*

those of the Sultan and of Prester John, can be held up as examples of certain behaviors that Western Christians would be well advised to emulate.

44 I do not mean to suggest that Jews are not 'normal' humans. However, as many scholars have suggested, the Jews are the only group singled out as truly unacceptable by the Mandeville author; their communities are not meant to be compared, except in negative ways, to the other communities in the narrative.

45 DiMarco comments on the noble chastity of the Amazons in de Vitry, noting that even in *Mandeville* their contact with men from other communities serves primarily as a means for reproduction, and is limited to only a few days per year (74). Higgins offers a similar commentary: 'just as the Amazons' admirable chastity depends on historical accident, as it were, the Calonakan king's procreative accomplishments stem from his having many wives. What this particular juxtaposition suggests, then – since it shows *The Book* depicting both sexual restraint and (divinely enjoined) sexual indulgence favorably – is that many of the text's wonders resemble speculative explorations into recognizably possible worlds characterized by diverse forms of human and sometimes natural Otherness. The result, for modern as well as medieval readers, is a vicarious journey through a marvelous gallery that offers a shifting mix of pleasure, puzzlement, repulsion, instruction, and (historically-specific cultural) Self-criticism' (*Writing East* 149). I would argue, however, that the Amazons fit into a different category from the sexually 'indulgent' Calonakan king, as he is clearly human, while they have bodies that cannot fit comfortably or easily into 'normal' human communities. Therefore the juxtaposition of sexual practices made by Higgins, while interesting, is also troubling because these are very different kinds of communities.

145). The Amazons are not only convenient to the location of the Enclosed Tribes, but worthy and capable of serving as guardians for Christianity. While their monstrosity and transformation figure positively, they are not ideals. Higgins claims that it is because of their violence alone that they cannot serve as a true ideal for Christian communities: 'the image contains a disabling flaw: the origins of Amazonia are self-inflicted violence' (146). It is this 'self-inflicted violence' – to their bodies and to the men remaining in their community – that keeps them from truly serving as an ideal community, although some of their structures and practices are worthy of Christian attention.

The 'self-inflicted violence' of the Amazons is what makes them monstrous, but it is also what makes them more socially acceptable. Killing the lower-class men of their community simultaneously destroys and defends it. Once these men are dead, the community is permanently altered. However, it is when the Amazons cut off their breasts that they become both monstrous and admirable. In marking their bodies as monstrous, they develop clearly articulated social boundaries that separate them from human communities, and that designate their internal class structure in a way that is clearly visible and impossible to transgress. These women cannot, and will not, pass as 'human' into human communities, leaving the traffic of women and the circulation of marriage and reproduction intact in all but their own community. The transformation the Amazons undergo makes their bodies more threatening, as they disrupt ideas about gender and the body, and less dangerous, as they cannot be mistaken for 'normal' human women, like the dragon woman of Cos or the poison virgins. The bodies of these women establish clear boundaries: between women and men, between Christians and Jews, and between Amazons and human women. Transformation visibly identifies the Amazons as Other, rather than making monstrosity invisible, unpredictable, or impossible to detect.

PENETRATING THE COMMUNITY:
THE POISON VIRGINS

As we have seen, critics have consistently underestimated the social significance of the transformative monstrous body. These bodies are most often discussed as part of the Mandeville author's predilection for marvelous 'distractions' – they are seen either as diverting episodes included to appeal to base audience demands for entertainment, or as examples of the diversity in the world that the author hopes to paint for his audience. The same underestimation holds true for the most intriguing set of monstrous bodies in *Mandeville's Travels* – the poison virgins. Although a few critics make mention of these strange women, when they do, it is rarely to comment on their social or communal significance.[46] For most critics,

---

[46] Higgins includes them in his defense of the Mandeville author's decision to depart from his source, Odoric's itinerary. He claims that the strange creatures included in this original

their presence in the text merely reflects diversity rather than holding any narrative significance, and they are often reductively categorized as marvelous animals. However, to disregard monstrous human communities or to conflate them with the animal world seriously ignores the central premise of the text. Rather than simply charting the diversity of the world, *Mandeville's Travels* examines the social practices of communities that instruct, rival, or outdo the civilized behaviors of Christians at home. The poison virgins are part of one of the most instructive communities in the text: a community that has been invaded by transformative monsters and has accordingly restructured its entire practice of the trafficking of women.

Indeed, this community is described in very positive terms; they are a 'faire folk and good' (Defective 122) [fair and good people], 'good' (Egerton 200), and 'full fair & gode & gret' (Cotton 90) [full fair and good and great]. This is a human community: its citizens do not obviously possess strange physical forms, and they enjoy a social structure bolstered by civilized practices like marriage. They have one strange practice that Mandeville elucidates: although they have a desire for monogamous marriage, the men of the community require another man to sleep with their wives on the first night of their marriage: 'þe maner is siche þat þe firste niȝt þat þei be þy weddid, þei takiþ a certeyn man þat is yordeyned þerto and lete hem lye by here wyfes to haue here maidenhood' (Defective 122) [the practice is such that the first night that they are wedded, they take a certain man who is ordained for this purpose and let him lie by their wives to have their virginity]. Although this act is not in accordance with Christian practice, it is institutionalized in such a manner that it seems both as chaste and as civilized as possible; there is a special class of men 'ordained' for this social function. The term 'ordained' invokes Christian terminology, but also clearly establishes these men as a separate and distinct class of people, with its own codes of behavior.[47] Thus, these men are inherently separate from the rest of the community.

---

section are not frivolous; rather, he says, 'one can probably assume that the *Mandeville*-author wanted to offer a diverting change of pace and focus after the considerable attention given to a very few figures of unmatched power and religious influence. In addition, since the survey contains an inventory of exotic animals – "cocodrilles," chameleons, lions, elephants, and so on – one might likewise suppose that the author was overwriting the closing sections of Odoric's *Relatio* so as to make them better reflect the world's copious diversity' (*Writing East* 203). According to Higgins, then, the poison virgins are merely grouped with other strange creatures and have little to do with the Mandeville author's commentary on those 'few figures of unmatched power and religious influence.' Josephine Bennett makes a similar comment, but instead relates the poison virgins to other sexually provocative wonders. She too comments on the author's refusal to comment upon their nature, attributing this refusal to a desire to simply list interesting creatures and practices: 'He does not have the zest for crudities of the flesh, and especially for the scatological, which possessed Rabelais. He mentions the taboo of virginity, and the races of the hermaphrodites, but he does not elaborate. He simply includes them among the wonders of the earth' (75).

47 According to the *Middle English Dictionary*, 'ordeinen' means 'To put in order, organize; list in order; to regulate, control, or govern; subordinate (one's will to God's will); conform to God's

Although the role might seem like a powerful and coveted one, Mandeville reveals almost immediately the common perception of this role: the men are known as 'gadlibiriens' (Defective 122), translated for us (not in the Defective version) as 'the foles of wanhope' (Cotton 90) [fools of wanhope], 'a foule dispayr' (Bodley 467) [a foul despair], and ' "fools despaired" ' (Egerton 200).[48] These sexually potent men, who are handsomely paid, are known as the 'fools of despair' because of the danger their work entails: 'for men of þat cuntre holdiþ hit a grete þynge and a perilous to make a woman no mayde' (Defective 122) [because men of that country hold it a great and perilous thing to make a woman not a virgin]. Although these men's bodies are problematic in terms of circulation, it is not the bodies of the fools of despair that are truly monstrous. They are merely human men who have been given a particular social function. Rather than being monstrous, they are expendable: they fulfill a social purpose and protect more important members of the community from the dangers of their wives' bodies. It is the bodies of the virgins that are monstrous – they are indeed 'perilous' according to Defective, Cotton, Bodley, *and* Egerton.[49]

The virgins of this community are dangerous, although not threatening in the same way as the Amazons, or even Hippocrates' daughter or the mother of the Head of Satalia. Whereas the bodies of these women are clearly marked as dangerous – the Amazons by the removal of one breast, Hippocrates' daughter by her transformation from woman to dragon, and the mother of the head by her reproductive but dead body – the women of this community appear to fit in. In fact, they are considered safe after the fools of despair have done their job, so no

will.' The term is used in non-religious circumstances, but most frequently seems to suggest a larger ordering of the world, relating often to the arrangement of the stars or the will of God. It can also mean 'To create; to build, construct, form, make'; this seems like the intended sense of the word in this passage. As with 'to organize,' this sense of the word also relates most frequently to religious contexts, and is used in biblical references and religious commentaries.

48 According to Letts, editor of the Egerton, 'Cotton calls them "fools of wanhope." The name is unexplained. The Paris text has "desesperes." The source of this unedifying story has not been traced, but there is something like it in Vincent of Beauvais ... Dr. N.M. has an interesting note in his *Poison Damsels*, 1952, p. 37. He traces the story back to Solinus and Pliny (vii, ch. 2. 17, 18) where the damsels had poison in their eyes as well as elsewhere, and associates the story with the fear of defloration, the presence of evil influences, or the dread of impotence in the man' (200, note 1). Josephine Bennett comments more extensively on their possible sources, and the Mandeville author's decision to relocate them, geographically: 'sometimes Mandeville may make a bold transfer of a bit of folklore; for example, he attributes to a tribe in India a superstition about the breaking of maidenheads which Julius Caesar had attributed to the Britons. The historians of travel literature have been particularly outraged by this transposition, but Mandeville was certainly right in putting the belief in a far away country. In fact, he may not have been following Caesar at all, but Solinus, who tells a slightly different version of the story about the Augyles, who live next to the Troglodites in Ethiopia (which in the Middle Ages was considered to be a part of India)' (52–3).

49 Metrical does not include this story, which is not unexpected in a text that leaves out many stories contained in the longer prose versions.

immediately visible transformation seems to have taken place. But in fact these women hide their monstrous forms inside their bodies, only to be revealed in defense of their 'maidenhood.' Because of the danger presented by their bodies, it was 'here custome to make oþer men to asaye þe passage bifore þat þei were put in auenture' [their custom to make other men try the passage before they were put to that adventure] (Defective 122). Sex with these women is described by all the versions considered here as 'auenture' [adventure] – a dangerous quest.[50] Here, a man goes forth into the dangerous and unknown body of a woman, risking his life to the dangers that reside, unseen, within.

The virgins' bodies do provide adventure and danger for those who attempt to enter them, at least according to the tradition of the community. Sir John, upon asking, learns the threat of these monstrous bodies that do not appear to be monstrous:

> And Y askyd what was here cause whi þei dide so, and þei seide somme housbandis lay by here wyfes [first] and non oþer but þei, and somme of here wyfes hadde naddris in here bodyes þat twengid here housbandis vpon here ȝerdys in þe bodyes of þe wymmen, and so was many a man yslawe.
> (Defective 122–3)

> [And I asked what was the cause why they did so, and they said some husbands lay by their wives first and no other but they, and some of their wives had serpents in their bodies that stung their husbands upon their yards (penises) in the bodies of the women, and so were many men killed.]

The virgins' bodies conceal their monstrosity: no one claims to have seen the serpents, but their effect is seen on the bodies – in fact, the 'yards' – of their husbands. It is not clear which women's bodies contain these serpents and which do not; it is only *some* of the wives, not all, who necessitate the tradition of the fools of despair. It is absolutely unclear to the eye which women present a danger and which do not. The possibility of danger is so great that, according to both Cotton and Bodley, if the fools of despair fail to do their duty (because of 'dronkenness' (Cotton 90) [drunkenness]), the husband can react 'as þough the officere wolde haue slayn him' (Cotton 90) [as though the officer would have slain him]. Leaving the virgin's body untested, whether or not it contains a serpent, is tantamount to an act of attempted murder.

The women of this community *do* circulate; they are a part of its marital economy. There are two dangerous possibilities for their bodies, however, and one must be acted out. Either they transfer too little or too much. If the serpent in a woman's body kills her husband in his attempt to take her virginity, then she

---

50 According to the *Middle English Dictionary*, the term *aventure* carries the meanings 'fate, fortune, chance'; 'an event or occurrence'; 'danger, jeopardy, risk'; 'a knightly quest'; 'a marvelous quest'; and 'a tale of adventures.'

does not and cannot circulate – she is no longer married and does not bear children. On the other hand, if a fool of despair successfully performs his work on her wedding night, then the woman circulates in excess. Although such an occurrence is not mentioned explicitly, it is possible that a woman could bear a child that is not her husband's. The dangerous result of their over-circulation, then, is a physical kind of openness that can be counteracted or controlled only by isolating them. They are kept so strictly after their marriages that, according to Cotton, they have no contact with men other than their husbands: 'But after the firste nyght þat þei ben leyn by þei kepen hem so streytely þat þei ben not so hardy to speke with no man' (90) [But after the first night that they are laid by, they keep them so strictly that they speak with no men]. Bodley points out the danger of the over-circulated body, saying that 'aftir the first nyght that they arn so defoulid, they are kepid streyte aftir' (467) [but after the first night that they are so befouled, they are kept strictly afterwards]. The bodies that potentially contained snakes that might sting men are, after their deflowering, 'foul' in an entirely different way. As Brundage argues, legal statutes reflect ideologies that 'women are sexually more voracious than men, that they desire intercourse more ardently and enjoy it more, and that in consequence their sexual behavior requires stricter supervision than that of men' (*Law* 492). This fear, and the corresponding statutes, derive not only from anxieties about male inadequacy, or notions of their superiority – although these are both implied – but also because medieval social stability relies on the soundness of lineage. If women are indeed more voracious, then they are seemingly less in control of their own sexual behavior; the parentage of their children easily can be uncertain. Therefore, the exchange and subordination of women is designed to delimit women's control over their own bodies, so as to assure the legitimacy of their husband's children. The traffic in women is designed to keep women as effective cogs in the process of inheritance. As Rubin suggests:

> If women are exchanged, in whatever sense we take the term, marital debts are reckoned in female flesh ... It would be in the interests of the smooth and continuous operation of such a system if the woman in question did not have too many ideas about whom she might want to sleep with. From the standpoint of the system, the preferred female sexuality would be one which responded to the desire of others, rather than one which actively desired and sought a response. ("Traffic" 182)

The successful trafficking of women relies on a woman to be compliant, not active in the process by which she is traded. Because she has over-circulated, by necessity, in this community, a woman's body is always just slightly out of the control of her husband, and requires extreme supervision. Before their wedding night, the danger was that they could not circulate; afterwards, the danger is that they are always potentially in circulation unless they are 'kepid streyte' (Bodley 467) [kept strictly].

Like the Amazons, the bodies of the poison virgins are transformative in a less traditional sense. The Amazons are not born with monstrous bodies; they design and execute the transformation of their bodies through the removal of a breast. While one must suppose that the poison virgins are born with the serpents inside them, the serpents remain invisible, concealed. These women's physical forms do not reveal them to be monstrous to the observing eye – it is only the intimate experience of their monstrous bodies that gives them away. Therefore, the bodies of *all* women in the community are suspect, and their bodies remain dangerously in need of surveillance and control. The poison virgins, then, serve as more than frivolous distractions from the *real* work of *Mandeville's Travels*. The poison virgins inform readers that the monstrous can be invisible and sexual – it no longer declares itself through an obvious and visible physical aberration as in the case of *Wonders'* tusked women or Grendel and his mother. Although the bodies of the poison virgins transform themselves by being divested of their serpents after they are visited by the fools of despair, they exist, unidentified in the community, for many years beforehand. They have infiltrated a human community – which has notably undertaken efforts to protect its members.[51]

I began this discussion of the poison virgins by suggesting that *Mandeville's Travels* is a text concerned not simply with Eastern diversity, but also with the social practices of communities which instruct, rival, or outdo the civilized behaviors of Christians at home. The Mandeville author here does not seem to suggest that Christian women have poisonous serpents inside them, or that there should be a caste of men to deflower women before their husbands can have intercourse with them. Instead, this portion of the text suggests that monstrous bodies are not as obvious or as permanent as Christians might suppose. Monsters are capable of entering and endangering communities. Although there is a system in place to protect against the poison virgins, they also represent a new possibility for the monstrous – that although monstrosity is physical, it can also be disguised or invisible. Because the bodies of the poison virgins must be entered by a stranger before they can be used by their husbands for reproduction, they contradict the notion of marriage and of legitimate reproduction. The problem is not so clearly defined as Sir John's relatively uncomplicated refusal of the Sultan's offer of a Prince's non-Christian daughter; monsters no longer remain in the East, clearly marked by physical difference. Monstrosity, with the bodies of the poison virgins, has moved to the inside of a creature, rather than being easily identified by its outside appearance.

---

51 It might be argued that the fools of despair too have developed monstrous bodies in that their bodies are 'immune' to the poison virgins. It seems more likely to me that these men are expendable. If a serpent happens to be inside the virgin, its venom will be spent on an unmarriageable man who will then have served his life's purpose.

CONCLUSIONS:
THE PRESENCE OF THE MONSTER

In each of these four episodes, monstrosity and reproduction are intimately related to the problem of transformation. These bodies are so very monstrous and so very threatening because they are undeniably connected to human communities. The dragon woman and the fecund dead woman are residents of the communities of Cos and Satalia before their transformations, which hold serious repercussions for both of these communities: the woman's transformation to dragon removes her from the line of succession and prohibits the island kingdom from passing to a proper heir, while the birth of the monstrous head in Satalia literally destroys the entire community. These consequences come from the inside of the community, not from the outside. The monsters do not come from far away and attack, as does Grendel; they are always already there, inside the community, simply waiting to be drawn forth.

While the monstrous potential for the dragon woman and the dead woman is externally imposed, the Amazons take advantage of this potential through their own agency. They transform themselves, reacting to significant changes to the make-up of the community. They too are fundamentally bound to the community in which they exist, which they significantly alter by transforming their own bodies. Their reproductive practices perpetuate their monstrous community, but the marking of their monstrous bodies so as to be unmistakable makes them acceptable and understandable to Christian communities. Unlike the poison virgins, they cannot exist unrecognized in human communities. Of all of these transformative female monsters, the poison virgins represent the greatest danger. Their transformative monstrosity is physical but unrecognizable, and thus impacts their community and its social structure in essential ways. The community's reproductive order and marital practices result from the monstrous potential of the women's bodies.

Although the bodies of the poison virgins are transformed again when their serpents are dispatched by the 'aventure' of the fools of despair, they had existed unidentified in the community for many years beforehand. They are a part of a human community – which has notably undertaken efforts to protect its members. The lesson of the poison virgins is that monsters no longer remain outside of human civilization, clearly marked by a visible physical difference. While it is reassuring that these monstrous women are rescued by their transformation, the process of transformation has over-circulated bodies that can never be trusted again. However, they no longer have to pass as human, because they *seem* to have passed back into humanity.

All of these monsters complicate notions of humanity and hybridity because of their transformative status. As the dragon woman, the monstrous head, and the Amazons pass out of humanity, so do the poison virgins pass into it. In fact, two of these monsters pass as human at some point – the dragon woman, when she lures a doomed sailor to her castle, appearing as a beautiful woman, and the poison virgins before they are penetrated by the fools of despair. The audience knows that these women's transformative bodies are not entirely human – they are hybrid specifically in their conflation of the bestial with the human, be it dragon or internal serpent. And yet all of these female monsters have a provisional human status – the dragon woman before she was cursed, the woman of Satalia before she died, the Amazons before they remove a breast, and the poison virgins after their deflowering. However, this human status is indeed provisional: once the monstrous form is introduced, the body becomes hopelessly hybrid. The dragon woman teaches us that her body, once bestial, becomes implicated in her human identity. Similarly, the second episode reveals a hybrid between living and dead, between reproductive and destructive: it is the enduring human identity of the woman's corpse in Satalia that draws the burgess's son to her grave. While the Amazons' humanity is retained to a degree because they copulate and thus procreate with human men, they are simultaneously marked as monstrous by the removal of a breast. The Mandeville author suggests too that the poison virgins' bodies – although no longer a physical threat to their husbands – still are not entirely trustworthy. The narrator points out the danger of their over-circulated bodies by assuring the audience that the women are 'kept strictly' after their first night with a fool of despair. The bodies that potentially contained snakes that might sting men are, after their deflowering, tainted in another way entirely. Where their bodies are dangerously hybrid before they are transformed, they are clearly sexually polluted after this necessary transformation.

While Bynum in *Metamorphosis and Identity* argues that the hybrid and the metamorphic are two different categories of transformation, I argue that the meta-morphic monster is always in some way hybrid. The body that may *seem* to be human is never really entirely human after its transformation. The monstrous form is always implicated in bodies that can, or that have, taken on monstrous attributes. Thus, although the dragon woman may *appear* human to the sailor she draws in, the dragon is always already present – she has internalized the identity of the dragon body when she causes the death of the knight of Rhodes. Similarly, when the poison virgins are divested of their dangerous serpents by the fools of despair, their bodies retain a 'foulness' that must be carefully guarded and controlled by their husbands. So although these transformed women may seem to be human, they are in fact only *passing* as human. They are always already monstrous. And because the bodies of human women have such a potential to transform and become monstrous, communities cannot defend against them.

In each of these cases, the monstrous bodies of women are closely tied to human communities through the transformative nature of their monstrosity. They are not exiled to a single location in the monstrous and exotic East, but exist in various geographic locations, both to the East and to the West of Jerusalem. The Mandeville author offers a range of test cases of reproduction involving monsters, and while each situation is a little bit different, the point is the abiding theme of their existence. No single type of transformative monster unifies the text, but they all make the same point in different ways. The Mandeville author provides an anatomy of issues, a handbook of reproductive monsters from England to the East, which argues for the widespread nature of the phenomenon of the monstrous.

While Old English texts manage to erase their monsters, *Mandeville's Travels* depicts monsters that cannot be erased. It is one of the few medieval texts that does not attempt to resolve the problem of the monstrous. Instead, because of their new ability to transform, monsters not only continue to exist, but they do so within human communities. Transformative monsters disrupt the stability of human communities by interrupting the proper circulation of women's bodies, and by suggesting that the boundaries of these communities can no longer be maintained. Transgressive identity which is no longer easily visible and identifiable even in literary texts demonstrates just how little control communities have over the bodies that comprise them and circulate within them. The bodies of these transformative monsters reveal new possibilities for human bodies, human gender, and human sexuality, articulating that neither bodies nor identity are entirely stable, and that their circulation is both necessary and dangerous. Because monsters are, at times, indistinguishable from humans, they cannot be erased: moreover, they can reproduce. Transformation enables monsters to appear human, and it is this that makes them most monstrous.

Chapter 4

PATERNITY AND MONSTROSITY IN THE
ALLITERATIVE *MORTE ARTHURE* AND *SIR GOWTHER*

Mandeville's Travels features the bodies of four kinds of monstrous women whose transformative bodies have the potential to seem, rather than be, human. In *Mandeville*, transformation permits monstrous women to transgress the boundaries between monstrous territories and human communities, demonstrating medieval anxieties about miscegenation and the potential for monstrous-human procreation. However, male monsters also embody these fears about miscegenation and procreation – and many of them appear in texts set far closer to home than the monstrous transformative women who populate the distant and mysterious East. Indeed, the forests of medieval Europe, as represented in medieval romances, teem with enormous men – giants who rape, murder, consume, and attempt to penetrate the communities that surround their lonely haunts in mountains or forests. Killing and dismembering are popular means of disabling the threat of the giant, as happens in the Alliterative *Morte Arthure*. Alternatively, the author of the romance *Sir Gowther* employs the thematically necessary trope of transformation to dispatch his eponymous giant in a way that seems, superficially, more reassuring. These two Middle English texts seek to rid human communities of their monsters in safe and final ways. The male monsters in both the Alliterative *Morte* and *Sir Gowther* are dispatched – one through death and one through transformation – and yet, these monsters of excess appetite and sexuality continue to haunt the communities they once terrorized after they are removed from the narratives. While the violent emasculating death of the Giant of Mont St Michel in the Alliterative *Morte* forces readers to recognize all-too-human acts of terror and the resulting disruption of lines of inheritance, the preservation of Gowther's material body after his spiritual and physical transformation leaves more than just a specter of the monster in the middle of the text. In *Gowther*, the monster's physical body, now transformed to a human one, acts as a trace of its former self.

Where *Mandeville's* transformative female monsters pass as human and infiltrate human communities, the sexualized male monsters in the Alliterative *Morte* and *Sir Gowther* disrupt the hierarchy of paternal inheritance. Both male monsters, creatures of excess, threaten communities through their hypermasculine and sexual bodies. The violating monster, the giant envisioned as the origin of masculinity, possesses a destructive virility rather than a creative or procreative one. His desires cause him to destroy communities and lineage, and to insist that his own attempts at reproduction be foiled by virtue of his surfeit

159

potency. By examining the two possibilities of treatment of the monstrous body – erasure and transformation – I show the flaws and gaps in each. While erasure leaves behind traces of the monster in the body of the man who castrates and kills him, transformation appears to effectively resolve the problem of the monstrous body: the terrifying body of the monster becomes instead the body of a good man. However, as with the monstrous bodies in *Mandeville*, transformation may not be as finite or complete as it seems. A body once changed may change again. Even though the author of *Gowther* seems to suggest that monstrosity can be replaced with sainthood, the trace of the monster's body remains, threatening to reappear. The ontological problem of the category, that a body is changeable, serves to make the body doubly dangerous.

THE BODY OF THE GIANT AND THE MYTH OF MASCULINITY

Giants are a strange kind of monster because they are so terrifyingly human, and yet so clearly more than human. They do not have faces on their chests, like the *blemmye*, nor do they possess bestial body parts, like tails or talons. Their bodies are recognizably whole and also wholly human – they are merely much larger, and often much hairier, than a normal man. They commonly appear in medieval romance, a genre that thinks self-consciously about ideals both social and physical: ridiculously beautiful women, obscenely brave and strong men, the best kings, or the most evil regents. Giants too serve as extreme: violent threats to the community, they remind men of the unquestionable masculinity they wish to possess, and that they might achieve by conquering the body of the monster. The giant acts as a mirror to humanity and to human desires, possessing bodies that are under-civilized and over-determined. They seem to represent the natural state of man – a lost origin of masculinity and authority. They usually carry a mace or club rather than a sword, which shows them to be 'ignorant of chivalric weapons and the military customs of civilized Westerners' (Friedman 33). They are not a part of the institutionalized and mannered violence of the court, but seem more like its forebear. Unlike the smooth and crafted weapons of their opponents, they use tools associated with the natural world that are readily available and that exceed human strength and ability. While Walter Stephens sees the figure of the giant as entirely inhuman because he opposes man in every way (58), Jeffrey Jerome Cohen finds him troubling precisely because he 'cannot be fully banished from, or integrated into, those identity categories that his body constructs' (*Of Giants* xiv). Because the giant is both human and more-than-human, he cannot be dismissed from the category of humanity, but he also consistently exceeds it. The giant is that which man both abjects and desires: his physical excess is both gross and aspirational. He is the self that man longs to be, the ultimate patriarch and the perfect vision of masculinity and unity that he wants to achieve. The giant's body is the more complete self to which the human man never can measure up.

The giant's monstrosity arises from his excessive body; he is larger than a normal man, and usually has extreme appetites for food, violence, and even sex. Medieval giants are most often excessively male; they are bigger, stronger, better, but also more driven by masculine desire. The prototypical figure of the giant is a vanguard of what it means to possess and employ masculinity, in terms of either gender or sexuality. In the giant, we find a figure that makes no room for gender-blurring; rather, we see the opposite: he has a 'violently gendered body' (Cohen xii) that is almost exclusively male.[1] The primary purpose of the giant is to act as the limit of undisputed masculinity. The giant is often linked with the popular transhistorical figure of the 'Wild Man,' a being who is traditionally associated with nature and excess.[2] The giant is prior to, but also lesser than man because he is removed from civilization. Louise Fradenburg, drawing from the Wild Man's appearance in pageantry, designates the wild man as 'a liminal figure: he appears on the borders and edges; he guards limits; he ushers in and out' (235). The giant defines the boundaries of humanity, like most monsters, exhibiting those attributes that cannot or should not be incorporated in the civilized world. However, he is also foundational; he both prefigures and destabilizes masculine identity. Even though the giant is always killed by the knight, usually violently, the knight and his kingdom are never really rid of the giant because he is originary. Indeed, the giant is the first inhabitant of Britain, defeated by first Brutus and then Arthur in Geoffrey of Monmouth's *Historia Regum Britanniae.*[3]

Although the giant serves as an origin for masculinity, he is an exaggerated construct meant to confirm heterosexual identity, an empty ideal that cannot be achieved. The giant is both the norm against which all men are measured (and found lacking) and abnormal because of his impossible excess. If, as Judith Butler suggests, bodies are manifestations of dominant social codes, then the giant figures as simultaneously the code itself and the Other against which the code is defined. He acts as an origin, but, as Butler notes, the origin is an illusion, since identity is constructed through the repetition of behaviors that are infinitely different, nuanced, and 'non-self-identical' ('Imitation' 1712). He performs what we might consider to be a kind of drag gender, a performance of stereotypical gender that at once enhances and simultaneously destabilizes the precepts upon which gender relies. Butler argues that 'drag is not an imitation or a copy of some prior and true gender ... drag enacts the very structure of impersonation by which *any gender* is assumed' (1713). The giant, therefore, presents the idea of a true gender, but at the

---

1 Although female giants are rare, they do exist. In *Of Giants*, Cohen notes, for example, the existence of the female giant, Barrock, in *The Sowdon of Babylon.* They appear far more frequently in Old Norse literature, which generally depicts women in a significantly different light from Old or Middle English literature.

2 Finlayson states, in reference to Bermheimer, *Wild Man*, that 'confusion between wild men and giants was ... almost inevitable, so that the attributes of the two became mixed up' (116). In addition to Cohen's cogent discussion of the wild man figure in *Of Giants*, see Bernheimer; Husband, *The Wild Man*; Sprunger, 'Wild Folk'; and Fradenburg, 'The Wild Knight' in *City, Marriage, Tournament.*

3 See Cohen, *Of Giants*, xx.

same time the very excess of this performance indicates the flawed nature of all performances of gender. She elaborates:

> Drag constitutes the mundane way in which genders are appropriated, theatricalized, worn, and done; it implies that all gendering is a kind of impersonation and approximation. If this is true, it seems, there is no original or primary gender that drag imitates, but *gender is a kind of imitation for which there is no original*; in fact, it is a kind of imitation that produces the very notion of the original as an *effect* and consequence of the imitation itself … in this sense, the 'reality' of heterosexual identities is performatively constituted through an imitation that sets itself up as the origin and the ground of imitations. In other words, heterosexuality is always in the process of imitating itself – and failing. (1713)

Thus, the giant, set up in the human imagination as the origin of human masculinity, guarantees that the human man can only fail. If the giant is origin, then this status indicates that masculinity is flawed, incomplete, and unattainable. He presents a particular kind of problem for the construction of human identity, for he reveals the destructive nature of norms, and the impossibility of achieving them.

The Giant of Mont St Michel from the Alliterative *Morte Arthure* is an exemplary giant: he is grossly hairy: 'His fax and his foretoppe was filterede togeders' (1078) [His hair and his forelock were matted together] and 'His berde was brothy and blake, þat till his brest recede' (1090) [His beard was bristly and black, and reached down to his breast]; he carries a club made 'all of clene yryn' (1105) [all of clean iron], and he is excessive in size, as he is deemed to be 'Fro þe face to þe fote was fyfe fadom lange' (1103) [From the head to the foot, he was five fathoms long], with 'Ruyd armes as an ake' (1096) [Arms as stout as an oak] and 'Thykke these as a thursse, and thikkere in þe hanche' (1100) [Thighs as thick as a monster, and even thicker in the haunch].[4] In this description, he is also notably bestialized, as

---

4   The Alliterative *Morte Arthure* exists in only one manuscript, number 91 in the library at Lincoln Cathedral. The manuscript seems to be the work of a fifteenth century scribe, Robert of Thornton, who has signed the text. The manuscript is dated between 1430 and 1440 (Krishna 1). The story itself is the final portion of Geoffrey of Monmouth's chronicle of Arthur's life, although, as Krishna notes, 'the immediate source of the *Morte Arthure* is uncertain' (17). Monstrosity is deemed by many twentieth and twenty-first century scholars to be a sign of the ridiculousness of a story – an irrelevant or distracting element that draws the audience away from the real work of the text. Many of these scholars clearly point to Arthur's contest with the Giant of Mont St Michel as a less-than-serious element of the narrative. Göller claims, 'the battle with the giant of Mont St Michel is certainly a very twisted "romantic element in the story." Arthur's humour and irony, the emphasis on bawdy and grotesqueness, all this turns the episode into a burlesque *aventure*' ("Reality" 22), while Ritzke-Rutherford dismisses it as 'a mock-heroic parody of the conventional type-scene' (89). Notably absent from this list of dismissive scholars is John Finlayson, who strenuously argues for a serious consideration of this particular scene. I argue that the episode with the Giant of Mont St Michel should not be dismissed as too fantastic to bear relevance to the chronicle-historical concerns of the poem as a whole, but instead should be recognized as a fulfilling the larger

he is likened in appearance to at least eleven different animals, including a hawk (1082), a bear (1089), and even a sea-hog (1091), emphasizing the crudity of his visage and form, without suggesting that his body comprises animal parts.[5] His body is hyperbolic in every possible way – it is huge, thick, uncivilized, and animalistic.

While we know little of the Giant of Mont St Michel beyond his aggressive actions and his excessive appearance, the same is not true of Gowther, whose life we trace from his conception to beyond his grave.[6] Indeed, Gowther's story demands that we consider his origin; he is born not into the race of giants, but rather to a human mother. Unable to conceive with her husband the Duke and therefore threatened with dissolution of the marriage, his mother prays to Mary, asking that she 'Schuld gyffe hur grace to have a chyld. On what maner scho ne roghth' (65) [should give her grace to have a child. She didn't care in what manner]. While the prayer is to Mary, its resolution is not so holy: a demon who looks like her husband appears in the garden in which she prays and he seduces

themes of the Alliterative *Morte Arthure*. The question of genre has been an important one in the study of the late fourteenth century poem. Scholars have identified it variously as a chronicle, a romance, a tragedy, a *chanson de geste*, and an epic, to name only a few. As Kennedy has pointed out, recent critical work rarely attempts to classify or limit the poem through the category of genre. Krishna's edition offers an excellent overview of the genre debate concerning the poem (19–22).

5 I would like to note that never does the poet say that the Giant actually possesses animal parts, but only that his parts are like those of whichever animal. The Giant's body, while hybrid as are all monsters, is a body of human excess, not of bestial intervention.

6 This is perhaps a function of genre: the Alliterative *Morte Arthure* follows the chronicle romance tradition, in which the Giant serves an episodic function, whereas *Gowther*'s genre is much more closely aligned with either a saint's life or a romance. For a thorough discussion of the question of genre, see Bradstock, 'Secular Hagiography' and Marchalonis, 'Process of Romance.' Indeed, scholars struggle to align the romance's obvious penitential message with its violent secularity. This divide is particularly pronounced because of the deep variation between the two existing manuscript versions of *Sir Gowther*, designated here as Royal and Advocates. The two manuscripts are British Library Royal MS 17.B.43 and National Library of Scotland MS Advocates 19.3.1. Both versions of the poem are written in twelve-line tail rhyme stanzas, and both derive from the Northeast Midlands (Laskaya and Salisbury 263). Hopkins notes the benefits of each manuscript, stating that the scholars who use Royal do so because it is more 'refined,' while other scholars use Advocates because it is 'less corrupt' (144). Royal suppresses some of the more explicit elements of the story, including the raping of the nuns – Laskaya and Salisbury attribute the 'gentler' treatment in this manuscript to a possibly 'more cultured and refined audience' (263). Advocates, alternately, uses graphic descriptions, and, in fact, seems to revel in its vivid depictions of sex and violence, emphasizing Gowther's monstrosity, which is often sexualized and therefore cut or elided in Royal. Advocates is used most frequently, because Royal only seems to cut explicit moments rather than adding anything significant to the poem (although its elisions do offer interesting possibilities for interpretations like Blamires'). Most contemporary scholars use Advocates. While it is the penitential impulse that allows us such intense knowledge of Gowther as a character, it is the violence and monstrosity shown in Advocates that makes Gowther's transformation so astonishing and important.

her. He immediately transforms[7] into his own form and announces her impregnation: 'When he had is wylle all don/ A felturd fende he start up son,/ And stode and
hur beheld;/ He seyd, "Y have geyton a chylde on the/ That in is yothe full wylde
schall bee,/ And weppons wyghtly weld" ' (73–8) [When he had done what he
wanted, he leapt up quickly as a shaggy fiend, and stood and beheld her; he said, 'I
have gotten a child on you that in his youth shall be fully wild and wield weapons
skillfully'].[8] The Duchess immediately seduces her own husband to cover her
conception, and the ruse is successful. The Duke accepts the child as his own.

The Duke is a father in name only to Gowther; his real father is the demon.
While some scholars argue for a hybrid paternity because the demon takes on the
appearance of the Duke, the poem asserts that the demon is the true father of
Gowther.[9] He both engenders and predicts his progeny's 'wild youth' and his skill
with weapons – attributes that Gowther certainly fulfills. Moreover, the poet
confirms Gowther's status as the demon's child by illuminating his larger family
tree: 'This chyld within hur was no nodur,/ Bot eyvon Marlyon halfe brodur'
(97–8) [This child within her was no other than Merlin's half brother]. Gowther's
demon-father is also the father of Merlin, making Gowther and Merlin brothers.
By invoking Merlin's name, the poet produces an unmistakable cultural reference
for an audience well acquainted with the hybrid identity and mysterious and
dangerous powers of that magician.[10] They can only expect that Gowther will have

---

7 Although the fiend is a fascinating and transformative figure, fiends and demons present a
problem quite distinct from the problems of human monsters. At the most basic level, fiends
or demons are not human in any way. In fact, Cohen, in 'Gowther Among the Dogs,' Corinne
Saunders, and McGregor note that the fiend is usually a figure who simply takes on other
forms but is rarely featured in his own – therefore *Sir Gowther* is unusual in its depiction of a
fiend's 'natural' form. For more information on fiends and demons, see Elliott, *Fallen Bodies*.
8 Many scholars acknowledge that this is an act of rape. Saunders offers an excellent discussion
of this element.
9 McGregor acknowledges the demon as Gowther's literal parent, but she argues that, because
of the demon's disguise, the Duke is implicated in his conception: 'the Fiend's appearance
cannot obviate the guise in which he approached the Duchess; he did so in the form of the
Duke so that, eerily, both Duke and Fiend are present at the child's conception. Both are
Gowther's "real" father; both create his paternal inheritance' (73–4). Blamires argues unconvincingly that the Royal version mitigates the demon's paternity and shows the Duke to be
Gowther's real but corrupt father. He works at a metaphorical level, associating what he terms
as the Duke's 'arrogance' with being a fiend (52). Alternatively, Cohen complicates the issue of
Gowther's paternity by suggesting that when the demon assumes the Duke's form, he takes
not only his appearance but some of his essence, and this essence is transmitted in the sex act.
Although the fiend performs the act, he does not produce his own sperm, but rather steals the
essence of the Duke ("Gowther" 229). Therefore, the fiend is both a kind of father, and merely
a corrupt conduit for paternity. Both Cohen and McGregor demonstrate the difficulties
presented by the changeable body of the fiend, but I suggest that such manipulations are
neither satisfying nor necessary. The Duke heretofore has been unable to procure an heir for
himself, and his wife's prayer does not seem to have changed his physical ability.
10 Charbonneau argues that *Gowther* is an ill-put-together romance, filled with unrelated details.
She sees the references to Merlin as one of these useless but 'titillating' details: 'The allusions to

skills beyond human ken. He takes on physical markers of his demonic parentage, but also essential internal traits; as Hopkins claims, Gowther 'is presented as having inherited from his father a really evil nature' (147).[11] Although Gowther is christened under the Duke's authority, and he thus takes responsibility for naming him, the demon clearly remains the literal and spiritual father of Gowther.[12] It is Gowther's hybrid identity – his status as both human and more than human – that enables him to exist in a human community, however disruptive he might be to its function. Unlike the Giant of Mont St Michel, who unsuccessfully tries to assume human social roles (as king, as lover, as parent), Gowther, through his hybrid nature and his potential for transformation, can and does fit into human roles in human communities, though he also exceeds the limits of humanity.

EATING THE OTHER:
DESIRE AND CONSUMPTION

Both the Giant of Mont St Michel and Gowther, creatures of excess size, are also monsters of surfeit appetite. Their bodies, large and frightening, define them as monsters. However, these bodies require a kind of maintenance significantly beyond the capabilities and capacities of the human body. Both monsters consume rapaciously – an activity whose consequences are far-reaching in the communities that surround them. The appetites of these giants, affiliated with their exaggerated bodies, also hold significance in terms of gender, sexuality, and reproduction. The Giant of Mont St Michel's consumption reveals the excesses of his body and gender, but it also lays bare his desires, both physical and social. Similarly, the extreme habits of consumption by the infant Gowther show him to be a danger to

---

Merlin, similarities to Robert the devil stories, and evocations of incubus lore seem pointless if the reason for the references is not sharply and immediately understood by an audience ... perhaps the original audience would have been satisfied with a few titillating tidbits to make the story more interesting, but modern readers demand more than throw-away bits of sensationalism and expect instead a narrative filled with coherency and meaningful details' (22). I argue that this reference is indeed very meaningful and emphasizes the demonic paternity of Gowther; it attempts to make familiar the demonic impregnation for the audience by invoking a known magical half-demon figure. As Laskaya and Salisbury argue, 'Demonologists in the late Middle Ages considered him [Merlin] a figure for the antichrist, prophesied in the *Book of Revelation* to signal the end of the world ... The fraternal relation between Gowther and Merlin and their shared paternity with the fiend would most certainly presage disaster for a medieval audience' (266).

11 Hopkins notes this issue of paternity as one of the significant differences between the Robert the devil sources and *Gowther*; Gowther is 'actually the son of the Devil rather than owed to him as a debt' (147).

12 Montaño discusses strange physical differences in children fathered by Saracens upon Christian women (121). However, once these children are baptized, these physical aberrations are resolved and their fathers usually convert. Baptism does nothing to curb Gowther's monstrosity, which reveals a clear difference between Saracen fathers and the demon as father.

women, and to the processes of reproduction and circulation. The linkage between desire and appetite shows the danger presented to the human community by the dangerous body of the hypermasculine monster.

In the Alliterative *Morte*, our first vision of the Giant of Mont St Michel links his excessive and sexualized body with his practices of obscene consumption. The monstrous desire to consume in mass quantities is less of a problem than what is consumed: the bodies of humans. This act is most appalling and transgressive if it is cannibalistic, which confers a semi-human status on the eater; like Grendel, the Giant of Mont St Michel eats humans to absorb their qualities and assert his status as not only human, but also as a figure of authority. In *Beowulf*, Grendel's desire to eat thirty men, including their hands and feet, demonstrates not only the breadth of his depravity, but also his desire for possession and incorporation of the human body into his own monstrous one. Similarly, in the Alliterative *Morte*, the Giant's consumption of humans operates performatively: it articulates his place at the top of the food chain and effectively rids him of competition. As such, what he ingests bolsters his own masculine prowess and sexual authority. Our first vision of the monster, through the eyes of Arthur, shows him to be a creature of complete indulgence and physical and sexual excess, as he feasts while he warms his bare body by the fire: 'His bakke and his bewschers and his brode lendez' (1047) [his back and his buttocks, and his big loins]. The Giant's enormous size is denoted in explicitly sexual terms: his large loins are connected immediately with his perverse appetite.[13] It is the potential for extremes – violence and consumption – inherent in the monstrous body that makes him so very dangerous. As a contrast, we immediately see man's impotence against him, for he sits munching on a human leg: 'þe thee of a manns lymme lyfte vp by þe haunche' (1046) [the thigh of a man's leg he lifted up by the haunch]. Compared with his own huge thighs and masculinity, the human haunch seems tiny, and its possessor has obviously been ineffectual in defeating the Giant. The monster's masculinity is affirmed by the way in which he displays his sexed body while he consumes a male victim whose dismembered body shows the deconstruction of not only human form, but human male authority and prowess.

The problem with the Giant is not just that he is monstrous and uncivilized, but that he desires to take part in human systems. He mimics human behaviors, yet does so with an obscene twist: he eats off 'a chargour of chalke-whytt syluer' (1026) [a charger of chalk-white silver], seasoning his meat with 'pekill and powdyre of precious spycez' (1027) [sauce and powder of precious spices], but this meat is 'seuen knaue childre, / Choppid' (1025–6) [seven knave children, chopped]. He has truly noble pretensions, but underneath these are his monstrous impulses. In addition to his taste for human flesh, he has sexual impulses for human women, seen in the form of the kidnapped Duchess as well as maidservants forced to do his bidding. However, his lust has terrible consequences, as we learn about the servants, about whom we are told, 'Siche foure scholde be fay within foure

---

[13] Bartlett, too, comments on both his 'insatiable sexual appetite and monstrously oversized penis' (66).

hourez,/ Are his fylth ware filled that his flesch yernes' (1031–2) [Four of such would be lifeless within four hours, before his filth would be fulfilled for which his flesch yearns]. The Giant's sexual desire, like his appetite for food, invades the boundaries of human communities. The problem, then, is not that the Giant is impotent, but that he is too potent – he is simply too large for a woman.

The Giant's excessive size and masculinity make it literally impossible for him to engage in successful intercourse with a human woman, despite his excess of fertile desire. Arthur is later told by the Duchess' grieving nurse that 'He hade morthirede this mylde be myddaye war rongen,/ Withowttyn mercy one molde – not watte it ment./ He has forsede hir and fylede, and cho es fay leuede;/ he slewe hir vnslely and slitt hir to þe nauyll' (976–9) [He murdered this mild thing without any mercy on earth before midday was rung out. He violated her and defiled her, and she is left dead; he slew her savagely and slit her to the navel]. It is literally his desire that kills her; his penis not only penetrates, but tears her in half. This lustful but perhaps also dynastic impulse results not only in the loss of heirs, but also of the potential mother. While his sex is certainly monstrous, its result links him to Arthur, who also fails to engender a line of heirs. Both the Giant and Arthur remain childless, despite obvious efforts to beget heirs. The Giant's childlessness, however, results from 'extra'-potence, demonstrating all too clearly Arthur's impotence, which in turn 'suggests the failure of his manhood' (Westover 313). Arthur's physical impotence is set in contrast to the Giant's excessive masculinity, or, as Bartlett calls it, his 'pathological virility' (66). Despite the impossibility of reproduction for the Giant, he remains a potent threat to the kingdom, in what he does to its people, as well as how he compares to its King. Both threats originate in his extreme masculinity and his profound desire to consume and possess.

Like the Giant of Mont St Michel's acts of consumption and rape, Gowther's appetite and rapid development have consequences for the women of his community, but these behaviors come from instinct, not malicious desire. In addition to his excessive growth rate (he is the size of a seven year old by the age of one), or even possibly to enable it, Gowther possesses an insatiable appetite. Through his extreme physical need, he not only sucks his wet-nurses dry, he kills them: 'He sowkyd hom so thei lost ther lyvys,/ Sone had he sleyne three!' (113) [He sucked them until they lost their lives, soon he had killed three!]. Killing one nurse through such an appetite might be explained, but three seems ridiculous – yet these three nurses represent only Gowther's first few months of life. As we know, he grows incredibly quickly, and 'Be twelfe monethys was gon/ Nine norsus had he slon/ Of ladys feyr and fre' (118) [By the time twelve months passed, he had slain nine nurses, ladies both fair and noble]. Gowther's consumption of these nine women is all the more significant because they are noble women.[14] His actions

---

[14] Uebel argues for a different kind of monstrosity for Gowther, when he claims that Gowther 'vampirically' sucks nursemaids dry (100). While Gowther does seem to be sucking the life-force from these women, he certainly does not consume their blood.

deplete the community of noble wives and mothers, reminiscent of the Giant of Mont St Michel's crimes against the reproductive community of nobles from which he draws his companions and victims. However, Gowther's crime is one of immoderate appetite for breastmilk, a desire that is instinctual, not intentional.

Unlike the Giant, Gowther's hungers here are indiscriminate; although he damages the community in his consumption of its noblewomen, his uncontrolled hunger also threatens his mother's life. Gowther's hunger has political repercussions: the 'Knyghtus of that cuntre' (121) [knights of that country] demand that the Duke procure no more nurses for his son, and his mother is compelled to nurse her son, putting her own life in jeopardy. While he does not kill her, it is against her body that his early dentition is first deployed: when Gowther is finally offered his mother's breast, he bites off the nipple: 'His modur fell afowle unhappe,/ Upon a day bad hym tho pappe,/ He snaffulld to hit soo/ He rofe thos hed fro tho brest' (127–30) [His mother fell afoul unfortunately, One day she gave him her breast, he suckled it so that he ripped the nipple from the breast]. The poet ascribes no will in Gowther to harm his mother; rather, the language here suggests a desperate rooting: he 'snaffles' to her breast, an onomatopoeic word that seems to be unique to this text.[15] Despite his lack of intention, his infantile inability to control this impulse figures him, from the start, as a threat to women's bodies.

These early acts of violence against women prefigure Gowther's future treatment of women, but they are not attached to desire to harm. His appetite is uncontrollable largely because, as an infant, he is too young to control it. And yet these early violent incidents establish patterns of behavior by which he may construct his identity; they are signs of a prescient and dangerous masculinity.[16] In this early act, Gowther rejects his proper place in the hierarchy – this is the first moment in which he fails to be a proper heir and steward of his kingdom. The poet notes no purpose or pleasure on the part of the infant, but merely his growth, which reiterates only his insatiable appetite as it is driven by sheer physical need.[17] Saunders

[15] No other quotation appears in correlation to 'snafful' or its immediate variations in the *Middle English Dictionary*.
[16] Most critics read Gowther's violence against the women who nurse him as willful acts of identity construction. Blamires reads the nipple-biting as a rejection of the maternal: 'Here is the heir who will not imbibe maternal pedigree aright, who asserts "self" violently against that pedigree' (53). Cohen similarly reads this early violence as a reaction against nurturance and the domestic: 'The physical violence that attends every attempt at nurture demonstrates that no place exists for him within the domestic spaces represented by the parade of nurses and his mother; Gowther, from infancy, resists familialism' ("Gowther" 225). Uebel, however, reads this as more than resistance: for him it is 'sadistic' and violent in a truly intentional way: 'Considered together, Gowther's preoedipal crimes represent a sadistic rebellion against the maternal, the earliest indication of his urge toward annihilation' (101).
[17] Uebel continues to link Gowther's acts to specific kinds of monsters: werewolves and vampires: 'Premature dentation, often associated with canine qualities …, had folkloric significance as a sign of vampirism, lycanthropy, or the intervention of sorcery' (101). Although the poet certainly wants the audience to notice Gowther's monstrous impulses, he does not demonize Gowther in these specific ways. Gowther does not transform from human to

reads these acts as evidence of his 'evil and unnaturalness' (298), and, in a sense, she is right. Gowther simply acts out his physical identity, which is 'evil' and 'unnatural' in that he is only half human. He does not willfully declare himself against society, the maternal, or family, although his acts do rebel against these systems. Gowther's early acts are not acts of will, but are artifacts of his true parentage, and of his identity as it is grounded in his physical form. His violence, though it has implications for the entire community, is often hereafter directed at the bodies of a woman. Even his infant body is set against the bodies of women early – taking too much and penetrating flesh meant to be treated gently. Gowther's body is always already defined by its violation of women's bodies; even as an infant, his excessive masculinity presents itself in his appetites and desires.

Both the Giant of Mont St Michel and Gowther exhibit inflated masculinity in the ways that they consume the bodies of humans. However, the forms that this masculinity takes are presented very differently. The Giant, an adult, eats human bodies out of appetite, but also as an attempt to acquire their human qualities. In his mimesis of the courtly feast, his use of a silver platter and expensive spices, he incorporates human practices *and* human bodies. However, in attempting to artic-ulate his authority over human bodies to carve out a place for himself in the human hierarchy, he demonstrates the *differance* by which his body is defined.[18] Gowther's consumption of his wet-nurses is a far less premeditated act: he does not kidnap, kill, and dismember them, roasting them over the fire and serving them on platters. Instead, his insatiable appetite, driven by a body growing at excessive rates, causes the demise of women procured for him by his human family. While the results are the same for both the Giant and Gowther, the consumption of a generation of nobles, Gowther's youthful innocence recommends that we see him in a different way. Both monsters' acts are dictated, at least in part, by the cravings of their exces-sive bodies; Gowther's early appetites, however, are instinctual rather than willful, and we see early on that he is at the mercy of this body.

THE DYNASTIC IMPULSE OF THE GIANT:
THE GIANT, THE PHALLUS AND HUMAN AUTHORITY

Both in the Giant of Mont St Michel and in Gowther, we see creatures of excess – excess size, excess appetite, and excess masculinity. These features are inherently related: size necessitates appetite, and both size and appetite are implicated in the

---

monster, as do the werewolf and the vampire – his monstrosity results not from a traumatic attack, but rather is inherent in his parentage. Moreover, Laskaya and Salisbury claim that this same attribute is linked with another category: that of the demon-father: 'According to folk belief the presence of teeth at an early age functioned as proof of demonic paternity' (267).

18 As I have discussed earlier, Derridean *differance* indicates the quality which distinguishes similar items and prevents them from being the same. It is the quality of identification.

problems of masculinity that both monsters embody. These qualities lead to each monster's consumption and destruction of women, which in turn disrupts community practices of the proper circulation of women, and therefore reproduction. However, the consumption of women is only a part of the problem they present: they subvert the larger social order by usurping and wielding authority and the symbols of authority. Both the Giant and Gowther appropriate and deploy symbolic phalli to take over human power structures, just as they use their monstrous masculinity to destroy the bodies of women. In taking up the symbols of power, masculinity, dynasty, and indeed paternity – the Giant's kirtle of kings' beards and Gowther's falchion – the monsters infiltrate and endanger human communities. Through these means, they damage the communities in and near which they exist by violating social codes, subverting and replacing the titular authorities of these communities, and undoing the proper circulation of women and the processes of reproduction. Their excess masculinity, then, works to undermine the proper function of community and society.

The phallus is at once symbolic and literal, particularly in these medieval poems. Just as in *Beowulf*, it is a sign of authority, linked to both the male body (the penis) and the male position of social power (the patriarchy). As Butler argues, the connection between the body and the law is one that is constructed, and that requires maintenance to uphold both masculinity and social function: 'The law requires conformity to its own notion of "nature". It gains its legitimacy through the binary and asymmetrical naturalization of bodies in which the phallus, though clearly not identical to the penis, deploys the penis as its naturalized instrument and sign' (*Gender Trouble* 135). While the phallus can function without its obvious attachment to the male body, it is fundamentally related to social operations of power. However, this structure of power and authority that locates the body of the giant as its origin is flawed in one fundamental way: the giant, though well endowed, is generative in neither the Alliterative *Morte* nor *Sir Gowther*. The phallus, although not necessarily a literal penis, is connected to ideas of masculine sexual potency. Lacan states:

> The phallus is the privileged signifier of that mark in which the role of the logos is joined to the advent of desire. It can be said that this signifier is chosen because it is the most tangible element in the real of sexual copulation, and also the most symbolic in the literal (typographical) sense of the term, since it is equivalent there to the (logical) copula. It might also be said that, by virtue of its turgidity, it is the image of the vital flow as it is transmitted in generation. (*Ecrits* 287)

Lacan argues here that the phallus links logic, authority, and reason with desire, and therefore the penis is the referent by which the symbolic phallus can function. This correlation works because authority and desire rely on potency – on the ability to penetrate, generate, and procreate. However, in these poems, both monsters occupy positions of power and authority by seizing symbolic phalli and using them to destroy, while both fail, in the most basic sense, to procreate. As we have seen above, in the description of the Giant of Mont St Michel, the phallus that is too big destroys women and the possibility of generation. Gowther's sexual masculinity, as we shall see, is also destructive to the bodies of women, just as his phallic falchion is to the community at large. Neither monster can, in the end, set up a lasting legacy; neither successfully fathers any children. Therefore, the monster phallus, envisioned as the origin of masculinity, is truly a kind of non-functional masculinity that destroys communities rather than expanding them.

The Alliterative *Morte Arthure* is a text concerned with questions of masculinity, especially chivalry, kingship, and paternity. These themes occur in other accounts of the end of Arthur's life, but they are particularly highlighted in the Alliterative version.[19] Although based on chronicle sources, the Alliterative *Morte* significantly alters them. This poetic account emphasizes certain thematic elements by making Mordred into a reluctant regent, dramatizing the Queen's farewell to Arthur, incorporating into the figure of the Giant 'the hobby of collecting kings' beards,' and developing a mutual and productive relationship between Gaynor and Mordred (Fries 35). These changes all accentuate the themes of masculinity and potency already embedded in the larger narrative. The phallus, and its presence or absence, is consistently of concern in the Alliterative *Morte*. As Göller claims, 'the author seems to have been mildly obsessed with wounds "below the belt" ' ("Reality" 23). The most obvious phallus in the poem is that of the 'breklesse' (1048) [breechless] Giant of Mont St Michel. On his way to confront the tyrant Lucius of Rome over lands that he has the right to rule, Arthur is informed of the crimes of a giant who is rapidly depopulating the area. In seven winters he has eaten more than 'fyfe hondrethe' (845) [five hundred] people and 'als fele fawntekyns of freeborne childyre' (846) [as many children of freeborn knights]. More importantly, he has killed all the male children of the clans, 'ne kynde has he leuede ... That he ne has clenly dystroyede all the knaue childyre' (848, 50) [not a family has he left ... of which he has not cleanly destroyed all the male children]. His most recent affront, in addition to the continuing cannibalism of knights and children, is that he has kidnapped the Duchess of Brittany in order 'To lye by that lady aye whyls hir lyfe lastez' (855) [To lie by that lady while her life lasts]. The Giant's gustatory and sexual appetites are exorbitant, and the targets of each are the noble classes.

This passage demonstrates Arthur's faulty kingship, chiefly his failure to protect the lives of his people and the lineage of the noble community. Arthur's

---

19 Finlayson nicely summarizes other redactions' treatment of the fight with the Giant: 'In Wace and Layamon a general picture is given of the terror and damage caused by the giant (Wace's is more detailed). Geoffrey of Monmouth simply states that a giant from Spain had carried off Helen. Though it has been argued that there is a close correspondence at this point in the narrative between Layamon and our poem, this claim is not supported by close examination of the relevant passages. In fact AM seems to owe little but the general outline of the incident to either W or L, much less to G, and develops the episode in a manner which indicates that our author attaches far more significance to the encounter than did the writers of other chronicles' (113).

goal in the poem is to regain his rightful lands because his ancestors were rulers of Rome (272–87), but also because, as King Angus says, 'Thow aughte to be ouerlynge ouer all oþer kynges,/ Fore wyseste and worthyeste and wyghteste of hanndes' (289–90) [You ought to be overlord of all other kings, being wisest, worthiest, and most skilled of hands]. However, Arthur has already failed to protect his people in the nation closest to England – France. While the killing and consumption of children is meant to demonize the Giant, the significance is not only in their age. He kills all the male children, the heirs of all the noble families. Moreover, he kidnaps the Duchess not to consume, as he does the children and the knights, but to 'lay with.' We will later learn that she descends from 'the rycheste' (865) [the richest], most powerful bloodlines, and is, in fact, a cousin of Arthur's wife. The Giant desires the removal of existing heirs, perhaps with the goal of replacing them with his own. This is more than an impulse of monstrous consumption and immediate satisfaction for carnal desire; it is a political and dynastic impulse precisely because it targets only noble mothers and their sons. Moreover, these acts directly threaten Arthur and invite his intervention – an intervention that is notably delayed for seven years.

The Giant has proved a threat to other kings, those underkings for whom Angus suggests Arthur should be overlord – he has assumed their authority by demanding that they give up to him phallic symbols of their masculinity that are simultaneously intimate and public. According to the Duchess' nurse, the Giant wears a garment 'bordyrde with the berdez of burlyche kyngez, Crispid and kombide, that kempis may knawe/ Iche kyng by his colour' (1002–4) [bordered with the beards of strong kings, curled and combed so that warriors may know each king by his color]. In this poem, the taking of hair is representative of defeat and emasculation, as is the case when Arthur causes the defeated Romans to have their hair shorn.[20] The Giant's beard-collecting introduces the pattern of emasculating hair-taking. Not only has he defeated these kings, whether or not they faced him in battle or sent their shorn beards in response to his demand for such tribute, but he has assumed their power as his own in the wearing of their beards for any warrior to recognize. As Westover claims:

> The coat is a token of the masculine, since the beards with which it is embroidered serve as synecdoches for individual men. Their cumulative effect is to increase the heroic, eminently masculine prestige of the coat's owner ... at the same time, however, the coat is fraught with ambiguity, since it signifies tyrannous injustice as well as manhood. (315)

The Giant wears the kirtle as a badge of authority, which is only powerful in its excess of masculinity. It takes the beards of many kings to construct the masculine authority necessary to satiate the Giant, but he will not be satisfied until he has the

---

[20] See Bartlett (62), who also observes 'those conquered in battle are routinely forced to participate in rituals of symbolic emasculation' (57).

beard of the most powerful king – Arthur. The element that most defines the kirtle and perhaps the Giant is the absence of Arthur's beard, or the presence of lack.[21]

Arthur's lack of involvement at Mont St Michel has resulted in the deaths of innocent civilians and noble men and women, but more significantly, in the depletion of the next generation of nobles. The Giant, it seems, has been demanding Arthur's beard as tribute for the past seven years: 'And he has aschede Arthure all þis seuen wynntter:/ Forthy hurdez he here, to owttraye hys pople,/ Till þe Bretons kyng haue burneschte his lyppys,/ And sent his berde to that bolde wyth his best berynes' (1009–12) [And he has asked for Arthur's these seven winters; because of that he hides here, to injure his people, until the king of the Britons has polished his lips and sent his beard to that bold one via his best warriors]. Arthur's impotence in defending his people is compounded by the Giant's direct challenge to him.[22] Such a loss is inexcusable; Patricia Ingham argues that the poem points to the inevitability of loss within the Arthurian system, claiming that certain kinds of losses are acceptable, while others are 'catastrophic,' like that of Gawain later in the poem (89–90). She counts the death of the Duchess as one of those acceptable losses. However, this loss is neither acceptable nor singular, because it is not simply the loss of a lone noblewoman, nor of the pathos-inspiring children. It is the loss of posterity for the nation, and the gap left by her never-to-be-born children echoes Arthur's own heirlessness and lack of paternity. He tolerates this lack of progeny in both cases, leaving his kingdom significantly devoid of heirs; this is indeed a catastrophic loss. Although the Giant does not, in the end, achieve Arthur's beard – and therefore does not subsume the power affiliated with this phallus – he assumes the authority of all the other kings, and uses this power to purge the entire region of its posterity.

While the Giant clothes himself in the authority achieved by other men, Gowther creates his own, in the form of a falchion that both suits and exceeds the social order into which he is born. Unlike his consumption of women as a child, his creation of the falchion is entirely intentional and purposeful – and it is noticeably linked to his coming of age as a young man. At fifteen, he creates his own weapon, 'A fachon bothe of style and yron,/ Wytte yow wyll he wex full styron/ And fell folke con he feyr' (142–4) [A falchion both of steel and iron, you should know that he grew full fierce and terrorized many people]. This falchion suits only

---

21 It is perhaps more than ironic that this is Lacan's formulation for women in relation to the phallus: women are constituted by lack of a phallus. In this case, it seems that Arthur is repeatedly affiliated with lack, and is thus perpetually feminized. It is this identification that seems to drive him to increasingly excessive acts of violence in order to achieve a kind of mastery and therefore masculinity.

22 Arthur responds immediately and vehemently to Rome's demands for tribute, setting off on a crusade to regain his forefathers' lands, but for seven years he has not responded to the Giant's demands. Some readers might suggest he does not know of these threats; I argue that if he does not, his lack of knowledge of this kind of internal threat to his authority betrays a serious flaw in his governance.

someone of his size and excessive strength; we are told that no other man can wield it because of its heft: 'No nodur mon might hit beyr' (141) [No other man might bear it]. This size and heft of this sword compare with the sword of giants that Beowulf finds and uses in Grendel's mother's mere, but which melts, revealing Beowulf's own human inadequacies. However, Gowther is no mere human; he does not simply find and use the sword; he crafts it himself. It is tailored to his own form and function. While the falchion is certainly a Saracen signifier, as many scholars have suggested, Gowther's frightening hybrid identity is not racial, Saracen–Christian, but special, demon–human.[23] The falchion marks Gowther as Other, invoking the Saracen, but its primary significance is in its size and excess. These qualities indicate Gowther's physical difference and the problems inherent in his physical and spiritual make-up.

Gowther's use of this falchion is not effectively governed or proscribed; he uses it to create his own law. Just as his physical growth – representative of his demonic paternity – is uncontrolled, so is his violent behavior. The Duke has no real authority over him. In an attempt to control Gowther's wicked behavior, the Duke tries to direct the boy's aggression into an acceptable outlet: he knights him: 'Tho Duke hym might not chastise,/ Bot made hym knyght that tyde' (149–50) [The Duke could not chastise him, but made him a knight at that time]. Knighting him, however, does nothing to curb Gowther's violence; instead, the poet suggests immediately after mention of this knighting that no one in the kingdom can survive one of his blows (153). The failure of this attempt does not designate a failure of the knightly class, but instead, the false paternity of the Duke. McGregor suggests that this impotence points to a problem inherent to paternity;[24] however, we have no situation in the poem through which to test this claim: the only father who fails here is not actually a father – he is instead shown to be impotent, physically and symbolically, from the first lines of the poem. This powerlessness is even more clearly marked when the Duke simply expires, his attempt to circumscribe Gowther's violence having failed miserably: 'For sorro tho Duke fell don ded' (154) [The Duke fell down dead from sorrow]. The institution of knighthood has no power to control the physical monstrosity of one of its knights because Gowther is governed by a far stronger force: his real and indeed superhuman

---

23 The falchion has significant symbolic connections with the cultural and religious Other, the Saracen: Cohen notes that it is 'an Eastern weapon, suggestive of Saracens and other fiendish heathens' ("Gowther" 225), while Montaño argues that it represents Gowther's racial identity (123). Although the sword has Saracen implications, Gowther's parentage is demonic and Christian. He may be symbolically connected to the Saracen as he performs anti-religious acts, but he is neither religiously nor racially Saracen. Alternatively, Laskaya and Salisbury suggest that it is representative of his identity as a 'wild man' (269). Significantly, however, the falchion is forged using conventional and 'civilized' metals into a form that is recognizable as a sword – it is nothing like the rude club used by uncivilized Wild Men.

24 McGregor argues, 'As Gowther's continued violence demonstrates, the symbolic dimension of paternity the Duke tries to employ remains impotent. The Duke is quite literally his father in name only, an empty placeholder' (71–2).

paternity. Gowther's demonic father does not so much predict Gowther's future behavior as notify Gowther's mother of Gowther's identity: 'He seyd, "Y have geyton a chylde on the/ That in is yothe full wylde schall bee,/ And weppons wyghtly weld" ' (76–8) [He said 'I have gotten a child on you that in his youth shall be fully wild and wield weapons skillfully']. Gowther, at his conception, is defined by his demonic father, and, in his creation and use of the falchion, forces his titular father to vacate his position of authority so that Gowther may occupy it.

Upon the Duke's death, Gowther takes up his social position of authority; he replaces his false father both literally and figuratively, also replacing order with crisis. In the midst of describing Gowther's most horrible deeds, the poet assures us that 'He wold wyrke is fadur wyll' (176) [He would do his father's will]. We are therefore reminded that Gowther is not administering the law as a duke should, but rather he dispenses corruption as befits the child of a demon, even if he does not yet know of his true father. While Gowther is violent before the Duke dies, his crimes grow significantly more troubling when this false heir becomes Duke himself. This new responsibility puts Gowther's crimes into sharp focus: not only does he fail to protect his people and those who cannot protect themselves – the function of a knight – but he terrorizes them himself. His crimes are both sexualized and violent, and they are generally played out against people affiliated with or reliant upon the Church. He does not fail merely as a proper signifier of knighthood and right belief by refusing to hear mass or matins, but he actually beats up priests: 'And men of holy kyrke dynggus down/ Wher he might hom mete' (172–3) [And smites down men of the holy Church whenever he meets them]. Gowther's law and authority are subject to no moral center, and particularly oppose the Church, an institution notably under the authority of an entirely different father, one diametrically opposed to Gowther's demon patriarch.

More than just abusing those he meets by chance, Gowther courts conflict, using his social status to his advantage, and purposefully directs his violent impulses at the bodies of women. He visits a convent, and because of his position, the nuns are obligated to meet him: 'Thos pryorys and hur covent/ With presescion ageyn hym went/ Full hastely that tyde' (184–6) [The prioress and her convent went to meet him in a procession quickly that time]. Gowther abuses this honor: not only do he and his men rape the nuns, but they also lock them inside the church and set it on fire: 'Thei wer full ferd of his body,/ For he and is men both leyn hom by –/ Tho soothe why schuld y hyde?/ And sythyn he spard hom in hor kyrke/ And brend hom up, thus con he werke' (187–92) [They were afraid of his body, because he and his men both lay with them – Truly, why should I hide it? And then he enclosed them in their church and burned them up, thus did he work]. Gowther, in effect, hunts down these nuns, using and perverting the rules of the previous social order to his advantage. Here Gowther particularly subverts the order of the circulation of women: by raping nuns, he puts women who ought to remain out of circulation back into it, against their and the Church's will, locating himself as an authority above that of the Church. Then, once he has asserted his own law over these women's bodies, he destroys them utterly and thereby removes them from any other subsequent challenges to his own law. Through his position of authority, upheld by his use of the falchion, he resists the ultimate social authority, the Church, and reconfigures the circulation of women in transgressive but ultimately unproductive ways.

However, after Gowther learns of his true parentage, he realizes that the phallus he wields is not really under his own control, but under the governance of his father the fiend. He determines to defy his strongest impulses and accept wholly that which he had abjected: the Church. He recognizes at this moment the necessity of salvation, setting the possibility of future good action and penitence against the evil nature of his body. Aware of the danger of having a fiend for a father, he begins to pray for the first time: 'To save hym fro is fadur tho fynde;/ He preyed to God and Mare hynde,/ That most is of poste,/ To bring is sowle to tho blys' (242–4) [To save him from his father the fiend, he prayed to God and gentle Mary, that have the most power to bring his soul to bliss]. Still clearly the son of a demon, Gowther desires to come under the protection of a different set of parents. He determines in this moment that the authority he perceived to be his own is controlled instead by his demonic father. He learns that his falchion, though made by his own hands, is not entirely under his own control. His body and its behaviors have been determined by his demon father at his conception: he has fulfilled the demon's early claims ' "That in is yothe full wylde schall bee,/ And weppons wyghtly weld" ' (73–8) ['That in his youth he shall be fully wild and wield weapons skillfully']. In order to reclaim his weapon, and therefore his masculine authority and independence from his rapist father, he will have to become subject to another law entirely.

In each situation, the Giant and Gowther assume a kind of authority from phallic objects. The Giant's kirtle of kings' beards asserts his mastery over their weaker and lesser bodies, and displays their impotence in managing his threat. Because none of these kings can defeat him, the Giant is able to kidnap and rape his way through their communities, causing only destruction. He is entirely incapable of generation because of his monstrous size and hypermasculine body and identity. Gowther too grows early into an excessively masculine body and an identity that is not entirely integrated into the values and structures of his community. When he crafts and uses his falchion to terrorize the countryside, he destroys the man that he believes to be his father and inherits this father's position of leadership and authority. However, once Gowther assumes the position of the law and authority, gained by the administration of his falchion, he uses it to twist and pervert this position of authority, rerouting the lines of circulation and reproduction decided by the community. Both of these masculine monsters place themselves at the center of authority and power through usurpation and violence. However, Gowther's decisions to give up his position of authority and pursue penance begin to show the humanity engendered in him by his mother, not his father. Although physically rapacious like the Giant, Gowther's existence within the community, his desire for repentance, and his hybrid status as a creature already part human make him alone a candidate for successful transformation and recuperation.

HOW TO SUBDUE A GIANT:
CASTRATION AND TRANSFORMATION

Despite the profound similarities present in the bodies of the Giant of Mont St Michel and Gowther, each of their stories represents an alternate means of managing the monster. In both cases, the monster's problem is one of excessive masculinity located in and manifested through the phallus. Therefore, in order to control the monster and re-appropriate authority into human hands, the phallus must be removed. The monster must be castrated. However, in Middle English literature, this reconfiguration of the monster's body can happen in two ways: (1) the monster can be literally dismembered and thereby erased from the narrative, and the authority which he had taken on can be reintegrated into the human community; or (2) the monster's body can be transformed and the hypermasculine phallus he once possessed can be redeployed in the name of another father who now holds the authority he had usurped. The act of castration and dismemberment is one that is permanent, and that articulates, as in the Old English texts, the permanent monstrosity of the giant. Not all Middle English monsters are transformed, as we can see in the case of the Giant. However, the possibility of transformation allows us to see the monstrous body in an entirely different way. Through transformation, the monster has a chance to become man, and to change his monstrous ways along with his monstrous form. Transformation implies a certain kind of plasticity, an openness to the processes of change and adaptation. With the promise of transformation, however, comes the implication that a body once changed might change again. The trouble with transformation is that, as with the women's bodies in *Mandeville's Travels*, what is monstrous and what is human is not clearly visible, and therefore the line between the monstrous and the human is no longer entirely firm. With the possibility of change comes the probability of instability. Thus, while the castration of the Giant of Mont St Michel removes his threat by reacting against his body, the transformation of Gowther holds both more potential for hope, and for uncertainty.

The violence with which Arthur undertakes the castration of the Giant reveals that this battle is about more than justice: it is about masculinity and authority. After an exchange in which Arthur barely avoids blows and manages to stab the Giant in the forehead through 'to þe brayne' (1114) [to the brain], he drives his sword into the Giant's thigh and slices upwards: 'Hye vpe on þe hanche with his harde wapyn,/ That he hillid þe swerde halfe a fote large –/ The hott blode of þe hulke vnto þe hilte rynnez;/ Ewyn into inmette the gyaunt he hyttez,/ Iust to þe genitals and jaggede þam in sondre' (1119–23) [High up in the haunch with his hard weapon, so he buried the sword in half a foot, the hot blood of the hulk runs over the hilt, even into the innards of the Giant he hits, right to the genitals and cut them apart].[25] Arthur's response to the Giant's consumption of noble heirs and

---

[25] The use of the term 'genitals' clearly refers to the phallus and masculine potency; the other two

the attempted rape of the Duchess is, effectively and primarily, a castration: he cuts the Giant's genitals asunder.[26] While the sexual punishment for the sexual crime is a clear incentive, castration for rape, it seems that Arthur acts perhaps a little too violently for his motivation to be impersonal. In addition to being the appropriate punishment for rape, perhaps here we see Arthur engaging in an eye-for-an-eye kind of justice. The Giant's goal is Arthur's beard, which he desires to complete his collection. The beards he has already obtained represent his authority over the kings who have lost their beards; they have submitted to him, have given up their potency as leaders. The Giant has castrated them, and intends the same for Arthur. Arthur responds to the threat to his beard by removing the literal signifier of the Giant's masculinity and potent authority. No more can the Giant impose himself in the place of a male noble and assume the privileges thereof.

Castration does not immediately kill the Giant, and, significantly, it does not end the threat to Arthur's life: the sexualized battle thus calls into question the efficacy of Arthur's phallus. The enraged Giant grabs the King and they engage in a violent wrestling match. Never having struck Arthur with his club, the Giant embraces Arthur in a way that is far more life-threatening:

> Thane he castez the clubb and the Kyng hentez:
> On þe creeste of þe cragg he caughte hym in armez,
> And enclosez hym clenly, to cruschen hys rybbez –
> So hard haldez he þat hende þat nere his herte brystez. (1132–5)

[Then he throws down the club and seizes the King, on the crest of the crag, he caught him in his arms, and encloses him tightly to crush his ribs, and he holds him so hard that his heart nearly bursts.]

The watching maidens, who had been the Giant's spit-turners, cry and pray for Arthur's life (1136–9), and Sir Kay, who has just rushed up to the scene, is convinced that Arthur is dead (1152–5). The language of the wrestling match combines elements of the sexual and the violent. This is not the noble battle of knights, but an intimate grappling, much like that which occurred between Beowulf and Grendel's mother. The verbs, obviously chosen for alliteration, nonetheless reflect the double nature of the fight, for Arthur and the Giant wrestle together, toss around, wallow, tumble, turn over, tear each other's clothes, tilt together, and exchange places on top and bottom: 'Wrothely þai wrythyn and

mentions of this word in the Middle English corpus are from Gower (*Confessio* V. 801–900), where it refers specifically to a castration, and from a medical remedy from *Secreta Secretorum*.

[26] In fact, Arthur lists his complaints in order of importance when he first approaches: first, he mentions the unclean food (1063); next, the killing of children (1065–6); thirdly, that he has killed many people and made Christian martyrs; and, almost as an afterthought, he adds his revenge for the Duchess: 'And for this faire ladye, þat þow has fey leuyde,/ And þus forced one foulde, for fylth of þi selfen' (1070–71) [And for this fair lady, that you have left lifeless, and thus forced in the dust, for your own filth].

wrystill togederz,/ Welters and walowes ouer within þase buskez,/ Tumbellez and turnes faste and terez þaire wedez;/ Vntenderly fro þe toppe þai tiltin togederz,/ Whilom Arthure ouer and oþerwhile vndyre' (1141–5) [With anger they writhe and wrestle together, welter and wallow over within the bushes, tumble and turn fast and tear their clothes, untenderly on the top they tilt together, sometimes with Arthur on the top and sometimes underneath]. The physical connection between Giant and King asserts the struggle for authority that is this contest over beards.

This fight will decide much more than physical superiority; it is a fight over threatened masculinity and the patriarchy of a nation. However, it is a fight that reveals dangerous flaws in Arthur's identity and masculinity. Strangely, Cohen claims this is Arthur's 'most heroic battle' (*Of Giants* 152). Certainly the stakes of this fight are high: if Arthur fails here, he cedes superiority and rule to a rapist and cannibal and fails to avenge a dead noblewoman, but he also fails to confront Lucius and confirm his right to his lands. In essence, if Arthur loses, he fails as a king in all ways, from simple justice to dynastic collapse. With such noble stakes and 'heroism,' however, we might expect a more noble fight. Instead, as Manfred Markus remarks, 'the brutality of the fight, the blows to brains and bowels and the splitting of genitals throw rather a negative light on Arthur' (64). We do not see heroic swordplay, even as Arthur fights against all odds, but rather we get blows below the belt and rather undignified wrestling, with bushes being rolled through and clothes being torn. Arthur gives up his sword and his dignity, his failures as a king and a fighter having been revealed. The match culminates only when Arthur pulls a dagger and jams it into the Giant 'vp to þe hiltez' (1149) [up to the hilt]. Arthur cannot defeat the Giant through wrestling (he is, after all, not a giant himself!), but must use a tiny weapon to penetrate the monstrous body which is too large to effectively penetrate a woman.[27]

Although the poet emphasizes the Giant's physical superiority, he also rein-scribes Arthur's status as a civilized and potent knight at this moment. Arthur's authority is rewritten not with a sword, but with a dagger – with cunning, no doubt, but not exactly with nobility. If this battle is about not only who will win, but also about who possesses more masculine authority, then Arthur loses. His sword might castrate the Giant, but it does not defeat him. Arthur's best weapon is small and concealed; although he defeats the Giant, the way in which he does so shows the audience the extent of his phallus. His own insecurity over his mascu-linity and authority is borne out when he attempts to supplement his masculinity by 'appropriating the symbols of the Giant's sexual prowess' (Bartlett 68) in his assumption of the Giant's most potent possessions, the kirtle of kingly beards and the iron club: ' "Haue I the kyrtyll and þe clubb, I coueite noghte ells" ' (1191) ["If I have the kirtle and the club, I covet nothing else"]. Even though Arthur's defeat of the Giant is total – the Giant is after all castrated not once but twice, as his head is

---

27 This wrestling match may remind us of Beowulf's successful wrestling match against Grendel, but the desperate use of a weapon also recalls Beowulf's fight against Grendel's mother.

removed and put on display – Arthur is unable to solve the problems of his own kingdom, and indeed his own family, as I shall demonstrate. He gains no more masculinity by defeating the Giant than he does in conquering Lucius early in the narrative.

Arthur's biggest failure, ultimately, is at home. The Giant is simultaneously dread and pleasure, simultaneously human and more than human. The Giant thus represents that which opposes Arthur, but also, as Cohen suggests, the masculine authority that always already comes before him.[28] And yet, if the origin and pinnacle of masculinity is overcome by a late-comer with a dagger, then what does that say about the stability of masculinity? Arthur's castration and defeat of the Giant articulates his victory over the body of the monster, but it cannot bolster his own flagging masculinity. The Giant's phallus is castrated, removed like the penises of the male monsters in *Wonders of the East*, and thereby he and his human pretensions undergo a vehement act of erasure by Arthur. Thus, the Giant is erased from the narrative, also like Grendel and his mother, but the problems of masculinity that his body indicates remain and trouble the rest of the narrative.

Sir Gowther, alternatively, presents us with a transformative monster for whom different possibilities exist. Unlike the Giant, he recognizes and abhors his own monstrous body and behavior upon learning about his demonic origin. Because he undertakes his own revision, he is not erased, but rather transformed both physically and spiritually. Although transformation provides frightening possibilities for the monstrous body in *Mandeville's Travels* and other medieval texts,[29] the fifteenth century romance *Sir Gowther* rewrites the scene of transformation. In this text, the monstrous body is transformed into the spiritually penitent body. The nature of transformation itself is revised: instead of a seemingly human body being made horrifying by its ability to transform, a body that is terrifying and hybrid is saved through the healing power of transformation. Instead of being killed, the body of the monster is revised and rewritten into something recognizable, understandable, and not only safe, but saintly.

Gowther's recognition of his monstrous origins marks the beginning of his

---

[28] Cohen argues that the abstract figure of the giant is representative of the Lacanian concept of 'extimite': 'the monster appears to be outside the human body ... thus he threatens travelers and errant knights ... But closer examination reveals that the monster is also fully within, a foundational figure; and so the giant is depicted as the builder of cities ... the origin of the glory of empire' (*Of Giants* xii). This claim contrasts starkly with Finlayson, who associates the Giant with 'Evil' and thus Arthur with 'Good.' He argues that this scene is so relevant to the larger narrative because it makes clear that 'Arthur is not only a great conqueror, but is also, more significantly, the champion of Christianity and the redeemer of his people' (119). He mentions neither Arthur's killing of Mordred's children nor his notable delay in responding to the problem of the Giant in the first place.

[29] For instance, Chaucer's *Wife of Bath's Tale* introduces multiple transformative bodies, including fairies that magically appear, and a woman who can be ugly or beautiful (as well as faithful or unfaithful) by day or by night, depending on the choice of her betrothed. Similarly, *Sir Launfal* depicts the lovely and 'awe-ful' disappearing body of the fairy-lover, which resolves but complicates the problematic identity of the titular knight.

process of conversion from sinner to saint – but even as his behavior changes, his identity as the son of a demon does not. He travels to Rome and supplicates the Pope on his knees, asking for 'schryfte and absolyscion' (269) [shrift and absolution]. He identifies himself as a christened person, saying ' "Yey,/ My name it is Gowther; Now y lowve God" ' (278–80) ['Yes, my name is Gowther, now I love God'], and confesses his parentage. Uebel rightly observes that Gowther does not confess his own actions but dwells upon his conception: 'Notably, Gowther confesses to no crimes ... but he does confess his fiendish origins by rehearsing his familial history ... Gowther presents himself as victim rather than sinner' (104). Gowther's problems certainly derive from his parentage and his monstrous body, but this confession nonetheless seems incomplete: he leaves aside his own choices in pursuing the direction his monstrous body urged on him. This distinction, present in Gowther's omission, reveals a strikingly new notion: that one might be led astray by one's body, but that perhaps the body is not entirely to blame. Gowther's ability to recognize his misdirection and to seek penitence, however poorly he might be doing thus far, indicates that he is not as defined by his body as are the monsters in earlier English literature. Regardless of Gowther's omission of his sins, however, the Pope recognizes the damage Gowther has done to the Church. When he says, ' "For thu hast Holy Kyrke destroyed" ' (283) ['For you have destroyed Holy Church'], we must assume that the Pope refers to more than the fact of Gowther's birth, as Gowther is not the only child of a demon ever to be born. He must also know of the insults inflicted on the religious people in Gowther's dukedom. Gowther begs for penance and promises to hold to the penance given him, but he refuses when the Pope asks him to lay down his falchion. His refusal is logical, ' "My frendys ar full thyn" ' (294) ['My friends are full thin']; Gowther, after all, has made many enemies since his infancy. Still, the falchion is more than a symbol of his knighthood; it is the signifier of his monstrous masculinity. The falchion serves as a symbol of his physical difference, his propensity for excess, and his usurped and misused masculine authority – qualities he is unable to simply put aside, because they reside in his monstrous body.

Despite the Pope's absolution, Gowther's forgiveness can only come from God because of the nature of his monstrous body. His case requires the very highest authority; a priest cannot confer this kind of transformation. The penance Gowther receives circumscribes his interaction with the outside world; he can neither eat nor speak like a human: ' "Wherser thu travellys, be northe or soth,/ Thu eyt no meyt bot that thu revus of howndus muthe/ Cum thy body within;/ Ne no worde speke for evyll ne gud,/ Or thu reyde tokyn have fro God,/ That forgyfyn is thi syn" ' (295–300) ['Wheresoever you travel, be it north or south, eat no meat but that you receive from a dog's mouth, (none but that should) come within your body; Nor speak any word either for evil or good, until you have received a sign from God that your sin is forgiven'].[30] Even the Pope, it seems, is unsure if

---

[30] Uebel demonstrates the appropriateness of this particular kind of penance, although he argues that it is ultimately unsuccessful: 'Remarkably, the pope attempts to turn the sadistic Gowther

Gowther's sins can be forgiven because of his physical identity. Although he gives Gowther penance to perform, its duration is indefinite – the end will only be achieved through God's own intervention.[31] Gowther's identity as a half demon, half human confounds even the Pope: a permanent change in behavior for Gowther does not necessarily guarantee his forgiveness because his very body is shaped by a deep and profoundly different kind of sin.

Gowther's step in the process of transformation is behavioral: he must give up his pride, even if he cannot give up his falchion. Gowther leaves Rome and wanders into another country, but he dutifully obeys the terms of his penance; although Cohen states that he 'becomes dog' ("Gowther" 232), in truth, he merely acts like one. He is fed by a greyhound each night of his travels, which reveals to the audience that God watches his penance with approval. That it is a greyhound that feeds him also confirms his status as (at least half) noble.[32] Gowther does indeed live *like* a dog, but he clearly exists in a significantly more human category. When he first enters the Emperor's castle, having waited meekly to be invited in by the porter, he immediately settles himself under the high table without speaking a word: 'Unto tho hye bord he chesse,/ Ther undur he made is seytt' (332–3) [Unto the head table he went, and under it he made his seat]. The odd behavior earns him threats from the head porter, who nonetheless notes his noble appearance when he reports the strange man's presence to the Emperor: ' "a mon,/ And that tho feyrest

---

into a masochistic knight by compelling him to focus his identity on one part of his body, his mouth, transforming the site of his original sins (the oral attacks on his nurses and mother) into a sign of penance' (104). Blamires sees the penance as appropriate to what he perceives as Gowther's most significant crime: his arrogance. He gains a new humility through a 'series of moments of interior self-suppression' (55).

31 Charbonneau notes that 'Gowther's dilemma then is not a typical human one, but rather the playing out of that tricky theological question of whether despite unintentionally fulfilling his devilish patrimony and committing the most heinous sins, he can be forgiven. He is no Everyman – and by his very birth cannot be – so that the text explores the precise nature of his ambiguous, semi-determinate nature as not quite human' (25).

32 Salter argues that the greyhound 'can also be viewed as an emblem of Gowther's noble nature, drawing attention to his role as an aristocratic hero of romance, as well as his identity as a saint' (80). Uebel sees this transition as neither productive nor positive, however; he claims that 'Gowther contaminates his soul – for he cannot do otherwise – by abjecting himself as a dog. The hybrid dog–man was, throughout the Middle Ages, seen as an image of the punishment that submission to sin brings down upon mortals' (108). Alternatively, Cohen sees this state as a successful overcoding of the human body, necessary for Gowther to obtain true humanity. He argues that 'all of the forces that are transmitted through the canine body rebound to overcode the human. An interstitial monster springs temporarily into being: a dog–man, a cynocephalus, a werewolf. But once the overcoding "takes," the body passes out of its freakish hybridity to be inscribed more fully than ever into the secure space of the Human' ("Gowther" 232). Thus, Cohen sees him as a dog, Salter sees him as a high-status dog, and Uebel sees him as a degraded hybrid dog – and yet, in no way has Gowther's body been transformed. Uebel concedes that Gowther's dog-status is not literal: 'Yet Gowther's "becoming-dog" is, of course, purely demonstrative; he cannot, unlike a conventional lycanthrope, actually, that is to say physically let alone mentally, become canine' (107).

that ever y sye" ' (339–40) ['a mon, and that is the fairest that I ever saw']. Gowther is not so 'humiliated' by this dog-status that his social status is not recognizable; indeed, his unwillingness to give up his falchion demonstrates that he has yet to give up his possession of authority, even though he has temporarily laid aside his performance of its authority. His comportment, however, is almost immediately recognized as penance: ' "And yet mey happon thoro sum chans/ That it wer gyffon hym in penans" ' (346–7) ['And yet it may be through some chance that it was given him in penance']. Gowther's behavior has an audience able to interpret it, and to understand it in human, not animal, terms.

Gowther's muteness and connection to the dogs, and thus to both the Emperor's daughter and his Saracen enemies, confirms his double status as human and Other. Like Gowther, the Emperor's daughter is mute, but unlike Gowther, her muteness is not penitential: 'Scho wold have spokyn and might noght' (376) [She would have spoken, but could not]. It is this young woman that provides the means for Gowther's final redemption. She is the cause of a war between her father and a great Sultan who desires to marry her. Her father absolutely refuses this alliance in the name of Christ: ' "And y wyll not, be Cryst wonde,/ Gyffe hor to no hethon hownde" ' (391–2) ['And I will not, by Christ's wounds, give her to any heathen hound']. This phrase, 'heathen hounds,' familiar enough in Middle English literature,[33] is a phrase that serves to link Gowther with the Saracens. Gowther is first connected to the Saracens through his blade, the falchion, as Uebel suggests:

> The blade itself is foreign; curved like a sickle, it symbolizes the brutality of the Saracen other, whose very identity, as Norman Daniel has shown, was imagined throughout the Middle Ages to inhere in the double threat of violence and sexuality. Gowther has in effect become Saracen, his sadism and his fetishism interanimating him to the point of a pure will to power. (103)

While possessing this kind of Eastern blade might imply a strange and Saracen identity for the transgressive Gowther, it does not 'transform' him into a Saracen – it merely indicates his status as Other in comparison to normative Christian identity. However, this connection, when paired with Gowther's enforced bond to the castle dogs, does link him to the 'heathen hounds' who oppose the Emperor. The dogs' symbolism is double: through the muteness and humility of the dogs, Gowther is associated with the mute daughter and the injunction of the Pope, but through their bestial nature and the metonymic tie to the Saracens, Gowther is linked to the non-Christian. These connections highlight Gowther's troubled and

---

33 The phrase appears in *Merlin: or, the history of King Arthur: a prose romance*, chapter XXIX, and chapter XXXII, in *Octovian* Cambridge University Library Ms. Ff.2.38, between lines 1401 and 1500, in *Þe Liflade of St. Juliana*, the Royal manuscript, and at least three times in *Layamon's Brut* (*Middle English Dictionary*). Friedman, too, comments on the link between the term 'dog' and Moslems (67). See Montaño for further discussion (124–6).

double identity: he is human and able to be forgiven, but he is also demon, and thus inherently (and physically) opposed to the Christian. No matter how humble his behavior, this physically dual nature makes redemption, in such a state, impossible.

Gowther lives a double life while in the Emperor's household, employing his sword skills this time to the benefit of a community, rather than to its destruction. This second life is recognized only by the mute daughter. When the war begins, Gowther prays for a means to help the Emperor (406–7), a prayer that is answered immediately: Gowther finds a black horse and armor at his chamber door (411). As he rides out to war, the audience is assured that 'Non hym knew bot that meyden gent' (419) [None knew him but that gentle maiden]. In battle, Gowther earns violent success, which recalls his former violence. However, this time the violence is directed not inward, toward his own community, but outward, to the enemies of the Christian community at large. Thus, Gowther continues his employment in extreme and violent deeds, chopping off heads and bursting brains: 'Mony a crone con he stere' (425) [Many a head did he remove] and 'He gard stedus for to stakur/ And knyghttus hartys for to flakur/ When blod and brenus con brast;/ And mony a heython hed of smott' (427–30) [He made horses stagger and knights' hearts flutter when blood and brains burst, and many a heathen head off smote]. The poet does not hesitate to describe these actions in detail, as Gowther violates the integrity of the bodies of his opponents, just as he did in his own lands, to his own people. When he is done with this bloodshed and the Sultan retreats, Gowther returns humbly to his spot under the table. No one else has recognized him, so this behavior does not seem strange to any but the maiden. She rewards him within the terms of his penance: 'Tho meydon toke too gruhowndus fyn/ And waschyd hor mowthus cleyn with wyn/ And putte a lofe in tho ton;/ And in tho todur flesch full gud' (445–8) [The maiden took two fine greyhounds and washed their mouths clean with wine, and put a loaf into the one and in the other, good meat]. Thus, in the structure of the narrative, Gowther behaves rightly – he maintains the terms of his penance, does not boast of his valiant fighting or demand recognition, and is rewarded for his behavior by the symbol of peace and humility within the poem: the silent Christian virgin. Yet in truth, his behavior has changed very little. He still enacts his violent and excessive physical nature, but this time it is on a condoned battlefield against an appropriate enemy.

Gowther's defeat of the Saracens sets him, unequivocally, as a Christian warrior who has learned to judge aright the 'real' enemy and not to be that enemy himself. While the kind of violence enacted by Gowther constitutes a release of his inherently violent and demonic tendencies, these actions are undertaken in a socially and morally sanctioned forum. Because his use of the falchion is guided by God's response to his prayer and reaffirmed by the reward of the Emperor's daughter, Gowther's battle-performance is not only allowed but also commended. Gowther sets himself against the Saracens, and, indeed, is perhaps so successful because he turns his own 'Saracen' blade against them. Gowther does not symbolically kill himself by killing the 'heathen hounds'; he defines himself against their unchristian and now dead bodies. Indeed, Salter takes the approval of Gowther's killing to suggest an affinity between Gowther's role here as warrior and his later role as saint: 'Thus, not merely does the poem claim that there is no conflict between Gowther's dual roles as knight and saint, it actually seems to imply that God grants him a place in heaven as a reward for so conscientiously discharging the morally burdensome obligations expected of a knight' (76). Gowther does what a good knight should do, but he does it more successfully and with more humility. He is no longer the enemy of Christian communities, but rather, their defender.

On Gowther's third and final day in battle, he combats the Sultan, who figures as Gowther's final battle against his own impulses. The Sultan is dressed richly, in 'sabull blacke' (577) [sable black], the color in which Gowther first appeared in battle. As Cohen claims, 'The Sultan takes the place of the giant which Gowther no longer is' ("Gowther" 233). While Gowther is still physically aberrant, he is no longer behaviorally linked to the Sultan. Just before the final moment of battle, the poet interrupts the narrative to remind the audience of Gowther's attention to the Pope's instructions: 'Bot he wold not for yre ne tene/ No worde speke, withowt wene,/ For dowtte of Godus wreke;/ If all he hongurt, noght he dyd eytte/ Bot what he might fro tho howndus geyt;/ He dyd as tho Pwope con hym teche' (607–11) [But he would not for anger or injury speak any word, without a doubt, for knowledge of God's divine judgment. If he hungered, he ate nothing but what he might get from the dogs; he did as the Pope taught him]. This description comes not because we see a moment in which we suspect Gowther might eat or speak when he should not. It comes as a reminder of Gowther's sanctioned and controlled behavior, which then makes him worthy to ride beside the Emperor to protect him from harm (614). Gowther does not decide his own course of actions for his body; he no longer presumes this place of authority, either in terms of the Church or the state. He acts in service of both, presuming to lead neither. In defense of the Emperor, Gowther silently lops off the Sultan's head: 'Tho dompe Duke gard hym ley a wed,/ Stroke of his hed anon,/ Rescowyd is lord, broght hym ageyn' (629–31) [The mute Duke made him remain a hostage, then struck off his head, rescued his lord, brought him back again]. Through appropriate use of the falchion, Gowther defeats that with which he was metonymically and symbolically allied through the entire narrative. Notably, in doing so, he remains steadfast to his bargain with God, but his violence is not diminished. He acts to castrate the authority of another pretender – the Sultan – through dismemberment. In acting in the service of his lord, he removes the representation of power from his enemy, and relocates it in a socially and religiously acceptable vessel. He does not assume it for himself.

Although he is not yet forgiven, Gowther acts not of his own authority, but allows his actions to be dictated by socially correct authorities. He performs under the direction of the Pope, and of Christianity, and his falchion, once the symbol of his hybrid danger and his demonic father, works in the service of the Christian community. As McGregor suggests, his weapon 'becomes the weapon with which he defends the emperor in God's name' (75). Gowther has changed his behavior; he has become a soldier for God instead of a soldier for Satan. Although he has reformed his behavior, he cannot change his physical status. Gowther remains the son of the demon; perhaps he directs his use of violence, but that extreme violence remains a fundamental part of his identity. It is true that at this point Gowther remains a hybrid being, but he cannot be absolved while this multiple identity exists. He is physically still the son of the demon, still a physically hybrid creature: Gowther remains a monster.

Gowther's redemption and transformation come only through the medium of the broken body of the Emperor's daughter. Saving the Emperor, Gowther is hit by a Saracen spear through his shoulder (635); the maiden witnesses this event and tumbles from her tower. She falls into a kind of coma without stirring for two days, lying more still 'Then ho deyd had ben' (642) [than if she had been dead]. Blamires, who sees the arrogance of the noble class as Gowther's major sin, claims that the maiden 'takes the fall' for Gowther (56), acting as a kind of sacrifice, but one directed not at his religious failings, but rather his social ones. Gowther's flaw, however, is not arrogance, as Blamires suggests, but hybridity. The maiden's fall is not a fall into humility, which Gowther has already achieved through his silent service and submission under the table. Her fall makes possible Gowther's redemption not only because it allows for a miraculous recovery – in itself, a kind of transformation – but also because it necessitates the presence of the Pope.

The once-mute princess, then, serves as a conduit for the word of God, who also uses the Pope as a means to transform the body of the repentant Gowther. After the Pope arrives to absolve the princess before her burial, she miraculously awakens, and even more miraculously, speaks. The miracle resulting from her fall transforms her not only from being nearly dead to being alive, but also from being mute to being able to speak. Her transformation, too, is a physical one – a transformation aimed at righting a body that is constituted by lack. It is not only that she speaks but what she says that allows for Gowther's redemption. She brings a message from God to Gowther, whom she addresses; it is the message the Pope bade him wait for: 'Hoe seyd, "My lord of heyvon gretys the well,/ And forgyffeus the thi syn yche a dell,/ And grantys the tho blys;/ And byddus the speyke on hardely,/ Eyte and drynke and make mery;/ Thu schallt be won of His"' (657–66) [She said, 'My lord of heaven greets you well and forgives you your sin in each part, and grants you blessing; and bids you speak on bravely, eat and drink and make merry; you will be one of his own']. With these words, Gowther's transformation begins: he is not merely forgiven, but he will become one of God's own. Her verb here indicates a new state of being for Gowther: he is not accepted *as* one of God's own – instead, he will *be*. Her language shows the transformation that is incipient.

This transformation begun by the princess is confirmed and carried out by the words of the Pope: these two are the purest members of the community, and are closest to God. They serve also as parallels to and traces of the priests and nuns Gowther tormented and raped, reminding us just how significantly his behavior has changed. The Pope authoritatively shrives Gowther and announces his new status in the eyes of the Church: he kisses Gowther 'And seyd, "Now art thu Goddus chyld;/ The thar not dowt tho warlocke wyld,/ There waryd mot he bee" ' (670–75) [And said, 'Now you are God's child, you need not fear the wild devil, there changed must he be']. Through Gowther's penance and the miracle of the mute maiden's recovery of both consciousness and speech, Gowther is forgiven and literally transformed, 'waryd,' from the son of a demon to 'God's child.' This word seems to be a form of 'varien,' 'to undergo a change in form, attribute, status, etc., be altered; undergo successive or alternate changes' (*Middle English Dictionary*). While Gowther's status has certainly changed, it is the first term in this definition that shifts most significantly for him: his form.

Gowther's body has been altered precisely because his paternity has changed. Gowther is a new man because now he is entirely man, a child of God, not the son of the demon. The demon in him has been 'vanquished,' thus he is no longer hybrid. With this change of paternity comes a change in physicality; Gowther is no longer a human–demon hybrid, prone to the excessive strength and growth of the giant. He becomes entirely human, under the authority of the Pope and at the word of God, pronounced by the revived virgin. The paternity of God erases the presence of the fiend, his father, as the Pope's blessing clearly indicates: Gowther no longer needs to fear the 'warlocke wyld' because he is no longer present in his body. He has been replaced. Gowther has undergone what Caroline Walker Bynum would term a 'replacement change' (*Metamorphosis* 29): his hybridity has been replaced by singularity. Cohen suggests that 'Because "geyton with a feltyrd feynd" and sanctified after a long journey through a series of transitional bodies, Gowther has come to signify a transformative, corrective, normalizing principle' ("Gowther" 236). I would argue that although Gowther does indeed represent a normalizing and corrective principle, he has not actually had transitional bodies: his body, always the son of a demon, has been controlled through penitential behavior until it is transformed through a miracle and the blessing of God and the Pope.

The monster in Gowther is removed through transformation, not erasure. Still, in both the Alliterative *Morte* and *Sir Gowther*, Christian communities are rid of monsters through acts of excision. The Giant of Mont St Michel is removed from his position of terror through Arthur's multiple acts of castration. The penis and head, both phalli, are both removed, articulating that the Giant's crimes are not just sexual, but also social. He does not only aim to eat and rape humans; his threat has serious social implications, and these must be addressed through the dismemberment and display of his body. The Giant's masculine authority is seated not only in his head but also in his phallus. As he has removed the beards of the surrounding kings, Arthur will remove not only one beard, but the other as well. Gowther's hypermasculine and monstrous identity is removed, too, by excision: however, this excision is less violent and less intrusive. He is transformed *because* of his deeds of repentance, but is only actually transformed *through* the word of God, carried by a virgin and the Pope. While Gowther might make his own choice to act rightly and to turn his misused authority over to socially and religiously condoned and established sources, his physical body can only be transformed through external and far more powerful means. Once the son of a demon, his paternity is removed by God and relocated to another source. Through this transformation, Gowther becomes a child of God, and his body and actions are refigured in the service of Christian community. Thus, transformation is established as an alternative to removal constituted by dismemberment and death for the monstrous and physically transgressive. Bodies that exceed the limits of nature and society must no longer be destroyed, necessarily: they can be reformed. Transformation of the monstrous body makes this possible.

THE TRACE OF THE MONSTER
AND THE PROBLEM OF REPRODUCTION

Although the Alliterative *Morte* and *Sir Gowther* present two possibilities for managing the body of the excessively male monster – erasure and transformation – both texts also reveal that the monster cannot be entirely removed from the text, or perhaps from the body. The monster remains as a Derridean trace in both poems, echoing the problems of overly masculine and dangerous bodies. While the Giant's masculinity in certain ways informs Arthur's choices and actions in the rest of the Alliterative *Morte*, Gowther's reformed behaviors impact his community in a multitude of positive ways. And yet, both texts end with the dilemma of heirlessness, and particularly heirlessness that leaves their respective communities without effective and appropriate leadership – precisely the same problem created by the phallic authority of the monster.

The Giant of Mont St Michel acts as a focal point for these problems of masculinity both before and after his death. By dispatching the monster, Arthur does not dispose of the problems the Giant embodies. Instead, the way in which the monster is killed continually indicates the problems inherent in the community and kingdom he has terrorized. This encounter with the Giant indicates Arthur's failures as a king – it shows that he is able to take care of neither what is at home nor what is away. He cannot protect his noble subjects, but he also cannot protect or fulfill his own position as a husband and a father. Although the Giant has been literally erased from the landscape of Brittany by his double dismemberment and death, he haunts the rest of the narrative. Like the Giant, a tyrant who usurps lands and bodies, Arthur becomes tyrannical and insatiable after he conquers Rome. Arthur performs his own version of beard-collecting by shaving the two Roman senators who submit to him after his victory: 'They schouen thes schalkes schappely theraftyre;/ To rekken their Romaynes recreaunt and ȝolden;/ Forthy schour they them to schewe, for skomfite of Rome' (2333–5) [Then they shaved these creatures as was fitting in order to prove these Romans cowardly and defeated; therefore they shaved them to show the humiliation of Rome]. The taking of these men's hair asserts Arthur's authority over them and their government, just as the Giant took the beards of the kings as a marker of their submission

188

to his authority. Arthur's own sense of masculine inferiority, anxieties over his tiny dagger, and beleaguered sense of authority turn him into a tyrant.

More than marking the bodies of the defeated senators, Arthur's new tyranny is enacted in the taking of lands and kingdoms that do not rightfully belong to him, just as the Giant attempted to hold authority of many kingdoms by de-bearding their kings. After his defeat of the Emperor of Rome, he plans to take Lorraine, Lombardy, and Tuscany, saying of Lorraine, ' "The lordschipe es louely, as ledes me telles./ I will that ducherye devyse and dele as me likes" ' (2399–400) [His lordship (land) is lovely, as the people tell me. I will divide that dukedom and deal it out however I like]. Although Arthur later gives the explanation that the Duke has been a 'rebel' (2402) to the Round Table, the initial impulse seems to be about possession of something valuable and lovely, with the authority to do as he likes with it. In a sense, he treats these lands as the Giant treated the body of the Duchess, tearing it apart for his own pleasure and purposes. After taking Lorraine and Lombardy, Arthur demands that the citizens be treated well (3081–3), but Tuscany does not fare so well. There he and his men 'take townnes full tyte' (3151) [take over towns quickly] and 'Towrres he turnes and turmentez þe pople' (3153) [Tear down towers and torment the people]. They do not treat the citizens well, but they 'spryngen and sprede and sparis bot lytull' (3158) [spread and disperse and spare but little] and 'Spoylles dispetouslye' (3159) [plunder mercilessly]. Arthur and his men are without mercy and without respect for the people of these lands, just as the Giant treated the people of Brittany. Arthur's desire to take what is rightfully his has turned into an 'insatiable appetite for world domination which has in fact come more to resemble the Giant's indiscriminate cruelty than its original motive' (Bartlett 70).

Moreover, during Arthur's pursuit of 'world domination,' his own kingdom has fallen into disarray. He does not behave as a proper patriarch of his people; he leaves Mordred behind as a reluctant regent,[34] ignoring Gaynor's conjugal plea not to deprive her of her 'wedde lorde' (700) [wedded lord]. When Arthur is informed of Mordred's usurpation of kingdom as well as wife, Arthur's impotence as a ruler is revealed. He fails to protect his people and his wife, and as a consequence, his lands are in utter disarray – Danes, Saracens, Saxons, Picts, 'paynims' (3533) [heathens], and Irish outlaws rule and rout his kingdom under Mordred's command. This affects not only the despoiled monks and ravished nuns (3539) and the ravaged poor (3540), but the castles (3543) and woodlands (3544) of the wealthy. Mordred has most clearly revealed Arthur's impotence by impregnating Gaynor (3552), a feat Arthur had proved unable to perform. Her fertile body here serves as a reminder of the sacrificed body of the Duchess, usurped by the Giant – another body that Arthur failed to protect and retain for proper circulation.

---

34 Mordred begs Arthur to choose another regent and to allow him to go with Arthur to fight the Romans, saying 'To presente a prynce astate my powere es symple' (683) [My power is weak to act the prince's part].

Perhaps the most alarming link with the Giant is the way in which Arthur dies: he is symbolically castrated. In the contest between Mordred and Arthur, Mordred lacerates Arthur's loins: 'The felettes of þe ferrere side he flassches in sondyre' (4237) [The loins to the other side, he slashes apart].[35] As Westover notes, the recent editors of the poem gloss *felettes* as 'loins,' which is 'one of the secondary meanings listed under *filet* in the MED' (310). He argues that 'the definition of the word "loins" may be taken by metonymy to mean "genitals"' (311). Thus, Arthur's procreative capacity is slashed by the very man who has impregnated his wife. However, his wound parallels that which he inflicted on the Giant for his crimes against Arthur himself and his kingdom. Arthur's death by a wound 'below the belt' to a part of the body linked with masculinity not only raises the specter of the Giant, but also recalls Arthur's excessive, castrating response to the potent body of the Giant.

The trace of the Giant is most strongly felt in the conclusion of the poem, when Arthur demands the killing of children, the very crime he punishes the Giant for committing. The final emasculation of Arthur is not Mordred's usurpation of his kingdom, but of his sexual rights. The fact that Gaynor bears Mordred children points expressly to Arthur's impotence, which was first revealed on Mont St Michel. Arthur's response, the murder of Mordred's children, reflects the problems inherent in the episode with the Giant. The problem for Arthur is paternity and succession; there is no generation after Arthur, not of his own line, and certainly not in the vicinity of Mont St Michel because the Giant has killed all the kings and their heirs. The poem ends at line 4346, extolling Arthur's lineage; he 'was of Ectores blude, the kynge son of Troye,/ And of Sir Pryamous the prynce, praysede in erthe;/ Fro thythen broghte the Bretons all his bolde eldyrs/ Into Bretayne the Brode, as þe *Bruytte* tellys' (4343–6) [was of Hector's blood, the King of Troy's son, And of Sir Priam the Prince's, praised on the earth; From Troy the Britons brought all their brave elders into Britain the Great, as the Brut says]. With Arthur, his line ends. However, this noble listing of paternity is flavored by Arthur's dying words, only forty lines before: 'And sythen merke manly to Mordrede children,/ That they bee sleghely slayne and slongen in watyrs;/ Latt no wykkyde wede waxe, no writhe one this erthe' (4320–22) [And then mark strongly that Mordred's children be secretly killed and thrown into the sea; let no wicked weed grow, nor flourish on this earth]. As Lee Patterson suggests, through this killing of Mordred's innocent Christian children, 'we are forced to recall … the giant of Mont St Michel, [who,] in a detail unique to this version, feeds on "crysmede childyre" (line 1051)' (223). These children, not Arthur, are the final descendants of the noble line. Therefore, in deciding to kill the children and end the noble line, Arthur enacts vengeance against Mordred's usurping potency rather than permitting a succession in which he himself is not directly implicated.

---

[35] Goller lists the 'wounds below the belt' in the text. He offers at least three instances, one of which concerns the Giant's castration ("Reality" 23–25). Westover adds the cut to the *felettes* to Goller's list.

Like the Giant, Arthur's body ends in castration and dismemberment, and also like the Giant, he ends as a tyrant and usurper of power he does not rightly possess or employ. The Giant, though removed from the poem through castration and removal, remains a central figure of masculinity, reflecting the problems of the main characters through to the very end of the poem.

Gowther's physical body, however, is not removed from the text, but remains present, in various ways, until the end of *Sir Gowther*. Although the demon is excised from his body, his once-monstrous form is not extracted from the poem. Like Arthur, he ends his days childless, but, unlike Arthur, he affects his community in positive and constructive ways. Gowther's first act after his transformation is to abide by his social contract as a noble: he marries. When he marries the Emperor's daughter, 'Of all hur fadur londus eyr' (680) [Heir of all her father's lands], he becomes heir to those same lands. He gives away his own Dukedom to the old Earl who questioned his parentage, upon whom he also bestows his mother's hand (686–90). He symbolically restores the body of this woman to proper circulation, articulating both that her body is under the direction of the proper male authority, and that it is no longer at the mercy of the demon. Next, he makes reparations for his horrible crimes against religious people by building an abbey and filling it with monks (691–4). Despite the forgiveness he has received from God and the Pope, he remains haunted by what he did to the nuns: 'All yf tho Pope had hym schryvyn/ And God is synnus clene forgevon,/ Yett was his hard full sare/ That ever he schuld so yll wyrke/ To bren tho nunnus in hor kyrke' (697–701) [Even though the Pope had shriven him and God had forgiven his sins, still his heart was pained that he should ever have done such a terrible deed as to burn the nuns in their church]. He builds them an abbey, which becomes known as a center for wisdom (703–8). In this way, the acts of the monster serve as a trace of what he once was and did, but because of his transformation, this trace can also be transformed into something good and generative. Gowther's former monstrous identity and acts are thus replaced too, with the replacement of destroyed churches and bodies. These items act as monuments, commemorating the transformative power of God, but also reminding us of the destructive power of the demonic Gowther.

Gowther spends the rest of his days as an exemplum of Christian knighthood, an identity that is ultimately replaced by sainthood. Upon the Emperor's death, Gowther becomes 'lord and emperowr,/ Of all Cryston knyghttus tho flower' (712–13) [lord and emperor, the flower of all Christian knights]. He stands ready against Saracens, supports the poor and rich, helps the Church, and 'Thus toke he bettur reyd' (720) [Thus he took better counsel]. When he dies after many years of wise rule, he is buried in the abbey he first destroyed then rebuilt. Gowther's burial alone stands as a miracle, for this Christian became one only through his miraculous transformation: 'God hase done for his sake/ Myrrakull, for he has hym hold;/ Ther he lyse in schryne of gold/ That suffurd for Goddus sake' (729–32) [God has done a miracle for his sake, for he has him in his hold; there he, who suffered for God's sake, lies in a shrine of gold]. The war within Gowther is won by God and religious powers on earth through the physicality of penance; this victory causes the transformation, which is both physical and spiritual.

Gowther's miraculous transformation is not the only one in this text, however: his transformed body conducts miraculous transformations for other bodies constituted by lack. After his death, Gowther acts as a kind of intercessor for God. We are told that Gowther has power through the Holy Ghost to help the suffering of those 'Who so sechys hym with hart fre' (733) [Who so seek him with a free heart]. Specifically, Gowther transforms troubled bodies: 'For he garus thos blynd to see/ And tho dompe to speyke, parde,/ And makus tho crokyd right,/ And gyffus to tho mad hor wytte,/ And many odur meracullus yette, Thoro tho grace of God allmyght' (739–44) [For he causes the blind to see and the dumb to speak, also, and makes the crooked straight and gives to the mad their wit, and many other miracles also, through the grace of God almighty]. Although Gowther had no power to transform himself, after his death, through the power of God, he enables the transformation of other bodies. None of these bodies, notably, are hybrid bodies, but they are bodies that lack specific qualities: the powers of sight and speech, straightness, and wit. Gowther's transformation serves as a singular example of monstrous transformation and conversion. The specific kind of transformation he undergoes is not meant to be repeated, but to be a comfort to others, and to enable other kinds of physical transformation for bodies that are already human. Transformation here is positive, reassuring, and, finally, available through God's grace and through the intercession of pope or saint.[36]

However, some elements of Gowther's body and transformation leave certain readers unsettled, precisely because they do not trust the integrity of this new body. In essence, the narrative begs the question if and how Gowther 'can become a man, not a devil, and whether as a half-devil/half-man who has been baptized, he can attain salvation at all' (Charbonneau 25). This very question implies that such a change is unbelievable because of the monstrous nature of the body. And yet, what is unsettling in this story is not really *if* Gowther can be transformed, but rather what that transformation means. As I noted above, 'varian' means 'to undergo change in form …,' but the same word holds other definitions that are less reassuring. The *Middle English Dictionary* offers further definitions, listing as second and third, respectively, 'to exist in a variety of possible forms, conditions,' and 'to be unstable, inconsistent, or inconstant; of persons: be inconstant or erratic in behavior, opinion, etc., waver, alternate … tending to change, unstable.' Thus, while Gowther is 'waryd,' transformed, the nature and indeed permanence of that change are questionable. If a body is changed once, why would it not change again? After all, 'varian' can mean to alternate, and may even imply an

---

[36] Blamires cautiously suggests a late fourteenth century date for the poem, based on its emphasis on Papal authority: 'Like the Charlemagne romances, it could be said to promote papal authority (damaged at the time by the schism) and to warn against tyrannical lordship (a phenomenon, to be sure, of the last decade of the century)' (57). Charbonneau also remarks that this seems like 'church propaganda' (27).

inherent tendency toward change. Moreover, if we consider the second definition, 'varian' can suggest that a body exists in a variety of possible forms. This definition suggests a kinship with Bynum's other possible type of change: hybridity. She uses this term to indicate a visible kind of simultaneity – as embodied in something like the werewolf, which is both man and wolf at the same time (*Metamorphosis* 29–30). It seems, initially, that Gowther's transformation follows her definition of metamorphosis, affiliated with mutation and temporal change (30); he is a half demon sort of giant, and then, through transformation, he is a man and a son of God. However, this second definition that notes the possibility of various forms, along with Bynum's alternate type of change, asks us to consider just how permanent, and indeed, how complete, Gowther's transformation is. Indeed, is all trace of the fiend really removed from this once-hybrid body? Through the process she terms metamorphosis, is the problem of his hybridity actually removed?

While certain critics do not trust that Gowther is ever truly changed, I argue that the question is less about his initial change, and more about the complex nature, and, indeed, the finality of that change. Charbonneau finds the narrative unsatisfying, saying, 'How could an author expect us to believe this hopelessly ill-prepared transformation from devil's son to saint, from burner of convents to builder of them, from disfigurer and mutilator of women to caretaker of them?' (21). Readers are not being asked to believe that Gowther is casually reformed through his own hard work and penance. We are meant instead to recognize an alternative to condemnation and dismemberment through the safe process of transformation. We are meant to see the power of God and Church over the body of the monstrous. In *Sir Gowther*, the body ultimately cannot and does not infiltrate and destroy; the monstrous body is overtaken by the grace of God. Despite his transformation, however, Gowther's body continues to remain liminal, in certain ways. He does not return to his home and act in the capacity that a son of his earthly mother and father should, as an heir and leader of the community – but this choice may be explained by denoting that he is truly not a real heir to his titular father, the Duke. He does not act as a proper heir in his original kingdom, or, truly, in his adopted one. He never produces heirs or participates in the economy of reproductive circulation, the one desire that drove his mother into her initial encounter with the fiend. The fact is, with Gowther, something *does* remain unfinished.

The problem with Gowther is that the disappearance of the monstrous from his body is never really tested. The trouble in this romance begins with the struggle of an infertile noble couple who have no child; Gowther is born through a mother's desperation to fulfill her part of the marital contract and the couple's obligation to succession. The Duke is ready to leave his wife of ten years in order to find someone who might bear a child, because otherwise ' "Eireles mon owre londys bee" ' (59) ['Heirless must our lands be']. The monstrous body of Gowther is the result of this dangerous anxiety, but in his body, the problem of heirlessness is never resolved. Gowther and his wife never conceive a child. The poet wants to make doubly sure that Gowther's monstrosity is excised from both body and community. While we can reasonably trust that Gowther's body has been transformed, the poet cannot take the risk of Gowther's reproduction. So while Gowther's own paternity is resolved by the power of God, it is not so absolute that Gowther himself can father an entirely human child. His body, despite seeming human, retains a trace of the monster. This is not to say that Gowther would certainly father a monstrous child – but he might. The poet resolves this dilemma of transformation by removing Gowther from reproductive circulation, redeeming him, but not quite trusting the stability of his body. Just as the dismembered Giant haunts the body of the Alliterative *Morte* and Arthur, so too does Gowther's former monstrous self remain as a trace in both the narrative, and, perhaps, in the plastic body of the redeemed Gowther.

TRANSFORMATION AND ITS DISCONTENTS

The problem of sexual and reproductive circulation is never far away from either the Alliterative *Morte* or *Sir Gowther* – nor, for that matter, from *Mandeville's Travels*. The problem of the reproductive body is one that is writ large, it seems, in these examples of Middle English literature. Middle English texts that represent the bodies of monsters as well as the potential for their transformation also express consistent concern with human bodies that do not reproduce or circulate as they should. Thus, if the monster, a representative in the Alliterative *Morte* and *Sir Gowther* of excessive and violent masculinity, is quelled through processes of castration or transformation, then what is to be done about bodies that underperform? The monsters threaten human masculinities, to be certain, but they also demonstrate the inadequacy of men's bodies. Killing or transforming the monster, then, may protect the community from his ravages, but it does not, in any particular sense, restore potency to the bodies of castrated and beaten men.

The literal murder and figurative erasure of the Giant from Mont St Michel and the narrative does not entirely remove the Giant from the text. Arthur's excessive sexualized violence in his meeting with the Giant reveals his own impotence, and makes it impossible to forget the Giant for the rest of this poem. Instead, the Giant is a specter of excess masculinity, constantly reminding the audience of Arthur's shortcomings – reminders ultimately fulfilled by Arthur's own failure to reproduce and his murder of Mordred's innocent children. Although he is not transformative, the Giant of Mont St Michel *does* try to enter the human community – not subtly as do the transformative female monsters in *Mandeville's Travels*, but violently, through ridding the land of kings and heirs, and through the overwhelming (and unsuccessful) attempt to engender his own heirs through the rape of noblewomen. Killing the monster does not rid the land of the problems he indicates, although it does put an end to the immediate dangers his body presents. The Giant could not have been killed more completely; beheaded not once but twice, but even this does not successfully remove him from Britain. The body of this Giant, because it is doubly dangerous and thus doubly castrated, acts a trace of the unachievable origin of masculinity. In his excessive body, he suggests the comparative fragility and vulnerability of human masculinity. His castration only reminds the reader of what Arthur always already lacks. Therefore, the dead and dismembered body of the Giant does not affirm Arthur's authority, but instead marks his impotence. The damning trace of the Giant remains when Arthur attempts to rub him out. In order to resolve the problem of the monstrous, it is not erasure but transformation that is required.

Gowther's transformation is fascinating because it reverses the process of most monstrous transformations in Middle English literature. These other transformations feature a human-seeming body that then disastrously is revealed to be monstrous. Instead, Gowther transforms from a monstrous human into a wholly and holy human one. The transformative monster presented by *Sir Gowther* revises the threatening process of the transformation through the authority of God and the Church. Yet one trace of the monster remains. Uebel suggests that through Gowther's status as a fetishistic devotional subject, 'Gowther … continues to have a contaminative effect, outlasting his death, on the people around him' (110). Gowther's 'contaminative effect' is not his status as a saint and miracle worker, but rather his body. Gowther's body retains traces of his demon parentage – as with the sad dragon woman in *Mandeville's Travels*, the monster always returns. We cannot be certain if transformation truly removes the monster, or just the appearance of the monster. Once transformation becomes possible, then monstrosity can also become invisible, located in the recesses of a body once visibly marked by monstrous attributes. Although transformation seems a solution to bodies that are transgressive and exceed the boundaries of humanity both physically and socially, that solution may be merely cosmetic. Once monstrosity is no longer a strictly physical quality, as it is in Old English literature, then any body, at any time, might be monstrous. Transformation seems a humane way of ridding medieval texts and towns of the problem of monsters, but that transformation also means that no body, even a human one, is ever truly stable.

CONCLUSION

Transformation and the Trace of the Monster

I BEGAN THIS BOOK with a description of Johannes Hartlieb's painting of Alexander the Great, in which Alexander is depicted with tusks. This fifteenth century painting presents us with an Alexander dressed in the trappings of nobility, but whose hair is disheveled and whose body has been infiltrated by the monstrous creatures he so desired to witness, report, and dominate. Although Alexander is the prototypical conqueror, the invader, in this image it is his own body that has been invaded and colonized by the monstrous. This portrait shows Alexander as a human whose body is no longer completely human after prolonged exposure to the monstrous East. He is now a hybrid creature, a monster whose body is both animal and human – but he is also transformative. His once-human body is shown to have been porous, susceptible, open to dangerous outside influences. The boundaries of his body have been breached and the myth of its integrity exploded. This tusked Alexander shows us that the monstrous is contaminative, but also demonstrates that the category of humanity is not discrete; its boundaries, like the limits of Alexander's body, are flexible and contingent. If a human body can be changed to a monstrous one, then humanity itself is in danger of contagion and perhaps disintegration.

The tusked Alexander is a warning – against excessive pride and greed, probably; perhaps against colonization; but certainly against contact with the Other. He warns that influence moves in both directions, that conquering and conversion leave one's body and indeed one's society open to outside influences. The safeguards of the body and society can be and have been breached. Neither is any longer impermeable and permanent; both are subject to invasion and change. Transformation, in the fifteenth century, is not only possible and imminent, it is underway.

But this representation of Alexander is only one piece of a larger cultural and historical puzzle. The portrait reveals late medieval attitudes toward the body and toward the monster, showing that transformation is possible, and that human bodies and human communities are not immune to the influence and indeed 'contamination' of the monster. Earlier medieval English versions of Alexander's story and body reveal a different sense of his connection to the world of monsters: while he is not monstrous himself, he has been affected by his congress with

197

monsters. He appears several times in the Old English canon, most notably in *Wonders of the East* and the *Letter of Alexander to Aristotle*.[1] In *Wonders*, he appears twice, once to exterminate the tusked women with 'indecent' bodies and once to receive a human woman as a kind of welcome gift. This second appearance shows Alexander in the context of a human community. Though Eastern, this community is ubiquitously generous with its women, for:

> gyf hwylc mann to him cymeð þonne gyfað hi him wif ær hi hine onweg lætan. Se macedonisca Alexander, þa ða he him to com, þa wæs he wundriende hyra menniscnysse, ne wold he hi cwellan ne him nawiht laðes don.
> (Orchard, "Letter" 200–202)

[if any man comes to them, then they give him a woman before they let him go on his way. When Alexander of Macedon came to them, then he was astonished by their humanity. He would not kill them nor do them any injury.]

This description shows the community to be hospitable and civilized. The boundaries of the community are fluid and its people do not seem to fear the over-circulation of their women, whom they give freely to strange visitors. But it seems that it is this extreme generosity that saves them from Alexander's impulse to conquer and destroy. He admires their 'mannishness,' their humanity, a quality that holds particular meaning because the human community is surrounded by monsters, both in the narrative structure and in their geographical location. Indeed, only two of the thirty-seven monstrous creatures separate the description of this community from that of the tusked women whom Alexander must destroy because they, with their indecent bodies, will not come to him willingly. While this community's borders are wide open to the monsters around them, they remain entirely human – a fact by which Alexander is 'astonished.' The human body, in this Anglo-Saxon text, cannot and will not become monstrous. Transformation to and from the monstrous is not possible in Old English.

However, that does not mean that Alexander remains unchanged by his previous contact with the monstrous. The illustration that accompanies this description is strangely similar to Hartlieb's, though no tusks are in evidence. In

---

[1] *The Letter of Alexander*, in Old English extant only in Cotton Vitellius A.xvi alongside *Wonders* and *Beowulf*, has its origin in Greek and Latin works. However, we cannot assume that direct translation is the intent of the Old English author. Orchard comments, 'as pure translation, the *Letter* is clearly flawed in its frequent departures of style and substance from the original text. The effect of these alterations, however, requires close consideration to determine whether the anonymous translator was working with a clear purpose in mind or (as previous scholars have been all too quick to assume) was simply unskilled' (*Pride and Prodigies* 132). He finds that these previously identified 'stylistic flaws' contribute to a Christian interpretation of Alexander as prideful and violent rather than simply establishing an ignorant translator. Most significant here is the phrase 'pure translation.' It should become obvious to us that the value of the *Letter* is not in the purity of its translation from Latin and Greek, but in its 'corruptions,' which may reveal Anglo-Saxon attitudes toward the story and character.

Tiberius, we see three men on the right side of the picture handing over a single woman to a fourth man, who stands on the left. The three men, members of this generous community, are well dressed and groomed. The man closest to the left has short curly brown hair and wears a long-sleeved, knee-length light-brown tunic. His hose and leg-bindings come almost to the knee and he wears small black shoes, as do each of the members of this community. The man to his right has curly blonde hair and also sports one of the few beards and mustaches of the manuscript. The mustache, like his hair, is neatly kept. The third man, painted in profile, wears a knee-length light-green tunic and carries a bowl. The woman that these obviously civilized men present to the fourth man is slightly shorter than they and wears a long loose-sleeved, ankle-length pink garment. Her hair is modestly covered by a bone-colored cloth. That she is a woman is obvious in more than just her clothing: her face is shaped differently from the men's. It is smaller, heart-shaped, and her eyes are smaller and eye-brows more precise. She even has a little dimple line on her chin. Her sex is further marked by the outline of her breasts through her modest tunic. Like the men, she wears small black shoes. None of these four seems affected by any of the qualities of the monstrous that surround them in the manuscript. The woman does not appear to resist her transfer to the fourth man, and all of them are marked by the ability of their community to weave cloth, design clothing, and to make leather shoes and pottery. The gendered differences in clothing suggest a community that follows, roughly, the social norms of an Anglo-Saxon sexual difference. The fourth man, Alexander, however, gives us pause. He does not look like the other three men in the picture. His hair is black, and longer and messier than the other men's, although not excessively so. He wears a knee-length tunic – yellow – as he reaches for the woman's right hand with his left. But this man does not wear shoes. He is barefoot. Even more surprisingly, he does not carry a sword, but a club in his right hand. These are markers of the less-than-human in this manuscript. Monsters are naked and barefoot, but men are clothed and shod. Some men carry swords, but only monsters carry clubs. Alexander as he is depicted in this picture has not exactly sprouted tusks, but he is not the civilized man we expect. He has been affected by his congress with the monstrous – the trace of his travels through their territories is marked upon his body.

Like Beowulf, Alexander is not the same after his contact with the monstrous, and, particularly, after his thwarted desire for the beautiful and transgressive tusked women, whom he consequently massacres. Like Grendel and his mother, these women are erased from the manuscript, both through revision and through death. But they leave a trace – a trace that is visible and written on the still-human body of their killer.

While *Wonders* shows Alexander's sexual circulation as he happily accepts the woman given to him (although he perhaps feels desire for a more monstrous woman), the Old English *Letter of Alexander to Aristotle* shows him abstaining from sexual circulation. Indeed, so important is his sexual purity that the final moments of the narrative unequivocally demand it. For the entirety of the narrative, Alexander travels through the marvelous East fighting human enemies, watching his men be consumed by monstrous animals, and encountering communities of monstrous humans. This narrative is marked by Alexander's constant desire to know, see, and thereby possess, so when he learns about a place of prophecy, he is determined to find it and know as much about the undiscovered territory of his future as he does about the mysterious East.[2] The place of prophecy, the garden of the trees of the sun and the moon, relies upon strict binaries between male and female, masculine and feminine: 'Oþer þara is wæpnedcynnes sunnan trio, oþer wifkynnes þæt monan trio, 7 hie gesecgað þæm men þe hie frineð, hwæt godes oþðe yfles him becuman sceal' (Orchard, "*Wonders*" 246) [The tree of the sun is of the male-kind, and the tree of the moon is of the female-kind, and they say to the people who ask them what good or what evil will come to them]. In this passage, masculinity is equated with the common term *wæpned*, probably to avoid the confusion of the more general term, *man*, but the term also carries connotations of masculinity, violence, and potency.[3] Prophecy relies on the balance between the sexes, but the Old English text subtly connects masculinity with violence, with penetration, and with knowledge.

And yet, access to knowledge relies on Alexander's ability to remain sexually pure. When Alexander asks the attendant bishop if he may enter the grove of trees, he is told that: ' "gif þine geferan beoð clæne from wif gehrine, þonne moton hie gongan in þone godcundan bearo" ' (248) ['If your companions are pure of the touch of woman, then they may go into the sacred grove'].[4] His ability to know his future hinges on his ability to remain out of sexual circulation. Even more

---

2   Butturff, in "Style as Clue to Meaning", and Orchard, in *Pride and Prodigies*, see Alexander as an earthly representation of pride because of this desire for possession. In 1970, Butturff turned to the matter of style in order to prove that 'not only is the Old English version of the *Letter* focused on the figure of Alexander, but that the translator intended to provide by his work an *exemplum* on the *superbia* of earthly rulers; and that he did so by consistently exposing the egotism of the Macedonian potentate who was humbled by the inevitable fate of mortals' (82). He built on Sisam's 1916 observation that 'the ideal leader of the Greeks and Romans thinks first of his army, but our English translator felt that the general should come first' (quoted in Butturff 86).

3   In the rest of the text, the word for men is only modified by the term *wæpned* as Alexander nears the garden: this specific noun occurs only when both men and women are being described as members of a strange community, and this only happens twice, both times in close proximity to the garden. Alexander must avoid the temptations of the communities of men and women closest to this garden.

4   Gunderson's summary of the various Latin and Greek recensions of the *Letter* notes the requirements for addressing the trees in the Latin and Greek versions thus: 'Whoever is to enter must be free of sexual contact with a boy or women. His further instructions about proper religious observances included the removal of the rings and all of their clothes, as well as their shoes' (62). While the requirements concerning clothing, shoes, and women remain, those about the rings and the boys are dropped in the Old English *Letter*. The possibility of male sexual partners is one cultural difference between a Greek audience and an Anglo-Saxon one that is made fascinatingly clear, but it also demonstrates that the Anglo-Saxon author made editorial changes to this section appropriate to his own social context – and that Alexander's purity remained important for him.

interesting here is the notion that contact with a woman would be somehow read-able on his body – that perhaps the tree would be able to sense such impurity. Sex writes upon the body, limiting its ability to achieve knowledge. However, Alex-ander passes this test, and is granted access to the trees. His body has not been contaminated by contact with a woman. What really matters here, though, is not just Alexander's ability to remain pure, but also the geographical and narrative context in which he must remain pure.

Alexander's masculinity is challenged implicitly by the presence and proximity of female monsters. They do not exist in communities of their own, as they do in *Wonders*, but female members of the communities are worthy of separate mention only as Alexander nears the place of prophecy. Once he has passed through and conquered the more civilized communities of the East and subdued the attacking beasts, he finds himself near communities of monstrous humans, like the *Ictifafonas*. Monstrosity is marked in several ways on the bodies of the *Ictifafonas*. Not only are they monsters of excess, they are also human–animal hybrids, of a sort. They are nine feet tall, a state of excess confirmed by the fact that they also eat whales (Orchard, "*Wonders*" 242). Their hybridity is more complex because they are described as shaggy: 'ruge wifmen, 7 wæpned men wæron hie swa ruwe 7 swa gehære swa wildeor' (242) [rough women and men, who were as shaggy and hairy as wild beasts]. These people have excessive amounts of hair, hair that is like that of wild animals. But what is most compel-ling about the *Ictifafonas* is the writer's need to clarify that this is a community made up of both men and women, something he has not done in the preceding eleven pages of Orchard's fifteen-page edition. Because of what will happen at the garden of the trees of the sun and the moon, the stakes of sex and gender are higher at this position in the text, and in the journey. It is entirely possible that Alexander might come into contact with a woman here, and that this could prevent him from reaching the space of prophecy. However, this grammatical construction sets the men and women of the community apart: *ruge* describes *wifmen*, thus we have hairy women, but *men* is modified directly only by *wæpned*. Therefore, the men of this community are affirmed as male, masculine, manly men, while the women are *ruge*, shaggy. Later both the men and women are all described as *ruwe* and *gehære* as animals, so the construction does not so much suggest that the men are not shaggy, as it does suggest that what makes the men monstrous is their 'weaponedness,' and what makes the women monstrous is their shagginess. It seems particularly important that we see the women here as hairy, something women usually are not, and the men here as excessively mascu-line. Thus, this community of naked, nine-foot-tall people who grab not just fish, but whales out of the water with their bare hands, is made up of women who have taken on a signifier of not only bestiality, but possibly also masculinity in their hairiness, and men who are even more masculine, *wæpned*, than their women. The transgressive gendering of this community reveals the troubling potential for contact with a woman in the marvelous East. To do so would be to place Alexander's own masculine identity in a precarious position. The necessity of purity, then, seems to be a means of curtailing and condemning miscegenative circulation with sex and gender hybrid female monsters like these.

In the *Letter of Alexander*, the touch of a woman, given the potential that she might be monstrous, is depicted as disruptive and contaminative. Alexander needs to get to the trees of the sun and the moon, and if he should come into contact with one of these women in any significant way, he will not be able to complete his journey and to know his future. So it seems the monstrous feminine, more than just the feminine, signals contamination. This idea of contamination is further reflected in Alexander's inability to return home, foretold to him in the garden of the trees of the sun and the moon. He is changed because of his contact with the wondrous and his desire to possess and to know the marvelous East and its monsters. I do not argue that he himself becomes a monster in this text: Hartlieb may give him the features of a monster in the fifteenth century, but the *Letter* certainly does not. Rather, I argue that it is congress with the monstrous that changes him, not by making him less human, but perhaps by making him less whole. His time in the marvelous East has exposed in him a desire to know and possess things that he cannot or should not. For this reason, he can never go home again.

Unlike Alexander, most of the human men I have discussed in this book do return home, but like Alexander, they are changed by their contact with the monstrous. Beowulf returns from Grendel's mother's mere to Heorot, and then to Geatland, telling, retelling, and retooling the stories of his fights with Grendel and his mother. Sir John Mandeville completes his journey through the Holy Land and the marvelous East, writing his story thirty-four years after its occurrence. Arthur returns to his kingdom after fighting the Giant of Mont St Michel and journeying to Rome. Sir Gowther returns to the kingdom of his birth after performing penance in a country besieged by Saracens. Of these men, only Beowulf and Mandeville remain in the homes to which they return, whereas Arthur returns home to battle his usurping son Mordred before dying, and Gowther returns only to surrender his legacy to the old man who stood up to him, before returning to rule his adopted country. One common quality marks the bodies of all of these men, transformative or not: none has heirs. Through their connections to sexed and gendered monsters, both male and female, human men's physical and symbolic authority is questioned and found lacking. As the only creature who is both monster and main character, Gowther produces no children because of the peril presented by his once-monstrous body. However, both Beowulf and Mandeville eschew marriages and produce no children, despite strong imperatives, particularly in Beowulf's case, to do so. These men are affected by the monstrous men and women with whom they come in contact. Beowulf gains and loses his phallic authority and masculinity through his contact with Grendel and his mother, producing no heir to protect his kingdom from an onslaught of attackers after his death. However, Mandeville's lack of sexual circulation reflects the danger of the transformative monstrous body – for how could he be certain that he, and his community might not be infiltrated by a woman whose body could conceal her monstrosity? Contact with the monstrous, and perhaps desire for these monstrous bodies, have rendered men's own bodies impotent, unproductive, and out of circulation.

In contrast to the heirless bodies of the male main characters, each of these texts features women's bodies that are monstrously productive. *Wonders* names community after community in which monsters *beoð akende* [are born], a phrase, in variation, used seventeen times out of thirty-seven sections. Grendel's mother's greatest threat is her perhaps autonomous ability to engender grendels. Similarly, Mandeville's story is filled with the reproductive bodies of women, from the dead woman who gives birth to a head, to the Amazons, who give away any sons they engender with men of neighboring countries, to the poison virgins, whose bodies might at any moment produce either a snake or perhaps an illegitimate child. In fact, Gowther's mother so longs for a child that she gets (a monstrous) one with a demon. These texts demonstrate that contact with fertile and monstrous female bodies removes men's masculine potency and their ability to reproduce.

The figure of the castrating woman is nothing new – she is featured in film, song, and story, in medieval texts and contemporary ones. What is new here is the way her monstrosity performs the emasculation: these female monsters not only take the potency of men, often by appropriating a phallus of some sort, be it sword, dagger, arrow, tail, or snake, but they also replace human reproduction with their own monstrous procreation. The problem with these women is not just that they are fertile, or that they are phallic, but rather that they are both. Their bodies fit uneasily into the binary paradigm; thus, they nudge the paradigm of social and sexual behavior for women, just as they simultaneously confirm the limits beyond which women should not tread.

Monstrous women, however, are not the only threat to human masculinity; most of the male monsters I have discussed here are problematic in their excessive masculinity and their assumption of the phallic authority of human men. While a male monster who features a denuded performance of masculinity, or who is both feminine and masculine, is certainly possible, and would seem to challenge the very tenets of masculinity, he does not appear in these texts. Perhaps he would be the most taboo of all monsters. Instead, all of these texts present us with male monsters who are larger than human men, and whose phalluses and penises challenge the human social order. However, a trace of compromised masculinity is present in the bodies of male monsters. Unlike the female monsters, these male monsters are not generative. Grendel begets no children; the Giant of Mont St Michel is too big to have successful sexual intercourse; and Gowther, as monster, kills off the victims of his rape (the nuns), and dares not produce a child once he has been transformed. These male monsters show human men to be impotent in an entirely other arena: the political one. Grendel wants Hrothgar's giftseat, while the Giant of Mont St Michel takes the beards and authority of surrounding kings, demonstrating his control over their lands and behavior. Gowther uses his inherited political position as Duke to run rampant over his lands, raping, killing, and destroying the country ruled by his supposed father. The male giant's excessive masculine potency is directed not at procreation, but at destruction of the social order. And though he is defeated by either man (Beowulf and Arthur) or God (in the case of Gowther), the stability of the kingdom is shaken by the encounter with the male monster.

Thus, the bodies of these monstrous humans destabilize both the bodies and the communities of humans. They break down the boundaries of society by means of bodies that exceed social and physical limits, and they tear down the existing structure, only to replace the productive and masterful human male authority with the dangerous bodies of monsters born again and again from phallic women. Bodies that transgress social boundaries of the 'normal' or the acceptable clearly present problems to both the individual and the nation. These are bodies that must be controlled. The monstrous serves as a threatening category in medieval literature – but writers of different periods respond in significantly different ways to it. The primary response to the monstrous is a desire to erase it – from the text, from the community, from memory. An alternative – transformation – attempts to take away those elements that constituted the monster, allowing the body to appear human. But monstrosity is not so easy to escape. Even when monstrosity is erased or transformed, a trace of it remains and constitutes a clear presence within the text, in the blank spots left behind on the manuscript page and the story told by the returning hero, on the bodies of women and men who seem to be human, but whom we suspect might be something more, or on the vulnerable human bodies of the men who resist these monsters.

Erasure is a possibility in both Old English and Middle English, but transformation is possible in only the Middle English texts. Erasure, because it is often so violent, seems to be more thorough – after all, once a monster has been killed, he can no longer be a real physical threat to the kingdom he once challenged, whereas a transformed body threatens to revert to its monstrous form at any time. And yet both leave telling traces, implying that the monster can always return. The Giant of Mont St Michel is killed, but the masculinity and potency that he both embodies and symbolizes haunt the remainder of the narrative. The Giant, a monster who is not transformative, cannot be easily erased from the text of the Alliterative *Morte Arthure*, much like Grendel, or the monstrous male bodies of *Wonders*. In Arthur's excessive excision of the monster from the text, we become increasingly aware of how he continues to affect and reflect the reproductive failures within the narrative. It is the violated body of the Giant that serves as a trace, reminding the audience of Arthur's failures to protect his people and impregnate his wife. Although the Giant is not transformative, and thus does not have a body that is tricky and troublesome to identify, the desire to erase it yields a constant reminder of it. Whenever we see assertions of masculinity and paternity for the remainder of the text, and particularly in its conclusion, we remember the castrated body of the overly potent Giant.

Sir Gowther, then, offers a consoling solution to the problem of the monstrous body. Transformation in this text is neither monstrous nor threatening, as it is in *Mandeville's Travels*. Transformation in this text is controlled by the will of God through the authority of the Pope and the Church. *Sir Gowther* not only provides a solution to the problem of the transformation, but it also allows for the successful erasure of the monster not through death, but through Bynum's category of replacement change. When Gowther's paternity changes – when he becomes the 'child of God' – the change is more than philosophical or spiritual. The change in paternity is a change in biology; Gowther literally becomes a different being. The demon is evacuated from his form and thus Gowther's physical excess is no more. The body of the demon's son is replaced by the body of a child of God, just as the ruined convent and its raped and burned nuns are replaced by a more renowned convent, known for its wisdom and goodness. However, when one thing is replaced by another – for instance, when the new convent replaces the old one – the viewer is reminded of what was once there. Something transcends the replacement: the trace. In Gowther's case, although his biological identity has changed, the poet never suggests that his appearance changes. Thus, the problem with replacement is that it always holds traces of that which it once was. Its very presence, then, reminds us of another presence. While we are reassured that the previous presence has been replaced, a hint of former identity remains. It is precisely the problem of the trace that makes Gowther's body safe, but not safe enough to reproduce. Transformation, a quality that serves to highlight the danger of gendered monstrosity in other medieval texts, is called on by the poet of *Sir Gowther* to replace instead of erase monstrosity. Replacement certainly functions more effectively, allowing Gowther to achieve the forgiveness of God and the acceptance of the community. Although Gowther replaces the demon as father with God the father, he himself never becomes a father. While his monstrous identity has been replaced by a holy one, his body still holds traces of its dangerous former presence. His body, it seems, is always already monstrous – even though it has been transformed by God.

The problem of the monstrous body is not one that is easily resolved. In Old English texts, writers, readers, and characters attempt to rid themselves of the monstrous through acts of erasure, both literal and figurative. But when a figure is excised from a text, the evidence of that erasure remains: such is the case with the erased genitals in *Wonders of the East* – we can literally see where these body parts are covered over or scratched out. Figurative traces of Grendel and his mother, too, remain in the text after they are erased from the story by Beowulf. Grendel's arm and head, displayed for the Danes, serve as traces of a body that is never really drawn for the audience. On the other hand, no body part of Grendel's mother serves as a trophy. Although her body is left decapitated in the mere, she returns to the text every time Beowulf retells and revises the story of their fight, and ultimately reveals Beowulf's own failure of paternity.

Killing the monster does not remove it entirely from the text. In Middle English, these monstrous bodies resist erasure through transformation. They come closer and closer to the communities and bodies of humans through their ability to look like them; thus in *Mandeville's Travels* the woman who becomes a dragon can appear human to draw in unlucky knights, and the poison virgins can disguise their secret and fatal monstrosity inside their bodies, thus disrupting the reproductive practices of the community in which they live. These bodies remain unresolved and utterly dangerous to those humans with whom they interact. *Sir Gowther* attempts a solution to the problem of the monstrous body; through penance, the child of a demon and a noblewoman transforms physically and spiritually into a child of God. In the end, however, the transformed body remains hybrid; the traces of what it was before linger in the new and different body. Most of these texts attempt to dispel the threat of the monster through erasure, be it the literal removal of the monstrous image, the killing of the monster, or the rehabilitation of the monster through religious means. These attempts are doomed to fail because not only does the monster always return, as Cohen suggests, but the monster never departs.

What does this mean, then, for human bodies and human communities? After all, the monsters discussed in this book are not real, but fictional. However, they embody cultural anxieties regarding the potential of real human bodies. In Old English, the insistence that monstrous bodies are permanent and can only be resolved through acts of erasure serves as both a representation of beliefs about the nature of the body, as Bynum has argued, and as a means to control and direct human behavior. Neither the body nor one's social station can transform: they are set and stable, established at birth. The monstrous bodies warn people to stay within their communities, literally, and to abide by their rules of gender and sexuality. To exceed the boundaries of the 'normal' social body is to require erasure. However, in articulating the dangers of these monstrous bodies that refuse to abide by the limits of the actual or social body, Old English writers confirm the possibilities and indeed the power of such bodies.

The possibility of censure and erasure of the body remains in Middle English literature, but it is supplemented by a new attitude toward the individual and society. Laws like the sumptuary codes articulate the need for social division and preservation of the existing order; they suggest that bodies and social positions should not change, and they attempt to naturalize such assumptions by making the body a visible display of the internal and innate state of social class. However, the need for such codes reveals that people's bodies exceed the limits placed on them, and thus require policing. The fourteenth and fifteenth centuries in England are times of massive social changes, changes that are manifested in the bodies of monsters, but also in the bodies of humans. People's bodies and social positions are capable of change, of transformation. They might begin as one thing, but through some means, magical or otherwise, become something entirely other. This is not to suggest that the rules of gender and sexuality are radically altered. Still, the new possibility of transformation is not without its dangers. The possibility of transformation allows for an alternative to stagnancy and the status quo, but it also displays the weakness of the foundation of social order. If transformation is possible, then what body can be trusted as real, complete, or stable? Where are boundaries to be drawn – and indeed, even if boundaries are drawn, can they be maintained? Transformation is a productive new potential for the individual and social body, but it also places communities in peril. An identity that is flexible and fluid is also an identity that can blow apart presumptions not only of social class, but of gender, sex, and sexuality – the division of the sexes upon which the patriarchy relies.

Monstrous bodies – bodies that break the boundaries of humanity – confirm the necessity of those boundaries, but they also demonstrate the potential of the human body to exceed them. That potential is sometimes frightening, sometimes destabilizing, sometimes surprising, and sometimes productive. Just like the monstrous body, the human body that does not fit neatly into existing categories of gender, sex, and sexuality not only disrupts the social and sexual order, it reveals the gaps and flaws in the architecture of society. These bodies – like acts of erasure – destroy something that was, but also create something new. The bodies of monsters, erased themselves, act as traces of the bodies of humans that do not abide by strict categories established for the maintenance of the social order. In truth, no human body or identity fits completely into the niche created for it by any social construction. Bodies resist categories – and if that is the case, then we are all monsters.

BIBLIOGRAPHY

EDITIONS AND TRANSLATIONS

Ælfric. *The Catholic Homilies*, vols. I and II. Ed. Malcolm Godden. London: EETS, Oxford UP, 2000.

Augustine. *De Civitate Dei.* Ed. R.A. Green. Cambridge: Harvard UP, 1960.

Bately, Janet M., ed. *The Anglo-Saxon Chronicle: A Collaborative Edition, Vol. 3, MS A.* Cambridge: D.S. Brewer, 1983.

Beowulf and the Fight at Finnsburg, third ed. Ed. Fr. Klaeber. Lexington, MA: D.C. Heath and Company, 1950.

Bradley, S.A.J., trans. *'Beowulf.' Anglo-Saxon Poetry.* London: Dent, 1982. 403–94.

Butturff, Douglas R. 'The Monsters and the Scholar: An Edition and Critical Study of the *Liber Monstrorum*.' (Unpublished Ph.D. dissertation from University of Illinois, 1968).

Cockayne, T.O. *Leechdoms Wortcunning, and Starcraft of Early England Being a Collection of Documents, for the Most Part Never Before Printed Illustrating the History of Science in this Country Before the Norman Conquest*, 3 vols. London: Rerum Britannicarum Medii Ævi Scriptores (Rolls Series) 35 i–iii, 1864–6 (reprint 1965).

Crawford, S.J., ed. *The Old English Version of the Heptateuch, Ælfric's Treatise on the Old and New Testament and his Preface to Genesis.* London: EETS, Humphrey Milford, OUP, 1922.

Dobbie, Elliott Van Kirk, ed. *Beowulf and Judith.* New York: Columbia UP, 1965.

Donaldson, E. Talbot, trans. *Beowulf: A Prose Translation.* Originally trans. 1966. Ed. Nicholas Howe. New York: W.W. Norton, 2001.

Gibb, Paul Allen. *Wonders of the East: A Critical Edition and Commentary* (unpublished Ph.D. dissertation, Duke University, 1977).

Griffith, Mark, ed. *Judith.* Exeter: Exeter UP, 1997.

Gunderson, Lloyd L. *Alexander's Letter to Aristotle about India.* Meisenheim: Verlag Anton Hain, 1980.

Hamelius, P., ed. *Mandeville's Travels, Translated from the French by Jean d'Outremeuse.* Edited from MS. Cotton Titus c. XVI, in the British Museum. 2 vols. EETS, os 153–4. London: Oxford UP, 1919–23.

Heaney, Seamus, trans. *Beowulf.* New York: Norton, 2000.

Howe, Nicholas, ed. *Beowulf: A Prose Translation.* Trans. E. Talbot Donaldson. New York: W.W. Norton and Co., 2002.

James, Montague Rhodes, ed. *Marvels of the East: A Full Reproduction of the Three Known Copies, with Introduction and Notes.* Oxford: Oxford UP, 1929.

Kiernan, Kevin, with Andrew Prescott *et al*, eds. *The Electronic Beowulf.* Ann Arbor: U of Michigan P, 1999.

Krapp, G.P. 'Genesis A.' *The Junius Manuscript*, ASPR 1 (1931): New York: 1–87.

Krishna, Valerie. *The Alliterative Morte Arthure: A Critical Edition.* New York: Burt Franklin and Co., 1976.

Laskaya, Anne and Eve Salisbury, eds. *'Sir Gowther.' The Middle English Breton Lays.* Kalamazoo, MI: Medieval Institute Publications, 1995.

209

McGurk, P.M.J., D.N. Dumville, and M.R. Godden, with Ann Knock. *An Eleventh Century Anglo-Saxon Illustrated Miscellany (British Library Cotton Tiberius B.V Part One*. EEMF 21; Copenhagen: Rosenkilde and Bagger, 1983.

Mitchell, Bruce and Fred C. Robinson. *Beowulf: An Edition with Relevant Shorter Texts.* Oxford: Blackwell Publishers Ltd, 1998.

——, eds. 'Cynewulf and Cyneheard.' *A Guide to Old English.* Fifth ed. Oxford: Blackwell, 1992. 208–12.

Orchard, Andy, ed. and trans. *'The Letter of Alexander to Aristotle.' Pride and Prodigies: Studies in the Monsters of the Beowulf-Manuscript.* Ed. Andy Orchard. Cambridge: D.S. Brewer, 1995. 224–53.

——. *'Liber Monstrorum.' Pride and Prodigies: Studies in the Monsters of the Beowulf-Manuscript.* Cambridge: D.S. Brewer, 1995. 254–317.

——. *'The Wonders of the East.' Pride and Prodigies: Studies in the Monsters of the Beowulf-Manuscript.* Cambridge: D.S. Brewer, 1995. 175–203.

Rogers, Bertha, trans. *Beowulf.* Delhi, NY: Birch Book Press, 2000.

Rypins, Stanley. *Three Old English Prose Texts.* London: EETS, os 161, 1924.

Seymour, M.C., ed. *The Defective Version of Mandeville's Travels.* EETS, ns 319. London: Oxford UP, 2002.

——. *The Metrical Version of Mandeville's Travels.* EETS, ns 269. London: Oxford UP, 1973.

Timmer, B.J., ed. *The Later Genesis.* Oxford: Oxford UP, 1948.

Tupper, Frederick, ed. *The Riddles of the Exeter Book.* Boston: Ginn and Company, 1910.

The Wonders of the East. London, British Library MS Cotton Tiberius B.v, fols. 78v–87r.

——. London, British Library MS Cotton Vitellius A.xv, fols. 98v–106v.

——. Oxford, Bodleian Library MS 614, fols. 36r–48r.

Wulfstan. *The Homilies of Wulfstan.* Ed. Dorothy Bethurum. Oxford: Clarendon P, 1957.

SECONDARY SOURCES

Acker, Paul. 'Horror and the Maternal in *Beowulf.' PMLA* 121:3 (2006), 702–16.

Akbari, Suzanne Conklin. *Seeing through the Veil: Optical Theory and Medieval Allegory.* Toronto: U of Toronto P, 2004.

Alfano, Christine. 'The Issue of Feminine Monstrosity: A Reevaluation of Grendel's Mother.' *Comitatus: A Journal of Medieval and Renaissance Studies* 23 (1993), 1–16.

Almond, Richard. *Medieval Hunting.* Thrupp: Sutton P, 2003.

Arnason, David. 'Derrida and Deconstruction.' Online. March 18, 2005. http://130.179. 92.25/Arnason_DE/Derrida.html.

Austin, Greta. 'Marvelous Peoples or Marvelous Races? Race and the Anglo-Saxon *Wonders of the East.' Marvels, Monsters, and Miracles: Studies in the Medieval and Early Modern Imaginations.* Eds. Timothy Jones and David Sprunger. Studies in Medieval Culture XLII. Kalamazoo, MI: Medieval Institute Publications, 2002. 27–54.

Bammesberger, Alfred. 'The Half-Line *Grendeles Mægum* (*Beowulf* 2353b).' *Notes and Queries* 243:1 (1998), 2–4.

——. 'Further Thoughts on *Beowulf,* line 1537a: GEFENG ÞA BE [FEAXE].' *Notes and Queries* 246:1 (2001), 3–4.

Bartlett, Anne Clark. 'Cracking the Penile Code: Reading Gender and Conquest in the Alliterative *Morte Arthure.' Arthuriana* 8:2 (1998), 56–76.

Beal, Rebecca S. 'Arthur as the Bearer of Civilization: The *Alliterative Morte Arthure,* ll.901–19.' *Arthuriana* 5:4 (1995), 32–44.

——. 'Guenevere's Tears in the Alliterative *Morte Arthure:* Doubly Wife, Doubly Mother, Doubly Damned.' *On Arthurian Women: Essays in Memory of Maureen Fries.* Eds. Bonnie Wheeler and Fiona Tolhurst. Dallas: Scriptorium P, 2001. 1–10.

Bibliography

Bennett, Josephine Waters. *The Rediscovery of Sir John Mandeville.* New York: MLA, 1954.

Bennett, Judith M. *History Matters: Patriarchy and the Challenge of Feminism.* Philadelphia: U of Pennsylvania P, 2006.

Benshoff, Harry. *Monsters in the Closet: Homosexuality and the Horror Film.* Manchester: Manchester UP, 1997.

Bernheimer, Richard. *Wild Men in the Middle Ages.* Cambridge: Harvard UP, 1952.

Biernoff, Suzanna. *Sight and Embodiment in the Middle Ages.* New York: Palgrave Macmillan, 2002.

Bildhauer, Bettina and Robert Mills, eds. *The Monstrous Middle Ages.* Toronto: U of Toronto P, 2003.

Blamires, Alcuin. 'The Twin Demons of Aristocratic Society in *Sir Gowther.' Pulp Fictions of Medieval England.* Ed. Nicola McDonald. Manchester: Manchester UP, 2004. 45–62.

Bond, J.M. 'Burnt Offerings: Animal Bone in Anglo-Saxon Cremations.' *World Archaeology* 28:1 (1996), 76–88.

Bonjour, Adrien. *The Digressions in Beowulf.* Oxford: Blackwell, 1950.

Bosworth, Joseph and T. Northcote Toller, eds. *An Anglo-Saxon Dictionary based on the Manuscript Collections of the Late Joseph Bosworth, edited and enlarged by T. Northcote Toller.* London: Oxford UP, 1972.

Bovey, Alixe. *Monsters and Grotesques in Medieval Manuscripts.* Toronto: U of Toronto P, 2002.

Bradstock, E.M. '*Sir Gowther*: Secular Hagiography or Hagiographical Romance or Neither?' *AUMLA* 59 (1983), 26–47.

Bredehoft, Thomas A. ' "Ellorgæstas": The Grendel Family and Abjection.' Unpublished essay.

Bremmer, Rolf H., Jr. 'Grendel's Arm and the Law.' *Studies in English Language and Literature: 'Doubt Wisely': Studies in Honour of E.G. Stanley.* Eds. J. Toswell and E. Tyler. London: Routledge, 1996. 121–32.

Broderick, Herbert. 'Some Attitudes toward the Frame in Anglo-Saxon Manuscripts of the Tenth and Eleventh Centuries.' *Artibus et Historiae* 5 (1982), 32–43.

Brundage, James. *Law, Sex, and Christian Society in Medieval Europe.* Chicago: U of Chicago P, 1987.

——. 'Playing by the Rules: Sexual Behavior and Legal Norms in Medieval Europe.' *Desire and Discipline: Sex and Sexuality in the Premodern West.* Eds. Jacqueline Murray and Konrad Eisenbichler. Toronto: Toronto UP, 1996. 23–41.

——. 'Sexual Equality in Medieval Canon Law.' *Medieval Women and the Sources of Medieval History.* Ed. Joel Rosenthal. Athens: U of Georgia P, 1990. 66–79.

Burnett, Charles and Patrick Gautier Dalche. 'Attitudes Towards the Mongols in Medieval Literature: The XXII Kings of Gog and Magog from the Court of Frederick II to Jean de Mandeville.' *Viator: Medieval and Renaissance Studies* 22 (1991), 153–67.

Butler, Judith. *Bodies that Matter: On the Discursive Limits of 'Sex.'* New York: Routledge, 1993.

——. *Gender Trouble.* New York: Routledge, 1990.

——. 'Imitation and Gender Insubordination.' *The Critical Tradition: Classic Texts and Contemporary Trends* third ed. Ed. David Richter. Boston: Bedford/St. Martin's, 2007. 1707–18. Originally published in *Inside/Out: Lesbian Theories, Gay Theories.* Ed. Diana Fuss. New York: Routledge, 1991.

——. *Undoing Gender.* New York: Routledge, 2004.

Butturff, Douglas R. 'Style as a Clue to Meaning: A Note on the Old English Translation of the *Epistola Alexandri as Aristotelem.' English Language Notes* 8 (1970–71), 81–86.

Bynum, Caroline. *Metamorphosis and Identity.* New York: Zone, 2001.

——. 'Why All the Fuss about the Body?: A Medievalist's Perspective.' *Critical Inquiry* 22:1 (1995), 1–33.

211

Byron, Gay L. *Symbolic Blackness and Ethnic Difference in Early Christian Literature.* London: Routledge, 2002.

Camille, Michael. 'Obscenity Under Erasure: Censorship in Medieval Illuminated Manuscripts.' *Obscenity: Social Control and Artistic Creation in the European Middle Ages.* Ed. Jan M. Ziolkowski. Leiden: Brill, 1998. 139–54.

Campbell, Mary B. *The Witness and the Other World: Exotic European Travel Writing, 400–1600.* Ithaca: Cornell UP, 1988.

Caputi, Mary. *Voluptuous Yearnings: A Feminist Theory of the Obscene.* Lanham, MD: Rowman and Littlefield, 1994.

Chance, Jane. *Woman as Hero in Old English Poetry.* Syracuse, NY: Syracuse UP, 1986.

Chance Nitzsche, Jane. 'The Anglo-Saxon Woman as Hero: The Chaste Queen and the Masculine Saint.' *Allegorica* 2 (1980), 139–48.

Charbonneau, Joanne A. 'From Devil to Saint: Transformations in *Sir Gowther.' The Matter of Identity in Medieval Romance.* Ed. Phillipa Hardman. Cambridge: D.S. Brewer, 2002. 21–8.

Clark-Hall, J.R. *A Concise Anglo-Saxon Dictionary.* Fourth Revised Ed. H.D. Meritt, Repr. Medieval Academy Reprints for Teaching 14; Toronto: Toronto UP, 1984.

Clayton, Mary. 'Aelfric's *Judith*: Manipulative or Manipulated?' *Anglo-Saxon England* 23 (2007), 215–28. ·

Clover, Carol. 'The Unferþ Episode.' *Speculum* 73:2 (April 1998), 297–337.

Cohen, Jeffrey Jerome. 'Decapitation and Coming of Age: Constructing Masculinity and the Monstrous.' *The Arthurian Yearbook, III.* Ed. Keith Busby. New York: Garland, 1993. 173–92.

——. 'Gowther Among the Dogs: Becoming Inhuman C. 1400.' *Becoming Male in the Middle Ages.* Eds. Jeffrey Jerome Cohen and Bonnie Wheeler. New York: Garland, 2000. 219–44.

——. *Medieval Identity Machines.* Medieval Cultures, vol. 35. Minneapolis: U of Minnesota P, 2003.

——. 'Monster Culture (Seven Theses).' *Monster Theory: Reading Culture.* Ed. Jeffrey Jerome Cohen. Minneapolis: U of Minnesota P, 1996. 3–25.

——. *Of Giants: Sex, Monsters, and the Middle Ages.* Minneapolis: U of Minnesota P, 1999.

Cooke, William. 'Three Notes on Swords in *Beowulf.' Medium Aevum* 72:2 (2003), 302–8.

Craib, Ian. *Psychoanalysis and Social Theory: The Limits of Sociology.* Amherst: U of Massachusetts P, 1990.

Crane, Susan. 'The Human–Animal Relationship in Hunting.' Medieval Academy of America Annual Meeting. Miami Beach, March 2005.

——. 'The Meaning of Medieval Hunting.' Center for Medieval and Renaissance Studies Lecture Series. The Ohio State University, February 2005.

Creed, Barbara. *The Monstrous Feminine: Film, Feminism and Psychoanalysis.* London: Routledge, 1993.

Cronan, Dennis. 'The Origin of Ancient Strife in *Beowulf.' NOWELE: North-Western European Language Evolution* 31 (1997), 57–68.

——. 'The Rescuing Sword.' *Neophilologus* 77:3 (1993), 467–78.

Cummins, John. *The Hound and the Hawk: The Art of Medieval Hunting.* New York: St. Martin's P, 1988.

Damon, John Edward. '*Desecto Capite Perfido*: Bodily Fragmentation and Reciprocal Violence in Anglo-Saxon England.' *Exemplaria* 13:2 (2001), 399–432.

Daston, Lorraine and Katharine Park. *Wonders and the Order of Nature 1150–1750.* New York: Zone Books, 1998.

Davis, Glenn. 'The Exeter Book Riddles and Sexual Idiom.' *Medieval Obscenities.* Ed. Nicola McDonald. York: York Medieval Press, 2006. 39–54.

Davis, Lennard J. 'Constructing Normalcy: The Bell Curve, the Novel, and the Invention of the Disabled Body in the Nineteenth Century.' *The Disability Studies Reader.* Second ed. Ed. Lennard J. Davis. New York: Routledge, 2006. 3–16.

Day, David D. 'Hands Across the Hall: The Legalities of Beowulf's Fight with Grendel.' *Journal of English and German Philology* 98:3 (1999), 313–24.

De Pauw, Linda Grant. *Battle Cries and Lullabies: Women in War from Prehistory to Present.* Norman: U of Oklahoma P, 2000.

Deleuze, Gilles and Felix Guattari. *A Thousand Plateaus: Capitalism and Schizophrenia.* Trans. Brian Massumi. Minneapolis: U of Minnesota P, 1987.

Derrida, Jacques. '*Differance.*' *The Critical Tradition,* third ed. Ed. David H. Richter. Boston: Bedford/St. Martin's, 2007. 931–49.

——. *Of Grammatology.* Trans. Gayatri Spivak. Baltimore: Johns Hopkins, 1976.

——. 'Structure, Sign and Play in the Discourse of Human Sciences.' *Writing and Difference.* Trans. Alan Bass. Chicago: U of Chicago P, 1980. 278–94.

Diamond, Arlyn. 'Heroic Subjects: Women and the Alliterative *Morte Arthure.*' *Medieval Women: Texts and Contexts in Late Medieval Britain.* Ed. Jocelyn Wogan-Browne *et al.* Turnhout, Belgium: Brepols, 2000. 293–308.

Dictionary of Old English Corpus Online. U of Toronto. 2005. Online. http://ets.umdl. umich.edu.proxy.lib.ohio-state.edu/o/oec/.

DiMarco, Vincent. 'The Amazons and the End of the World.' *Discovering New Worlds.* Ed. Scott Westrem. New York: Garland, 1991. 69–90.

Dinshaw, Carolyn. *Getting Medieval: Sexualities and Communities, Pre-Modern and Post-Modern.* Durham, NC: Duke UP, 1999.

——. 'Got Medieval.' *Journal of the History of Sexuality* 10:2 (2001), 202–12.

Dockray-Miller, Mary. 'Beowulf's Tears of Fatherhood.' *Exemplaria* 10:1 (1998), 1–28.

——. 'Breasts and Babies: The Maternal Body of Eve in the Junius 11 *Genesis.*' *Naked Before God: Uncovering the Body in Anglo-Saxon England.* Eds. Benjamin C. Withers and Jonathan Wilcox. Morgantown: West Virginia UP, 2003. 221–56.

Elliott, Dyan. *Fallen Bodies: Pollution, Sexuality, and Demonology in the Middle Ages.* Philadelphia: U of Pennsylvania P, 1999.

Fausto-Sterling, Anne. *Sexing the Body: Gender Politics and the Construction of Sexuality.* New York: Basic Books, 2000.

Finlayson, John. 'Arthur and the Giant of St. Michael's Mount.' *Medium Ævum* 33:2 (1964), 112–20.

Fleck, Andrew. 'Here, There, and In Between: Representing Difference in the *Travels* of Sir John Mandeville.' *Studies in Philology* 97:4 (2000), 379–400.

Foley, Michael. 'The Alliterative *Morte Arthure*: An Annotated Bibliography, 1950–1975.' *The Chaucer Review* 14:2 (1979), 166–86.

Fradenburg, Louise Olga. *City, Marriage, Tournament: Arts of Rule in Late Medieval Scotland.* Madison: U of Wisconsin P, 1991.

Frank, Roberta. 'Sex in the Dictionary of Old English.' *Unlocking the Wordhoard: Anglo-Saxon Studies in Memory of Edward B. Irving, Jr.* Eds. Mark Amodio and Katherine O' Brien-O'Keeffe. Toronto: U of Toronto P, 2003. 302–13.

Frantzen, Allen. *Before the Closet: Same-Sex Love from Beowulf to Angels in America.* Chicago: U of Chicago P, 1998.

——. *Desire for Origins: New Language, Old English, and Teaching the Tradition.* New Brunswick: Rutgers UP, 1990.

Freud, Sigmund. *Psychopathology of Everyday Life (1901).* Trans. A.A. Brill. New York: New American Library, 1951.

——. 'Repression' (1915). *The Freud Reader.* Ed. Peter Gay. New York: W.W. Norton, 1989. 568–73.

——. 'The *Uncanny*' (1919). *The Critical Tradition,* third ed. Ed. David H. Richter. Boston: Bedford/St. Martin's, 2007. 514–32.

———. 'Fragment of an Analysis of a Case of Hysteria ('Dora').' *The Freud Reader.* Ed. Peter Gay. New York: W.W. Norton, 1989. 172–238.

Friedman, John Block. *The Monstrous Races in Medieval Art and Thought.* Cambridge: Harvard UP, 1981.

Fries, Maureen. 'The Characterization of Women in the Alliterative Tradition.' *The Alliterative Tradition in the Fourteenth Century.* Eds. Bernard S. Levy and Paul E. Szarmach. Kent: The Kent State UP, 1981. 25–45.

———. 'Female Heroes, Heroines and Counter-Heroes: Images of Women in Arthurian Tradition.' *Popular Arthurian Traditions.* Ed. Sally K. Slocum. Bowling Green: Bowling Green State U Popular P, 1992. 5–17.

———. 'The Poem in the Tradition of Arthurian Literature.' *The Alliterative Morte Arthure: A Reassessment of the Poem.* Ed. Karl Heinz Göller. Cambridge: D.S. Brewer, 1981. 30–43.

Gade, Kari Ellen. 'The Naked and the Dead in Old Norse Society.' *Scandinavian Studies* 60:2 (1998 Spring), 219–45.

Giacone, Margaret Bridges. 'Woman in a Boat: Incest, Miscegenation, and Hybridity in Early Medieval Narratives of the Coming of the Saxons.' *Crossover: Cultural Hybridity in Ethnicity, Gender, Ethics.* Ed. Therese Steffen Tübingen: Stauffenburg, 2000, 117–33.

Gilmore, David. *Monsters: Evil Beings, Mythical Beasts, and All Manner of Imaginary Terrors.* Philadelphia: U of Pennsylvania P, 2003.

Glare, P.G.W., ed. *Oxford Latin Dictionary.* Oxford: Clarendon P, 1983.

Godfrey, Mary. '*Beowulf* and *Judith*: Thematizing Decapitation in Old English Poetry.' *Texas Studies in English Language and Literature* 35:1 (1993), 1–43.

Göller, Karl Heinz. 'The Dream of the Dragon and Bear.' *The Alliterative Morte Arthure: A Reassessment of the Poem.* Ed. Karl Heinz Göller. Cambridge: D.S. Brewer, 1981. 130–39.

———. 'A Summary of Research.' *The Alliterative Morte Arthure: A Reassessment of the Poem.* Ed. Karl Heinz Göller. Cambridge: D.S. Brewer, 1981. 7–14.

———. 'Reality versus Romance.' *The Alliterative Morte Arthure: A Reassessment of the Poem.* Ed. Karl Heinz Göller. Cambridge: D.S. Brewer, 1981. 15–29.

Gordon, E.V. 'Old English Studies.' *The Year's Work in English Studies* 5 (1924), 66–72.

Greenblatt, Stephen. *Marvelous Possessions: The Wonder of the New World.* Chicago: U of Chicago P, 1991.

Haas, Renate. 'The Laments for the Dead.' *The Alliterative Morte Arthure: A Reassessment of the Poem.* Ed. Karl Heinz Göller. Cambridge: D.S. Brewer, 1981. 117–29.

Haddlesey, Richard. 'The Black Death in England: c1348–50.' *British Medieval Architecture.* (Online) www.medievalarchitecture.net/black_death.html. 2008.

Hala, James. 'The Parturition of Poetry and the Birthing of Culture: The *Ides Aglæcwif* and *Beowulf.*' *Exemplaria* 10:1 (1998), 29–50.

Halberstam, Judith. *Female Masculinity.* Durham, NC: Duke UP, 1998.

———. *Skin Shows: Gothic Horror and the Technology of Monsters.* Durham, NC: Duke UP, 1995.

Hall, Kim F. *Things of Darkness: Economies of Race and Gender in Early Modern England.* Ithaca: Cornell UP, 1995.

Haraway, Donna. *Simians, Cyborgs and Women: The Reinvention of Nature.* New York: Routledge: Free Association Books, 1991.

Hardman, Phillipa. 'Introduction: The Matter of Identity in Medieval Romance.' *The Matter of Identity in Medieval Romance.* Ed. Phillipa Hardman. Cambridge: D.S. Brewer, 2002. 1–8.

Harris, Joseph. ' "Double Scene" and "*mise en abyme*" in Beowulfian Narrative.' *Gudar pa jprden: Festskrift till Lars Lonnroth.* Eds. Stina Hansson and Mats Malm. Stockholm: Brutus Ostlings Bokforlag Symposion, 2000. 322–38.

Harwood, Britton. 'The Alliterative Morte Arthure as a Witness to Epic.' *Oral Poetics in Middle English Poetry.* Ed. Mark C. Amodio. New York: Garland, 1994. 241–86.

Higgins, Iain Macleod. 'Defining the Earth's Center in a Medieval "Multi-Text": Jerusalem in *The Book of John Mandeville.' Text and Territory: Geographical Imagination in the European Middle Ages.* Eds. Sylvia Tomasch and Sealy Gilles. Philadelphia: U of Pennsylvania P, 1998. 29–53.

——. *Writing East: The 'Travels' of Sir John Mandeville.* Philadelphia: U of Pennsylvania P, 1997.

Higley, Sarah. 'The Wanton Hand: Reading and Reaching into Grammars and Bodies in Old English Riddle 12.' *Naked Before God: Uncovering the Body in Anglo-Saxon England.* Eds. Benjamin C. Withers and Jonathan Wilcox. Morgantown: West Virginia UP, 2003. 29–59.

Hill, Joyce. ' "Þæt Wæs Geomuru Ides!" A Female Stereotype Examined.' *New Readings on Women in Old English Literature.* Eds. Helen Damico and Alexandra Hennessey Olsen. Bloomington, IN: Indiana University Press, 1990. 235–47.

Hollywood, Amy. 'The Normal, the Queer, and the Middle Ages.' *Journal of the History of Sexuality* 10:2 (2001), 173–79.

Hopkins, Amanda and Cory Rushton, eds. *The Erotic in the Literature of Medieval Britain.* Cambridge: D.S. Brewer, 2007.

Hopkins, Andrea. *The Sinful Knights: A Study of Middle English Penitential Romance.* Oxford: Clarendon P, 1990.

Horner, Shari. 'Voices from the Margins.' Originally appeared in *The Discourse of Enclosure.* Albany: State U of New York P, 2001. 65–100. Republished in *The Postmodern Beowulf.* Eds. Eileen Joy and Mary Ramsay. Morgantown: West Virginia UP, 2006. 467–500.

Howard, Donald R. *Writers and Pilgrims: Medieval Pilgrimage Narratives and their Posterity.* Berkeley: U of California P, 1980.

Howe, Nicholas. *Migration and Mythmaking.* New Haven: Yale UP, 1989.

——. *Writing the Map of Anglo-Saxon England: Essays in Cultural Geography.* New Haven: Yale UP, 2008.

Huisman, Rosemary. 'The Three Tellings of Beowulf's Fight with Grendel's Mother.' *Leeds Studies in English* 20 (1989), 217–48.

Husband, Timothy, with Gloria Gilmore-House. *The Wild Man: Medieval Myth and Symbolism.* New York: The Metropolitan Museum of Art, 1980.

Ian, Marcia. *Remembering the Phallic Mother: Psychoanalysis, Modernism and the Fetish.* Ithaca: Cornell UP, 1996.

Ingham, Patricia Clare. 'Disavowing Romance: Colonial Loss and Stories of the Past.' *Sovereign Fantasies:Arthurian Romance and the Making of Britain.* Philadelphia: U of Pennsylvania P, 2001. 77–106.

Irving, Edward B., Jr. *A Reading of Beowulf.* New Haven: Yale UP, 1968.

——. *Rereading Beowulf.* Philadelphia: U of Pennsylvania P, 1989.

Jones, Timothy S. and David A. Sprunger, eds. *Marvels, Monsters, and Miracles: Studies in the Medieval and Early Modern Imaginations.* Studies in Medieval Culture XLII. Kalamazoo, MI: Medieval Institute Publications, 2002.

Karkov, Catherine E. 'Exiles from the Kingdom: The Naked and the Damned in Anglo-Saxon Art.' *Naked Before God: Uncovering the Body in Anglo-Saxon England.* Eds. Benjamin C. Withers and Jonathan Wilcox. Morgantown: West Virginia UP, 2003. 181–220.

Karras, Ruth Mazo. *Sexuality in Medieval Europe: Doing Unto Others.* New York: Routledge, 2005.

Kear, Adrian. 'Eating the Other: The Fantasy of Incorporation.' *Border Patrols: Policing the Boundaries of Heterosexuality.* Eds. Deborah Lynn Steinberg, Debbie Epstein, and Richard Johnson. London: Cassell, 1997. 253–74.

Kennedy, Edward Donald. 'Generic Intertextuality in the English Alliterative *Morte Arthure*: The Italian Connection.' *Text and Intertext in Medieval Arthurian Literature.* Ed. Norris J. Lacy. New York: Garland, 1996. 41–56.

Kim, Susan. 'The Donestre and the Person of Both Sexes.' *Naked Before God: Uncovering the*

Body in Anglo-Saxon England. Eds. Benjamin C. Withers and Jonathan Wilcox. Morgantown: West Virginia UP, 2003. 162–80.

——. 'Man-Eating Monsters and Ants as Big as Dogs.' *Animals and the Symbolic in Mediaeval Art and Literature.* Ed. L.A.J.R. Houwen. Groningen: Egbert Forsten, 1997. 39–52.

Kirkup, Gill, *et al.*, eds. *The Gendered Cyborg: A Reader.* London: Routledge, 2000.

Klaeber, Fr. 'Die christlichen Elemente im Beowulf.' *Anglia* 35 (1912), 111–36.

Kline, Naomi Reed. *Maps of Medieval Thought: The Hereford Paradigm.* Woodbridge, UK: Boydell, 2001.

Knoppers, Laura Lunger and Joan B. Landes, eds. *Monstrous Bodies/Political Monstrosities in Early Modern Europe.* Ithaca: Cornell UP, 2004.

Koeberl, Johann. 'The Magic Sword in *Beowulf.' Neophilologus* 71 (1987), 120–28.

Kordecki, Lesley. 'Losing the Monster and Recovering the Non-Human in Fable(d) Subjectivity.' *Animals and the Symbolic in Mediaeval Art and Literature.* Ed. L.A.J.R. Houwen. Groningen: Egbert Forsten, 1997. 25–38.

Kristeva, Julia. *Powers of Horror.* New York: Columbia UP, 1982.

Kuhn, Sherman. 'Old English Aglaeca-Middle Irish Olach.' *Linguistic Method: Essays in Honor of Herbert Penzl.* Eds. Irmengard Rauch and Gerald F. Carr. The Hague, New York: Mouton Publishers, 1979. 213–30.

Lacan, Jacques. *Ecrits.* New York: W.W. Norton, 1982.

——. *The Seminar of Jacques Lacan, Book III, The Psychoses 1955–56.* Trans. Russell Grigg. New York: W.W. Norton, 1988.

Lant, Kathleen Margaret and Theresa Thompson, eds. *Imagining the Worst: Stephen King and the Representation of Women.* Westport, CN: Greenwood P, 1998.

Lapidge, Michael. *The Anglo-Saxon Library.* Oxford: Oxford UP, 2006.

——. '*Beowulf* and the Psychology of Terror.' *Heroic Poetry in the Anglo-Saxon Period: Studies in Honor of Jess B. Bessinger, Jr.* Eds. Helen Damico and John Leyerle, *Studies in Medieval Culture* 32 (1993), 373–402.

——. '*Beowulf*, Aldhelm, the Liber Monstrorum and Wessex.' *Studi Medievali, Serie Terza.* Spoleto: Centreo Italiano di sull alto Medioevo, 1982. 151–91.

Lees, Clare. 'Men and *Beowulf.' Medieval Masculinities: Regarding Men in the Middle Ages.* Ed. Clare Lees. Medieval Cultures vol. 7. Minneapolis: U of Minneapolis P, 1994. 129–48.

Lees, Clare and Gillian Overing. *Double Agents: Women and Clerical Culture in Anglo-Saxon England.* Philadelphia: U of Pennsylvania P, 2001.

Lerer, Seth. 'Grendel's Glove.' *English Literary History* 61:4 (1994), 721–51.

——. *Literacy and Power and Anglo-Saxon Literature.* Lincoln: U of Nebraska P, 1991.

Letts, Malcolm. *Mandeville's Travels: Texts and Translations.* 2 vols. London: Hakluyt Society, 1953.

Lionarons, Joyce Tally. '*Beowulf*: Myth and Monsters.' *English Studies* 77:1 (1996), 1–14.

Lochrie, Karma. *Covert Operations: The Medieval Uses of Secrecy.* Philadelphia: U of Pennsylvania P, 1999.

——. *Heterosyncrasies: Female Sexuality When Normal Wasn't.* Minneapolis: U of Minnesota P, 2005.

Lockett, Leslie. 'Grendel's Arm as "Clear Sign" in Feud, Law, and the Narrative Structure of *Beowulf.' Latin Learning and English Lore: Studies in Anglo-Saxon Literature for Michael Lapidge.* Eds. Katherine O-Brien O'Keeffe and Andy Orchard. Toronto: U of Toronto P, 2005. 368–88.

Macksey, Richard and Eugenio Donato, eds. *The Languages of Criticism and the Sciences of Man: The Structuralist Controversy.* Baltimore: Johns Hopkins UP, 1970.

Magennis, Hugh. ' "No Sex, Please, We're Anglo-Saxons": Attitudes to Sexuality in Old English Prose and Poetry.' *Leeds Studies in English* 26 (1995), 1–27.

Marchalonis, Shirley. '*Sir Gowther*: The Process of Romance.' *Chaucer Review* 6 (1971/72), 14–29.

Margherita, Gayle. *The Romance of Origins: Language and Sexual Difference in Middle English Literature.* Philadelphia: U of Pennsylvania P, 1994.

Markus, Manfred. 'The Language and Style: The Paradox of Heroic Poetry.' *The Alliterative Morte Arthure: A Reassessment of the Poem.* Ed. Karl Heinz Göller. Cambridge: D.S. Brewer, 1981. 57–69.

Mathews, Karen Rose. 'Nudity on the Margins: The Bayeux Tapestry and Its Relationship to Marginal Architectural Sculpture.' *Naked Before God: Uncovering the Body in Anglo-Saxon England.* Eds. Benjamin C. Withers and Jonathan Wilcox. Morgantown: West Virginia UP, 2003. 138–61.

Mauss, Marcel. *The Gift: The Form and Reason for Exchange in Archaic Societies.* Trans. W.D. Halls. New York: W.W. Norton, 1990.

McDonald, Nicola. 'Introduction.' *Medieval Obscenities.* Ed. Nicola McDonald. York: York Medieval Press, 2006. 1–16.

McGregor, Francine. 'The Paternal Function in *Sir Gowther.*' *Essays in Medieval Studies* 16 (1999), 67–75.

McKinley, Kathryn L. 'Manuscripts of Ovid in England, 1100–1500.' *English Manuscript Studies, 1100–1700* 7 (1998), 41–85.

Menzer, Melinda. '*Aglæcwif (Beowulf* 1259A): Implications for *–wif* Compounds, Grendel's Mother, and other *aglæcan.*' *English Language Notes* 34:1 (1996), 1–6.

Mezciems, Jenny. ' "'Tis not to Divert the Reader": Moral and Literary Determinants in Some Early Travel Narratives.' *Prose Studies* 5:1 (1982), 1–19.

Middle English Dictionary. Ann Arbor: University of Michigan P, 2005. Online. http://ets.umdl.umich.edu.proxy.lib.ohio-state.edu/m/mec/.

Mittman, Asa Simon. *Maps and Monsters in Medieval England.* New York: Routledge, 2006.

Moi, Toril. *Sexual/Textual Politics: Feminist Literary Theory.* London: Routledge, 1985.

Montaño, Jesus. '*Sir Gowther:* Imagining Race in Late Medieval England.' *Meeting the Foreign in the Middle Ages.* Ed. Albrecht Classen. New York: Routledge, 2002. 118–32.

Morey, Robert. 'Beowulf's Androgynous Heroism.' *Journal of English and Germanic Philology* 95:4 (1996), 486–96.

Morgan, Gwendolyn A. 'Mothers, Monsters, and Maturation: Female Evil in *Beowulf.*' *Journal of the Fantastic in the Arts* 4 (1991), 54–68.

Mulvey, Laura. *Visual and Other Pleasures.* Bloomington: Indiana UP, 1989.

O'Keeffe, Katherine O'Brien. 'Body and Law in Late Anglo-Saxon England.' *Anglo-Saxon England* 27 (1998), 209–32.

Olsen, K.E. and L.A.J.R. Houwen, eds. *Monsters and the Monstrous in Medieval Northwest Europe.* Leuven, Belgium: Peeters, 2001.

Orchard, Andy. *A Critical Companion to Beowulf.* Cambridge: D.S. Brewer, 2003.

——. *Pride and Prodigies: Studies in the Monsters of the Beowulf-Manuscript.* Cambridge: D.S. Brewer, 1995.

O'Sharkey, Eithne M. 'King Arthur's Prophetic Dreams and the Role of Mordred in Layamon's *Brut* and the Alliterative *Morte Arthure.*' *Romania* 99 (1979), 347–62.

Ott, Norbert H. 'Encounters with the Other World: The Medieval Iconography of Alexander the Great and Henry the Lion.' *Demons: Mediators Between this World and the Other. Essays on Demonic Beings from the Middle Ages to the Present.* Eds. Ruth Petzoldt and Paul Neubauer. Frankfurt: Lang, 1998.

Overing, Gillian R. *Language, Sign, and Gender in Beowulf.* Carbondale: Southern Illinois UP, 1990.

——. 'Swords and Signs: A Semiotic Perspective on *Beowulf.*' *American Journal of Semiotics* 5:1 (1987), 35–57.

——. 'The Women of *Beowulf:* A Context for Interpretation.' *Beowulf: Basic Readings.* Ed. Peter Baker. New York: Garland, 1995. 219–60.

Parks, Ward. 'The Flyting Contract and Adversarial Patterning in the Alliterative *Morte*

Arthure.' Traditions and Innovations. Eds. David G. Allen and Robert A. White. Newark: U of Delaware P, 1990. 59–74.

——. 'Prey Tell: How Heroes Perceive Monsters in *Beowulf.' Journal of English and Germanic Philology* 92:1 (1993), 1–16.

Pasternack, Carol and Lisa M.C. Weston, eds. *Sex and Sexuality in Anglo-Saxon England*. Tempe: Arizona Center for Medieval and Renaissance Studies, 2004.

Patterson, Lee. 'The Romance of History and the Alliterative *Morte Arthure.' Negotiating the Past: The Historical Understanding of Medieval Literature*. Madison: The U of Wisconsin P, 1987. 197–230.

——. *Chaucer and the Subject of History*. Madison: U of Wisconsin P, 1991.

Petzoldt, Ruth and Paul Neubauer, eds. *Demons: Mediators Between this World and the Other. Essays on Demonic Beings from the Middle Ages to the Present*. Frankfurt: Lang, 1998.

Platt, Colin. *King Death: The Black Death and its Aftermath in Late-Medieval England*. Toronto: U of Toronto P, 1996.

Porter, Elizabeth. 'Chaucer's Knight, the Alliterative *Morte Arthure*, and Medieval Laws of War: A Reconsideration.' *Nottingham Medieval Studies* 27 (1983), 56–78.

Puhvel, Martin. 'The Might of Grendel's Mother.' *Folklore* 80 (1969), 81–8.

Richards, Mary P. 'The Body as Text in Early Anglo-Saxon Law.' *Naked Before God: Uncovering the Body in Anglo-Saxon England*. Eds. Benjamin C. Withers and Jonathan Wilcox. Morgantown: West Virginia UP, 2003. 97–115.

Richardson, Peter. 'Point of View and Identification in *Beowulf.' Neophilologus* 81:2 (1997), 289–98.

Ritzke-Rutherford, Jean. 'Formulaic Macrostructure: The Theme of Battle.' *The Alliterative Morte Arthure: A Reassessment of the Poem*. Ed. Karl Heinz Göller. Cambridge: D.S. Brewer, 1981. 83–95.

Roberts, Jane, Christian Kay and Lynn Grundy. *A Thesaurus of Old English*. Atlanta: Rodopi, 2000.

Robinson, Fred C. 'Did Grendel's Mother Sit on Beowulf?' *From Anglo-Saxon to Early Middle English*. Eds. Malcolm Godden, Douglas Gray, and Terry Hoad. Oxford, Clarendon, 1994. 1–7.

——. 'Elements of the Marvellous in the Characterization of Beowulf: A Reconsideration of the Textual Evidence.' *Old English Studies in Honour of John C. Pope*. Eds. Robert B. Burlin and Edward B. Irving. Toronto: U of Toronto P, 1974. 119–37.

Rogers, H.L. 'Beowulf's Three Great Fights.' *Review of English Studies* 6 (1955), 339–55. Reprinted in *An Anthology of Beowulf Criticism*. Ed. Lewis E. Nicholson. Notre Dame: U of Notre Dame P, 1963. 233–56.

Rondolone, Donna Lynne. '*Wyrchipe*: The Clash of Oral-Heroic and Literate-Ricardian Ideal in the Alliterative *Morte Arthure.' Oral Poetics in Middle English Poetry*. Ed. Mark C. Amodio. New York: Garland, 1994. 207–40.

Rosen, David. 'The Armor of the Man-Monster in *Beowulf.' The Changing Fictions of Masculinity*. Urbana: U of Illinois P, 1993. 1–26.

Roy, Bruno. 'En Marge du Monde Connu: Les Races de Monstres.' *Aspects de la Marginalité au Moyen Age*. Paris: Gallimard, 1989.

Rubin, Gayle. 'The Traffic in Women: Notes on the "Political Economy" of Sex.' *Toward an Anthropology of Women*. Ed. Rayna R. Reiter. New York: Monthly Review P, 1975. 157–210.

——. 'Thinking Sex: Notes for a Radical Theory of the Politics of Sexuality.' *The Lesbian and Gay Studies Reader*. Eds. Henry Abelove, Michele Aina Barale and David M. Halperin. New York: Routledge, 1993. 3–44.

Russell, Jeffrey Burton. *The Devil: Perceptions of Evil from Antiquity to Primitive Christianity*. Ithaca: Cornell UP, 1977.

Salisbury, Joyce. *The Beast Within: Animals in the Middle Ages*. New York: Routledge, 1994.

Bibliography

Salter, David. 'Sir Gowther.' *Holy and Noble Beasts: Encounters with Animals in Medieval Literature*. Cambridge: D.S. Brewer, 2001. 71–81.

Salvador, Mercedes. 'The Key to the Body: Unlocking Riddles 42–46.' *Naked Before God: Uncovering the Body in Anglo-Saxon England*. Eds. Benjamin C. Withers and Jonathan Wilcox. Morgantown: West Virginia UP, 2003. 60–96.

Saunders, Corrine J. ' "Symtyme the fende": Questions of Rape in *Sir Gowther*.' *Studies in English Language and Literature: 'Doubt Wisely'. Papers in Honour of E.G. Stanley*. Eds. M.J. Toswell and E.M. Tyler. London: Routledge, 1996. 286–303.

Saunders, Michael William. *Imps of the Perverse: Gay Monsters in Film*. Westport, CT: Praeger, 1998.

Schildrick, Margrit. *Embodying the Monster: Encounters with the Vulnerable Self*. London: Sage, 2002.

Schultz, James A. 'Heterosexuality as a Threat to Medieval Studies.' *Journal of the History of Sexuality* 15:1 (2006), 14–29.

Schwetman, John W. 'Beowulf's Return: The Hero's Account of his Adventures Among the Danes.' *Medieval Perspectives* 13 (1998), 136–48.

Scragg, D.G. '*Wifcyþþe* and the Morality of the Cynewulf and Cyneheard Episode in the Anglo-Saxon Chronicle.' *Alfred the Wise: Studies in Honour of Janet Bately on the occasion of her sixty-fifth birthday*. Eds. Jane Roberts and Janet L. Nelson, with Malcolm Godden. Cambridge: D.S. Brewer, 1997. 179–86.

Sedgwick, Eve Kosofsky. *Epistemology of the Closet*. Berkeley: U of California P, 1990.

Sedinger, Tracey. 'Nation and Identification: Psychoanalysis, Race, and Sexual Difference.' *Cultural Critique* 50 (Winter 2002), 40–73.

Shoaf, R. Allen. *Chaucer's Body: The Anxiety of Circulation in the 'Canterbury Tales.'* Gainesville: U of Florida P, 2001.

Sisam, Kenneth. *Studies in the History of Old English Literature*. Oxford: Clarendon P, 1953. Repr. by Sandpiper, 1998.

Skeat, Walter W. *An Etymological Dictionary of the English Language*. fourth ed. London: Oxford UP, 1910.

Smith, Gregg. 'Death and Desire: The Thematic Function of the Dead in Medieval Icelandic and Irish Literature' (unpublished Ph.D. dissertation from University of Washington, 1996).

Sobecki, Sebastian I. 'Mandeville's Thought of the Limit: The Discourse of Similarity and Difference in *The Travels of Sir John Mandeville*.' *Review of English Studies* 53:211 (2002), 329–43.

Spivak, Gayatri. '*Translator's Preface.*' *Of Grammatology*. By Jacques Derrida. Trans. Gayatri Spivak. Baltimore: Johns Hopkins UP, 1976. ix–lxxxvii.

Sprunger, David. 'Wild Folk and Lunatics in Medieval Romance.' *The Medieval World of Nature*. Ed. Joyce Salisbury. New York: Garland, 1993. 145–66.

Stanley, E.G. 'Two Old English Poetic Phrases Insufficiently Understood for Literary Criticism: *Þing Gehegan* and *Senoþ Gehegan*.' *Old English Poetry: Essays on Style*. Ed. Daniel G. Calder. Berkeley: U of California P, 1979. 67–90.

Stephens, Walter. *Giants in Those Days*. Lincoln: U of Nebraska P, 1989.

Stern, Elizabeth Jane. 'Legends of the Dead in Medieval and Modern Icelandic'. (unpublished Ph.D. dissertation from UCLA, 1988).

Tanke, John. '*Wonfeax Wale*: Ideology and Figuration in the Sexual Riddles of the Exeter Book.' *Class and Gender in Early English Literature*. Eds. Britton Harwood and Gillian Overing. Bloomington: Indiana UP, 1994. 21–42.

Taylor, Keith P. '*Beowulf* 1259a: The Inherent Nobility of Grendel's Mother.' *English Language Notes* 31:3 (1994), 13–25.

Thompson, Rosemarie, ed. *Freakery: Cultural Spectacles of the Extraordinary Body*. New York: New York UP, 1996.

Bibliography

Tolkien, J.R.R. '*Beowulf:* The Monsters and the Critics.' *Proceedings of the British Academy* 22 (1936), 245–95.

Tzanaki, Rosemary. *Mandeville's Medieval Audiences: A Study on the Reception of the* Book *of Sir John Mandeville (1371–1550).* Aldershot: Ashgate, 2003.

Uebel, Michael. 'The Foreigner Within: The Subject of Abjection in *Sir Gowther.*' *Meeting the Foreign in the Middles Ages.* Ed. Albrecht Classen. New York: Routledge, 2002. 96–117.

Vale, Juliet. 'Law and Diplomacy in the *Alliterative Morte Arthure.*' *Nottingham Medieval Studies* 23 (1979), 31–46.

Verner, Lisa. *The Epistemology of the Monstrous in the Middle Ages.* New York: Routledge, 2005.

Wallace, David. *Premodern Places: Calais to Surinam, Chaucer to Aphra Behn.* Oxford: Blackwell, 2004.

Warner, Michael. *The Trouble with Normal.* New York: The Free Press, 1999.

Weisner-Hanks, Merry E. *Christianity and Sexuality in the Early Modern World.* London: Routledge, 2000.

Weston, Lisa. 'Queering Virginity.' *Medieval Feminist Forum* 36 (2003), 22–4.

Westover, Jeff. 'Arthur's End: The King's Emasculation in the Alliterative *Morte Arthure.*' *The Chaucer Review* 32:3 (1998), 310–24.

Westrem, Scott D. 'Against Gog and Magog.' *Text and Territory: Geographical Imagination in the European Middle Ages.* Eds. Sylvia Tomasch and Sealy Gilles. Philadelphia: U of Pennsylvania P, 1998. 54–78.

Williams, David. *Cain and Beowulf: A Study in Secular Allegory.* Toronto: U of Toronto P, 1982.

——. *Deformed Discourse: The Function of the Monster in Medieval Thought and Literature.* Montreal: McGill-Queen's UP, 1996.

Withers, Benjamin C. and Jonathan Wilcox, eds. *Naked Before God: Uncovering the Body in Anglo-Saxon England.* Morgantown: West Virginia UP, 2003.

Wittkower, Rudolf. 'Marvels of the East: A Study in the History of Monsters.' *Journal of Warburg and Courthald Institutes* 5 (1942), 159–97.

Wright, Glenn. '*Gefeng þa be eaxle – nalas for fæhðe mearn*: Getting to Grips with Beowulfian Litotes.' *In Geardagum: Essays on Old and Middle English Language and Literature* 20 (1999), 49–63.

Wurster, Julia. 'The Audience.' *The Alliterative Morte Arthure: A Reassessment of the Poem.* Ed. Karl Heinz Göller. Cambridge: D.S. Brewer, 1981. 44–56.

Ziolkowski, Jan. 'Literary Genre and Animal Symbolism.' *Animals and the Symbolic in Mediaeval Art and Literature.* Ed. L.A.J.R. Houwen. Groningen: Egbert Forsten, 1997. 1–24.

——. *Talking Animals: Medieval Latin Beast Poetry 750–1150.* Philadelphia: U of Pennsylvania P, 1993.

INDEX